why ANIMALS MATTER

Cathy —

Thanks for all your work for animals!

— Eri...

why ANIMALS MATTER

the case for animal protection

Erin E. Williams & Margo DeMello

 Prometheus Books

59 John Glenn Drive
Amherst, New York 14228–2197

Published 2007 by Prometheus Books

Inquiries should be addressed to
Prometheus Books
59 John Glenn Drive
Amherst, New York 14228–2197
VOICE: 716–691–0133, ext. 210
FAX: 716–691–0137
WWW.PROMETHEUSBOOKS.COM

11 10 09 08 07   5 4 3 2

Library of Congress Cataloging-in-Publication Data

Williams, Erin E.
    Why animals matter : the case for animal protection / by Erin E. Williams and Margo DeMello.
        p. cm.
    Includes bibliographical references and index.
    ISBN 978–1–59102–523–8 (alk. paper)
    1. Animals rights—United States. 2. Animal welfare—United States.
I. DeMello, Margo. II. Title.

HV4764.W55 2007
179'.3—dc22

                                                                            2007008738

Printed in the United States of America on acid-free paper

CONTENTS

ACKNOWLEDGMENTS

This book is the result of two lifetimes' worth of accumulated knowledge of and interest in issues that affect animals. Both of us are longtime animal advocates who have spent much of our lives working to better the conditions of nonhuman animals. And both of us are longtime animal lovers who share our homes with rabbits, dogs, cats, birds, guinea pigs, and rats. The enrichment that we have experienced as a result of living with animals has played no small part in the creation of this book.

Other hands and minds guided this book as well. Our friends and colleagues in the animal protection world shared their knowledge and experience with us, offering valuable insight and commentary on the material in this book. We would like to thank, in no particular order: Paul Shapiro, Andrew Page, Heidi Prescott, Stephanie Shain, Dr. Martin Stephens, Jonathan Lovvorn, Nancy Perry, Kitty Block, Naomi Rose, Peter Petersan, Dawn McPherson, Kathleen Conlee, John Goodwin, Dr. Michael Greger, Paul Petersan, Gowri Koneswaran, Peter Brandt, Sarah Uhlemann, Annie Judah, Norm Phelps, Carter Dillard, Kristie Stoick, Patrick Sullivan, Gaverick Matheny, Tricia McCarthy, and Michael Markarian. While the authors deeply appreciate all of this generous help, our inevitable errors or omissions are solely our own responsibility.

A number of people provided stories about animals whom they rescued, and others provided pictures for the book. For sharing their stories and photos with us, we wish to thank: Marji Beach and Kim Sturla of Animal Place, Tricia Ritterbusch of Farm Sanctuary, Judy Paulsen of Greyhound Companions of New Mexico, Richard Farinato of the Humane Society of the United States, Carol Buckley of the Elephant Sanctuary, Karen Courtemanche of Harvest Home Animal Sanctuary, Danielle Bays, Kate Turlington of People for the Ethical Treatment of Animals, Lynn Cuny of Wildlife Rescue & Rehabilitation, Inc., Terry Cummings from Poplar Spring Animal Sanctuary, and Kristin Von Kreisler.

For allowing us the use of their photos, we also thank: Han-Yu Loo, Rachel Hess, Nels Akerlund, Paula Jaworski, and Beth McNulty of the Humane Society of the United States, Erica Meier of Compassion Over Killing, and Tal Ronnen.

We are also grateful to Steven L. Mitchell of Prometheus Books and his wonderful staff, for their encouragement, flexibility, and kindness.

Finally, we have to acknowledge our loved ones, without whom we could not have written this book. Margo thanks her husband, Tom, who patiently lived through Margo's tantrums and breakdowns as she completed two books in one year, as well as all of her companion animals, who provided the inspiration necessary to complete this book. She also thanks her parents, who have never stopped supporting and loving her, through thick and thin. Erin would like to thank her father, who taught her on her family's dairy farm that animals are thinking, feeling individuals—and for his support as she became an animal protection advocate. She considers herself incredibly fortunate to have so many caring friends—especially Anna—who supported her not only through writing this book, but in all her other endeavors. And most of all, she thanks her partner, Andrew, who has always provided unfailing encouragement, love, and inspiration. This book is for all of them.

Chapter 1

WHY CARE ABOUT PROTECTING ANIMALS?

We cannot just do whatever we want with them. . . . Certainly, a sort of industrial use of creatures, so that geese are fed in such a way as to produce as large a liver as possible, or hens live so packed together that they become just caricatures of birds, this degrading of living creatures to a commodity seems to me in fact to contradict the relationship of mutuality that comes across in the Bible.[1]
—Joseph Cardinal Ratzinger, now Pope Benedict XVI

Are we ready to send our animals and pets back to the natural state of running loose? . . . being wild. Breeding at will? Are we ready to give up our pets, food, life style, all for animal rights? Are we ready to be legislated and controlled by a few animal rights people, that we are financially supporting them in their goals and hidden agenda.[2]
—From the Animal Owners United Web site

Our treatment of animals in modern America is full of contradictions. In the early twenty-first century, companion animals are a central feature of our lives. Many benefit from the most luxurious food and accessories and revel in the love and companionship from their human families. Yet at the same time, many of the animals with

11

whom we share this planet suffer as a result of human exploitation. Most animals raised for food or clothing are born, are reared, and then die in the most extreme forms of confinement, never experiencing even the slightest bit of kindness or mercy. Animals used for medical experiments and product testing often live painful, lonely lives in small cages from birth until death. Other animals, such as those used in circuses or rodeos, live only to entertain us, receiving little, if anything, in return for the amusement they provide. And wild animals suffer in other ways—they lose their lives as their habitats disappear, they are removed from their homes for the exotic animal trade, and they are hunted for trophies. Even those animals whom we welcome into our families suffer through the conditions of the pet industry that produces them. We buy millions of animals as if they were furniture or clothes, keep many of them in inadequate conditions, and discard them when we grow tired of them.

Things haven't always been this way. People have relied on animals for food and clothing for hundreds of thousands of years, but when we first domesticated animals for food and labor, approximately ten thousand years ago, the human-animal relationship began to fundamentally change. At this point, the belief that animals are property became more widespread, creating a relationship marked by dominance and control. But it wasn't until the nineteenth and twentieth centuries, with the development of industrial methods of animal husbandry, that the relationship between humans and other animals became as intensely exploitative as it is today.

We can see this transition perhaps most clearly in the meat, egg, and dairy industries, where factory farms have displaced small farmers as our nation's appetite for these products has swelled. Today, farm animals are "produced"—not raised—in massive operations that control virtually all aspects of the animals' lives. They often have no fresh air, do not feel the earth under their feet, and do not enjoy sunlight. Hundreds of millions of them are virtually immobilized. They can hardly perform any of their most important natural behaviors or experience even the most basic pleasures. Animals under these conditions have become meat-, egg-, and dairy-producing machines with all aspects of their lives and deaths orchestrated according to the economics of industrial efficiency. The relationship between farmer and farmed animal is now a strictly profit-driven relationship, with the animals themselves and the sites of their production and death hidden away from the public.

The same forces that have turned small farms into animal factories have wrought enormous harm on the planet and, ultimately, on humanity. Factory farms confine tens or even hundreds of thousands of animals, producing staggering amounts of animal waste as well as excreting dangerous levels of water and air pollution into surrounding communities. And as pastureland is lost to both development and factory farms, many of the benefits of rural living—such as sense of community, clean air, and lack of congestion—are permanently lost.

Humans suffer from industrial animal agriculture in a host of ways: modern farm workers are forced to inhale high levels of ammonia and other pollutants; workers in slaughterhouses and packing plants suffer some of the highest injury rates among all industries; and people living downwind from factory farms suffer increased rates of health problems. And thanks to the industry's ever-increasing demands for profit, once-unionized meatpackers increasingly find that their previously high-paying, skilled jobs are disappearing and are replaced by low-paid jobs for unskilled workers.

Factory farms, too, cut their labor costs since much of the work has been mechanized. The remaining workers surely suffer some consequences from a job that entails overseeing the misery of countless animals—a far cry from the life of small-scale farmers. And as factory farming spreads around the world, human suffering and environmental degradation increase even more.

Animals in factory farms are stripped of their "animalness"—their ability to reproduce on their own, to raise their young, and, in many cases, to socialize with their own kind. They are denied the pleasures of running, sleeping in the sunlight, and playing. As the animals are turned into profit-producing objects, we are stripped of some of what makes us human: our sense of right and wrong, and our ability to show compassion to those who are less powerful than we are.

Perhaps most astonishing is the scale of animal agribusiness. Each year in the United States, nearly 10 billion land animals are raised and killed for their meat, eggs, and milk.[3] Globally, the figure is 50 billion, or more than 95,000 animals per minute. Farm animals represent 99 percent of all the animals humans raise to exploit: nearly 10 billion animals compared to about 218 million killed in all the other industries we will discuss—combined.[4] Animal agribusiness is thus the most extreme example of institutionalized animal abuse. But it is not the only one.

The modern medical, pharmaceutical, and product-testing industries also depend on the specialized production of animals to serve their needs. Here, animals are purpose-bred and supplied to universities, product-testing companies, and research labs. Known by lab animal suppliers as "research models," these animals too become machines. Purchasers can request animals who are genetically modified to be pathogen-free, inbred or outbred, hybrid or mutant. These animals are viewed as tools without which human health and scientific discovery would be severely compromised. Yet, much animal research is of dubious value, and in many cases, sophisticated alternatives are available. While the use of animals in medicine may have resulted in the discovery of some drugs and treatments used today, the reliance on animals—at the expense of focusing on technological, cellular, and other models that more closely replicate the human body—may have caused many other treatments to be overlooked. In addition, because no animal is completely similar to humans, once products and drugs have been tested on animals, there is no way to know whether they will still be safe for our use without some sort of human testing.

Industrialization and our society's views of animals have also had an irreversible effect on wildlife. We have cleared millions of acres of wildland to create housing developments, shopping centers, and business parks, which have displaced or killed untold millions of wild animals. As wildlife is decimated in this losing battle with development, those animals who remain find themselves hunted by a small but powerful minority of sportsmen who see their mission as solving the wildlife "problem" as well as "conserving" the same dwindling populations that they are killing. The rest of us must be content to see what remains of wild animals by visiting zoos.

In fact, we have created whole industries in which animals—both wild and domestic—are transformed into entertainment. While many of us derive pleasure from watching wild animals in captivity at zoos, others watch horse and dog races. Many of us like watching animals perform stunts in circuses or in other animal attractions, and still others enjoy watching animals like dogs or roosters fight each other, often to the death. Yet these industries too are rife with problems, with millions of animals enduring miserable fates so that we can experience a few fleeting moments of excitement or a trivial pleasure.

Finally, with Americans' mass migration in the last century from the country to the cities and suburbs, the only way for many of us to connect with an animal is by having a pet. As we will see, the American pet industry has a notoriously bad history of abusive breeding practices; this industry also relies on cutting costs in order to maximize profits, which results in a great deal of suffering to produce the pets whom we cherish so much. The pet industry, like the animal agribusiness and lab animal suppliers, relies on sophisticated marketing to increase demand so that more and more animals are produced as pets. Even wild animals are increasingly being transformed, via the exotic pet industry, into pets as well. But supply still outpaces demand, and animal shelters are forced to destroy millions of unwanted pets each year.

Why should we care about all this animal suffering? Like us, animals have the capacity to both suffer and feel pleasure. Their physiological capacity to experience these sensations is virtually identical to our own. One would be hard-pressed to find any biologist who would take seriously the once-popular claim that animals are insensitive machines. Federal legislation such as the Animal Welfare Act, Humane Methods of Slaughter Act, and the anticruelty codes of all fifty states is predicated on the fact that animals *feel* pain. Animals can also feel pleasure. According to ethologist Dr. Jonathan Balcombe, in his book *Pleasurable Kingdom*, "From the play of animals to their food preferences, from their sexual behavior to their anticipation of rewards, it is clear that they, too, have richly positive experiences. We are not the only species to feel exhilaration's rush, anticipation's pull, or paroxysms of delight."[5]

Animals suffer not just because of individual human cruelty, but on an institutional level as well in order to provide corporations with profits. These same corporate profits often result in human suffering as well. Welfare critics sometimes contend that animal advocates don't care about people because they care so much about animals. The human capacity for compassion, however, is not so limited. In this book, we demonstrate that caring about animals also entails caring about people and the environment. Conversely, if one is concerned about many of the issues facing humanity today, then one should be concerned about animal exploitation. By exposing the ways animal industries harm not only animals but also people and the environment, we can see that we can share the same interests.

Matthew Scully, former speechwriter for President George W. Bush and author of *Dominion: The Power of Man, the Suffering of Animals, and the Call to Mercy*, provides a good example:

> A secular philosopher like Peter Singer can oppose factory farming because it's unethical by his theories of justice. An environmentalist can oppose factory farming because it's reckless stewardship. A conservative can oppose factory farming because it is destructive to small farmers and to the decent ethic of husbandry those farmers live by. A religious person can oppose factory farming because it is degrading to both man and animal.[6]

The irony is that while humans once needed animals for their meat, fur, and labor, we no longer need to use animals to satisfy our basic needs. Thanks to technological advances, today we can choose from an enormous range of foods, apparel, household products, and entertainment that do not cause animals to suffer. Yet, while we no longer need animals, we raise them in more factory-like conditions than ever before and in far greater numbers. All at a time when alternatives to eating meat, wearing fur, or testing cosmetics on animals are more prevalent than ever.

This is a consequence of industrial methods that make animal production extraordinarily cheap. The cheaper it is to produce animals and products from them, the more they are produced and consumed. As a consequence, more lives are wasted and we too become cheaper, as we measure the value of existence in profits and pennies. As animals have less and less monetary value (the cage, after all, is worth more than the chickens it confines), they become trifling commodities. Countless "spent" egg-laying hens are now left to smother in dumpsters because it is not cost-effective to at least kill them before discarding them. For the factory owners, these animals have no value other than monetary. Without value, why should we care about what happens to them or about the conditions in which they live?

One goal of this book is to demystify the realities of animal exploitation in modern America—to demonstrate how animal industries maximize profit and cut costs, and how that causes animal suffering, environmental destruction, and human misery. As Matthew Scully points out, "Man, the rationalizing creature, can justify just about anything when there is money in sight. It's only easier when your victims are so completely out of sight and unable to speak for themselves."[7] Industries mystify the conditions in laboratories, in slaughterhouses, and on factory farms because many of us don't want to see or know what goes on in these places. Yet our instincts tell us the way we use animals is simply not right.

We also show, through the rescue stories featured in every chapter, some of the real animals who have experienced life on a factory farm, in a puppy mill, or in a product-testing laboratory. By telling the stories of Lucky, Eileen, Truffles, Rudy, and Timber, we hope to give readers a sense of individual lives affected by cruelty. Like your own companion animals, these animals have their own histories, desires, preferences, and wills, and they deserve more than they had been given. Luckily, the animals whose stories we tell are those who were rescued by caring people and who now enjoy lives filled with love and kindness. We think all animals' stories deserve to have happy endings.

Why Animals Matter does not engage in complicated philosophical arguments. Instead, we focus, from a commonsense perspective, on how the human-animal relationship during the last few hundred years has become ever more industrialized. The animal, human, and environmental devastation resulting from this shift is something we need not and should not accept. Mere common sense and common decency tell us the situation is not working. While we can purchase cheaper meat from animals who never experienced the sun or fresh air, while we can buy virtually any animal we want as a pet, while scientists can create mice with human genes and even with human tissue, and while rich hunters can pay thousands of dollars to shoot an endangered, tranquilized animal, most of us, if we knew the realities behind those choices, would take a step back and reconsider. But just because we can do all these things, should we? Most people would choose to live more compassionately if given the information about what our choices really entail.

Our goal is simple. Just as Dorothy pulled back the curtain to expose the little man behind Oz, we are attempting to expose the industries that profit from and the myths that buttress the most extreme forms of animal exploitation today. At the same time, we wish to show another face: the faces of the individual animals who have directly experienced this exploitation. Our shared humanity allows sensitivity and compassion to guide our choices and actions, and the animals with whom we share this earth deserve nothing less.

Chapter 2

THE MEAT INDUSTRY

Animals as Food

Our inhumane treatment of livestock is becoming widespread and more and more barbaric. Six-hundred-pound hogs—they were pigs at one time—are raised in two-foot-wide metal cages called gestation crates, in which the poor beasts are unable to turn around or lie down in natural positions, and this way they live for months at a time. On profit-driven factory farms, veal calves are confined to dark wooden crates so small that they are prevented from lying down or scratching themselves. These creatures feel; they know pain. They suffer pain just as humans suffer pain. Egg-laying hens are confined to battery cages. Unable to spread their wings, they are reduced to nothing more than egg-laying machines.[1]

—US Sen. Robert Byrd (D-WV)

The prospect of a virulent flu to which we have absolutely no resistance is frightening. However, to me, the threat is much greater to the poultry industry. I'm not as worried about the US human population dying from bird flu as I am that there will be no chicken to eat.[2]

—Yvonne Vizzier Thaxton, executive editor, *Poultry* magazine

INTRODUCTION

For the great majority of people in this country, the only interaction we have with the animals who became our dinner is the preparation and consumption of them. Separated from the production process by geography and often misled by slick industry marketing, Americans consume billions upon billions of animals each year. Our supermarket meat, neatly covered in plastic wrap on its Styrofoam tray, bears little to no resemblance to a dead animal, let alone a living one. Our milk and eggs come not from the farmer down the road but rather from massive sheds that the public cannot enter.

Yet Americans are concerned about the welfare of farmed animals—according to a 2003 Zogby poll, 52 percent of Americans are concerned about "the treatment of farmed animals raised for food consumption." Of the poll respondents, 82 percent believe that "there should be effective laws that protect farmed animals against cruelty and abuse." And nearly two-thirds agree that "farms should be inspected by government inspectors to ensure that laws to protect animals from cruelty are being followed."[3]

higher cost food.

Corporations are increasingly listening to these concerns. An amazing variety of vegetarian foods is available at nearly every supermarket, and restaurants across the country offer tantalizing vegetarian fare. Sales of these products are exploding, and animal products offered by producers that comply with progressive welfare standards are occupying an ever-growing market share.

While these businesses' ranks are growing, they are the exception rather than the rule. In the past several decades, virtually every aspect of the meat industry has become increasingly consolidated, with a very small number of companies controlling the markets for eggs, dairy, and milk. According to the United States Department of Agriculture (USDA), the largest 2 percent of factory farms produce more than 40 percent of all farm animals.[4] A small number of powerful chicken, pork, and beef producers and processors dominate the American market, edging out not just the small family farms but the medium-sized farms as well. These corporate giants like Cargill, Tyson Foods, IBP, and ConAgra are now "vertically integrated," owning the facilities that produce the animals, the feedlots to fatten them, and the meatpacking facilities to slaughter them and package the meat. This type of integration allows massive companies like these to control every aspect of production, making it nearly impossible for smaller farms to compete.

This industry consolidation emphasizes ever-increasing productivity at the expense of animal welfare. Dr. Bernard Rollin, a prominent animal scientist, explains, "[I]n industrial agriculture, this link between productivity and well-being is severed. When productivity as an economic metric is applied to the whole operation, the welfare of the individual animal is ignored."[5] Today's farmed animals are genetically selected to be productive in even the worst conditions; for example, factory-farmed laying hens can continue to produce eggs even if their legs are broken.

Industrialized factory farms that embrace this ethic overlook animal welfare in favor of the bottom line. They also systematically undermine human health, the environment, and social welfare, as we demonstrate later in this chapter. The Worldwatch Institute explains that industrialized animal agribusiness "is a driving force behind virtually every major category of environmental damage now threatening the human future—deforestation, erosion, fresh water scarcity, air and water pollution, climate change, biodiversity loss, social injustice, the destabilization of communities, and the spread of disease."[6]

Perhaps the most troubling aspect of this perspective is that we've entirely lost our understanding of these animals as individuals. For the millions of Americans who have companion animals, we see that each dog or cat has her own preferences and needs—her own uniqueness. And like dogs and cats, farmed animals too have their own personalities; they are much more intelligent than we historically have acknowledged. They can be curious, affectionate, playful, outgoing, withdrawn, lonely, frightened, and more. Most important, they can suffer and feel pleasure. Yet most of us will never meaningfully interact with farmed animals. As B. R. Myers, a contributing editor of *Atlantic Monthly*, puts it, "98 percent of the animals that Americans interact with are farmed for food."[7] It is when we purchase and prepare pieces of them, which bear no resemblance to the living beings they once were, that we have the greatest amount of "interaction."

There's ample reason why most of us prefer our meat to come pre-butchered and wrapped in plastic, or increasingly, precooked and pre-pared. We simply want to maintain a comfortable distance, and we don't want to think about the animals we are eating or how they lived and died. And when we do in fact consider where our food comes from, we imagine the Old MacDonald's farm cliché. There's comfort in the myth that the animals at least had a life worth living, and that small farms still provide us with our food. But family farmers have become nearly extinct in this country, their ranks comprising less than 2 percent of the population.[8]

The tragic reality is that the vast majority of farmed animals in this country live a fraction of their normal life span, and their lives are filled with suffering that is nearly impossible for us to even imagine. Brought into existence by corporations that consider them mere units of production, they endure routine, institutional—yet terrible—abuses. Old MacDonald and his farm have become bygone figments of an earlier era. Not only do animals pay the price, but so do people and the environment.

LAWS

Despite the fact that nearly 10 billion animals are raised and killed for food each year in the United States, there are virtually no laws that pro-tect them from even the worst abuse. Only a small handful of federal laws exist. Most state cruelty codes exempt common agricultural prac-tices, so cruelty that would result in criminal prosecution if the victim were a dog or a cat is standard business practice at factory farms.[9]

The United States lags far behind Europe in its treatment of farmed animals. The European Union has already passed legislation banning barren battery cages, the intensive confinement of calves in veal crates, and the use of gestation crates to confine female pigs. As B. R. Myers points out in his *Atlantic Monthly* piece, "If we do less than the Europeans to protect our livestock, then, it is not because we are callous but because we believe that the average factory-farm owner—and most of us are indeed likely to imagine a 'rancher' instead—will not cause the animals in his care MORE suffering than is necessary. . . . This complacency, which is encouraged by the meat industry's PR machine, reflects one of our most cherished national myths."[10]

Only two federal laws do exist to protect farmed animals: the Twenty-eight Hour Law of 1873, which regulates treatment of animals during transport, and the Humane Methods of Slaughter Act of 1958, which requires that processors render animals unconscious before slaughtering them. Yet there are absolutely no federal protections for animals on farms. Other areas cry out for regulation, such as intensive confinement and genetic manipulation of animals used for food. These receive little legislative attention at all.

Transport

Each year, US factory farms transport tens of millions of live pigs, cows, and sheep to slaughterhouses, and billions more birds, such as chickens and turkeys, make similar journeys. The hauls are routinely many hundreds and sometimes more than a thousand miles; animals may be shipped from Canada to the United States, from the United States to Mexico, or coast-to-coast.

For the great majority of American farmed animals, the trip from the factory farm to the slaughterhouse is terrifying and abusive. Crowded into trailers and hauled for long distances, most farmed animals do not receive food, water, or an opportunity to stretch their limbs. Even worse, they are often packed together so tightly that they trample and injure each other. And they are often completely exposed to the elements; in 2006, about 150 pigs from Ohio died in Brownsville, Texas, on the way to Mexico. After being left on trucks for up to two days in temperatures exceeding 90 degrees—with no access to water—the animals died from heat exhaustion and dehydration.[11] Not only does transport cause stress and injury, but the stress involved in the crowded, unfamiliar conditions harms the animals' immune systems, which increases their susceptibility to disease.[12]

Animals in trucks are also injured in traffic accidents or when they fall off vehicles, such as a Thanksgiving 2005 incident in which two dozen turkeys fell off a truck and stopped traffic in New Jersey. As a state official pointedly quipped, "I think we should be investigating this as an escape attempt."[13]

In 1873 Congress passed the Twenty-eight Hour Law, which requires that for every twenty-eight hours of interstate transport, shippers must offload animals and provide them with at least five hours of rest, food, and water. Yet each year, millions of animals travel for days in cramped, squalid conditions without access to food or water. Exhausted and often injured, many animals do not survive the trip. The USDA has the responsibility of enforcing this law, but until 2006, it interpreted the law as not applicable to trucks—despite the fact that the law states that transporters "may not confine animals in a vehicle or vessel for more than 28 consecutive hours." Railroads were the primary means of transporting animals in 1873, since there were no trucks. Today nearly all farmed animals in the United States are shipped on trucks.[14] And despite the USDA's reversal of its position, it has not yet enforced the law.

As a result of the crowding and mistreatment during transport, hundreds of thousands of cows and calves become too injured or ill to move on their own each year. At slaughterhouses or animal auctions, workers often drag these "downed" animals off the trucks using ropes, chains, or even forklifts or tractors. Since the USDA has temporarily banned the use of downed cows for human consumption, these animals possess no economic value. Many of these operations simply leave the animals to die. They may take days to perish, with no access to food, water, veterinary care, or pain relief.

States such as California, Colorado, Florida, Illinois, Indiana, Maryland, Oregon, and Washington have enacted legislation regulating the marketing and transport of downed animals, but the federal government has yet to do so. Following the first confirmed American case of mad cow disease in 2003, the USDA issued a temporary ban on the use of downed cows for food. The agency has not yet made this ban permanent. Although federal legislators have introduced the Downed Animal Protection Act in subsequent years, the bill has yet to pass both the Senate and the House.

Slaughter

In 1958 Congress passed the Humane Methods of Slaughter Act (HMSA) in order to ensure that slaughterhouse workers render animals insensible to pain before shackling and slaughtering them. The HMSA explicitly states that "cattle, calves, horses, mules, sheep, swine, and other livestock" receive protection from inhumane slaughter practices. Yet, the USDA interprets the term "other livestock" to exclude chickens, turkeys, fish, and other animals—thereby allowing more than 9 billion animals to be slaughtered every year using the same inhumane methods that Congress declared in 1958 to cause needless suffering.

Slaughterhouses across the country systematically abuse birds by shackling and hanging them upside down on a conveyor belt, electrically stunning and paralyzing some of them, cutting their necks with mechanical blades, and drowning them in tanks of scalding hot water—all while they are completely conscious. In 2004 the *New York Times* reported on a People for the Ethical Treatment of Animals investigation that documented workers practices at a West Virginia Pilgrim's Pride slaughterhouse, the second-largest chicken processor in the United States. Video depicted slaughterhouse workers "jumping up and down on live chickens, drop-kicking them like footballs and slamming them into walls, apparently for fun."[15]

Biotechnology and Cloning

New developments in animal science are aimed at increasing the productivity of food animals, and the field ranges from animal behavior to
genetics, nutrition, physiology, growth, and more. One new development is the use of antibiotics to prevent illness in otherwise healthy
farmed animals. For the past forty years, penicillin, tetracycline, and
other antibiotics have been routinely used to keep farmed animals
healthy in unhealthy factory conditions. While Europe has banned the
use of hormones such as testosterone and estrogen, US animal producers commonly use them to stimulate growth and meat production.[16]

Genetic engineering and cloning of farmed animals is another relatively recent development. Genetic engineering involves changing animals' genetic makeup by manipulating and transferring selected genes
from one animal to the next. Although proponents claim that it allows scientists much greater control over traits, such as tenderness of flesh, disease resistance, and amount of fat, it remains extremely controversial,
both among the public as well as a number of scientists who are concerned about unintended consequences of using these methods.
According to a 2006 Pew Initiative on Food and Biotechnology poll, 64
percent of American consumers are uncomfortable with animal cloning.[17]

Some scientists have promoted the cloning of farmed animals to
increase yields since Dolly the sheep was successfully cloned in 1996
in Edinburgh, Scotland. She was euthanized at the age of eight due to
a degenerative lung condition.[18] Only about 6 percent of cloned farm
animal embryos survive.[19] Offspring often suffer from deformities,
diabetes, immune deficiencies, dysfunctional organs, circulatory and
respiratory problems, and more.[20] In addition, the availability of
genetically modified animals who have higher disease resistance could
encourage factory farms to keep them in even worse, overcrowded
conditions. So far, the focus has been to clone prized breeder animals.
Yet, since 2001, the Food and Drug Administration (FDA) has only
imposed a *voluntary* moratorium on sales of milk or meat from cloned
animals—which means that it's legal to sell these products.

In late 2006, the FDA released a report concluding that meat and milk from cloned animals and their offspring are safe—and that they should be sold without any labeling. A *New York Times* editorial blasted the FDA's move as a "victory for biotech companies and a loss for everyone else. Like many decisions on the cutting edge of agricultural technology, it was hurried along in a way that is more sensitive to political and economic pressure than to the long-term welfare of animals, humans and the world they inhabit. Asking whether cloned meat and milk are safe is not even the right question. The right question is, why clone at all?"[21]

BIRDS

Birds are both the most misunderstood and most abused farm animals in the country, with more than 9 billion of them killed for human consumption each year.[22] Recent research indicates that their intelligence in some ways surpasses that of dogs and cats, and that they exhibit advanced behavior similar to primates.[23] Yet virtually no laws protect them during their lives or slaughter. From birth until death, they endure daily systematic abuse in ways that would result in prosecution if the victims were companion animals.

Research indicates that birds are much more socially complex and intelligent than we previously believed—they can use tools, solve mathematical problems, deceive, and learn and teach vocal communication.[24] According to animal scientist Joy Mench, "Chickens show sophisticated social behavior. That's what a pecking order is all about. They can recognize more than a hundred other chickens and remember them. They have more than thirty types of vocalizations."[25] When chickens are allowed ample space outside, they spend their time interacting with other birds, establishing a social hierarchy, scratching about on the ground looking for insects, dust bathing, nesting, preening, and resting.

Until the twentieth century, many families raised chickens and turkeys on farms throughout the country. The animals lived outside or in coops. It wasn't until the 1920s in the mid-Atlantic Delmarva region of the East Coast that mass poultry production became commonplace. In the decades since, industrialized factory farms containing tens of thousands of birds have replaced smaller flocks. These operations control every aspect of the birds' existence, from hatching to slaughter.

While this allows for a minimal amount of work, it also creates a multitude of health problems, suffering, and institutional vulnerability; if something as simple as power failure affects a chicken shed, tens of thousands of animals can die from excessive heat in as little as an hour and a half.[26] This tight management, while effective for the bottom line, puts productivity ahead of welfare at the expense of the birds. As one animal scientist stated, "[O]n the balance of the evidence, we must conclude that approximately one quarter of the heavy strains of broiler chicken and turkey are in chronic pain for approximately one third of their lives. . . . [T]his must constitute, in both magnitude and severity, the single most severe, systematic example of man's inhumanity to another sentient animal."[27]

Not only has production moved indoors to vast sheds, but the industry has become increasingly consolidated as our collective appetite for chicken meat has skyrocketed—since 1955, US annual chicken meat production has increased from 2,412 million pounds to 35,800 million pounds in 2005.[28] Today, just four companies—Pilgrim's Pride, Tyson, Perdue, and Sanderson Farms—produce 58.5 percent of chickens used for meat.[29]

For the egg-laying hens, nearly 300 million of whom comprise the nation's egg-laying flock, conditions are much more bleak. First invented in the United States in the 1930s, the *battery cage* (named for the large numbers of cages in one shed, as in a "battery" of tests) has become the standard in egg production. Approximately 95 percent of egg producers now use these wire cages to confine several birds for the duration of their lives. Despite the overwhelming number of chickens used for food and eggs, they are virtually unprotected from even the worst cruelties. No federal laws exist to protect them while on factory farms. As we've seen, the USDA interprets the Humane Methods of Slaughter Act to exempt birds.

There are some signs of progress, however. Thanks to the efforts of animal welfare organizations, corporations such as Wolfgang Puck's and Burger King have raised welfare standards for laying hens, and these policies are reflective of broad consumer concern regarding farm animal welfare. As of this writing, more than 150 schools across the country have enacted policies to eliminate or greatly reduce their use of eggs from caged hens. Many retailers and food service providers have done the same, and their numbers are skyrocketing. A 2005 poll found that more than four-fifths of Americans support covering birds under the Humane Methods of Slaughter Act.[30] And according to a 2000 Zogby poll, an even higher percentage agreed that "crowding 8–10 chickens in cages, about the size of an open newspaper, so tightly that they cannot stretch their wings . . . [is] unacceptable."[31] Even still, birds raised for meat and eggs in this country endure lives filled with suffering.

Broilers

In the United States, chickens comprise the vast majority of land animals killed for our dinners. Each year, more than 9 billion of these animals endure short, miserable lives on factory farms. While a chicken's normal life span is up to fifteen years, the average chicken raised for meat, called a *broiler*, lives for just forty-five days or less before heading for the slaughterhouse—forty-five days inside a barren, windowless, and filthy space with tens of thousands of other birds.[32] And the only escape from the factory farm is hardly a respite at all; they suffer further cruelty being caught and transported to the slaughterhouse before the often painful and terrifying end.

A typical chicken factory farm consists of several long "grower houses," or sheds, which can hold about thirty thousand chickens in a shed sixty feet wide by five hundred feet long.[33] While the sheds can be quite massive, the stocking density is high to increase profit—usually, each bird has less than one square foot of space.[34]

Since chicken producers do not clean out the sheds during each forty-five-day cycle—most do not clean them out between every flock turnover—the litter that covers the ground becomes saturated with feces. This in turn creates an environment rife with ammonia, bacteria, and dust, creating an inescapable toxic cloud. High ammonia levels cause a number of health problems, including skin diseases, heart problems, blindness, and hemorrhages. The high bacterial levels also lead to respiratory infections.

While this is bad enough, one insidious practice causes more suffering for broiler chickens than any other: the poultry industry's selective breeding for developing faster-growing birds.

Over the past five decades, the poultry industry has increasingly emphasized productivity, and the time it takes for a bird to reach slaughter weight plays an important role. As chickens and turkeys reach slaughter weight in shorter amounts of time, factory farms can save money on food and other resources, as well as produce a greater number of birds in the same amount of time. Since the 1950s, the average time to grow a broiler chicken to slaughter weight decreased from twelve weeks to six weeks. Birds are larger, too. While the average chicken weighed two pounds at slaughter in the 1970s, birds today can weigh up to thirteen pounds.[35]

So what's the problem with having them grow more rapidly, especially if the average broiler chicken only lives for forty-five days?

This unnaturally rapid growth wreaks havoc on birds, causing a tremendous amount of suffering packed into just a few weeks of life. Indeed, poultry expert Dr. Ian Duncan has concluded, "Without a doubt, the biggest welfare problems for meat birds are those associated with fast growth."[36] Rapid growth contributes to skeletal and metabolic disorders, and it can also lead to respiratory disease, parasitic infections, hepatitis, muscle tissue disease, organ disease, and eventually death.[37] These problems add up to chronic pain and suffering for billions of birds.

The principal problem with rapid growth is that the birds' muscles and fat grow faster than their bones. This leads to skeletal disorders resulting in chronic pain, immobility, and for many birds, early death.

Dr. Temple Grandin, likely the best-known animal scientist in the country, states, "Today's poultry chicken has been bred to grow so rapidly that its legs can collapse under the weight of its ballooning body. It's awful . . . lameness is a severe problem in chicken welfare. I've been to farms where half of the chickens are lame."[38]

As a result of this immobility, birds often develop painful lesions, blisters, and burns. And since producers do not clean sheds until the birds are taken to be slaughtered, the animals must stand in their own waste, often contracting disease from bacterial infections in these exposed wounds. Not only can they die from these problems, but they often cannot engage in some of their most important behaviors, including scratching, dust bathing, walking, and even eating and drinking.

After approximately forty-five days, workers collect the birds, stuffing the struggling animals by their legs into crates for their journey to the slaughterhouse on the back of a truck. Not only does the catching process cause terror and injury for the birds, but the truck ride also can cause further stress, injury, and even death.

It takes a team of workers, or catchers, a few hours to "depopulate" a chicken shed, loading birds into crates at a rate of a thousand to fifteen hundred animals per hour.[39] Catchers normally grab several birds in each hand and hold the terrified, flapping animals upside down by one leg. While the ride to the slaughterhouse can be many hours long, truck drivers do not stop to give the birds food, water, or a rest. They have no protection from extreme temperatures. Exposure to cold can cause freezing, leading to gangrene and necrosis. Many birds also perish from heart failure, hyperthermia, or hypothermia.

The slaughter process begins when workers unload chickens from the crates and shackle them upside down on conveyer lines. The lines move at dizzying speeds, up to fifty birds being placed on one line each minute, and this causes problems throughout the slaughter process.

Because so many of the birds have bone problems as a result of rapid growth—and since they may already be injured from catching or transport—shackling is a painful, terrifying business that can result in further injuries and broken bones. According to one study, there is a 44 percent increase in broken bones after shackling.[40]

After the chickens are shackled, the belt carries them down the line, where their heads are immersed in electrified baths of water to stun and immobilize them. While this makes the job easier for the workers, the birds are often simply paralyzed—unable to move but still conscious.

Then either workers or machines cut the chickens' throats. However, the rapid line speed prevents either from performing the job accurately on every animal. Many birds do not bleed to death quickly but instead are still fully conscious as they proceed down the line to the scalding tank. True to their name, these tanks are filled with hot water in order to loosen the chickens' feathers. Those animals unlucky enough to still be conscious when they reach the scalding tank finally die by drowning in excruciatingly hot water.

The way that broiler chickens are bred also creates suffering for tens of millions of animals. In the United States, factory farms use more than 58 million egg-laying chickens, or broiler breeders, to produce broiler chickens.[41] These animals suffer from the same welfare problems as broilers, with two additions: chronic hunger and mutilations.

Factory farms have found a simple solution to some of the problems associated with rapid growth: food restriction. Since unrestricted diets—where the birds can eat as much as they want—can cause obesity, joint strain, and reproductive disorders when coupled with their unnatural growth, producers provide as little as a quarter of the amount of food to the birds that they would normally eat.[42] Food restriction creates not only nutritional deficiency and malnourishment, but also chronic frustration. Even the most basic pleasure—food—is gone, leaving breeder birds with a pathetic existence laden with suffering.

Like other chickens, broiler breeders spend their lives in intensive confinement, but since they live for sixteen months on average, they are more at risk for developing disease and aggressive behavior. In order to reduce these problems, producers cut off the roosters' combs and leg spurs and remove part of the breeders' toes and beaks. Producers perform these mutilations without anesthetic, not only causing acute pain, but often causing chronic pain for the remainder of their lives.

Egg-Laying Hens

Throughout the United States, more than 95 percent of the nation's egg-laying flock of nearly 300 million hens spend their entire lives crammed in barren, wire battery cages.[43] For their twelve- to eighteen-month life spans, they are confined inside massive factory farm sheds, which can contain up to a hundred thousand animals. The hens cannot perform nearly any of their natural behaviors and, amazingly, they even lack the space to walk and spread their wings. As a result of this confinement, hens in battery cages endure intense stress and frustration, as well as suffer from a number of painful and debilitating physical problems.

In the United States, nearly 300 million egg-laying hens are confined in wire battery cages so restrictive that the birds cannot even spread their wings or walk. (Photo courtesy of Compassion Over Killing)

Animal rescuers gently loading chickens into
transport containers in the aftermath of Hurricane Katrina.
(Photo courtesy of Peter Wood, HSUS)

Chickens Pulled from Katrina's Devastation

In the wake of Hurricane Katrina's devastation, millions of farmed animals were left either dead or dying in factory farms in Louisiana and Mississippi. Each year, these two states slaughter more than a million pigs, half a million cows, and nearly a billion chickens raised for both meat and eggs. Yet, thanks to the efforts of a small number of volunteers, more than a thousand chickens were rescued from the ravages of the disaster.

Not only did the hurricane destroy hundreds of chicken sheds, but widespread power outages, coupled with the lack of food and water, caused millions of birds to suffer and die in excruciating heat. Across Mississippi—the nation's fourth-largest chicken meat producer—the smell of rotting corpses permeated the air. According to one resident who spoke with rescuers, there were so many chicken corpses in one area that it looked like a "field of cotton." And producers were already bulldozing sheds, killing countless birds who were still clinging to survival.

Rescuers from the Humane Society of the United States, Farm Sanctuary, and Animal Place obtained permission from a chicken producer contracted with Tyson Foods to rescue birds from his operation. Katrina had damaged several of his five long sheds that each confined tens of thousands of chickens.

Over a period of two days, rescuers caught more than a thousand chickens, searching out animals huddled in groups in the surrounding woods. At one point, rescuers used a pole and net to rescue twenty-one birds from a massive, steaming open pit that contained thousands of decomposing birds and even empty beer cans.

The rescued birds now live in permanent homes, including Farm Sanctuary's New York shelter and Animal Place's sanctuary in California, where they will spend the rest of their lives in comfort and protection.

Life begins for egg-laying hens in commercial hatcheries, which produce millions of chicks. Once the eggs hatch, workers sort the chicks, collecting the females for shipment to egg producers. Since the egg industry has no use for male chicks, they are killed almost immediately—the hatcheries usually gas them, grind them up, or simply

Rescued chickens enjoying the sunshine in Farm Sanctuary.
(Photo courtesy of Farm Sanctuary)

discard them in dumpsters to suffocate or dehydrate. In 1998 the commercial egg industry killed 219 million male chicks.[44]

At one to two weeks of age, nearly all of the female chicks who will become egg-laying hens endure painful debeaking, in which producers slice off part of their beaks with a hot blade. There is no anesthesia or pain relief, despite the fact that the procedure results in acute pain and distress for the chicks, who possess nerve endings throughout their beaks.[45] While the egg industry claims that debeaking is necessary to decrease cannibalism and reduce feed costs, caged hens rarely cannibalize each other.[46] Another reason to debeak birds is simply for profit—since debeaking results in chronic pain for the birds, they have difficulty eating. This reduces the hens' food consumption, saving money for the producer.

On a battery cage factory farm, each cage confines several hens—completely barren except for an automatic feeder and a water nozzle. An average battery cage is about twenty inches wide by twenty inches deep by fourteen inches tall, which provides each bird with less floor space than a sheet of letter-sized paper—about sixty-seven to eighty-six square inches per hen.[47] Depending on the number of hens, some birds have even less room. The cages are typically stacked on top of each other in rows up to seven cages high; since the cages are wire bottomed, feces from the upper cages sometimes drops down onto the birds below. Eggs roll from the cages onto conveyer belts that gently move the eggs out of the shed where they are automatically packaged. Indeed, more care is given to the eggs than to the chickens.

In order to keep operating costs down, sheds are typically climate controlled. Worker involvement is minimal. On most factory egg farms, a small team of employees walk the long aisles between battery cages once a day, collecting dead birds from cages. In 2006 one employee at a Michael Foods factory farm in Nebraska documented atrocious—yet not uncommon—conditions, including hens unable to untangle themselves from cage wires, hens trapped in cages with decomposing corpses, and immobilized birds dying from starvation and dehydration, inches away from food and water. The employee's job was simply to remove hundreds of dead birds from cages each day at the factory farm, which confined approximately a million hens in similar conditions.[48]

In addition to the constant stress that dominates their daily existence, caged hens suffer a multitude of health problems. The primary cause of death while they are confined in cages is a disease called fatty

Egg-laying hens confined in battery cages. Some of these animals from a Gilroy egg factory were fortunate enough to be rescued by volunteers with animal protection groups. (Photo courtesy of Animal Place)

Gilroy Hen Rescue

In August of 2005, a consortium of animal protection groups, led by Animal Place and including United Animal Nations and East Bay Animal Advocates, banded together to rescue egg-laying hens from a factory farm in Northern California. The owner of the property contacted Animal Place and gave permission to rescue some of the 160,000 hens housed in two dilapidated buildings.

For a week, rescuers loaded frightened birds from cages into crates for transport to sanctuaries and humane societies. We worked alongside catchers whose job it was to rip birds from metal prisons and send them to slaughter. It would only take a week for catchers to depopulate the facility. For the rescuers it was a monumental race against time.

The tiny twenty-three-by-nineteen-inch wire cages, stacked three high, were crammed with seven to ten birds—none of the animals had enough room even to stretch their wings. All had their sensitive beaks partially cut off, making feeding and cleaning themselves difficult. The feces from the top tiers dropped through the wire onto the birds below.

The facility itself became a health hazard for both the rescuers and the farm workers. Ammonia-laden dust particles wafted into noses, while rescuers plodded across planks of splintered wood perched over a manure pit that had never been cleared.

After a week of grueling labor, two thousand birds were saved from slaughter. More than two hundred became permanent residents at Animal Place's sanctuary, while the other eighteen hundred found permanent refuge in homes across the state. The media coverage was immense, with more than two hundred newspapers and television stations running the story.

For those of us who entered those dimly lit buildings, cacophonous with the frightened screams of tens of thousands of animals, it was a magical moment to witness the rescued birds experience freedom. These creatures had never seen the light of day, never touched the real earth, and had never flapped their own wings. When they emerged from the rescue crates, it was a joyous moment to watch as they made leaps into the air, pecked in the dirt, basked in the glow of the sun. It was their time—their time to finally be birds.

Marji Beach
Program Coordinator, Animal Place

These rescued Northern Californian egg-laying hens now enjoy safe, happy lives at Animal Place. (Photo courtesy of Animal Place)

liver hemorrhagic syndrome, which frequently follows forced molting.[49] And laying hens often suffer from uterine prolapse, a condition in which the bird's uterus is pushed outside her body.

While the inability to perform important behaviors such as dust bathing, perching, and even spending time outside creates tremendous psychological suffering for hens, it also leads to health problems. Since hens need to dust bathe in order to regulate their temperature and prevent feather loss, being deprived of this activity leads to these very same issues. And hens who cannot perch suffer from increased aggression and damaged feet. Since the birds are forced to spend their entire lives on wire floors, they can also develop painful foot problems and infections. Deficiency of vitamin D and exercise often causes bone weakness and breakage. Due to these conditions, as well as over-breeding for egg production, 80 to 89 percent of hens suffer from osteoporosis—one study even estimates that one in six laying hens suffers from broken bones before capture and transport.[50]

In their natural environment, hens will take great care to select the safest, most secluded place to lay their eggs, as well as spend time collecting materials with which to construct a nest. However, crammed in a wire cage with several other cage mates, each battery-caged hen can only search futilely each day for an appropriate nesting spot. Poultry welfare experts agree that this causes significant frustration and suffering, since the drive to find a nesting spot is a powerful motivation for hens, as with most female animals who have strong instincts to find a safe place to give birth and care for their young.[51]

A laying hen typically lives twelve to eighteen months, a fraction of the life expectancy for a healthy chicken in a natural environment. As the birds reach one year of age, they begin to lay eggs less frequently. In order to increase egg yield, some producers "force molt" the birds, starving the hens or feeding them only low-nutrient feed until they lose 30 percent of their body weight. After the weight loss is reached, producers begin feeding the birds their previous diet. Fortunately, the starvation method is now uncommon. Previously, producers starved hens for ten to fourteen days, and their mortality rates could nearly double.[52]

After the birds are no longer productive, factory farm workers "depopulate" the sheds, removing the birds and either killing them on site or shipping them to a slaughtering or rendering plant. For these "spent" hens, the removal from their cages causes injury and trauma. By the time workers catch them for slaughter, the hens have spent their entire lives crammed in cages without being able to walk or spread their wings, much less exercise. As a result, their bodies are frail, and the removal process breaks and dislocates bones, ruptures organs, and causes head trauma and other injuries.

Most "spent" hens are economically worthless, and many egg factory farms dispose of the birds on site. Workers sometimes compost the hens, burying them alive in mass graves. Other egg producers load them into dumpsters like garbage; in 2005 a Missouri man's videotape documented the country's third-largest egg producer, Moark, using a conveyor belt to load live chickens into a dumpster, where they were undoubtedly crushed or suffocated.[53] Spent hens may also be gassed with carbon monoxide and composted. However, gassing doesn't kill all the chickens. In 2006 Northern California residents were shocked to see chickens "crawling out of a mound of compost like the living dead" and staggering around. Witnesses called them "zombie chickens."[54]

Other egg producers ship egg-laying hens to one of the few slaughtering or rendering plants that accept "spent" hens. As the workers collect birds from their cages, they often hold several birds at once as they move them into crates and load them onto trucks for their journey. From here, their transport and slaughter is similar to that of broiler chickens, with all of the accompanying abuses.

A movement to eliminate battery cages is gaining momentum. More than 150 schools have enacted policies to eliminate or greatly decrease their use of eggs from caged hens. Burger King is switching some of its eggs to cage-free. Wolfgang Puck and Ben & Jerry's are ending their use of eggs from caged hens. A number of major retailers have eliminated their sales of cage eggs entirely, and even tech companies such as AOL and Google no longer use cage eggs in their corporate cafeterias. City councils in Maryland, Florida, and California have unanimously adopted resolutions condemning battery cages.

Moving away from battery cages won't solve all the problems with egg production, but the burgeoning opposition to this extreme factory farm cruelty is an important step forward.

Turkeys

In the wild, turkeys are agile, social creatures who can live up to ten years. Domesticated in North America since the early seventeenth century, today's turkeys are creatures far removed in appearance from their wild counterparts—misshapen, unable to fly or even to mate, and in chronic pain. In the United States, factory farms produce more than 255 million turkeys each year for our consumption.[55] The four largest turkey producers—Butterball, Hormel, Cargill, and Sara Lee—are responsible for 55 percent of US turkeys.[56]

Young turkeys, also called "poults," endure mutilations within the first days of life in commercial hatcheries. Their snoods—fleshy nubs above their beaks—and up to one-half of their sensitive beaks are cut off to help prevent aggression. Parts of their toes are sliced off to prevent them from damaging themselves, since their carcasses would decrease in value.

In just 132 days, turkeys reach their slaughter weight of thirty-five pounds.[57] As with broiler chickens, selective breeding for rapid growth causes the most severe welfare problems for turkeys. Turkeys suffer from skeletal disease, heart disease, immobility, and the resulting welfare problems.

In addition, US factory farms use approximately 4 million turkeys as breeders each year. Turkey breeders can suffer from similar problems as other turkeys and broilers. Since turkeys breeders live longer than their counterparts raised for slaughter, their skeletal problems can be more pronounced. Hip problems can affect all male turkey breeders in a flock, causing chronic pain. Like their chicken breeder counterparts, they suffer from chronic hunger. Producers provide as little as half the amount of food to turkey breeders than they might otherwise eat. Mortality rates among turkey breeders can vary between 25 and 66 percent before they are sent to slaughter.[58]

Due to selective breeding, male turkeys' breast muscles are so unnaturally large that they cannot mate normally—virtually every turkey in the country is born as a result of artificial insemination.[59] In this process, workers "milk" the birds to collect semen. About twice a week for nearly their entire lives, workers catch the toms, flip the struggling birds over, clamp them into position, and use a sucking device to collect semen. Once a week, the female turkeys endure a similar process, where workers also forcibly hold them upside down and then inject the liquid.

Americans view the turkey as an icon of our national character at Thanksgiving. Yet factory farming has reduced the wild turkey, an animal that Benjamin Franklin once proposed as our national bird, to a pathetically crippled, genetically manipulated creature who cannot even reproduce naturally, let alone live in the wild.

Foie Gras

Not many Americans are familiar with foie gras, an expensive pâté or liver dish, whose name is French for "fatty liver." Yet each year in the United States, hundreds of thousands of ducks endure miserable lives to satisfy the palates of affluent foodies willing to pay stratospheric prices for it—foie gras retails for up to thirty dollars per pound. True to its name, foie gras is the deliberately fattened liver of a duck or goose—an organ that is, quite literally, diseased.

US foie gras factory farms typically use male Mulard ducks, a cross between a Muscovy and a domestic duck. The process begins at the hatcheries, where workers separate ducklings according to sex and either sell females to meat producers or kill them.

When the birds are about fourteen weeks old, producers confine them in small pens and begin the month-long force-feeding process. Three times each day, workers use a metal or plastic pipe to shove tremendous quantities of ground-up cornmeal down their throats. Not only does force-feeding cause physical problems, but along with intensive confinement, it also causes psychological distress.[60]

After viewing undercover video taken at a US foie gras producer that documented appalling conditions, including floors covered in vomit and feces, rats tearing at the flesh of live birds, and live birds living in pens with corpses, a number of restaurants have removed foie gras from their menus.[61] Indeed, force-feeding and restrictive, filthy conditions cause a host of health issues. Since force-feeding involves the forcible insertion of a pipe, this trauma causes lacerations and bruises, and the pipe can even tear through the esophagus, causing more pain at each force-feeding. In addition, the birds' livers can swell to more than ten times their normal size; not surprisingly, the unnaturally massive size of the livers also impedes organ function. At the beginning of the force-feeding process, their livers weigh approximately three ounces. When the birds are slaughtered, they can weigh up to two pounds.[62] Their swollen livers engorge their abdomens, making it difficult for them to move. Many ducks also suffer from impaired mobility as a result of foot and leg problems, which cause additional pain. The European Union Scientific Committee on Animal Health and Animal Welfare found that the mortality rate of force-fed birds was ten to twenty-five times greater than conventionally farmed birds of the same age.[63]

Intensive confinement prohibits many ducks from participating in normal behaviors, such as interacting with one another, preening, and even walking and spreading their wings. And foie gras factory farms prevent ducks—waterfowl with a strong need to bathe and swim—from accessing water.

In 2003 the California legislature passed a measure banning the production and sale of foie gras, to be effective in 2012. In 2006 Chicago aldermen approved a bill banning its sale in the city. California and Chicago join more than a dozen other places, including the United Kingdom, Finland, Sweden, Denmark, Norway, Germany, Poland, Israel, and Switzerland, that have passed legislation addressing this cruelty. And high-profile chefs such as Wolfgang Puck and Charlie Trotter refuse to use foie gras due to animal welfare concerns.

There are currently three factory farms that produce foie gras in the United States: Hudson Valley Foie Gras and La Belle, both in New York, and Sonoma County Foie Gras in California. Of the three, Hudson Valley Foie Gras is the largest, producing three-fourths of all US foie gras.[64] The company uses more than three hundred thousand ducks each year with more than $12 million in annual sales and $1.5 million in annual profits. With an estimated $20 million in combined annual sales, a number of foie gras producers have joined together to form the North American Foie Gras Producers Association to protect their profits from the burgeoning movement away from foie gras.[65]

PIGS

The ancestors of today's factory-farmed hogs were active, highly social animals who spent a great amount of time each day foraging, rooting, mud bathing, and walking about, as well as engaging in complex social behaviors. Studies have shown, for instance, that pigs recognize other pigs, both in the wild and in confinement, and they base their behaviors with other pigs on previous interactions with those individuals, demonstrating both an advanced memory and strong social skills.[66]

In ideal circumstances in animal sanctuaries, domestic pigs live very similar lives. Rescued pigs enjoy interacting with people and other pigs, napping in hay-filled barns and lolling about in the mud. Unlike their wild counterparts who can live up to twenty years, the contemporary factory-farmed hog exists in a dark, often windowless shed for six months before being shipped to slaughter. Riddled with physical problems, more than 100 million pigs are slaughtered every year for our meals.[67]

While far removed from their natural environment by breeding and geography, factory-farmed pigs are still social and intelligent—some say they are even smarter than dogs.[68] This only makes their confinement that much more abusive. Intensive hog production has become commonplace in the United States since the 1980s, since the shift began from smaller, traditional operations to larger, more-consolidated factory farms. The four largest pork producers—Smithfield, IBP, Swift/ConAgra, and Excel/Cargill—control a majority of the market of nearly 70 percent. As with other farmed animal sectors, family farmers are becoming extinct as giant corporations control everything from semen production to slaughter. Here again, profit is the culprit. One researcher explained, "[I]t is the economic forces that drive pork producers to do things that hurt or stress their pigs."[69]

The life of a factory-farmed pig begins in a farrowing crate designed to separate mother pigs from their piglets. The crates are tiny, offering just enough room for the sow to stand up or lie down. At two to five days of age, producers cut off the tails of piglets and castrate the males; all of this is done without anesthesia. Tails are docked in order to discourage piglets from biting other pigs' tails, while the pigs are castrated both to reduce aggression and to reduce odor, or "boar taint," from the meat. Producers abruptly remove the piglets from their mother at as little as two weeks of age, about five and a half months before they would naturally wean themselves. The piglets are moved to growing pens, where they remain in groups.

After about six weeks, unless they are on a "farrow to finish" operation where they would remain for their entire lives, they are trucked to a finishing operation, where they live for about four and a half months until they reach market weight of 240 to 260 pounds. The pigs spend the rest of their lives in filthy, overcrowded metal pens, standing and lying on barren concrete with nothing to occupy their normally active, curious nature. This causes boredom, stress, and health problems. Respiratory disease is common since the air is thick with ammonia and dust. Months spent without exercise on concrete exacerbates arthritis for many pigs, which is caused by illnesses, bacterial infections, and trauma.

Truffles and Rudy, who were rescued after falling off of transport trucks.
(Photo courtesy of Farm Sanctuary)

Truffles and Rudy

Truffles and Rudy have been inseparable since they both arrived at Farm Sanctuary as young piglets in September 2005. Both piglets had fallen out of two different transport trucks in Indiana on their way to "finishing" farms, where they would be fattened for a few months and shipped to slaughter— likely destined to become holiday hams.

Truffles was a very young piglet when she fell off a truck on Indiana's Interstate 69, injuring herself as she hit the pavement. Fortunately, a brave and compassionate woman witnessed Truffles' fall, and she pulled over, ran across heavy traffic, and carried her back to the car. The exhausted, bloody piglet fell asleep as soon as she lay down on a blanket in the back-seat. Farm Sanctuary member Diane Evans agreed to foster Truffles until she could be transported to the organization's New York shelter.

Only a few days later, a kindhearted trucker found Rudy near an Inter-state 74 truck stop in Indiana and brought him to an animal shelter near Indianapolis. Although animal control officers originally made arrange-ments to send Rudy to a farmer who would raise him for food, the farmer missed the deadline to pick him up. Farm Sanctuary was able to intervene, and volunteers brought the lucky piglet who had escaped slaughter twice to Diane Evans's home.

Here, Truffles and Rudy met for the first time, and by the time the two piglets arrived at Farm Sanctuary, they were already bonded. Now the growing piglets rarely leave each other's side, and they enjoy days filled with playing in their mud bath, watching the other animals at the sanctuary, and reveling in attention. While most factory-farmed pigs live only six months before being sent to slaughter, Truffles and Rudy can look forward to spending the rest of their lives—perhaps more than ten years—happy, safe, and loved.

Like many other farmed animals, pigs are killed when they are still babies. These animals endure lives far removed from those of wild pigs or young animals fortunate enough to find homes in sanctuaries. Piglets normally spend much of their time playing, establishing a social hierarchy, learning how to root and dig mud holes, grazing, and traveling with a herd. Kept in confinement for their entire lives, these important, natural behaviors are completely thwarted.

Transport

Transport is one of the most stressful and traumatic parts of a pig's life. Hundreds of thousands of animals are injured and killed during the process annually. *National Hog Farmer* magazine reported that each year, 420,000 pigs are crippled and 170,000 die during transport.[70] Pigs can freeze to death on the trucks in cold temperatures, and they are especially susceptible to death and heatstroke in high temperatures.

Truffles and Rudy resting inside their barn.
(Photo courtesy of Farm Sanctuary)

Slaughter

Workers unload the pigs from the truck and herd them into a series of pens at the slaughterhouse. They move small groups of pigs into a small stunning pen and then electrically stun the pigs using a large pair of tongs that they clamp to both sides of a pig's head. Since slaughterhouse lines are fast—line speed can be up to twelve hundred pigs processed per hour—the workers must stun and shackle the animals quickly.[71] In their haste, they may not stun the pigs into unconsciousness, so some are chained and hoisted upside down onto overhead conveyor belts while still conscious. The belts carry the animals to the next worker, the "sticker," who cuts through their carotid arteries and jugular veins. The animals can take five minutes to bleed to death, and then they are dropped into scalding tanks that loosen hair. If the "sticker" does not cut all the way through the carotid and jugular, a pig may still be conscious and struggling as he or she enters the scalding tank and drowns.

Pig processing is increasingly consolidated. The four largest pig processors—Smithfield, Tyson, Swift & Co., and Cargill—slaughter 66 percent of pigs in the United States.[72]

Gestation Crates

Factory farm hog producers confine at least 60 to 70 percent of the nation's more than 6 million female breeding pigs, or sows, inside barren, metal gestation crates in massive, windowless sheds that can confine more than a hundred animals.[73] On average, these crates measure two feet wide, and they do not provide adequate space for the sows to turn around. Forced to live on concrete slatted floors above pits of their own feces, these intelligent animals can develop a range of devastating problems. In a 2006 talk, Temple Grandin explained, "Gestation crates for pigs are a real problem. . . . Basically, you're asking a sow to live in an airline seat. . . . I think it's something that needs to be phased out."[74]

Sows are artificially inseminated for the first time at approximately seven months of age, a method that more than 90 percent of hog factory farms use to induce pregnancy.[75] In order to collect semen, a "milker" essentially masturbates the animal, holding the boar's penis in his hand as the boar mounts a dummy and collecting semen as the boar ejaculates. Sows are inseminated almost immediately after their babies are taken from them, after fewer than two weeks of nursing, and they produce two to two and a half litters on average each year. Living for an average of four years in this state of confinement, they function only as breeding machines to churn out piglets.

Physical Problems

Sows in gestation crates suffer from a number of health problems that can cause a lifetime of suffering. Indeed, these health problems can often lead to higher mortality before slaughter. Since waste from the sows falls through concrete slats in the crates into a pit below, lying above the pit exposes sows to ammonia from decomposing feces, causing respiratory disease. And crated sows often suffer from urinary tract infections, a major cause of mortality, since they often do not drink enough water and are forced to lie in their own feces and urine.

In addition, a lifetime spent standing and lying on slatted concrete causes tremendous problems, with many crated sows suffering from cardiovascular disease, respiratory illness, foot lesions, joint disorders, and lameness. The inability to turn around or even walk reduces muscle and bone strength, impeding even the most basic of movements. Sows also often injure themselves by standing on the concrete floors, as well as rubbing against enclosure bars. And they may also be stepped on by other sows as they extend their legs into adjacent stalls when lying down.

Psychological Suffering

Not only does the intensive confinement cause physical problems for millions of sows, but it also harms their mental health. Since the animals are nearly immobilized throughout their lives, and producers routinely feed them about half the amount of food they might otherwise consume, they develop repetitive, stereotypic stress behaviors. These may include head-weaving, biting the bars of crates, repeatedly nudging drinking fixtures, and excessive chewing. Some of these actions can cause self-inflicted injury, while some sows become inactive and unresponsive, likely symptoms of clinical depression.[76]

Because of the obvious cruelty inherent in the intensive confinement of pigs, the European Union has banned the use of gestation crates, effective in 2013, and the United Kingdom and Sweden have already prohibited their use. In 2002, Florida voters overwhelmingly approved a constitutional amendment to phase out the use of gestation crates. And in a 2006 landslide, Arizona voters approved an initiative to prohibit gestation crates, effective in 2012.

Only a few months later in early 2007, Smithfield—the world's largest pig producer—sent shockwaves through agribusiness when it announced that it is phasing out the use of gestation crates over the next decade. Citing customer concern as the company's reason for the phaseout, Smithfield Foods' CEO C. Larry Pope stated in a press release, "While this will be a significant financial commitment for our company over the next ten years, we believe it's the right thing to do."[77] Maple Leaf Farms, Canada's largest pig producer, followed suit days later. Some retailers and restaurants, such as Whole Foods and Chipotle, only sell pork from producers that do not use gestation crates to confine sows.

COWS

Cows are social animals who rarely spend time alone. They stay with their herd while grazing, resting, and ruminating. While their intellect isn't the first attribute that many of us consider when we think about them, recent research indicates that cows are socially sophisticated, intelligent animals. They can maintain friendships over long periods of time; hold grudges; feel happiness, fear, and pain; and even worry about the future.[78] In a healthy environment, they can live up to twenty-five years.

Yet the small, family-owned dairy and the pastoral ranch of the American frontier—both of which, while not ideal, at least allowed for most of cows' natural behaviors—are rapidly becoming relics of the past, as factory dairies and feedlots replace them. These modern facilities, which can contain thousands of animals, thwart the animals' strong need for unrestricted social interaction, as well as create a host of welfare problems for the animals. Today's veal calves and dairy cows endure painful separation from their mothers after birth. Whether crammed into a restrictive crate, forced to live in knee-high muck on a concrete floor, or left to spend months on a dusty feedlot, many cows suffer miserably.

Veal

For most consumers, veal is synonymous with animal abuse—and with good reason. In 2006 more than 710,000 calves were slaughtered for veal.[79] The great majority of these animals are confined in crates so tiny, they cannot turn around, walk, or even lie down comfortably. This restriction, along with an unnatural diet, produces the anemic, tender flesh that is prized by the few remaining veal consumers. Veal consumption in the United States has plummeted as a result of widespread concern for the way in which factory farmers produce veal. In 2005, veal production set a new record low.[80]

Although calves typically nurse for about seven months, producers separate male calves from their mothers within a day or two after birth. The mothers return to the dairy herd to begin the next cycle of milking. The calves are shipped to an animal auction where they are purchased, then shipped to a facility where they will be grown to slaughter weight. Shipped at only few days of age, many calves are barely even old enough to walk by themselves, and often many die on the journey.

After arriving at the facility, the calves are tethered by their necks into barren wooden crates that measure two feet wide. They are unable to turn around and exercise, lie down normally, play, groom themselves, interact with other calves, and explore their environment. As a result of the complete lack of stimulation, calves can lose interest in eating and become depressed. They may also engage in stereotypic behaviors such as rolling their tongues about or bar biting.

Veal producers feed calves an all-liquid, iron- and fiber-deficient diet that induces anemia and a number of other health problems, including abnormal gut development, diarrhea, stomach ulcers, and

Jacob

In 1999 motorists found a tiny Holstein calf wandering around near a Massachusetts highway. Bruised and bleeding, the calf was only one day old, and his umbilical cord was still attached to his belly. He had fallen off a transport truck heading from a dairy farm to an auction, where he almost certainly would have been purchased and shipped to a veal producer, confined in a veal crate for about six months, and killed to become a "delicacy."

The passersby contacted animal control, and officers brought him to the local humane society. Workers there contacted Poplar Spring Animal Sanctuary in Maryland and arranged transport to their four-hundred-acre refuge for farm animals—a permanent, loving home for the calf who, like all calves confined in crates on veal factory farms, endured separation from his mother in the first days of his life.

Today, the small calf has become a big boy named Jacob. He weighs about fifteen hundred pounds and is still growing. He isn't as large as some of the other steers, such as his companion Norman, who was rescued from an auction when he was only a day old. Jacob's best friend is Minh, a Jersey steer, and the two of them enjoy meandering around their huge pasture with the other cows, chewing their cud under the shade trees, and enjoying attention from sanctuary visitors. Jacob loves eating timothy hay and, as a treat, sweet feed made from corn, oats, and molasses. Every once in a while, he indulges in his favorite "junk food": a piece of white bread.

Fortunately for Jacob, his tumble from the trailer resulted in a lifetime of care and companionship. He has the freedom to socialize, move about freely, and enjoy the earth and sunshine—all activities that are impossible for calves confined in tiny crates where they cannot even turn around.

increased susceptibility to disease. Producers keep calves inside wooden crates instead of iron ones, so that the calves cannot consume iron by licking the crate bars.

Calves are highly social animals who enjoy spending a great amount of time interacting with their mothers and other calves. They also spend time playing with other calves and grazing. Factory farms frustrate these social needs by separating the animals from their mothers and confining them in individual crates that restrict movement and prevent interaction with other animals.

Veal calves usually spend their entire five-month lives in these cramped, squalid conditions before being shipped to slaughter. As animals with a strong herding instinct, not only do calves suffer from isolation, but they also cannot do the things that calves would normally do: suckle, be groomed by their mothers, learn to graze, or play by

Once a calf destined for a veal crate, Jacob now enjoys roaming around a spacious pasture with other animals.
(Photo courtesy of Poplar Spring Animal Sanctuary)

running, kicking, and bucking. Animals raised for veal are among the most abused in the country, simply to satisfy the desire for pale white flesh at dinner.

There is hope that the situation is improving for calves raised for veal. The European Union has wholly banned veal crates, and in 2006, Arizona voters overwhelmingly approved a measure prohibiting the use of veal crates. Only a couple months later, Strauss Veal, the largest US veal producer, announced that it is phasing out the use of veal crates over the next two to three years. Another leading veal producer, Marcho Farms, quickly followed suit. Converting to crate-free housing won't eliminate every issue with veal production, but it will improve the lives of countless calves.

Dairy

Although the American public still holds dear an image of dairy cows spending their lives serenely chewing their cud and grazing in green pastures, the majority of these animals now spend their lives on factory farms. They often do not have access to the outdoors, let alone pastures, and many animals spend their lives on concrete floors. Factory dairies can confine thousands of animals, increasing the amount of milk that the cows produce and using highly mechanized processes that cut costs. As costs go down, the country's 9 million dairy cows suffer. One animal scientist has noted, "Poor welfare can be caused by cruelty or poor management but it is also commoner as production efficiency increases. Mastitis, lameness and reproductive failure tend to increase as milk yield increases."[81]

Like humans and other mammals, cows do not produce milk unless they have given birth. Female calves typically stay in the herd and become milking cows, and as we've seen, many male calves are separated from their mothers nearly immediately after birth for shipment to veal operations.

Over the past decades, the period between the time that cows stop lactating and the next time they give birth has decreased dramatically.

This means that the average dairy cow gives birth to one calf each year, lactating for about six months during her pregnancy before being artificially inseminated about three months after giving birth. Dairy cows generally live for four years before their productivity begins to diminish, and they head for the slaughterhouse.

Most factory farms keep dairy cows indoors. Tie stalls, the most common type of indoor housing, involves tethering the animals inside individual spaces in which they cannot turn around, walk, or lie down comfortably. Tie stalls can cause teat injuries and mammary infections, as well as other health problems. Open stalls, the second most popular housing system, allow cows more freedom of movement.

Most large-scale dairy operations confine cows to concrete flooring, which makes it difficult for the animals to stand up and lie down, and slippery, manure-covered surfaces can also cause them to fall and injure themselves. Extended time standing on concrete can cause circulatory problems, lesions, and lameness—which may be the most common cause of suffering for these animals.[82] Feces often fully or partially covers the floor, which can lead to foot and leg problems. In addition, it can cause mastitis, a painful udder infection that can sometimes be fatal.

Contrary to our notions of contented cows chewing their cud in a pasture, the most common type of outdoor housing of dairy cows is the drylot, which is similar to a barren, dirt feedlot used for beef cattle. These lots are overcrowded, and the vast amounts of manure and mud generated by hundreds of animals can cause infections and other health problems. In addition, high temperatures can cause heat stress. For instance, during the 2006 heat wave in California, so many animals died that several counties declared states of emergency due to the pileup of carcasses.[83]

Industrialized dairy operations frequently mutilate dairy cows. Producers may remove horns of calves under ten weeks of age with a caustic paste or a hot iron. Producers typically use a scoop, wires, shears, or a saw to amputate the horns of older animals. All of these methods cause tissue damage and pain. And while still relatively rare in the United States, one particularly inhumane practice is on the rise among factory farm dairy producers: tail docking. This procedure, intended to keep the cows' tails and udders cleaner, involves the unanesthetized amputation of up to two-thirds of the tail, typically performed by either a sharp instrument or the application of a rubber ring that cuts off blood flow and causes the tail to fall off. Tail docking can cause acute and chronic pain, distress, and increased fly problems.

Since the early 1970s, milk production per cow has more than doubled. Each dairy cow now produces more than nineteen thousand pounds of milk each year.[84] Genetic selection plays a role in ever-increasing milk yield, with producers breeding larger cows who are more susceptible to health problems, including mastitis and lameness. Many dairy producers inject cows with BGH, or bovine growth hormone, to increase yield artificially as well.

Beef

Each year in the United States, beef producers raise and slaughter more than 33 million cattle for beef.[85] Although the number of animals slaughtered—and the intensity of their suffering—is dramatically fewer than that of broiler chickens, egg-laying hens, and pigs, the cattle industry is still responsible for a tremendous amount of suffering. Tyson, Cargill, Swift & Co., and National Beef Packing Company are the country's largest beef packers, controlling 83.5 percent of the market.[86] In the past several decades, the number of smaller ranches has diminished.

Today's beef cattle usually live on the range for about seven months—again, an enormous improvement compared to the confinement of egg-laying hens, calves raised for veal, and breeding sows. They are then transported to feedlots, where they spend six months living in cramped, squalid conditions and eating an unnatural diet to gain weight rapidly. Feedlots are enormous operations, and they can confine more than a hundred thousand cattle. Barren except for feeding stations, watering troughs, and other cattle, the lack of stimuli in these operations can cause boredom and repetitive, stereotypic behaviors. After they reach market weight of approximately twelve hundred pounds, they are shipped to slaughter.

Many beef calves endure painful mutilations, usually without anesthesia. Producers usually perform castrations to improve weight gain. They use a knife or a rubber ring that cuts off blood supply to the testicles, causing them to become necrotic and then fall off. In addition, ranchers and feedlot operators may use a hot iron to brand cattle, causing painful third-degree burns, usually on the leg or hip. And like industrialized dairy operations, beef producers remove the horns of calves with caustic paste or a hot iron.

Feedlot operators typically feed cattle a high-calorie diet comprised of some mixture of corn, wheat, and other grains. Since a cow's natural diet is grass and roughage, the unnatural diet can cause digestive disorders and even lameness. As cattle rapidly gain a massive amount of weight, this growth and lack of exercise can cause cartilage damage, pain, and lameness. Nearly all feedlot operations use antibiotics and antimicrobials. However, animals still get sick with illnesses such as bovine respiratory disease, which can cause fever, pneumonia, and death. In addition to the unnatural diet, most feedlot operations implant cattle with growth hormones.[87]

Beef cattle typically must endure transport more often than dairy cattle, since they are shuttled back and forth among the cow-calf operation, animal auctions, the feedlot, and the slaughterhouse. Crowded conditions in trailers can cause injury and even death. Kept on trailers in crowded conditions for many hours, if not days, without access to food and water, cattle can become exhausted. Struggling to stand and jostling against other animals, cattle can fall and be trampled. Frightened, confused animals are at the mercy of workers who may yell, hit, kick, or use electric prods that deliver a painful jolt.

In 2004 the USDA counted 160,000 "downed" cattle and calves on beef operations.[88] These animals endured the same problems as downed dairy cows and calves, including rough handling and lack of food, water, and veterinary care. Like their counterparts in the dairy industry, downed beef cattle can take days to die.

Cattle who are still able to walk when they make it to the slaughterhouse face the possibility of a painful slaughter. In a typical beef slaughterhouse, workers unload cattle from trailers and herd them into chutes, where they proceed into the slaughterhouse for stunning, usually with a captive-bolt gun. Because of the rapid line speed, workers have only seconds to fire a metal rod into each animal's forehead and shackle the hind leg onto an overhead conveyor belt. Since captive-bolt guns demand a high level of precision and line production speeds can be four hundred cattle an hour, they have a high failure rate; one study indicated that "only 36 percent earned a rating of 'acceptable' or better, meaning cattle were knocked unconscious with a single blow at least 95 percent of the time."[89]

The belt carries the cattle down the line, where other workers cut their necks, bleed them, and butcher them. While the Humane Methods of Slaughter Act of 1958 requires that processors must render animals insensible to pain prior to slaughter, a 2001 *Washington Post* investigation obtained documentation of shocking violations throughout all steps of the slaughtering process: improper stunning, live cattle hanging from chains, and cutting and skinning of live cattle.[90]

In 2004 an undercover People for the Ethical Treatment of Animals (PETA) video taken at an AgriProcessors Inc. kosher slaughterhouse in Iowa documented abuses, such as workers pulling tracheas and esophagi out of still-conscious steers, who then staggered around and struggled with their windpipes hanging out of their throats.[91]

RABBITS

Many of us have fond childhood memories of rabbits who were part of our families when we were young. For an increasing number of people, rabbits are part of our households—about 6 million rabbits live as companion animals in the United States. Rabbits can live indoors as part of a family for more than ten years, be litter-box trained as easily as cats, and form incredibly close bonds with their guardians. As highly social animals, they thrive on a great deal of attention, like to play games, and are remarkably intelligent.

Yet each year, US rabbit producers raise and slaughter 8.5 million rabbits for meat under shocking conditions.[92] One producer's comments highlight the attitude of people who raise rabbits for meat: "To me, rabbits are dollar signs. I can't imagine anyone having a pet rabbit. They're mean. They're really mean."[93]

While the rest of the "livestock" industry has transitioned to massive factory farms, the rabbit industry is an exception—most rabbit meat producers and processors are small, backyard operations. In fact, most producers have fewer than a hundred rabbits at a time.[94] This is a $10 million industry in the United States, which has been declining steadily since its peak about sixty years ago.[95]

Rabbit meat isn't tremendously popular in the United States for a couple of reasons. First, its image is tarnished—most people still consider rabbits as companions and associate them with beloved cultural icons such as the Easter Bunny, Bugs Bunny, and Thumper. Second, many people associate rabbit meat with haute cuisine, which causes them to avoid it.[96] And since producers must pay for USDA inspection, the prices of the meat produced by the producers that are inspected are high.

At the same time, more restaurants are looking at rabbit meat as an addition to their menus. Some food journalists attribute this to the increased popularity of bistro-style restaurants that promote "game" meats. And the USDA found that in 2004, the United States' importation of rabbit meat more than doubled from the previous year, bringing in more than a million pounds of rabbit meat.[97] US rabbit growers are banding together to gain the economic clout they need to make rabbit meat more popular.

One recently formed group is the Tri-State Rabbit Growers Association, which originally included rabbit producers from Alabama, Mississippi, Tennessee, and later those from Georgia and Florida. Rabbit growers in the United States benefit from state and federal support; for instance, the USDA appointed a resource, conservation, and development coordinator to the Tri-State Rabbit Growers Association, and in 2007 the Alabama legislature provided the association with $25,000 in aid.[98]

The life of a rabbit fated for dinner is short and bleak. Producers often wean baby rabbits as early as four weeks so that their mother can be bred again quickly. This unnaturally early weaning—baby rabbits typically wean themselves at about eight weeks of age—is traumatic for the animals, who form close bonds with their mothers. One common side effect is "weaning shock," a condition where the baby rabbits fail to gain weight or even lose weight. In addition, they can develop illnesses such as enteritis—an often fatal digestive tract condition—and pneumonia.

US breeders generally house up to six rabbits together in a cage about 24 inches by 30 inches, affording each rabbit about 120 square inches—about the same amount of floor space as a sheet of legal-sized paper—in which to live out her entire three-month life.[99] Conditions become more cramped as the rabbits grow, and they cannot run, exercise, jump, or play. As a result of this intensive confinement, rabbits can develop problems such as spine deformation and mobility issues. They typically do not have anything solid on which to lie, so the continued exposure to bare wire cage floors can cause "hock sores," or open sores on their hind legs. Their nails may also break and become infected.

Rabbits can suffer from contagious diseases as a result of the confinement and poor living conditions. Intestinal coccidiosis is a parasitic infection that causes appetite loss, digestive upset, and diarrhea. Pasteurellosis causes sneezing, coughing, and other respiratory problems. The United Nations Food and Agriculture Organization explains, "The mere fact of raising five or six rabbits together in a cage one-third of a square meter in a room with 100 or 1,000 other cages acts as a sort of sound board to amplify (other stressors that affect rabbit health)."[100]

Producers keep breeding females and males in solitary cages, which is stressful for these highly social animals. In the wild, rabbits live in large groups called "warrens," which can consist of hundreds of rabbits. They have a highly stratified and complex social structure, and they form close relationships with their companions. Yet for nearly their entire two-year life span, breeder rabbits have little contact with other rabbits, causing a great deal of stress to these outgoing animals who crave each other's company.

After becoming sexually mature at about four months of age, female "breeders," or does, are bred for the first time. While 25 to 30 percent of does may die of pneumonia or other illnesses after their first or second litter, the survivors are typically bred again as soon as one to forty days after giving birth.[101] They produce up to twelve litters of babies each year for about two years, and as their production drops, producers slaughter them.

Most producers ship rabbits via truck, often depending on "bunny runners" to transport the animals to slaughter. Since there are only about fifty-five rabbit slaughterhouses in the United States, rabbits often endure truck rides that are several hundred miles to destinations several states away.[102] Rabbits are loaded onto trucks in cages that can be only six inches high, not even affording them enough room to stand. Crammed with up to eight other animals in tiny cages, rabbits tend to huddle tightly together, which can cause potentially fatal dehydration or heatstrokes.

Processors typically keep rabbits for up to a week before slaughtering them. Since the US government does not consider rabbits "livestock"—they fall under the jurisdiction of the FDA—they are excluded from the Humane Methods of Slaughter Act's protection. This means rabbits lack any sort of federal legal protection from even the most barbaric abuses throughout their entire lives and slaughter.

While many processors attempt to stun rabbits before slaughter, these methods are frequently ineffective and inhumane. Processors may stun up to one hundred rabbits an hour by pulling down on their heads while pulling back on their hindquarters, a technique called "cervical dislocation."[103] However, this method is only effective if the rabbits are less than 2.2 pounds, and by the time they reach the slaughterhouse, rabbits can weigh between 4 and 8.5 pounds. Other processors may stun rabbits by shooting them with captive-bolt guns. Backyard producers who do their own slaughtering may simply decapitate them, shoot them with pellet guns or .22s, or stand on broom handles laid across the rabbits' necks.

Finally, producers slaughter rabbits by hanging them up by their back legs and cutting their necks. Even twelve-year-old children raise and slaughter rabbits themselves, a situation that seems not only unnecessary but an easy way to promote animal cruelty in children.[104]

While the transition from small family farm to corporate factory farm has spelled disaster for most other "livestock" industries, the opposite situation, with similarly dire results, has happened with the rabbit meat industry. As a small industry characterized by growers and producers who operate out of their backyards, the industry is virtually exempt of any regulation. USDA inspection is completely voluntary, and producers must pay for inspections—an effective deterrent for any kind of inspection. So the rabbit meat industry involves a huge amount of cruelty, absolutely nothing in the way of welfare standards, and no government oversight whatsoever.

FISHING AND AQUACULTURE

More than 14 million American households keep fish as pets, spending countless millions of dollars on aquariums, food, and maintenance.[105] Yet our knowledge about where the fish on our tables came from is limited. Scientists are now increasingly recognizing that fish do indeed interact with each other as individuals, and they exhibit surprisingly sophisticated social characteristics. They live in complex social groups; recognize other individual fish; perform social behaviors such as cheating, altruism, and reconciliation; hunt cooperatively; and even use tools and manipulate their environment. Researchers have even noted, "Most phenomena of interest for primatologists are found in fish as well."[106]

In addition, animal scientists increasingly agree that although fish do not have a neocortex, they have a nociceptive system and can feel pain.[107] The World Organization for Animal Health determined, "It is beyond doubt that fish do have nociceptors and thus have the possibility to register pain, although the response and way of 'showing' pain is not expressed the same way as in terrestrial animals."[108]

Americans consume an average of more than sixteen pounds of sea animals each year, and the amount is increasing.[109] These animals are very similar or the same as their counterparts living in tanks in our living rooms. Both commercial fishing and aquaculture are multibillion-dollar industries that provide countless animals to satisfy American consumers' appetite. Many of these animals still come from our oceans, and global overfishing is decimating marine ecosystems. As fish populations in the oceans plummet to keep up with worldwide demand, an increasing number of fish are being raised in aquaculture systems in order to supply sea animals for human consumption.

Fishing

Commercial fishing is big business, and it is becoming as tightly connected to the economy as land-based animal agriculture. In 2001 America's commercial seafood industry was worth $28.6 billion.[110] Governments provide more than $20 billion annually to the worldwide fishing industry, with between 22 and 38 percent of fishing revenues being bolstered by government aid.[111]

Fishing alters the underwater ecosystem in several different ways: physical effects of fishing gear, mortality of target fish and bycatch (animals caught unintentionally), habitat destruction, discarded bycatch and entrails, and destruction of the food web.[112] And since the oceans are home to more than 90 percent of the earth's plants and animals, the problems that commercial fishing causes are on a global scale.

The process of capturing and killing fish creates massive amounts of suffering. Fish caught in trawls, which are nets that are dragged behind boats, usually die within one hour. Those caught in purse seines, in which the net is gathered together like a purse, can last up to four hours. Those caught on hooks can take from four to six hours to die. Those caught in other kinds of nets can take up to twenty-four hours to die.[113] Other fish may suffer and die from decompression when they are hauled up onto a boat. The fish who are still alive when they are hauled on board may remain conscious for fifteen minutes after being removed from the water.[114]

Overfishing

Despite a decades-long increase in world fish catch, years of systematic overfishing have resulted in a crisis for fish populations and marine biodiversity. In the last half of the twentieth century, total fish caught rose from 21 to 120 million tons, which even surpassed the total world beef and poultry production in 1994. However, wild catches reached a plateau in the 1990s; the overall increase is due to the relatively recent commercial aquaculture expansion, which now accounts for a quarter of total fish production.[115] Currently, eleven of the world's fifteen most important fishing areas are declining, and many species of fish are in jeopardy.[116]

Fishermen are also catching younger and "lower quality" fish that they previously would have rejected, engaging in a practice called "fishing down the food chain." As a result, populations of fish such as sardines, mackerel, and herring could become virtually extinct. Since carnivorous fish depend on these fish for survival, this could ultimately destroy the food web and the fragile ocean ecosystem.

Of 304 fish populations examined by the National Marine Fisheries Service, 93 are overfished or fished unsustainably, and the condition of another 655 populations is unknown. The United Nations estimates that more than two-thirds of the world's fish species are either depleted or fully exploited; one cause of this decline in population is the unreported, unregulated, and illegal fishing that is increasing globally, as fishermen attempt to avoid tighter regulations.[117] One 2006 study published in *Science* found that if current overfishing and pollution patterns continue, we can expect to see a complete collapse of world fish populations by 2048.[118]

Bycatch and Trawling

Bycatch is one of the most critical issues affecting fish populations. The Pew Oceans Commission defines *bycatch* as the "incidental catching, discarding, or damaging of living marine resources when fishing for targeted species."[119] Each year fishermen worldwide catch, kill, and discard about 60 billion pounds of unwanted fish, about one-fourth of the total amount caught.[120] There are no solid numbers for bycatch for US fishermen, but if the same ratio occurs in this country, then US fishermen toss about 2.3 billion pounds of injured or dead marine life back into the water annually.[121] More than half of the non-target animals die after fishermen throw them overboard. Conservative figures calculate that about 25 billion animals perish as "trash" each year.[122]

Not only do billions of fish suffer and perish as bycatch each year, but the practice also results in the dangerous decline of populations of sea turtles; marine mammals such as dolphins; birds such as shearwaters, auks, albatrosses, and petrels; and many other animals. In 2005 fishermen killed 100 million sharks and other fish for their fins, entangled 250,000 turtles in fishing nets, and killed 300,000 seabirds with illegal longline fishing, in which hundreds or thousands of hooks are suspended from a single long line.[123]

Trawling also decimates ocean habitats and marine populations. Fishermen use trawling to catch scallops, shrimp, and bottom-dwelling fish, and the equipment they use is massive. Some dredges can weigh more than a ton, and most boats drag two across the seafloor, tearing through reefs and other critical habitats. Not only do many nontarget animals end up in trawlers' nets, but habitat destruction drastically alters the ecosystem. The United Nations has reported that ocean habitats are cleared at twice the rate of forests.[124] The area that trawlers affect each year is as large as the United States.[125]

Aquaculture

Aquaculture, or fish farming, is surging worldwide as wild fish populations decline and consumers continue to demand fish. It now accounts for the production of more than 220 species of fish and shellfish, and between 1987 and 1997, global aquaculture more than doubled. According to the United Nations Food and Agriculture Organization, fish farms raise nearly half the fish consumed as food worldwide—more than forty-five metric tons of sea animals each year, worth about $63 billion.[126] In the United States, more than one-third of all aquatic animals consumed are farmed. At the same time, government handouts to the domestic industry have also increased to tens of millions of dollars annually.[127]

Although the industry is the fastest growing in agriculture, and the numbers of animals it produces is skyrocketing, there is little to suggest that aquaculture will actually alleviate the stress on wild populations.[128] And while the aquaculture industry promotes commercial fish farming as environmentally healthy, it is nothing more than underwater factory farming. Like terrestrial-based factory farming, the animals live in confined spaces, requiring the same inputs of feed, medication, and chemicals; they also excrete the same enormous amounts of waste. Both of these factors wreak havoc on the environment, as we will see later.

While many people eat farmed fish out of concern for dwindling wild fish populations, in most cases, aquaculture actually kills a greater number of wild fish than it produces. Many farmed fish are carnivorous, and they require feed. As a result, fishermen must catch wild fish in the oceans to feed the farmed fish, so for many types of aquaculture, we actually lose fish, not produce them. On average, 1.9 pounds of wild fish are required to produce a pound of farmed fish. Seven of the ten most commonly farmed species are carnivorous; aquaculture systems must feed them 2.5 to 5 times as much fish protein than they actually produce. Other farmed animals consume wild fish as well. The pig and poultry industries are the largest global consumers of fish meal.[129]

Suffering

The billions of aquatic animals confined in factory farm conditions suffer abuses just as other farmed animals do: an unnatural environment, overcrowding, rough handling, and often inhumane slaughter. While conditions vary depending on the species of fish, overcrowding is the norm. Salmon, for example, may be confined in sea cages with up to fifty thousand other fish. Each 2.5-foot animal has about as much space to swim in as a bathtub. Trout may be even more cramped, with up to twenty-seven of these foot-long fish allocated the same amount of space.[130]

Fry, or baby fish, emerge from eggs in hatcheries; they are then usually transported to farms. Here, they live in overcrowded, often filthy conditions, which can result in illness, such as bacterial disease and fungal infections, as well as injury. Fish may injure themselves against the cage walls or the other fish and develop lesions, fin damage, and infections. Farmed fish can develop skeletal deformations, eye lesions, blindness, and soft tissue malformations that can in turn lead to reduced tolerance to stress, impaired circulation, and heart failure.[131] Salmon can become infested with sea lice, parasites that cause lesions and scale loss; damage can be severe enough to cause a "death crown," a condition in which the fish's skull bones become exposed.[132] Nutritional deficiencies can lead to skeletal deformities and liver degeneration, as well as depressed immune systems.[133]

All of these unnatural conditions cause stress for the animals, leading to stunted growth, impaired disease resistance, panic behaviors, and aggression. Crowding can cause stereotypic behaviors, such as constant circling and fin-biting. Fish farmers may also reduce food availability and starve fish to reduce costs when the market is slow, and this can cause increased aggression and cannibalism.[134] In addition, producers may starve fish for up to ten days to clear their digestive tracts before slaughter.

The aquaculture system must also constantly medicate fish with antibiotics and chemicals. Like terrestrial animal factories, conditions at fish farms are unhealthy and prone to disease. Producers must give animals drugs to keep them minimally healthy. Fish farms use about fifty different kinds of antibiotics.[135]

Periodically, producers "grade" fish according to size in order to decrease aggression and cannibalism. The process involves netting or pumping the fish through a series of slats, in which the animals drop through according to size. Not only can rough handling during grading cause injuries, but it can also stunt growth and increase fry deformities and mortality.

Slaughter

At the slaughterhouse, workers offload fish from trucks, and the stress involved in handling can cause injuries and death.[136] The fish are held often in crowded, dirty holding tanks until sedation. Sedation methods work differently depending on species of fish, and workers typically use ice water, water pumped full of carbon dioxide, blows to the head, or electrical shock to stun them before slaughter.

These methods are far from foolproof. It can take some fish, such as trout, up to fifteen minutes to become unconscious in ice water or by being suffocated.[137] The carbon dioxide stunning method causes an escape response in fish before they lose consciousness, and they may still be conscious during slaughter, when their gills are cut and they bleed to death.[138] Since workers must hit individual fish in the head to stun effectively, individual error means that many fish remain conscious. If the current used in electric stunning is too low, the fish become paralyzed but are still conscious during slaughter. If the current is too high, they may hemorrhage and their backbones may fracture.[139]

Wildlife

Aquaculture can affect the surrounding wildlife in a number of other ways. The construction of farming systems destroys natural habitats. Aquaculturists must often use wild fry to stock farms, and the escape of exotic fish can dramatically affect a habitat in sometimes unpredictable ways. Most farmed fish are undomesticated and can survive in the wild. Escaped fish prey on and compete with native species, damage habitats, and introduce sickness and parasites. All these activities can eliminate other species and disturb ecosystems.

Fish can escape farms in small numbers by slipping through nets, or in larger numbers during storms or as a result of human error. In a 2000 storm, for example, about a hundred thousand salmon escaped from a single facility in Maine.[140] In the North Atlantic Ocean, nearly 40 percent of captured salmon are from fish farms.[141]

Not only do commercial fish farms affect other fish, but they also damage populations of birds and other animals. Commercial fish producers can legally use lethal controls for predatory birds. And while seals are protected by the Marine Mammal Protection Act, salmon farmers kill these animals because they feed on salmon.[142]

Pollution

Like other kinds of animal agriculture, aquaculture heavily pollutes the surrounding environment. While commercial shrimp farms are the biggest polluters, other farms also destroy ecosystems. Pollutants from shrimp and fish farms enter streams and rivers easily, depleting oxygen levels in water, causing toxic algae blooms, and contaminating water with pathogens and bacterial pollution.

Waste from these animals may be incredibly toxic, and, in some cases, the amount of waste has been reportedly equivalent to the amount of raw human sewage produced by a city of half a million people.[143] According to a study published in *Aquaculture Magazine*, "A mid-sized salmon farm with 200,000 fish releases an amount of nitrogen, phosphorous, and fecal matter roughly equivalent to the waste of 20,000, 25,000, and 65,000 people respectively." And in the United States and other countries, salmon farms simply use nets to contain the fish, allowing their feed and waste to directly enter surrounding waters without any treatment whatsoever.[144] Shrimp is the most-consumed sea animal in the United States, and most shrimp is imported from farms in Asia and Latin America, where millions of acres of land and mangrove forests have been cleared to create shrimp farms.[145]

Both antibiotics and chemicals can spread to the environment and humans. Approximately three-quarters of fish antibiotics used on US aquaculture facilities leach into the environment, spreading to wild fish and shellfish.[146] Fish facilities use chemicals to control algae and other aquatic plants. Like other pesticides, they can enter soil and water and harm other species.

THE MEAT INDUSTRY AND SOCIAL JUSTICE

As we've seen in this chapter, the meat, dairy, and egg industries slaughter billions of animals each year in a manner that causes massive suffering and trauma to nearly every animal who enters a slaughterhouse—as well as hundreds of millions more who suffer miserable lives inside cramped cages and crates. Yet animal welfare isn't the only issue. There are countless people whose lives are negatively affected by the meat industry, whether they are workers who are injured and lose their jobs, people who fall ill from eating contaminated meat, or neighbors of factory farms who become sick from environmental poisons.

Slaughterhouse and Factory Farm Workers

Hundreds of thousands of workers suffer abuses at the hands of these industries. Many of them are economically disadvantaged, undereducated, unskilled, unable to speak English, and/or undocumented immigrants—all characteristics that make them virtually defenseless from the orders of powerful companies that employ them. The meat industry exploits their vulnerability, paying them low wages to work in an environment in which the suffering and abuse of both humans and other animals go hand in hand—all the way from the contract growers and the factory farm employees through the processing line staff.

While the federal National Labor Relations Act protects the right of most private sector workers to engage in collective bargaining and organize unions to improve working conditions, it excludes all agricultural employees. So while some slaughterhouse workers are able to unionize, factory farm workers do not have the legal right to do so. And at the slaughterhouses, no federal agency oversees processing line speeds to protect workers.[147]

Worker Safety

There are approximately 5,700 slaughterhouses and processing plants in the United States, and the industry employs approximately 527,000 workers. These workers include not only people who stun, shackle, hoist, kill, disembowel, and cut apart the animals, but also people who clean the facilities. Pay is not good—according to the US Department of Labor, the median annual earnings of a slaughterhouse employee in 2004 was $21,440, and the median annual salary of a meat trimmer was only $18,660.[148] In addition to low pay, slaughterhouse work is among the most dangerous in the country.

Slaughterhouse workers spend long days doing repetitive work at rapid speeds using dangerous equipment and sharp tools. They are hurt in a number of ways: they slip and fall in the blood, feces, and other fluids that cover the floors; they are kicked and cut by animals struggling for their lives; they are cut by knives that disembowel and disassemble animals; and they endure painful and chronic repetitive motion injuries. The industry's ever-increasing line speeds increase the risk of being cut, bruised, burned, stabbed, blinded, dismembered, disfigured, and worse.

One recent example can be seen in a *Jewish Daily Forward* 2006 investigation into working conditions at an AgriProcessors Inc. facility. It revealed that while many of the company's eight hundred employees received the lowest wages of any slaughterhouse in the country, the company frequently shortchanged them on paychecks. Employees had little or no safety training, and coupled with fast line speeds, injuries and amputations were commonplace at the slaughter-house. The investigation indicated that supervisors were unsympathetic to sick or injured employees and were reluctant to send them to the company doctor. As with the rest of the meat industry, many AgriProcessors Inc. employees were undocumented immigrants.[149]

According to the US Department of Labor, more than 13 percent of slaughterhouse workers are injured or fall ill each year due to working conditions.[150] Not only is this one of the highest rates in the entire private sector, but slaughterhouses also have the highest rates of injury and illness in the food-manufacturing industry—an industry already notorious for having one of the highest incident rates.[151] Yet this figure is likely low since, as we'll see, management frequently prevents workers from filing injury claims or getting treatment for injuries. The Government Accountability Office (GAO) has criticized the Occupational Safety and Health Administration (OSHA) for not inspecting some high-risk facilities and only inspecting a small number of slaughterhouses with low injury and illness rates. This means OSHA may not be inspecting facilities that underreport data. And, according to the GAO, OSHA's data do not include injuries and illnesses affecting cleaning workers who are employed by outside contractors, since they are not employed directly by the meat industry.[152]

Slaughterhouse line speeds are constantly accelerating; for example, in chicken slaughterhouses, as many as fifty birds per minute can roll past workers. This means that employees must shackle, kill, or cut apart multiple animals every minute, for eight hours or more every day—often without breaks to check equipment, sharpen their knives, or rest for a few minutes. The noise level is high, and temperatures can soar to 120 degrees on the killing floor or drop below subzero temperatures in the refrigeration units. Since all birds and many pigs and cows are conscious as the workers shackle them, they are terrified—thrashing, kicking or flapping as they try to escape.

Despite the fact that the machines are large and dangerous—the purpose of the equipment is to kill and cut apart animals—management frequently does not adequately train employees. In some processing plants, training can consist of a video or nothing at all. And due to the rapid line speeds, workers close to each other can accidentally stab each other, causing "neighbor cuts."

The cleaners have what can be the most dangerous job. Working at night in dense steam fog, climbing onto equipment, hosing machines off, using harsh chemicals and pressurized water, and trying to retain footing on slippery bodily fluids, cleaners are at high risk for injury or death. Both Eric Schlosser's *Fast Food Nation* and Human Rights Watch's "Blood, Sweat, and Fear: Workers' Rights in US Meat and Poultry Plants" reference OSHA reports of cleaners being killed by hog-splitting saws, being crushed by conveyors, and losing legs in grinders.[153]

Illness and Disability

The air inside slaughterhouses is filled with dust, dirt, and airborne feces and blood particulates. As a result, workers can become infected with a number of illnesses. Often, animals on the line are sick. When they defecate or vomit on the workers, they can spread diseases such as *E. coli*, *campylobacter*, and *listeria*. Animals treated with antibiotics may become infected with bacterial illnesses that are resistant to antibiotics, and workers can become sickened by the same dangerous strains.

Since line workers repeat the same motions thousands of times in a single shift—lifting heavy, live animals and carcasses and cutting body parts—their likelihood of developing crippling, painful repetitive strain injuries is high. One industry article stated, "As recently as 2000, the meat industry led the country in repeated-trauma disorders, with meat plants logging injury rates of 92.2 injuries per 1,000 workers, compared with a national average of 3.3 injuries per 1,000. Poultry plants, by comparison, reported 53.5 injuries per 1,000."[154]

Systematic Abuse

While injury and illness figures are already too high, these problems often go unreported. Human Rights Watch, a nongovernmental advocacy organization, contends that the underreporting of these problems is considerable and cites constant intimidation by management to prevent workers from reporting injuries and illnesses. According to the organization, "The decline in official injury rates may be due as much to underreporting and nonreporting as to any improved conditions."[155]

The GAO notes that worker turnover can exceed 100 percent in a year.[156] High turnover means that workers often do not accrue sick or vacation time, nor are they at one job long enough to be covered by insurance.

Management often pressures workers to continue working and to ignore injuries. Since management may fire workers who take sick time, workers may simply continue working despite being in pain. Management may also force injured workers to quit. Some managers whose staff has fewer lost workdays even receive bonuses.[157] The meat industry is also notorious for union busting and for retaliating against employees who demand basic improvements in working conditions and pay.

Smithfield Foods' processing plant in Tar Heel, North Carolina, slaughters more than 32,000 pigs every day and employs more than 5,500 people, mostly poor and undereducated minorities. It is the largest hog slaughterhouse in the world. According to a *New York Times* piece, "The work is often brutal beyond imagining." One employee reported, "You have to work fast because that machine is shooting those hogs out at you constantly. You can end up with all this blood dripping down on you, all these feces and stuff just hanging off of you. It's a terrible environment." In order to prevent workers from unionizing, Smithfield fought efforts for more than a decade by threatening to shut down the plant, threatening Latino employees with deportation, and preventing fair union elections. A judge found that Smithfield had threatened, fired, and even beat up workers involved in unionizing activities.[158]

Factory Farm Workers

Factory farm workers endure many of the same problems as those in slaughterhouses: no organized representation, low wages, long hours, and dangerous work. Air from inside the sheds is a veritable pathogenic broth, and constant contact with manure often leads to illness. (In 2004 pig farming was the third most dangerous job in the private sector, with nearly 17 percent of workers becoming injured or ill.)[159] Factory farm workers have a higher rate of respiratory disease due to the presence of airborne hazards such as fungal molds, dusts, bacterial endotoxins, ammonia, and hydrogen sulfide. Hydrogen sulfide can build up and become toxic in underground manure storage pits, creating major health risks for workers. In fact, the National Institute for Occupational Safety and Health has deemed hydrogen sulfide a leading cause of death in the workplace.[160] The dust inside factory farms often contains animal, bird, and insect feces, microbes, mites, dander, pollen, antibiotics, pesticides, and other pollutants. As a result of breathing in this dust, workers can develop sinusitis, chronic bronchitis, and organic dust toxic syndrome. Factory farm workers are also exposed to infectious diseases such as anthrax, psittacosis, brucellosis, leptospirosis, swine influenza A, and avian influenza A, as well as several other diseases and conditions that result from exposure to the bacterium *Streptococcus suis*.[161]

Manure can also contain antibiotics, heavy metals, pathogens, volatile gases, mold, nitrogen, and phosphorus. These compounds cause serious respiratory problems for workers on factory farms, including asthma and nonchronic bronchitis. A 2005 study found that, in addition to consumption of tainted meat products and exposure to contaminated water near factory farms, "The inhalation of air within swine operations may serve as another exposure pathway for the transfer of multidrug-resistant bacteria from swine to humans." The study concluded that people who have direct contact with factory farms as well as neighbors of factory farms may become infected.[162] Employees can also develop skin infections from the bacteria present in manure.

One dairy factory farm, for example, can expose hundreds of workers to dangerous situations. Cows frequently kick workers. Although rare, workers have even drowned in manure pits as long as a swimming pool—such as when a dairy worker and his young son perished in a ten-foot-deep manure pit on a California dairy farm in March 2006.[163] They can develop permanent neurological damage from hydrogen sulfide, a toxic gas found in manure. Like their slaughterhouse counterparts, factory dairy farm managers force workers to work long hours for little pay and prevent them from taking time off and participating in collective bargaining—the process of negotiation between union leaders and employers. The labor laws intended to regulate the treatment of workers in other industries do not protect workers on factory dairy farms, since most of these laws exclude agricultural workers. As a result, dairies are not required to provide overtime pay, and employees do not have the right to form a union. In 2003 state and federal agencies inspected only 51 of the 86,300 dairy farms in the United States.[164]

Contract Growers

At the same time that the trend toward increasing consolidation has occurred, more and more companies are instituting a "supply chain" business model where the corporation controls everything from production to processing, creating a system in which the growers are powerless. While not common yet among cattle ranchers, pig, chicken, and aquaculture industries are beginning to follow this model more often. In this model, companies contract out to individual "contract" growers and provide the land, buildings, labor, and energy. The company owns the animals and provides the feed and the veterinary and technical services. The end result is that the individual growers assume all the risk if the company cancels a contract or leaves the area completely. Companies also quickly silence any organizing among producers.

Immigrant Labor

Meat companies recruit immigrants who are not aware of their rights and will accept lower wages. According to the GAO, more than one-fourth of slaughterhouse workers are foreign-born noncitizens.[165] Thirty-eight percent of the 304,000 production and sanitation workers in the meat industry are foreign-born noncitizens.[166] Many of them, unable to speak English and fearful of losing their jobs or being deported, are easy targets for intimidation and manipulation. Many workers are not aware of their protection under workers' compensation laws, and the language barrier can prevent workers who are sick or injured from communicating with management.

Meat companies have run radio ads in Latin American countries to attract workers, opened labor offices in Mexico, and even smuggled undocumented workers into the country as workers. According to the *New York Times*, "Industry experts said it has long been believed that American food companies recruit in Mexico and knowingly hire illegal workers. Some said the companies advertise on the radio in Mexico, distribute leaflets, show videos and hire immigrant smugglers, or 'coyotes.'"[167] In 2006 authorities detained at least thirty-six undocumented or falsely documented immigrants on a single Iowa egg farm—the third raid at the company since 2001.[168]

One example is Hudson Valley Foie Gras, which was in the middle of a debate in 2001 regarding its policy of not providing time off for the immigrant workers it employed. One of the workers told the *New York Times* that he had not had a day off since August 1999, one year and nine months previous. Immigrant workers force-fed ducks three times daily—that's more than a thousand ducks to feed every day—for a month. When the ducks went to slaughter after thirty days, the workers occasionally have one or two days off from feedings. Workers, however, did not spend this time resting or with their families but rather cleaning the sheds or unloading incoming ducks from delivery vehicles.[169]

Health Issues

As the meatpacking industry has consolidated, the corporations responsible for processing meat have jeopardized consumer health by failing to maintain adequate food safety standards. For example, food is contaminated at the slaughterhouse, where rapid line speeds increase the exposure of meat to feces, causing dangerous bacteria and viruses to enter the meat supply.

Some of the most common contaminants found in animal products can be deadly. Uncooked chicken and raw milk can carry *Campylobacter* bacteria, which are estimated to infect millions of Americans each year. *Campylobacter* can cause vomiting, diarrhea, abdominal cramps, and the rare but serious neurological disease Guillain-Barré syndrome, which can result in permanent nerve damage. *E. coli* O157:H7, present in the large intestines of cows, infects more than 70,000 Americans each year who eat or handle improperly cooked, excrement-contaminated meat. *E. coli* O157:H7 infections can cause severe, bloody diarrhea, kidney failure, and even death. Listeriosis causes serious sickness in 1,600 Americans each year, a quarter of whom die. And *Salmonella* infections cause cramps, diarrhea, and fever for an estimated 1.4 million Americans, killing 500 each year. According to the Food Safety and Inspection Service, more than 16 percent of US broiler chickens are contaminated with *Salmonella*, and millions of eggs are contaminated as well.[170]

Some bacteria, such as *E. coli* and *Salmonella*, can also contaminate vegetables and other plant-based foods, but the contamination is still of animal origin. For example, manure from dairy cows was the culprit in the 2006 *E. coli* outbreak that sickened eighty-one people who ate at Taco John's. Cow manure-contaminated spinach was responsible for killing three people and sickening more than two hundred people earlier that year.[171] Plants don't produce these bacteria; animals do.

While these food-borne illnesses sicken millions of Americans each year, the meat industry continues to benefit from a weak inspection process. For example, the USDA still does not have the ability to either order recalls of contaminated meat or shut down processing plants that violate food safety standards. And after the discovery of dangerous conditions, there often is a delay before the government requires the processing plants to clean up operations. This allows the meat companies to sell tons of potentially contaminated meat to unsuspecting consumers. In 2006, of the 2,853 total US slaughterhouses, only 793 were federally inspected.[172] And although federal law requires daily USDA inspection of processing plants, in 2007, USDA officials admitted that for thirty years, inspectors visited 250 plants only once every one to two weeks.[173]

Studies have shown that consumption or contact with fecal-contaminated meat have caused people to become infected with antibiotic-resistant bacteria.[174] In a 2003 *Consumer Reports* study of store-bought chickens, nearly half of the birds in the study were contaminated with *Campylobacter, Salmonella,* or both. Thirty-four percent of the *Salmonella* bacteria and ninety percent of the *Campylobacter* were resistant to one or more antibiotics.[175] Resistant bacteria can also leach from animal manure to soil and water, which can contaminate vegetables, fruits, and fish products.[176]

Antibiotics are critical to human health and are used around the world for treating infections such as pneumonia, meningitis, bacterial food-borne illnesses, and other often life-threatening infectious diseases. Yet each year, US meat producers use 24.6 million pounds of antibiotics for healthy animals alone.[177] These drug classes include many that are identical to those doctors prescribe for people, including penicillin, tetracycline, and erythromycin.

Research done by the Union of Concerned Scientists indicates that the greatest consumer of all antibiotics is animal agribusiness, which is responsible for an estimated 70 percent of all antibiotic use.[178] Factory farms use antibiotics for two reasons: first, to prevent and to treat illness, which is often caused by the stresses and unhygienic conditions of intensive confinement, and second, to promote growth.

As a result of the now-commonplace practice of using these antibiotics, not only do factory farm and slaughterhouse workers possess higher rates of antibiotic-resistant bacteria than the US population overall, but their resistance patterns are similar to those of the animals with whom they are in contact.[179] It's not just limited to meat industry workers. The GAO cites epidemiologic studies that indicate a correlation between changes in antibiotic use for farm animals and antibiotic resistance in humans.[180]

For example, in 2007 the Centers for Disease Control and Prevention announced that fluoroquinolones—a class of antibiotics used to treat gonorrhea—have become ineffective, leaving only one other class to treat the disease. The reason? A decade of factory farms adding the drugs to chicken feed to prevent respiratory problems. The editorial board of the *Columbus Dispatch* lamented, "An entire class of antibiotics has been sacrificed to the convenience of poultry and egg producers."[181]

According to Keep Antibiotics Working, a coalition of health, consumer, agricultural, environmental, humane, and other groups, antibiotic-resistant bacterial infections are responsible for at least $4 billion in increased healthcare costs each year.[182]

More than 350 organizations, including the American Public Health Association, American Medical Association, Sierra Club, National Catholic Rural Life Conference, and Center for Science in the Public Interest, have endorsed legislation that would phase out the use of antibiotics in healthy farm animals. And the World Health Organization has encouraged countries across the world to discontinue the use of antibiotics for growth promotion.[183]

The government largely ignores these entreaties. In 2007 the FDA advanced approval for the use of cefquinome (an important antibiotic for serious human infections) for use in cattle. The agency made the decision despite warnings from its own experts, the American Medical Association, and other health organizations that stated giving the drug to cows would be dangerous for people.[184]

Food contamination isn't the only public health issue associated with factory farming. Farm animals produce much more waste than the US population, and volatile gases in manure contain a number of potentially harmful compounds. Animal waste can spread more than forty different types of disease to humans. Factory farm workers as well as people living close to factory farms can have higher rates of tension, depression, mood changes, fatigue, cognitive problems, gastrointestinal problems, brain damage, skin irritation, and other health issues. Pregnant women may experience spontaneous abortions, and babies may suffer from methemoglobinemia, or "blue-baby syndrome." In addition, contamination from pesticides, hormones, nitrates, trace elements such as arsenic and zinc, ammonia, hydrogen sulfide, other odor-causing compounds, and air particulates can cause health problems. Some farmed animal pathogens, including *Streptococcus suis* and *Cryptosporidium parvum*, can cause fatal cases of meningitis.[185] Due to many of these health concerns, in 2006 the American Public Health Association advocated for federal, state, and local governments and public health agencies to pass a moratorium on building new factory farms.[186]

The two most sensational factory farm-related illnesses are bovine spongiform encephalopathy (BSE), better known as mad cow disease, and avian influenza, which have captured headlines and captivated public attention. Mad cow disease is a fatal degenerative disease that has been linked to the deaths of at least 150 people, who likely consumed tissue from infected cows. Mad cow disease may have an incubation period of up to forty years, cannot be cooked out of the meat, and infects cows when they consume feed made from cattle brains, spinal cords, eyes, and other tissues with high infectivity rates.

In 1997 the FDA published regulations on feeding cattle meat or byproducts to other cattle, although it's still permissible to feed cow blood to calves. Producers can also feed cattle by-products to chickens, for example, then in turn feed chicken waste back to cows. It's legal to feed most farm animals—not just cows—rendered animals of their own species, animal by-product meal, blood, hair, bone marrow, diseased or disabled animals, manure, fish, plastics, and heat-treated food adulterated with rodent or roach feces.[187] Think that's nauseating? The Union of Concerned Scientists points out that it's legal to feed farm animals rendered road kill and euthanized dogs and cats.[188]

While the United States and several other countries ban the feeding of most cow tissues to other cows, there is inadequate enforcement, and mad cow disease cases continue to appear. After authorities confirmed the first US mad cow disease case in 2003, the USDA issued a temporary rule prohibiting meat from downer cows to enter the food supply. The USDA has still not made this emergency rule permanent. In 2006 the USDA announced that it was slashing tests for mad cow disease by nearly 90 percent, from 1,000 tests per day to 110 tests per day—out of 35 million cattle slaughtered each year.[189]

A vastly more significant public health risk associated with factory farming is avian flu. While regular avian flu is a relatively common virus that affects wild birds, factory farming conditions can lead to the emergence of highly pathogenic strains such as the Asian strain, H5N1. The virus has already spread from birds to humans, causing many in the medical community to predict that the virus will become transmissible from person to person, which could trigger a global influenza pandemic.

From 1918 to 1920, a similar strain of flu killed as many as 100 million people in the worst disease outbreak in recorded human history. This flu killed less than 5 percent of its victims, but H5N1 has a mortality rate that is ten times greater than that of the "Spanish flu" outbreak. So how bad could a H5N1 pandemic be? In 2005 Dr. David Nabarro, the pandemic expert for the United Nations, warned, "We're dealing here with world survival issues—or the survival of the world as we know it."[190]

Tamiflu, the main medication used to treat H5N1 symptoms, is hard to come by and expensive. Another drug, Symmetrel, was easy to produce and inexpensive, but Chinese chicken producers rendered it useless when they spiked their birds' water supply with the drug to prevent infection, allowing a resistant strain to develop.

A 2006 World Bank report noted that consumption of birds had dropped by more than half in some European countries and estimated that a severe avian flu pandemic could cost about $1.25 trillion, or more than 3 percent of the global gross domestic product. This figure is based on only a 1 percent global mortality rate, which would still kill about 70 million people—approximately a quarter of the US population.[191]

CORRUPTION AND THE MEAT INDUSTRY

US animal agribusiness is a $100 billion-a-year business, and the companies involved are tremendously powerful.[192] Tyson Foods, for example, is the world's largest meat producer, and Cargill is the world's largest privately held company. While the family farmer has become nearly extinct in this country, his ranks comprising only a tiny fraction of the population, the special interests of industrialized agribusiness and factory farms has become one of the most powerful forces in Washington, DC. In a 2006 *Washington Post* article, Rep. Richard Armey (R-TX) stated, "The strength of the farm lobby in this town is really unbelievable. . . . I don't think there's a smaller group of constituents that has a bigger influence."[193]

As one of the most economically powerful industries in the United States and abroad, animal agribusiness enjoys close ties with a number of politicians. Often, the industry wields its economic clout in the form of campaign funds for a given candidate; once elected, the candidate is more likely to execute agribusiness' lobbying interests. Agribusiness gave more than $140 million to congressional and presidential candidates between 2000 and 2004.[194]

On the local level, factory farms are often located in states where regulations are weak and in communities of color, where residents possess little political power to refuse construction of facilities.[195] One study of the Mississippi hog industry found that there are approximately three times as many factory farms in poverty-stricken and largely African American areas.[196] Corporate animal interest groups also spend a tremendous amount in lobbying at state and local levels. And if states implement new regulations, factory farms can simply move to other locations. In some areas where factory farms are located, a high percentage of politicians enjoy close ties with the industry or are industry insiders themselves.

Regulation

Regulatory agencies often are staffed with former representatives from the very industries they are charged with regulating. Recent top-ranking USDA officials have included both the former public relations director and chief lobbyist of the National Cattlemen's Beef Association, a former president of the National Pork Producers Council, and other former meat industry leaders. *Fast Food Nation* author Eric Schlosser has criticized the USDA's inclusion of former meat industry executives as top administrators, stating, "Right now you'd have a hard time finding a federal agency more completely dominated by the industry it was created to regulate."[197] Since the passage of the 2002 farm bill, at least nineteen congressional aides who worked on the bill have been hired by agricultural lobbying organizations, commodity groups, or farm organizations.[198]

As a result of the "revolving door" between the USDA and industry, the agency has come under fire. A 2006 audit by the USDA Office of the Inspector General found that since 1999, the agency had only pretended to investigate anticompetitive behavior among stockyards and meat companies. USDA employees did not file complaints for hundreds of cases, and senior officials actually prevented investigations from being referred to the US Justice Department or from being filed as complaints. The inspector general found that officials instructed employees to enter letters and data reviews as investigations, essentially fabricating the appearance of enforcement and, according to the Senate Agriculture Committee's senior Democrat Tom Harkin, "cooking the books."[199]

Subsidies

The federal government began the farm subsidy program in the 1930s to provide a modicum of security to small farmers. Yet, over the past decade, the government has doled out $172 billion in subsidies. Most of this money goes not to family farms but to the large companies that are increasingly dominating agribusiness—only about one-third of all farms actually receive subsidies.[200] Only about 5 percent of some USDA research and grant programs (the Rural Business Enterprise Grant Program, the National Research Initiative, the Initiative for Future Agriculture and Food Systems, and the Value-Added Producer Grant Program) go to beginning farmers or farmers with small or medium farms.[201]

According a *Washington Post* investigation, in 2005 the government provided more than $25 billion in subsidies, despite the fact that pretax farm profits were at a near-record $72 billion. The investigation also found that farm subsidies "have altered the landscape and culture of the Farm Belt, pushing up land prices and favoring large, wealthy operators."[202]

These subsidies go not to the family farmers fighting for their financial survival but to factory farms, while lobbyists and interest groups use the image of the very same people they are putting out of business to gain more money in subsidies. Subsidies lower the prices of products such as corn and soy, which factory farmers use to feed cattle. And since most fruits and vegetables are not subsidized, consumers usually pay full cost for these foods.[203]

Factory farms aren't the only beneficiaries of taxpayer-funded subsidies. Ranchers lease the forage on public land for as little as one-fifth of what would be charged on the private market, and the government spends over ten times more on grazing programs than it actually generates from these grazing fees—this is where we get the term "welfare ranching." Indirect governmental subsidies account for more than $100 million, and this support comes in the forms of predator control, fire management, soil erosion aid, and road construction. In 2005 the US Forest Service administered more than 7,500 permits for grazing on more than 95 million acres of National Forest in thirty-four states.[204] Despite this small number of people with permits to use an enormous amount of public land, the federal government still pays millions of dollars each year to subsidize ranching. Recent studies indicate that this results in a cost of about $460 million per year to the American public.[205]

The farm bill, which sets the course of agricultural policy for the United States, is hashed out every five years behind closed doors in Washington, DC. Not surprisingly, it invariably favors major agribusiness interests. The implications of the farm bill could hardly be larger, affecting American and even global agriculture, the environment, immigration, poverty—and animal welfare. Yet most Americans pay no attention when the farm bill comes up for debate. Why? Michael Pollan, *New York Times* writer and author of *The Omnivore's Dilemma*, explains, "Because most of us assume that, true to its name, the farm bill is about 'farming,' an increasingly quaint activity that involves no one we know and in which few of us think we have a stake."[206]

In the past, the farm bill has been a vehicle for Congress to pass important animal protection legislation, such as the Improved Standards for Laboratory Animals Act in 1985. In 2001, the House Agriculture Committee killed popular measures from House and Senate farm bill versions that addressed downed animals, farm animal slaughter, and puppy mills.

Animal agriculture is one of the most powerful forces in Washington. Not only can we see its influence in the lack of protection for farmed animals and for the people who are affected by factory farms, but the lobby also affects environmental regulations, too—and as we'll see now, the effects of factory farms on the environment are profound.

ENVIRONMENTAL CONSEQUENCES OF MEAT PRODUCTION

While the United States has less than 5 percent of the world's population, we are directly responsible for the lion's share of the world's environmental problems, thanks to our voracious appetite for meat and our wasteful lifestyle. Americans, in fact, waste more food than most people eat in sub-Saharan Africa, with 48 million tons of human food wasted every year.[207] But it's not just Americans who contribute to this problem. Because of the enormous, growing gap between the rich and the poor in this country and around the world, the world's consumption habits vary widely. For example, the richest 20 percent of the world's population uses about 86 percent of the world's resources, while the poorest 20 percent use 1 percent, forcing the world's poor to cut down their trees, grow crops for export, fish, or graze cows—all to feed and produce "stuff" for the richest people.[208] Furthermore, since 1950, the richest 20 percent of the planet has doubled its per capita consumption of meat, so while the world's elite consume most of the world's resources and create the majority of the demand for meat, the planet as a whole suffers.[209]

Many of us have made changes in our daily lives to reduce our contribution to environmental destruction: recycling, installing energy-efficient lightbulbs, walking or taking the bus, or even switching to a hybrid car. Yet, as important as all these actions are, the evidence is stronger than ever that animal agribusiness and its use of ever-increasing numbers of animals is among the most serious causes of environmental degradation. A 2006 United Nations Food and Agriculture Organization (FAO) report detailed the overwhelming destruction that animal agribusiness poses to the environment. The FAO examined how this industry causes global land and water degradation, concluding that farm animal production is a greater contributor to global warming than automobiles and other forms of transportation. The report stated, "The livestock sector emerges as one of the top two or three most significant contributors to the most serious environmental problems, at every scale from local to global."[210] Despite the enormous scale of this problem and its implications for animals, the planet, and human health, there is little enforcement of pollution laws for animal agriculture. On the contrary, the industry takes advantage of lax regulations, loopholes, and industry-dominated government agencies to pollute our air, land, and water, all in the name of keeping operating costs down and profits up. And despite growing attention from the environmental movement, both the number of animals produced and the resulting ecological damage are increasing. Not only does this trend mean institutional cruelty to animals on a scale unprecedented in human history, but it also is responsible for ever-worsening global environmental destruction. As the entire world's agriculture systems make the transition to an era of corporate consolidation and increasing demand for animal products, this becomes a global problem. Each year, 56 billion land animals and countless more aquatic animals are killed for human consumption.[211]

For most Americans, the term "farm" brings to mind an image of a hardworking rural family, people who are invested in the health of their animals and the environment in which they live. Yet, as we've seen, our collective demand for animal products has increased to a point where it can no longer be satiated by our traditional system. The small-scale rural farm is nearly extinct in this country. Factory farms now produce the overwhelming majority of meat, dairy, and eggs, and the difference between the smaller operations of our rural heritage and the contemporary profit-hungry model is profound.

Factory farms consolidate all production in specific areas, concentrating the effects of environmental damages. According to the USDA, animals on US factory farms produce more than 500 million tons of waste annually.[212] This waste is hundreds of times stronger than untreated domestic sewage.[213] Arkansas broiler factory farms, for example, produce as much feces in one day as a city of 8 million people.[214] These operations produce a wide variety of pollutants, including ammonia, pesticides, antibiotics, hormones, pathogens, trace elements, nitrogen, phosphorus, and more."[215]

Consumption of Natural Resources

Animal agriculture consumes astonishingly high amounts of resources and energy. In the United States, meat production is responsible for the consumption of more than one-third of all raw materials and fossil fuels. While land used to grow grain produces five times more protein than meat does per acre, the rates for other foods are even higher.

Legumes yield ten times more protein per acre than meat, and leafy vegetables fifteen times more.[216] A recent study in the *American Journal of Clinical Nutrition* found that meat production takes 6 to 17 times more land, 4.4 to 26 times more water, 6 to 20 times more fossil fuel, and uses 6 times more biocides than processed soy protein.[217]

Animal producers use energy to power heating, cooling, water pumping, cleaning, transportation, and processing. In order to feed the billions of animals living in confinement, farmers use countless gallons of gasoline and diesel to power their tractors, and millions of barrels of oil to produce petrochemical fertilizer. The transport of feed to the factory farm, of the animals to the slaughterhouse, and of the carcasses to the distributors all consumes vast quantities of fuel. If the rest of the world adopted US agricultural production methods, our global oil supply would be sucked dry in about twelve years.[218] According to Michael Pollan in the *New York Times Magazine*, "Assuming (a steer) continues to eat 25 pounds of corn a day and reaches a weight of 1,250 pounds, he will have consumed in his lifetime roughly 284 gallons of oil. We have succeeded in industrializing the beef calf, transforming what was once a solar-powered ruminant into the very last thing we need: another fossil-fuel machine."[219]

While it takes thirty-five calories of fossil fuel to create a calorie of beef, the waste is even more extreme for pork: sixty-eight calories of fuel are necessary to make a calorie of pork.[220] And oil isn't the only waste in meat production. As a general rule, at each step up the food chain, energy is reduced by a factor of ten, so consuming animals who have consumed grains—or even other animals—is a waste of energy.

Factory farms use tremendous amounts of resources and contaminate the environment, yet the overall effect of the meat industry is even larger. Animal producers use nearly three-quarters of our annual grain harvest to feed farm animals.[221] This means that animal agriculture is responsible for the resource depletion and the environmental effects of feed production—whether it be pesticide use, water contamination, air pollution, soil erosion, or deforestation.

The Worldwatch Institute estimates that "if each American reduced his or her meat consumption by only 5 percent, roughly equivalent to eating one less dish of meat each week, 7.5 million tons of grain would be saved, enough to feed twenty-five million people—roughly the number estimated to go hungry in the United States each day."[222]

Water

There are thousands of factory farms in the United States.[223] All of the animals who live and die in this system consume vast quantities of water, and animal agriculture is one of the nation's biggest water polluters. Not only must factory farms use water for cooling facilities, cleaning equipment, and flushing waste from confinement areas into storage pits, but the animals themselves can drink an enormous amount of water. And farmers use a tremendous amount of water to grow the crops that feed the animals. As Michael Jacobson of the Center for Science in the Public Interest notes, "Together, irrigating feed crops and raising livestock consume over half of all freshwater. In contrast, domestic uses—all showers taken, toilets flushed, cars washed, glasses drunk, and lawns watered—consume less than one-tenth as much water as agriculture."[224] As a comprehensive 2007 study of agricultural water use warned, "Only if we act to improve water use in agriculture will we meet the acute freshwater challenges facing humankind over the coming 50 years."[225]

There is virtually no enforcement of regulations addressing waste from farmed animals. The federal government took action against only eight factory farms for Clean Water Act violations between 1997 and 2004.[226] Yet manure enters our water as spills, runoff, illegal discharges, leaks from storage pits, and fertilizer applications. This pollution can enter rivers and lakes, killing aquatic life, and it can even reach the ocean, where it causes devastation to marine ecosystems. Powerful compounds such as ammonia can evaporate from storage pits, traveling miles away before joining with rainwater and spreading to lakes and streams. In addition, chemicals from animal operations often contaminate groundwater, causing significant health issues.

The scale of the problem is massive. Factory farms must place the staggering 500 million tons of farm animal feces somewhere. At operations like feedlots, enormous piles of manure surround the confinement areas, and at facilities such as hog operations, the waste enters a storage pit, also euphemistically called a "lagoon." Storage pits can be small lakes of liquid feces several acres across. Other facilities use sprayfields, a technique where equipment sprays liquid waste onto crop fields. All of these systems leach nutrients into the surrounding waters, whether it is from runoff from piles or sprayfields, or from the leaking or bursting of storage pits.

Spills or illegal discharges at factory farms are all too common. Since the amount of feces can be so enormous, one spill can be deadly for a nearby river and its inhabitants. For example, a 1995 spill in North Carolina left 25 million gallons of hog waste in a local river, killing up to 10 million fish.[227] In 2003 Tyson Foods pleaded guilty to twenty felony violations of the federal Clean Water Act and agreed to pay $7.5 million in fines. The company admitted that it illegally discharged untreated wastewater from one of its Missouri poultry processing plants into a neighboring tributary.[228] In 2006 a factory egg farm was fined $105,000 for spilling 2 million gallons of chicken waste into Utah rivers.[229]

The EPA estimates that hog, chicken, and cattle feces has polluted thirty-five thousand miles of rivers in twenty-two states and has contaminated groundwater in seventeen states.[230] Phosphorous and nitrogen found in manure cause toxic algae growth that chokes off oxygen in water, poisons aquatic life, and destroys biodiversity. The Pew Oceans Commission estimates that manure runoff has degraded more than 60 percent of coastal rivers and bays. Each year, pollution from animal agriculture creates a "dead zone" in the Gulf of Mexico, killing much of the marine life in an area the size of Massachusetts.[231]

In the United States, state agencies typically regulate slaughterhouse waste more tightly than manure from confined facilities. However, this aspect of animal production also pollutes water with blood, offal, and water used to clean facilities, and some states allow plants to legally dump dangerous amounts of this material. While slaughter-house waste water is now cleaner than it was several years ago, the total amount of animals has increased so much that total pollution has increased. For example, one slaughterhouse that processes 220,000 chickens each day can generate more than 1.3 million gallons of waste water daily.[232] Some slaughterhouses deliver sludge to farmers for fer-tilizer, and a single slaughterhouse can produce 6,000 gallon loads of sludge in a single day.[233] All of this water and waste either enters rivers or streams directly, or it can run off fields into water sources.

While this problem is immense, it is often difficult to adequately enforce water pollution laws such as the Clean Water Act. In 2007 the State of New York fined Hudson Valley Foie Gras only $30,000—less than one-tenth of 1 percent of the available penalties for the viola-tions—for violating state and federal water pollution laws more than eight hundred times.[234] Some state agencies do not subject factory farms to stringent environmental regulations to begin with. For example, several states exempt poultry operations from regulations, simply because the chicken waste is dry and therefore not considered a discharge pollutant. However, farmers apply chicken waste to their fields and it then runs off into surrounding rivers and streams, causing phosphorous pollution that can poison aquatic ecosystems and lead to human health problems.

Air Pollution

While federal and state governments are remarkably lax about regu-lating air emissions from factory farms, raising animals for meat pro-duces a dizzying amount of air pollutants. Most of these compounds threaten not only the environment but also human health. USDA researchers have found that odors from factory farms may contain 170 separate chemical substances.[235] Production of farmed animals creates air pollution through the breakdown of enormous amounts of waste, as well as through the resulting particulates.

Waste storage pits like lagoons and sprayfields release pollutants

into the air, where they can join with rainwate
waterways. Some toxic gases such as hydroge
at unsafe concentrations even nearly five miles
Ammonia is another dangerous compound, wh
escapes from feces. After traveling through th
join with rainwater, where it spreads to land anc
ages algae growth and depletes oxygen in r   ...., killing
aquatic life. The EPA points to animal agriculture as the culprit for more
than 90 percent of North Carolina's ammonia emissions.[237]

Not only does the breakdown of animal waste generate air pollutants, but particulate matter is also involved in animal agriculture. For
example, tractors and animals both generate particulates through their
activity, and particulates choke facilities where millions of animals
may be confined inside. According to the EPA, in some areas such as
California's South Coast and the San Joaquin Valley, particulate matter
and ozone regularly exceed national health guidelines.[238] In the San
Joaquin Valley, dairies have passed cars as the primary producers of
smog-forming gases. The giant dairies are the top source of ammonia
particulates, which are associated with heart problems and increased
mortality in humans.[239] In 2004 Buckeye Egg Farm, Ohio's largest
commercial egg producer, agreed to pay a civil penalty and spent more
than $1.6 million to install pollution controls to cut particulate and
ammonia emissions at three giant confinement facilities. Buckeye is
typical among egg producers in that it is not a farm at all, but a massive factory system with more than 12 million chickens in more than
a hundred barns. The three facilities emit an annual total of more than
1,580 tons of particulates, as well as 1,450 tons of ammonia.[240]

Global Climate Change

Global climate change is one of the most critical environmental issues
that we face today. While many environmentalists are driving less or
switching to driving gas-sipping hybrids—both commendable steps—
evidence is piling up that meat production is actually worse for global

change than automobiles. A 2005 study by University of cago researchers found that eating vegetarian fare is more effective in reducing harmful greenhouse gas emissions than replacing a gas-guzzler with a compact car.[241] Raising cows for human consumption is now an important cause of the production of carbon dioxide, methane, and nitrous oxide—the three most powerful greenhouse gases.

Carbon dioxide is the top contributor to global warming, and the FAO estimates that animal agriculture produces 9 percent of carbon dioxide emissions. The crops grown to feed farm animals are produced in a highly mechanized, energy-consuming process that burns millions of barrels of oil each year. On-farm fossil fuel use produces as much as 90 million tons of carbon dioxide each year.[242]

Carbon dioxide is also produced when forests are burned and cleared to create grazing land. The agricultural industry is the largest cause of deforestation in the world, and rising meat consumption is the primary factor in agriculture's expansion.[243] Deforestation caused by animal agriculture may produce 2.4 billion tons of carbon dioxide each year.[244] Not only does deforestation release carbon dioxide into the air when plant material is burned, but it also destroys forests' ability to recycle carbon dioxide into oxygen—our planet's most important resource for this critical process. In 2001 the World Bank estimated that "since the 1960s, about 200 million hectares [nearly 500 million acres] of tropical forest have been lost, mainly through conversion to cropland and ranches, the latter especially in South and Central America."[245]

Methane is second only to carbon dioxide in causing global climate change. Its potential as a greenhouse gas agent is twenty times stronger than carbon dioxide.[246] Cattle release this gas in two ways—through digestive processes and through waste. In the United States alone, cattle produce 3.8 million metric tons of methane every year.[247] The FAO notes that animal agriculture produces 37 percent of worldwide methane emissions.[248]

Nitrous oxide is the third most common greenhouse gas, with an effect three hundred times stronger than carbon dioxide. Animal agriculture is responsible for 65 percent of nitrous oxide emissions.[249] Not only is manure a culprit, but the use of petrochemical fertilizers to grow crops for animal consumption also releases massive amounts of nitrous oxide into the atmosphere.

Overgrazing

While the vast majority of farmed animals spend their lives on factory farms, millions of cattle (as well as sheep and some goats) also graze on ranches and public lands in the United States. And although pollution from factory farms is responsible for serious problems, grazing is not without its own issues. Overgrazing can cause topsoil erosion, destruction of the water cycle, and the destruction of native plants and animals.[250] About 70 percent of the total land in eleven of the western states is grazing land. In the western states, the majority of federal lands are grazed, including land under the jurisdiction of the Bureau of Land Management (BLM) and the US Forest Service. Cattle also graze in many national wildlife refuges, federal wilderness areas, and some national parks—grasslands, deserts, wetlands, and forests.[251] This massive consumption eliminates food sources for native herbivores, destroying the food chain and ultimately killing predators who depend on smaller animals to survive.

The removal of native plants also decreases ground cover, causing erosion and destroying forests, wetlands, grasslands, rivers, and streams. Cattle trample the ground and create compacted, bare soil that is more susceptible to erosion, which renders the soil unable to absorb rain and support surface water and groundwater. Overgrazing is the primary cause of desertification in the United States.[252]

Imported beef is also responsible for the clearing of forests, which has an enormous effect on global climate change, as we've seen. Tropical rainforests of Central and South America lose an area about half the size of Florida each year, since cattle need an average of five acres apiece on which to graze.[253] Soybean farming has become the greatest source of deforestation in the Amazonian rain forest, with 80 percent of the global soy harvest used for feed for farmed animals. The issue in Central America is the most severe, because the rate of deforestation is so high and there is so much to be lost. Since 1950 cattle populations have doubled in Central America, and the amount of grazing land has increased from 3.5 million to 9.5 million hectares (8.6 million to 23.5 million acres).[254] A *Time* magazine article provides a good example: "Agriculture is the world's biggest cause of deforestation and increasing demand for meat is the biggest force in the expansion of agriculture."[255]

By altering fundamental ecological processes such as the water cycle, and by creating disasters such as erosion, pollution, and habitat loss, overgrazing also destroys the ability of the environment to support wildlife. On public lands alone, overgrazing threatens more than 175 threatened and endangered plant and animal species.[256] And for federally listed species, overgrazing is a contributor to the decline of 22 percent of them, which is nearly as much of a factor as mining and logging combined.[257]

CONCLUSION

As the meat industry continues to consolidate and squeeze out smaller farms, the animal welfare, social, and environmental problems only worsen. The primary beneficiaries are the companies that control the supply chain. To consumers, the only benefit is cheaper meat, dairy, and eggs.

And at what price do these foods come? Society bears the cost of pollution, antibiotic resistance, food-borne illnesses, crop subsidies, and more—all the hidden costs to taxpayers that make cheap meat seem so cheap. These costs don't factor into a ninety-nine-cent chicken sandwich, yet they are every bit as real.

There are other costs as well that are impossible to quantify: billions of animals each year pay the price in untold misery and suffering. Abuse of workers, public health risks, loss of rural heritage, and destruction of the environment also result from our desire for meat. And as our appetite increases, even the World Bank predicts that "under any scenario the increase in demand will put strong pressure on global natural resources. This increase might crowd out the poor, endanger global food security and food safety, and affect animal welfare."[258]

Of all the ways that humans exploit animals, the suffering endured by animals at the hands of the meat, egg, and dairy industries is the worst by an order of magnitude. The number of animals who we hunt, experiment on, wear as fur, use for entertainment, or abandon at shelters is but a tiny fraction of the billions of animals who we kill for food each year.

So what is to be done?

Ideally, the best-case scenario is for the country to transition to a plant-based diet, eliminating all of the terrible animal welfare problems associated with factory farms, as well as the social justice and environmental issues. There are a number of simple yet effective actions that we can take as individuals to reduce the amount of suffering on factory farms, and these are described below.

The meat, egg, and dairy industries should take the lead of the growing numbers of American consumers and retailers that are moving away from supporting the worst confinement practices. By eliminating the use of battery cages, gestation crates, and veal crates, as well as ending overbreeding for production traits, the industry can eliminate some of the most egregious abuses that affect billions of animals. It won't eliminate all the cruelty, but it's a start.

The government can eliminate the costly subsidies that go to the largest factory farms and instead subsidize smaller farms, fruit and vegetable producers, and farms that are transitioning to organic production. The USDA can improve the final minutes of billions of animals each year by following Congress's original intent and interpreting the provisions of the Humane Methods of Slaughter Act to apply to birds and other animals who are killed without any protection from even the worst abuses. Individual states can pass legislation banning the worst confinement practices.

There's still more to be done. And the increasing US population and the current voracious appetite for meat prevent us from going back to our traditional family farm system. But we shouldn't accept the current perversion of farming either.

What You Can Do

The following are a number of ways that readers can reduce the numbers of animals used in food production.

- Don't eat animals! Happily, vegetarian options have never been more delicious or plentiful. Nearly every restaurant serves vegetarian or vegan options, grocery stores offer delicious meat alternatives, and a huge selection of cookbooks, Web sites, and countless other resources are at your fingertips. Now is a better time to make simple, sustainable diet choices than ever before. If you want to become vegetarian, eliminate all but your favorite animal foods from your diet, or just generally reduce your consumption of animal foods. There are a number of ways you can get started:
  - Identify vegetarian foods that you already enjoy.
  - Make simple substitutions like vegetables, tofu, and faux meats in your favorite dishes to make them vegetarian.
  - Buy a vegetarian cookbook, and check out some of the great recipes available online.
  - Try some new vegetarian products from your grocery or health food store.
  - Try vegetarian or vegan dishes from your favorite restaurants.
  - Try new ethnic foods, like Italian, Mediterranean, African, Chinese, Thai, Mexican, and Indian foods that are often plant based.
  - Experiment with some of the simple dairy and egg substitutions that are available at natural food stores, and even at regular groceries.

- If you continue eating meat, reducing the amount you consume—even by pledging to eat vegetarian, say, three days a week, and by substituting some meat alternatives for some of your dinners—is a good way to alleviate these problems as well.
- Not all animal products are equal. Because most birds and farmed fish are small in size, there's more suffering per serving. For example, one chicken may die for a chicken dish, while the meat from one beef cow will feed many people. And a caged egg-laying hen or crated veal calf suffers far more than a grass-fed steer.
- Finally, switching your purchase of animal products from factory farm producers to producers that treat animals less inhumanely is a step in the right direction.

Chapter 3

HUNTING

Animals as Game and Pests

This is a child safety issue. Eight-year-olds don't have the coordination or attention span or physical ability to handle a gun. They are learning cursive writing and some of them believe in Santa Claus.[1]
—Joe Slattery, father of a fourteen-year-old who was shot and killed by a twelve-year-old while deer hunting, in response to a proposed Wisconsin bill lowering the minimum hunting age to eight

Hunting is revered in our country's character and economy. It's indelibly tied to conservation and is statistically safe. It adds richness to the lives of participants. We shouldn't allow youth prohibitions to compromise its future.[2]
—Doug Painter, President, National Shooting Sports Foundation

INTRODUCTION

About 12.5 million Americans, or 4 percent of the adult population of this country, hunt.[3] While that number is relatively

103

small and has been shrinking for decades, hunting in the United States was once a prominent part of the American economy. It also played a major role in the evolution of many natural sciences like biology and ornithology (most natural history museums in the United States got their exhibit collections from hunters), the development of the American conservation movement, and the destruction of the Native American cultures.

But American hunting is also a response to the European (primarily English) tradition of hunting. By looking at the history of hunting in this country, we can better understand why the killing of wild animals for trophies, sport, or profit remains such a powerful and protected part of American culture, even when the majority of Americans are opposed to it.[4]

In England hunting was an aristocratic tradition, and the concept of "public lands" did not exist; in other words, only wealthy landowners and their friends could hunt on private property. Because hunting was mostly reserved for the wealthy, the public considered wild animals the property of the rich, to the exclusion of the poor. Hunting, then, was not only a sign of prosperity and status, but it demonstrated mastery over nature and the lower classes as well. For English elites, hunting was a sign of masculinity, leadership, and a mark of a warrior.[5]

Later, as European powers colonized much of Africa and Asia, English aristocrats extended hunting to the colonial lands. English colonists and explorers hunted for sport and profit, focusing on large, dangerous animals who would confirm their "masculinity" and, in turn, the "mastery" of the British Empire. They also focused on animals whose hides, tusks, or trophies could bring profit. Elephants fit both bills and were a major target of English hunting during the nineteenth and early twentieth century. Historian Edward Steinhart notes that big-game hunting and colonial warfare were intimately linked in Africa; Europeans wanted to control both big game and native Africans, both of whom hunters could kill with little justification.[6]

The presence of European hunters transformed the native

Africans' views and uses of wildlife, which until that time had been important for subsistence as well as trade. After the arrival of the European trade in ivory, trophies, and other parts of animals, Africans also began to exploit these resources more intensively. In Africa as well as Asia, Europeans engaged native hunters to collect exotic live animals for display in Europe, and later in America. This was the beginning of modern zoos and circuses.

Hunting in the United States did not begin as an aristocratic tradition but as a democratic one. Hunting in this country has never been restricted to privately owned lands. At least in the early colonial days, most land was "public," since early Americans did not consider Native Americans as having ownership rights. Like voting, the public saw hunting as a political right of all Americans, as inalienable as voting.[7]

At the turn of the twentieth century, many Americans, even those living in the West, no longer needed to hunt for their food, as they moved to a lifestyle more dependent upon farming. Many others moved from rural areas into cities. Hunting turned into a sport, attracting a much smaller portion of the population and drawing the wealthiest adherents. Americans like J. P. Morgan and Cornelius Vanderbilt began a tradition of private game reserves and duck hunting clubs. This trend led working-class hunters and magazines like *Field and Stream* to worry that America was going to end up like Europe. There, hunting was restricted to the wealthy, who could afford not only to hunt on private reserves but could also hire hunting guides to do all of the manual labor for them. In some cases, these guides made the actual kills.[8]

During the second half of the nineteenth century, the growth of commercial hunting and trapping provided hide, fur, and feathers for the fashion industry. This occupied a smaller number of hunters but killed far greater numbers of animals, resulting in the near extinction of America's big-game animals before the twentieth century.

Like European hunting's links to colonialism, American hunting was connected to westward expansion in the nineteenth century. Just as European colonists had conquered both Africans and Native Americans as well as their animals, many American settlers felt a need to conquer and eliminate both Native Americans and large numbers of animals in order to fulfill the mandates of Manifest Destiny—the God-given right and duty to expand westward.

As settlers and miners moved west from the original colonies of the east, they often encountered Native Americans along the way. The official policy during the eighteenth and nineteenth centuries was to encourage Native Americans to "sell" their land to whites and become civilized. Settlers expected Native Americans eventually to stop hunting animals and become farmers, freeing up vast amounts of land for whites to use for farming, mining, ranching, and other forms of development. Both the presence of Native Americans and the animals they traditionally hunted were an economic hindrance to these activities. The new policy was to wipe out the bison from the plains, both to allow for cattle grazing and other uses and to discourage the Native Americans from using that land. Even though the US government and the Plains Indians had signed a series of treaties guaranteeing the

Hunters nearly exterminated the American bison in the nineteenth century. Today, they are hunted on game ranches. (Photo by Jack Dykinga, USDA)

Native Americans rights to hunt within certain areas, the treaties were just paper promises and mostly ignored.

The full-scale destruction of the American bison served a number of purposes. Within a span of about fifty years, thirty million were killed. Many American colonists saw Native Americans and bison as savage beasts civilization needed to conquer and control. By forcing Native Americans to stop hunting, it allowed for an easier process of displacement and confinement to reservations. In the annual report for 1873, Secretary of the Interior Columbus Delano wrote, "The rapid disappearance of game from the former hunting grounds must operate largely in favor of our efforts to confine the Indians to smaller areas, and compel them to abandon their nomadic customs." The newly developed railroads benefited because the presence of bison on or around the tracks created delays. White trappers and hunters flooded into open areas as native peoples were removed, and the newcomers benefited from killing thousands upon thousands of bison for their hides. Manufacturers used bison hides for rugs, clothing, and hats, and to create the industrial machine belts that helped power the factories of the nineteenth century, prior to the development of rubberized belts. And due to the development of large-bore rifles and the extension of the railroads to the Great Plains, the bison were easier to kill, and the products made from them were more easily shipped east. Because most Americans were supportive of the goal to advance westward and to move Native Americans onto reservations, the elimination of their major food source was thought to be good policy. Even the US Army got in on the act, killing bison as soldiers went about their other business in the West. Not coincidentally, the eradication of the bison freed up the land for cattle grazing, helping beef become one of the major food sources for whites.[9]

In a typical bison hunt, a hunter would stalk a group and select the lead cow, kill her first, destabilize the group, and kill the remaining shocked and frightened animals, one by one. After the killings, the skinners took over, skinning the animals and leaving the corpses to rot in the sun.[10]

As we have seen, one aspect of the nineteenth century hunter's philosophy was the destruction of wildlife in order to domesticate the environment; that legacy is still with us in the form of US Wildlife Service wildlife control measures, which have resulted in the deaths of millions of animals over the past century in order to protect grazing lands and other human interests. The fact that a few private herds of bison still exist in this country after such a concerted effort to wipe them out is only because of a group of naturalists and hunters in the early part of the twentieth century who formed the American Bison Society and created a number of bison preserves.[11] This story—of wild animals being virtually wiped out by hunters, only to be "saved" by hunters at a later date—marks one chapter of the history of hunting in this country.

President Theodore Roosevelt, an avid big-game hunter and a member of the upper crust, fought some of the most disturbing trends in hunting—the rise of commercial hunting and the extinction of species at the turn of the century, as well as the move toward hunting as an aristocratic tradition that should exclude working-class Americans. During his tenure as president, he helped create laws that restricted the amount of animals hunters could kill, established the US Forest Service to manage government forestlands, and used the Antiquities Act of 1906 to create dozens of national parks and wildlife refuges. The movement that he and others began later became the American conservation movement, but its early incarnations had nothing to do with preserving nature or wild animals for their own intrinsic value. The purpose was to preserve wild animals and their habitats for the use of Americans, who at that time were largely hunters. It was to ensure that the public owned the land and the wildlife on it, and that neither business interests nor the wealthy few could destroy them. Ironically, it was primarily the wealthy American hunters who made up the early conservation movement. They were concerned about the loss of wildlife and wildlands for their recreational desires, while working-class hunters viewed wildlife as an important economic resource for fur, skin, or feathers. Even Roosevelt, horrified by the loss of the bison of the northern plains, was originally drawn to the territory in order to kill a bison. He eventually added one of the few remaining animals to his own trophy collection.

Thanks to some of the regulations put into place in the early twentieth century to control commercial hunting and to limit the number of animals killed, hunting became less important as an economic activity and developed into a sport for a relatively few Americans. Contrary to Roosevelt's democratic ideals, a class division did in fact develop, with wealthier Americans focusing on sport hunting, trophy hunting, and the collection of exotic animals.[12]

Hunting Today

Today, 12.5 million Americans hunt animals. Of those, most (almost 11 million) hunt big-game animals, 82 percent hunt on private land, and 57 percent earn more than $40,000 per year.[13] In other words, most are middle income to wealthy, hunt large game animals for sport, or hunt on private property. Yet hunting, even while practiced by a small minority of Americans, continues to carry an enormous amount of symbolic and emotional weight. Because of hunting's symbolic value, as well as the number of wealthy and powerful hunters, this minority wields a disproportionate amount of political clout and is able to influence legislation affecting wildlife on the local, state, and federal levels. And that political clout translates into an industry devoted to encouraging the killing of millions of animals per year for recreation. At the same time, its lobbying power is decreasing, since the number of Americans who hunt is shrinking.

HUNTING HERITAGE

American hunters see themselves as inheritors of a great tradition—the hunting heritage. Because it is largely fathers or other male relatives who introduce most new hunters to the practice, participants see hunting as a sacred tradition embodying notions of family, history, and a love of the outdoors. Many hunting defenders call upon the history of the conservation movement and its connection to hunting as one of its most important justifications. Because turn-of-the-century hunters and conservationists like Teddy Roosevelt and Aldo Leopold were instrumental in establishing game management policies and protections for wildlife and wildlife habitats, the history of hunting is tied in most hunters' eyes to the conservation movement, which most Americans embrace, at least nominally. Of course, American hunting has another, equally valid history that is connected to the decimation of large numbers of species and the elimination of Native Americans from their land. Contemporary hunting advocates do not typically trumpet this history.

Other hunters see hunting as key to the development of the human species. For years, a key theory of human cultural and biological development was known as "man the hunter," which postulated that *Homo sapiens* evolved because of the social cooperation necessary for big-game hunting among our early ancestors. (Feminist archaeologists have since challenged this theory, demonstrating that women in foraging societies cooperate as much as or more than men to gather and to raise children.) Some hunting advocates promote this theory with statements like: "The heritage of hunting is not so much the size of the racks on deer and elk, but the fact that the modern sportsman is a descendent of thousands of years of human evolution and the power of the spirit of the hunt has forever etched its place in the human soul."[14]

Another strongly resonant idea about hunting has to do with the idea of self-reliance. Many hunters feel that they are re-living the pioneer lifestyle in which American settlers depended on their wits, skills, and perseverance to conquer nature and the American frontier.[15] Of course, very few hunters subsist on the animals they kill, which would be quite an expensive proposition given that the average expenditure per trip of an American hunter is $403.[16] The reliance of hunters on high-tech equipment, guides to lead them to animals, and even canned hunting operations, where tame animals are brought directly to them to kill, largely negates this hardy pioneer image.

With respect to conservation, it is true that hunters do participate in wildlife conservation today. Hunting fees and taxes on hunting equipment fund wildlife management programs in every state in the country. Hunters also support a wide array of conservation projects aimed at ensuring that there exists not only wildlife to hunt but also habitats for game animals. Most animal lovers and environmentalists, and indeed, most Americans, support causes such as habitat conservation measures. Hunters also see themselves as conservationists in the sense that through game management policies, hunting keeps populations that would otherwise spiral out of control in check and prevents starvation for some species. But hunters target healthy adult male animals rather than the sick or old whom "nature" would otherwise take or the females whose killings would result in a drop in population. These healthy animals would not typically starve to death, and survivors will respond to the reduction in numbers by bearing more young anyway. Finally, many animals hunted today are not considered to be overpopulated. In addition, over-hunting—whether commercial, private, or government sanctioned—has resulted in the decimation of species, including "pest" animals such as wolves, who prey on the same animals hunters target. It has also led to the unregulated killing of other "pest" species such as prairie dogs and coyotes.

Because hunting is a practice typically passed on from father to son, many hunting advocates see it as an important, sacred family tradition—like decorating the Christmas tree—made more sacred because it takes place in the Great Outdoors. Because hunters have traditionally been from rural areas (and still largely are, with 41 percent of all hunters living outside of major metropolitan areas),[17] many, following the tradition of Henry David Thoreau, see themselves as more connected to "nature" than urban dwellers, most of whom do not hunt and who show far less support of hunting than rural Americans.[18]

But enjoying nature with one's family can take many forms (such as camping, hiking, and wildlife watching), and most Americans evidently do not view killing animals with high-powered weapons to be either a family activity or a legitimate means of reconnecting with nature.

Finally, hunters see their sport as an ethical activity. On top of current laws, most hunters now follow a voluntary "code of ethics." It includes the concepts of fair chase (the killing of free-ranging wild animals in a manner that does not give the hunter a great advantage), not killing more animals than one needs, and leaving enough animals for the next hunter. Because hunters are a diminishing species, many hunting advocacy groups are concerned about their public image, making the dissemination of the hunter's code of ethics all the more important. This has also led to newer developments like helping the disabled to hunt, and "hunting for hunger" programs. (Matthew Scully calls this a "socially conscious sadism . . . like teaching cannibals to

---

Blue Boy

Blue Boy is a nilgai, a large antelope native to India. In the wild, nilgai can live up to twenty years. They are an exotic antelope commonly found on canned hunting operations, many of which are in Texas. Released in southern Texas in the 1920s, they have been highly sought after by trophy hunters—they are listed in Safari Club International's trophy record book.

In 1999 Blue Boy came to the Cleveland Amory Black Beauty Ranch from a Texas game farm. The operation had rejected him because of a broken horn, which meant that trophy hunters would not want to shoot him for a trophy.

Male, or bull, nilgai have a characteristic gray-blue coat—hence Blue Boy's name. However, Blue Boy was neutered to prevent him from reproducing with Princess, the female nilgai who also lives at Black Beauty Ranch. As a result, his coat is a deep brown color.

Blue Boy is now between ten and twelve years old and enjoys a spacious enclosure with addax, camels, and elands. He spends most of his time with Boogey, a Grevy's zebra, grazing and lying together in the sunshine. Both Blue Boy and Boogey are shy, preferring each other's company to people and other animals. And although Blue Boy's horn has grown back since his arrival at the sanctuary, he will spend the rest of his life in safety, without the threat of becoming a trophy on someone's wall.

use a table napkin and not take the last portion.")[19] As we shall see, the increase in the numbers of game farms and canned hunting opportunities in the United States mightily strain this concept of fair chase, since fair chase assumes that the "hunters occasionally succeed while animals generally avoid being taken," and most of these operations guarantee the hunter a trophy.[20]

Hunters fight any threats to their right to hunt with fierce determination, and many equate hunting rights with political rights. The Second Amendment to the Constitution, even though it says nothing about hunting (although some state constitutions specifically protect the right of hunting), is often interpreted by hunters as a guarantee to their right to hunt. Americans in general react strongly when any of their real or supposed rights are threatened, so it is no surprise that hunters react so strongly when their "heritage" is threatened, since it is as central to their identity as fireworks are on the Fourth of July.

It is true that hunting is a cultural tradition for a segment of the American population—but it's a tiny fraction. The question becomes: How much should Americans tolerate (and fund with taxpayer dollars)

Blue Boy and Boogey. Nilgai, or Indian antelope, are commonly hunted exotic animals on Texas game ranches. (Photo by Walter Larrimore)

a pastime that no longer provides subsistence to more than a handful of citizens, yet causes the deaths and suffering of tens of millions of animals per year?

SUBSISTENCE AND COMMERCIAL HUNTING

Humans lived as hunters and gatherers for most of our existence, until the domestication of plants and animals about ten thousand years ago. But even as societies in the Middle East, Asia, Europe, Northern Africa, and parts of Central and South America developed agriculture, there remained small, typically marginalized groups of people throughout the world who still largely lived off of the meat of wild animals and the fruits of the land.

How does such subsistence hunting differ from the sport hunting that is most popular among hunters in the United States today?

According to anthropologist Tim Ingold, traditional hunter-gatherers (or foragers, so called today because anthropologists now realize that the majority of their diets consisted of foraged plant foods rather than meat) see themselves as occupying the same world as animals rather than separating out and dominating nature, a world that is relational rather than oppositional. Ingold characterizes the relationship between hunter and animal as one of trust: "[T]he hunter hopes that by being good to animals, they in turn will be good to him" and will, at appropriate times, present themselves to the hunter in order to be taken.[21] On the other hand, if the hunter mistreats the animals, by, say, taking more than necessary, then the animals will desert him. The animal's spirit was believed to survive the hunt and could punish a greedy or disrespectful hunter.

Ingold contrasts the human-animal relationship in this worldview to the relationship that exists among farmers or pastoralists who have domesticated animals. Here, the relationship is not one of trust but one of domination: the animal is property of the farmer or herder and has lost all control over her own body. Those who keep domesticated animals determine their feeding, living conditions, whether or not they exercise, with whom and when they will mate, and when and under what conditions they will die. For Ingold and other writers, the domestication of animals by humans has turned the relatively equal hunter-animal relationship into a slave-master relationship.[22]

But how to compare subsistence hunters to modern hunters? Many modern hunters—even though the majority do not eat the animals that they kill—see themselves as continuing this tradition, and some even see hunting as a spiritual endeavor that puts them closer to nature.

The traditional subsistence hunter takes what he needs for his family but generally does not adversely affect the environment or the species (although it is true that the first inhabitants of the American continent likely wiped out North American megafauna such as the mammoth and the saber tooth tiger, who disappeared shortly after the arrival of humans to the Americas). Despite fueling some conservation measures as we've seen, the modern hunter and the modern sportsman's industries do indeed affect the environment, and negatively so. They create policies that artificially change the populations of animals, they cut roads into forests in order to allow access, and they eliminate natural predators of their preferred game species. More important, modern sport hunters kill animals in order to bring home trophies: the bigger the buck, the bigger the antlers, the greater the kill, even when the hunters do not consume the animal. The subsistence hunter and the sport hunter, then, belong to very different cultural traditions.

Today, many Native Americans still hunt for subsistence, but many legally hunt even endangered species for commercial purposes, under treaties that often protected native hunting traditions in exchange for giving up land to the government.[23]

Marine Mammal Hunting

One of the most controversial uses of subsistence hunting by native peoples is the killing of marine mammals like whales, dolphins, and seals. Native peoples who live in coastal areas have practiced whaling throughout history. Native Alaskans like the Makah traditionally hunted whales by using a harpoon attached to an inflated sealskin; the whale would swim around until he either tired enough so that they could lance him to death, or he bled to death from internal injuries. Europeans, Euro-Americans, and the Japanese used whales for meat, blubber, oil and bone, and these whalers eventually developed modern methods of killing, which involved using large ships to track the whales as well as using the ship itself as the "drogue," or large item attached to the harpoon; later, they regularly used guns and explosives. By the twentieth century, many whales were being overhunted and their population levels were being threatened, first in the Atlantic Ocean and then in the Pacific, thanks to the large commercial whaling industries. Because the vast majority of the whale populations are now gone combined with a declining market for whale oil and other products, commercial whaling has largely disappeared.[24]

Today, whaling is overseen by the International Whaling Commission (IWC), a commission formed as the result of the passage of the International Convention for the Regulation of Whaling in 1946. The stated purpose of the International Convention for the Regulation of Whaling is to regulate whaling and protect whale stocks for future generations. It is currently composed of seventy countries that have an interest in commercial whaling or in seeing whales protected. Thanks to the work of nonprofit organizations such as Greenpeace, Animal Welfare Institute, the Humane Society of the United States, and the dominance of anti-whaling nations such as the United States, the United Kingdom, and Australia, the IWC commercial-whaling ban took effect in 1986. The IWC accomplished this ban over the strenuous objections of Norway and Japan, the two leading whaling nations, as well as the former Soviet Union and Peru. Because of exceptions in the regulations that allow for the taking of whales for "scientific purposes,"[25] Japan and Iceland have been able to continue their whale hunts, even though the six to seven hundred whales killed by Japanese whalers every year have been used to supply the whale meat industry in that country and overseas. In 1982 the whaling ban was adopted, Norway objected, and therefore Norway was not bound by the moratorium. In 1993, acting on its objection, Norway resumed commercial whaling. The IWC has also given exemptions to native whalers who do not hunt whales for commercial purposes, as long as whale populations are not threatened.[26]

In every IWC meeting since the late 1980s, the commission debates the question of restoring commercial whaling, with Japan and Norway picking up more allies every year to support their contention that whaling should be allowed. Japan has been lobbying other countries—particularly Caribbean nations—to get support for its position, and it admitted providing overseas development aid to developing nations in exchange for a pro-whaling vote. Indeed, many developing nations also have strong fishing interests and have accepted Japan's self-serving and unsubstantiated argument that whales compete with humans for commercial fish stocks.

Years of lobbying combined with a perceived lessening of interest among some people in seeing whales protected appeared to have paid off for the pro-whaling nations. In 2006 the IWC for the first time since 1980 was dominated by pro-whaling countries, and the conservation minded countries were in the minority. In a non-binding, yet significantly symbolic vote, the IWC voted 33 to 32 to start efforts to return to commercial whaling. However, the commercial whaling ban cannot be overturned with a simple majority. It requires a three-quarter majority, and the pro-whaling countries only have a simple majority. However, given the increase in pro-whaling nations on the commission, a full restoration of commercial whaling may be imminent.[27]

While whaling nations see whales as just another economic resource, marine biologists and others who have studied whale social behavior know that many whales demonstrate a high level of intelligence and emotional complexity. For instance, sperm whales, a species of toothed whale covered by the IWC, vocalize through a series of clicks, moans, whistles, and other sounds. Baleen whales, another kind of whale covered by the IWC, do not have such highly structured social relationships, but their mother-calf bond is strong.

For example, in one notable case from 2005, a young humpback whale, a type of baleen whale, was killed when he was caught in a shark net off the coast of Australia; divers who were trying to retrieve the whale's body were initially thwarted by the dead whale's mother, who marine mammal experts said was trying to protect her calf.[28]

Although not covered by the IWC, seals are also hunted. Each year, a small group of Canadian seal hunters kills hundreds of thousands of harp seals for their pelts—used mostly for the fashion industry in Norway, Russia, and China—and seal oil. The sealers killed more than 325,000 seals in 2006, crushing their skulls with spiked clubs called *hakapiks* or shooting them.[29] Most of the seals are under three months of age when they are killed, and some may be only two to three weeks old.[30] Animal welfare organizations such as the Humane Society of the United States and the International Fund for Animal Welfare have documented sealers skinning seals alive and leaving pups to die slow deaths after being clubbed.

In 2007 the Canadian Department of Fisheries and Oceans, which authorizes the hunt, reduced the quota to 270,000 seals due to the fact that seal pups were falling from the ice floes and drowning before they were old enough to swim. Hundreds of thousands of seals drowned before the sealers even arrived. In some areas, the pup mortality rate approached 100 percent.[31]

Most Americans oppose the hunting of whales, seals, and dolphins. Even Canadians, whose media often defends its seal fur industry, are overwhelmingly opposed to commercial seal hunting.[32] Yet this opposition to hunting intelligent, friendly, and cuddly-looking animals on the part of Americans and Canadians begs the question asked by pro-whalers and pro-sealers: Why should we protect whales, seals, and dolphins when we kill billions of other animals for human uses? Why are they so special?

The answer is more complex than the fact that many of these animals are awe-inspiring and charismatic, although that is certainly the case. Whales are difficult to study, and we know very little about them because they spend the majority of their lives well below the surface of the ocean. On an ecological level, it is difficult to manage marine mammal hunts because they are particularly prone to abuse. If there were any negative effect to population numbers, it wouldn't become apparent for years, perhaps even decades, and so many of their populations are already low. In other words, their ecology and biology makes them uniquely and inherently unsuited to consumptive exploitation. Just as important, marine mammal hunting is inhumane. As unnecessary as it is to kill these animals in the first place, humans' awkwardness in the water means that we can't even kill them quickly, and therefore we cause them prolonged suffering and intense fear.

SPORT HUNTING AND EXOTIC GAME HUNTING

Sport hunting differs greatly from subsistence hunting, and even from the traditional way that hunting was practiced in the United States during early colonial times and through westward expansion. Sport hunting involves the killing of animals for recreation. Sometimes hunters consume the animal meat, but neither food consumption nor profit is the purpose of sport hunting. Instead, recreation or the acquisition of a trophy are the main goals.

Sport hunters explain their attraction to this activity by emphasizing the time spent outdoors, the excitement and challenge of tracking and ultimately catching prey, and the reward of bringing down a dangerous or smart adversary. Of course, they de-emphasize the pleasure they take in killing. Yet, without the killing and the trophy that the hunters so often prize, hunting would simply be wildlife watching and would certainly carry very little appeal for those who hunt.

Sport hunters focus on big-game animals such as deer, bears, and moose; small animals such as rabbits, squirrels, foxes, and mink; predators like mountain lions and coyotes; and birds such as pheasants, ducks, and geese. Sport hunters even kill mourning doves in large numbers as a form of target practice—in fact, doves are the animal most often killed by American hunters. The US Fish and Wildlife Service estimates that approximately more than 22 million mourning doves are killed each year.[33] While the number of hunted doves is decreasing, more doves are killed each year than all other migratory game birds combined.[34] Sadly, there is a very high wound rate in dove hunting and many are shot and left to die slow, painful deaths. Since many hunters neither consume nor make doves' bodies into trophies, they often make no effort to retrieve the animal, alive or dead.

State agencies are largely responsible for regulating hunting, and the federal government enforces prohibitions on hunting endangered species and establishes the rules that regulate the hunting of migratory birds. Hunters must purchase hunting licenses and a tag from the state for each big-game animal killed. Killing ducks entails the purchase of a state hunting license as well as a duck stamp from the US Fish and Wildlife Service. Finally, hunting is limited by season, by area, and by weapon.

Alaskan brown bear salmon fishing. These bears are commonly hunted for trophies. (Photo courtesy of Nels Akerlund Photography)

Some species, however, are unregulated or are under far less regulation, such as "varmints" like coyotes or prairie dogs, who hunters can often kill in unlimited numbers. Not only do most states have little to no restrictions on killing coyotes, but the USDA's Wildlife Services kills about eighty thousand coyotes each year.[35]

Trophy Hunting

The term "trophy" refers to the antlers, horns, tusks, heads, or bodies of animals the hunters kill, and many American hunters enthusiastically seek them. In fact, the United States is now the chief market for "trophy animals"—there are tens of thousands of animals whom hunters kill from all around the world and bring back, as trophies, to the United States. Some hunters call animals killed for trophies "wall hangers." There's even a game ranch called Wall Hanger Farms that invites hunters to "harvest a dream."[36]

Because of the trophy hunter's emphasis on bagging a trophy at all costs, they have evolved into a somewhat different species than the traditional American hunter. Many trophy hunters now use baiting, dogs, game farms, canned hunting ranches, guides, and technology in order to ensure a trophy at the end of the day. As the number of hunters declines in the United States, the number of trophy hunters increases —although they still only make up a minority of hunters.[37]

The notion of trophies in hunting is very different from the awarding of trophies in sports like baseball, bowling, or tennis. In these sports, the most skilled or talented athlete wins awards or prizes based on these attributes. Because so many wealthy but busy hunters now pay for a guaranteed kill at canned hunting establishments, trophies do not represent the talents of the hunter; they only demonstrate his wealth. Hunting trophies are not little aluminum statues handed out to the best athlete either; they are the actual bodies of animals prepared by a taxidermist and displayed, which makes them an especially gruesome marker of status.

The laws regulating international trophy hunting conflict, since it is usually illegal to kill an endangered animal in the wild in the United States. But it is perfectly legal to kill one in another country—sometimes it is even legal to bring the trophy animal back into the United States. For example, the 1988 African Elephant Conservation Act prohibits the import of ivory into the United States but allows the importation of elephant trophies thanks to the work of Safari Club International, the biggest sport hunting advocacy organization in the country, with more than $10 million in revenue in 2005. Furthermore, under the terms of the Endangered Species Act, it is legal to bring the carcasses of endangered animals into this country for scientific or conservation

---

Addax

In January 2004 four addax arrived at Cleveland Amory Black Beauty Ranch in Texas. The three females and one male came from another sanctuary that had encountered hard times and had to send its animals to other sanctuaries. They are antelope whose coats change color from brown to tan or white, according to the seasons.

Addax are common exotics in canned hunting operations, since they have long horns that dramatically spiral upward. Like the nilgai profiled earlier in this chapter, addax are listed in Safari Club International's trophy record book as "Introduced Trophy Animals of North America." Texas itself is home to hundreds of canned hunting operations, where customers pay a premium to shoot animals inside a fenced area.

In their native habitat in the Sahara Desert, addax are critically endangered, mostly due to hunting. They are also listed as endangered by the US Fish and Wildlife Service under the Endangered Species Act. Their range was once approximately 3 million square miles, but today there are likely not more than a few hundred addax remaining in the wild. Although they range over great distances and once gathered in massive herds, these animals are now found primarily in canned hunting operations.

The four addax at Black Beauty Ranch share a large, open enclosure with other hoofed animals, living on part of a 1,300-acre sanctuary that provides a safe, loving home for more than 1,300 animals. They nap in the Texas sunshine together, drink from one of the lakes, graze on the grasses, and rest comfortably in the shade when the weather is hot.

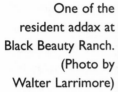

One of the resident addax at Black Beauty Ranch. (Photo by Walter Larrimore)

purposes (which is how many natural history museums continue to get specimens), and the US Fish and Wildlife Service sometimes issues permits to import trophy animals as well.[38]

At the time of publication, these permits are being issued on a more routine basis, due to the Bush administration's work to weaken protections for endangered species.

Trophy Records and Awards

Safari Club International (SCI) not only advocates on behalf of sport hunters by sponsoring hunting trips, holding an annual convention, and publishing a magazine, but since 1972 it has also offered the greatest number of hunting achievement awards of any hunting organization. Currently, it offers awards in twenty-nine major categories and hundreds of smaller awards as well. Some of the awards are for a single animal taken (i.e., antler size), but many awards are awarded for the killing of a combination of animals (i.e., the African Big Five, African Twenty-nine, North American Twenty-nine, Bears of the World, etc.). Earning an African Big Five Grand Slam means a hunter has killed an African lion, a leopard, an elephant, a rhino, and a Cape buffalo. In order to win a Bears of the World Grand Slam, a hunter must kill four different kinds of bears. Besides the main trophy categories is the Inner Circle awards, which are based on the number of animals taken; for instance, the Silver Circle means a hunter has killed ten different species of animal. The highest level, the Diamond Level, means you must kill seventy-six different species.

In order to win every SCI award and win the Crowning Achievement, a hunter has to kill 322 different animals.[39] Embarking on a SCI award mission is no easy feat. Hunters must pay expedition or safari companies to bring them to the animals, and companies like Valley Bushveld Safaris promise an "affordable and unforgettable South African safari hunting experience." Affordable is evidently a relative term, however, because Valley Bushveld's prices range from $2,600 (plus airfare) for three animals to hunt (kudu, wildebeest, and impala or blesbuck) to $5,300 for eight animals to hunt (wildebeest, springbuck, springbuck or mountain reedbuck, impala, gemsbuck, kudu, blesbuck, and grey duiker). Cheetahs, elephants, giraffes, lions, and rhinos are available through other outfits, but at substantially higher costs—upward of $10,000–$20,000 per animal.[40] Many companies tailor their safaris to match SCI's award categories, making it relatively easy to get listed in an award book.

SCI produces these trophy record books every year. Because the cost of winning these awards is so high, the organization offers raffle tickets at their annual events for one lucky winner to take all five for just the cost of a $250 ticket. Indeed, it can cost $100,000 to take the Big Five, yet only 10 percent of all hunters earn more than $100,000 per year.[41]

Except for the costs, winning an SCI award is easier than ever, thanks to the "intensive management techniques" many game ranches use, such as high fencing, selective culling, supplemental feeding and baiting, and artificially breeding of selected animals. Many game ranches now also offer guaranteed trophies; you don't pay unless you kill an animal.

SCI allows the inclusion of endangered species kills in its record books as long as hunters killed them prior to the date of listing by CITES (Convention on International Trade in Endangered Species of Wild Fauna and Flora) or the Endangered Species Act, or "under certain conditions." Other clubs offer hunting awards as well, but some, like the Boone and Crockett Club and the Pope and Young Club, will not consider animals shot at canned hunts for inclusion on their record lists. SCI has no such limitations.

Another organization that offers hunting awards is the Grand Slam Club, an organization of hunter-conservationists whose focus is wild sheep and goats. The Grand Slam Club gives out the Conklin Award, which "recognizes the world's greatest active hunter who pursues game in the most difficult terrain and conditions, exhibits the highest degree of ethics, and is a strong participant in wildlife conservation."[42] The 2005 winner, who has also won SCI's World Hunting Award Ring and SCI's International Hunting Award, has a "collection" that includes a great Rocky Mountain bighorn; a desert bighorn; two polar bears; three Alaskan brown bears; five muskox; a Central American whitetail; both species of brocket deer from the Yucatan; twelve or more free-ranging lions, leopards, and savanna elephants; more than four dozen Cape buffalo; both species of rhinoceros; three western bongo; all eight kinds of spiral-horned antelope; and ten forest duiker species.

Africa, due to its colonial history, has been stripped of much of its large-game animals over the past two hundred years. Much of the remaining population has been permanently transformed as a result of hunting for trophies such as elephant tusks. China, on the other hand, has been largely free from Western hunters, but that may soon change, as China announced plans in 2006 to auction licenses for foreign hunters to hunt rare and endangered species.[43]

Yaks, for example, would go for $40,000, because of their endangered status—there are only an estimated ten thousand left in the world. And while Chinese citizens have long hunted animals for meat and medicinal purposes, this would be the first time that the country would allow foreigners to kill these animals. (At the time of this writing, the auction was postponed due to controversy within China over the decision.)

One of the most egregious aspects of American trophy hunting has been the tax breaks—to the tune of several million dollars per year—provided to wealthy hunters to help offset the costs of their expeditions. After traveling to exotic locations to kill endangered or rare animals, trophy hunters had the animals appraised, often at incredibly inflated amounts, and donated them to nonprofit "museums" (sometimes set up in the hunter's own home) and other operations, claiming a tax deduction for the value of the animals. In addition, they claimed the entire "cost of replacement"—the entire price of the hunting trip made those trips completely tax deductible. One such museum is the Wyobraska Wildlife Museum in Nebraska, where more than eight hundred exotic animals were crammed into a railroad car at the back of the property. In 2004 stuffed animals appraised at more than $5 million arrived at the facility.[44]

Thankfully, in August 2006, the Senate passed the Pension Protection Act, which included a provision that allows hunters to deduct only the cost of the market value of the trophy or the cost of the taxidermy. The new law will save taxpayers up to $49 million over the next decade.[45]

Canned Hunts

Canned hunts refers to hunting operations that take place on private game farms or ranches that fence animals into a limited area so that hunters can more easily kill them. Canned hunting—also called high-fence hunting—is illegal or regulated in twenty states and challenges the notion of "fair chase" that is central to the American hunting philosophy.

The animals used in canned hunting operations generally come from two types of backgrounds: either they are raised on domestic game farms in order to be hunted, or they are purchased from animal dealers. Dealers buy them from a variety of sources, and they include former exotic pets, animals legally or illegally imported from Africa or Asia, former circus animals, and "surplus" zoo animals. A 1999 investigation found that 38 percent of all animals who left zoos from 1992 to 1998 ended up at game ranches and other undesirable locations.[46] On the other hand, it's not unheard of for animals who end up killed in canned hunts to start out their lives as pets. In 2007 an eleven-year-old boy killed a thousand-pound-plus hog on a ranch in Alabama. It was later reported that the hog, Fred, had been raised as a family pet and later sold to the ranch, where he was chased down a 150-acre fenced enclosure and shot eight times over three hours before he finally died.

There are about a thousand operations like this in the United States, and most are in Texas. These ranches offer traditional American animals to hunt such as deer and elk, as well as exotic animals such as oryx, addax, and zebras. The goal of these "hunts" is to bag a trophy. The cost to kill an exotic animal at a domestic canned hunting operation ranges from $250 for a small doe to $2,200 for a nilgai to $4,000 for a buck with a large rack—plus guide fees, lodging, meals, ammunition, and taxidermy. Even though killing a deer in the wild costs thousands of dollars less, the appeal here is not just the ease and guarantee of the kill. It's the fact that these operations allow the animals to grow to an age and size that guarantees the best rack.

While the very notion of wealthy hunters killing domestically raised animals (some of whom have been hand-raised) in an enclosed space is horrific to many hunters, some canned hunting operations go even further in manipulating the codes of commonly accepted hunting practices. They allow hunters to kill the animals at point-blank range, sometimes while the hunter is in a vehicle or while the animal is tied up or otherwise bound. Other operations use feeding stations and allow the hunter to kill animals while they're eating. Sometimes canned hunt operators have even drugged animals to immobilize them.[47]

Baiting—or using food to bring animals closer to the hunter, who is usually hidden behind or inside of a tree stand—has long been popular in hunting. And while most hunters oppose baiting deer, a majority feel that baiting bear is fine,[48] and dozens of bear hunting operations offer baited bear hunts. The Bear Buster Bear Baiter Buffet is even available for purchase online, and its automatic time-controlled feeding setting means that hunters will know exactly when to expect bears at the "buffet."[49] It is legal to bait bears with rotting food or even corpses on national forest land in ten states; eight states allow using dogs to tree the bear, or chase a bear into a tree where the hunter can easily shoot him. Other controversial practices found at canned hunting operations are "jacklighting," or shining a light on animals at night, using vehicles to herd or drive animals, and the use of electronic devices to attract or locate game.

At this time, other than the states that limit or prohibit canned hunting, there are no federal regulations whatsoever. However, the Captive Exotic Animal Protection Act, which is currently sitting in the Senate Judiciary Committee, would ban most forms of canned hunting in the United States by prohibiting the transfer or possession of a confined exotic mammal for hunting purposes. Representatives and senators have proposed similar legislation each year since 1995, but each year well-funded organizations like Safari Club International are able to convince Congress that it is every American's fundamental right to kill domestic or tame animals in enclosed spaces. Oregon is currently considering a complete ban on canned hunting. But the legislators and humane supporters who are in favor of it are being opposed by groups like the Safari Club International, the Oregon Hunters' Association, as well as private hunting ranches like Clover Creek Ranch. This operation offers Russian boars, Hawaiian black sheep, and water buffalo with prices starting at $500 and going to $2,000 and up.

One reason states have such a hard time banning the practice, which many hunters abhor, is because the animals are privately owned, whereas state game agencies that typically regulate hunting have authority only over the treatment of wildlife on public land.[50]

Another type of canned hunting is the practice of releasing domestically raised birds like pheasant, quail, partridge, and ducks for hunters to kill in large numbers. Dick Cheney is a fan of this type of hunting and has participated at least three times between 2003 and 2006 with fellow Republican heavyweights. Two of his trips were particularly noteworthy. In 2003 Cheney and a group of Republican donors flew on taxpayer money to a Pennsylvania ranch, where they killed in one morning more than four hundred farm-raised pheasants who were released in front of them; Cheney killed seventy himself.[51] Cheney was on a similar trip in 2006 at a Texas ranch when he famously shot a friend in the face. These hunts often require no licenses, and there are no bag limits.

Not only do canned hunts completely eliminate any notion of fair chase, but they also smack of the aristocratic style of hunting so hated by traditional American hunters. Indeed, wealthy hunters are allowed to kill whatever animals they like, at any cost, on private land where normal Americans cannot go, and with very little effort.

Exotic Game Farms

Game farming, or wildlife farming, is a relatively new practice in the United States in which wild animals (native and foreign) are raised on ranches, either to be used for hunting or for meat or skin. The first wild foreign animals brought to the United States were probably camels in the nineteenth century, followed by other animals like the nilgai antelope, who were bought from the San Diego Zoo by a Texas ranch in the 1930s.[52]

Even though these are usually wild animals, because private individuals own them and private ranches raise them, they are legally classified as "exotic livestock." As a result, many state game or wildlife agencies do not regulate them. There are even tax benefits for raising exotic livestock, as ranches can qualify for agricultural appraisal and thus receive a greatly reduced property tax rate.

Most of the ranches are in Texas, and the most common animals come from areas with a similar climate. They include Asian and African species of deer, antelope, and sheep, wild pigs from Europe, as well as more exotic animals like zebras, elephants, and giraffes.[53]

Whereas hunters and game agencies see wild animals as natural resources to be exploited and managed, game farmers see exotic ranch-raised animals as inventory. As "stock" levels change, game farmers are able to offer their customers a greater range of animals to choose from, and they can offer individual animals with specific rack sizes, for example.

Game farmers raise exotic animals for pleasure, for hunting (Texas's hunting directory lists more than one hundred such ranches), for meat to sell, for tourists to view, and, in an odd twist, some even claim they are sustaining endangered populations. Some species such

Many trophy hunters prize pronghorn antelope.
(Photo by Jack Dykinga, USDA)

as the nilgai are now more numerous in Texas than they are in their native India, and the oryx, now found in zoos and on Texas ranches, is thought to be extinct in its native Africa.[54] These animals are a $100-million industry in Texas alone;[55] they represent an increase in income from cattle ranching. Game ranchers typically acquired their original populations from zoos and later from animal dealers.[56] In some cases, they have allowed the animals to range free on public land, where, if they survive, they sometimes compete with local species for resources and have spread disease.

Sport hunters love game ranch-raised animals not only because of the ease of killing an animal in a fenced setting but also because the animals have been fed and medicated, leaving them bigger and healthier and making bigger trophies.

One good example of the shadiness of game farms is the Catskill Game Farm in New York. In 2006 the operation went under, putting nearly a thousand animals up for auction, including antelope, rhinos, yaks, rabbits, alligators, monkeys, and snakes. Many of them were tame and hand fed. Among the animals were representatives of about 150 endangered, threatened, or exotic species.[57] Investigators at the Humane Society of the United States who attended the auction saw several animals sold to allegedly unlicensed dealers who sell to canned hunt operations.[58]

One of the dealers was the high bidder at the auction for Boom Boom, a two-ton, thirty-five-year-old white rhino. Boom Boom was born at a Missouri circus and lived at Six Flags Great Adventure and Wild Safari in New Jersey before ending up at the game farm.[59] However, Ecko Unlimited, an urban clothing company with an interest in rhinos, purchased him from the dealer for $11,000.[60] Thanks to Ecko, he will enjoy the rest of his life in a spacious enclosure at an Arizona sanctuary. He now wags his tail "like a dog" and likes being pet behind the ears.[61]

Game ranches ultimately offer a unique perspective on hunting and conservation in the United States. On the one hand, they protect wild animals on public lands from hunters because they offer "farm-raised" animals for hunters to pay to hunt. On the other hand, they acquire new animals from wild populations. They pay animal dealers who buy exotic animals not only from zoos and private homes but also from collectors who travel to Asia or Africa to "collect" new specimens, where many can be killed in the process. Many ranches claim that they are providing a service by preserving animals who would otherwise be extinct or endangered in the wild. However, these animals are not being reintroduced into Africa or India; instead, they are bred to be shot and killed by wealthy American hunters on Texas ranches. And finally, if one of the major justifications provided by hunting is to keep population levels of wild animals at a manageable level, then how do we justify game farms that actually breed more animals in order to provide hunters with animals to kill? Game ranches also play a role in the decimation of predator species like wolves, bobcats, and coyotes, because these animals prey on the exotic wildlife and are killed by the ranchers.[62] How can this be justified in terms of conservation, population control, or species preservation?

Other Forms of Modern Hunting

Today, there are dozens of new ways that hunters can kill animals. One particularly egregious approach is remote hunting via the Internet. Promoted as a way to allow the physically disabled enjoy the sport of hunting, Internet hunting allows hunters from anywhere around the world to pay a fee and actually shoot animals via their computers. A gun and webcam is connected via remote control to the hunter's mouse, allowing him or her to control the weapon. As of June 2007, thirty-three states have banned the practice. In the 2005–2006 session, the Computer-Assisted Remote Hunting Act, which would prohibit Internet hunting nationwide, was introduced into Congress, where it has languished in the House Subcommittee on Crime, Terrorism, and Homeland Security.

Contest kills are another, much older sport hunting method, where hunters essentially use hundreds of "pest" animals such as pigeons or prairie dogs as live targets. In the notorious Hegins Labor Day Pigeon Shoot in Hegins, Pennsylvania, pigeons dazed after being confined in boxes for several days were released from traps thirty yards in front of hunters, who shot them in order to kill and score as many points as possible. As with doves, there is an extraordinarily high wound rate in pigeon shoots. Children wrung the necks of wounded pigeons who fell inside the scoring circle and threw them into the trash, and the wounded birds who flew outside the circle and were not retrieved died over a period of hours or days. The hunter who killed the most birds received a prize. After years of protests by animal rights groups and an appalled public, the shoot was permanently canceled in 1999.[63] Unfortunately, there are still several similar pigeon shoots still in operation in Pennsylvania.

In prairie dog kills, hunters sit near prairie dog colonies and shoot at them as they emerge from their underground burrows to eat, play, and rest in the sun. Many hunters consider this good target practice, but it's also an organized event where prizes are awarded for greatest number of kills. Some sport hunters even "mist" prairie dogs, using a high-powered rifle to explode the small animals into tiny, misty bits.

It's worth noting that lead shot used for hunting prairie dogs and other animals can be harmful to other species. Although it's illegal to use lead shot for waterfowl hunting, it's still legal to use lead shot for hunting other animals. This can cause lead to enter the food chain. The number-one cause of lead poisoning among raptors (such as hawks, falcons, and vultures) is ingesting lead fragments from the carcasses of hunted animals such as prairie dogs.[64] In 2006 a nontoxic shot advisory committee of the Minnesota Department of Natural Resources concluded, "It is inevitable that lead shot will have to be restricted for all shotgun hunting at some future time."[65]

Coyote calling contest participants use electronic calling devices that mimic the sounds of wounded animals or prey, luring coyotes to hidden shooters. Competitors can net thousands of dollars in prize money, and events can draw more than a hundred participants from across the country. There are approximately five hundred calling contests nationwide.[66]

WILDLIFE MANAGEMENT

There is no comprehensive federal law like the Animal Welfare Act that protects wild animals. Instead, a patchwork of laws covers everything from international conservation issues (such as the African Elephant Conservation Act) to issues surrounding human-animal conflict (Animal Damage Control Act) to laws protecting endangered species (Endangered Species Act) or specific species (such as the Marine Mammal Protection Act and the range of laws and treaties covering migratory birds) to laws protecting various habitats.

Wild animals for the most part are "managed" through the federal government by the US Fish and Wildlife Service and by individual state agencies. The agencies function under the assumption that wild animals are a resource that the public owns and that the states manage, while some wild animals are considered pests who the state also handles. In either case, wild animals ostensibly exist to benefit the public, and the wide range of state agencies tasked with managing wildlife carry this basic philosophy with them. The mission of the US Fish and Wildlife Service is to "conserve, protect and enhance fish, wildlife, and plants and their habitats for the continuing benefit of the American people."[67] The agency was established after the passage of the Fish and Wildlife Act of 1956, a comprehensive national fish, shellfish, and wildlife resources policy that emphasized oversight on the commercial fishing industry. In recent years, as many as 8 million people have engaged in consumptive wildlife use, or hunting, trapping, and fishing in the national wildlife refuge system each year. This may be due in part to the passage of the National Wildlife Refuge System Improvement Act of 1997, which includes hunting and fishing as two of the six priority uses for the national wildlife refuge system.[68] Furthermore, in 2006 the agency proposed creating new hunting and fishing programs on national wildlife refuges in New Jersey and Minnesota. The idea was to turn these two refuges into game parks and expand hunting opportunities at six additional refuges.

State Agencies

State wildlife agencies—such as fish and game departments, conservation departments, and natural resources departments—regulate hunting, manage wildlife, and work to minimize human conflicts with wildlife. They typically issue hunting and fishing licenses and oversee wildlife law enforcement.

The men and women who work for these agencies act as both law enforcement officers as well as conservationists by ensuring the continuation of wildlife as a renewable resource. This is why hunting fees support many of the activities of the state game agencies; it's the hunters who benefit from state wildlife programs, so much of the money for these programs comes from hunters in the form of fees and licenses.

For the individuals who work in this field, many see their role as keeping nature in balance. Because commercial and trophy hunting, development, and cattle ranching have eradicated most of the natural predators for many of this country's wild animals, wildlife managers now attempt to restore the natural balance by allowing hunters to kill game animals and keep their populations from exploding. Hunting, then, according to both hunters and wildlife agency employees, is necessary for wildlife.[69] State hunting regulations govern the where, when, who, and how of hunting. They distinguish between game animals and pest species (the latter is often not regulated at all). They may limit hunting to animals of a certain age, size, or sex. They regulate the type of weapon that can be used. They provide "bag limits," which regulate how many animals can be killed. They oversee the season when hunting a certain species can occur. And finally, they ensure that hunting takes place only where it is allowed. Hunters who hunt game animals must purchase hunting licenses, and big-game hunters must also purchase a "tag" for each animal they kill. Hunting of migratory birds involves the additional purchase of a duck stamp from the US Fish and Wildlife Service.

Hunting out of season, hunting prohibited animals, or hunting without a license is considered poaching, whether the poachers kill animals for personal use or profit. Poachers are a threat to both animals and legal hunters because many kill far more animals than regulated hunters and threaten populations. They are also a problem for states because their actions result in a loss of income from fees and licenses. Other violations that state fish and game agencies oversee include hunting with improper equipment, illegal baiting and using dogs or other advantages when prohibited. Criminologist Stephen Eliason notes that the number of reported violations of wildlife laws most likely pales in comparison to the actual number of violations and may even range as low as 1 to 2 percent of all actual poaching incidents.[70] Poachers may illegally kill wildlife in order to provide food for their families, but they may also do so to obtain a trophy for the thrill or because of an antagonism toward government control.[71]

The whitetail deer is the most common American large animal in the wild and a popular animal for big-game hunters. (Photo by Scott Bauer, USDA)

Human-Animal Conflict

On the other hand, some agencies exist to regulate conflict between humans and animals, ensuring that developers, ranchers, and others with economic interests don't have their interests impeded by the presence of wild animals. While these agencies use hunting as the solution to human-animal conflicts like the presence of deer in suburban developments, hungry bears approaching campers, prairie dogs digging holes in city parks, or coyotes eating pet cats and dogs, the agenda of these agencies is very different from fish and game departments: these animals are viewed as pests who must be eliminated because of human economic interests.

Congress passed the Animal Damage Control Act in 1931 to authorize the eradication of wolves, lions, coyotes, bobcats, prairie dogs, and other animals who pose a supposed threat to agriculture. The act created Animal Damage Control (ADC), which has, at different times, been implemented by a number of different federal agencies, most recently the USDA's Animal and Plant Health Inspection Service (APHIS). The predecessor to ADC was the Bureau of Biological Survey, created in 1905, with one of its goals being the destruction of pests and predator animals like wolves; within two years, the bureau, which employed professional hunters, eliminated 1,800 wolves and 23,000 coyotes from national forests. Between 1915 and 1942, hunters killed more than 24,000 wolves.[72] The bureau was responsible for the death of the last wolf in Yellowstone National Park in 1926. Even in these early days, the goals of the bureau were to protect livestock and to increase the animal populations for hunting. Sadly, from a modern perspective, those results were predictable: the deer population did balloon after the loss of the wolves, but tens of thousands of deer died the following year because there was not enough forage to support them. In a bit of bitter irony, after the federal government effectively wiped out the wolf population, the gray wolf was the first animal to be listed under the Endangered Species Act of 1973.[73]

Originally, the Animal Damage Control Act focused on animal damage to public lands, but today it operates on both public and private land. APHIS now administers Animal Damage Control, now called Wildlife Services, often in conjunction with state fish and game departments. Wildlife Services kills predators in Arizona, California, Colorado, Idaho, Minnesota, Montana, Nebraska, Nevada, New Mexico, North Dakota, Oklahoma, Oregon, South Dakota, Texas, Utah, Washington, and Wyoming. It has been responsible for the near extermination of all nineteen of the largest mammals in the West, as well as a large number of small animals such as prairie dogs.[74]

Even though the goal of hunting for animal damage control programs is very different than the goal of hunting for sport, ADC hunting benefits hunters and hunting advocates because it provides another way for hunting to be perceived as a valuable public service. It also benefits a small group of people—wealthy ranchers, politicians, and appointed state and federal officials—who cash in on a federal handout that helps ranchers stay in business.

Animal damage control advocates often characterize game animals as pest species. Deer, for instance, do not kill farm animals but are blamed for destroying gardens, bringing disease, causing car accidents, and creating other forms of havoc in suburbs. So, sport hunters are allowed to kill deer with public support—after all, no one wants to be involved in a collision with a deer. (Never mind that suburban development is the primary culprit for car-deer collisions, a situation that continues to worsen as housing developments gobble up more and more wild areas.) Unfortunately for deer, hunting doesn't necessarily control their populations. They can rebound soon after hunting season due to lessened competition for resources. And, of course, the animal damage control measures that wiped out much of their natural predators also play a role in their large numbers. There are numerous methods to prevent the damage that deer can cause, such as more responsible driving, speed limits, warning signs, roadside reflectors, as well as the use of fencing along roadways. Yet the fact remains that as long as developers continue to build on these areas, humans and wildlife will come into contact. Sadly, animal damage control programs have just one way of solving these problems—hunting.

In New Mexico alone, Wildlife Services kills more than twelve thousand animals every year at a cost of $2.2 million per year. This benefits only 7 percent of New Mexico's ranchers, who themselves make up only .04 percent of the state's population.[75] As is typical, the wealthiest and most powerful New Mexicans benefit the most from this program, with politicians and celebrity ranch owners receiving the most visits and wildlife kills on their properties. Furthermore, there is no incentive for ranchers or farmers to try to protect farm animals or crops on their own, since taxpayer money and government-hired hunters will come to their property to kill problem animals. The irony is that Wildlife Services' approach of targeting predators such as coyotes and wolves (using methods such as aerial shooting from helicopters, trapping, poisoning, and killing coyote pups in their dens) results in an increase of deer and other game animals, whose "overpopulation" provides another argument for hunting advocates to hunt.

Looking at the history of wolf eradication in this country provides an interesting window into the logic of animal damage control. The government has targeted various wolf species since the mid-seventeenth century. By 1800 the wolf had been largely eliminated from the East Coast because of the threat to the emerging cattle and sheep industries (which primarily grazed animals then, as now, on public lands). In the nineteenth and twentieth centuries, efforts to eradicate the wolf moved westward and picked up speed. As European Americans wiped out the bison, they also slaughtered wolves. Sportsmen joined with ranchers in supporting this policy, since they saw wolves as a threat to game animals.

Geographer Jody Emel points out that beyond the economic reasons for why wolves were slaughtered, the ferocity with which hunters killed them had to do with the way they were characterized—people considered them wasteful, vicious, and unsportsmanlike in the way they killed farm animals.[76] The public saw wolves as mean and treacherous animals who killed for pleasure. This was, by the way, very different from how many Native Americans saw wolves: they admired wolves for their endurance, strong family bonds, and bravery.

A US Fish and Wildlife program set up to reintroduce the Mexican gray wolf back into Arizona and New Mexico after last century's eradication continues. Yet, as a final irony, the same government agency is killing many of the wolves it has reintroduced due to farm animal deaths, reducing the new population from fifty-five to fewer than thirty.

Hunting as Conservation

Some hunting organizations do support many conservation efforts. As of this writing, the Congressional Sportsmen's Foundation was lobbying for the passage or reauthorization of a number of federal and state bills of strong interest to environmentalists, such as the Great Lakes Fish and Wildlife Restoration Act, the North American Wetlands Conservation Act, the Forest Emergency Restoration and Research Act, the Wetlands Loan Act, and the Federal Energy Natural Resources Enhancement Fund Act. The foundation is even concerned about global warming, demonstrating a commitment to environmental issues not found among many American conservatives.[77]

Yet, in recent years, this same group also worked to support bills that would shield gunmakers from liability lawsuits in cases of gun deaths and use taxpayer money to pay landowners to open up their land to hunters. Most critically, they have been pushing heavily the Threatened and Endangered Species Recovery Act of 2005, which has been passed by the House but never left a Senate subcommittee. It would essentially gut the Endangered Species Act by eliminating habitat protection measures and other key features. While the loosening of protections for endangered species would certainly be good news for hunters, it would also weaken protections of wildlands and open those lands up for development, something that conservationist-minded hunters traditionally oppose. The act was cosponsored by (now former) Rep. Richard Pombo, a California Republican, who in 1994 claimed before a Senate subcommittee that his family's ranch was declared a critical habitat for an endangered kit fox, which in turn endangered his family's finances. When an interviewer later pointed out that this statement was false, he was forced to retract the statement and to admit that he'd never been adversely affected by the ESA.[78]

The history of the environmental movement in this country is tied in many ways to hunting. But even in the days of Roosevelt, hunters had their own agenda: to conserve land in order to ensure that there remained animals to hunt. But these early conservationist-hunters didn't realize the role that natural predators played in the ecosystem. By eliminating predators in order to give themselves a bigger population of game animals to kill, manipulating population numbers via sex-selective killing, changing the lengths of hunting seasons, and manipulating habitats, they created problems that are still pervasive throughout ecosystems today.

The question for us remains: Without hunters and the funds that they pay to conserve habitats for their own use, would the environmental movement disappear? Would our public lands disappear, taking wild animals species with them? Of course not. The environmental movement in the United States is one of the most robust movements of its kind. Millions of Americans are committed to habitat preservation and wildlife conservation, and the vast majority do not hunt. Hunters and hunting advocates aside, most Americans and environmental groups would continue to fight to ensure the survival of our wildlife and the land that they live on—without pleading the case that certain animals need to be killed in order to allow others to survive.

POLITICAL INFLUENCE OF HUNTING ADVOCATES

Hunters and gun advocates are among the most powerful special interest groups in the United States today, even with the limited number of people they represent (as we've seen, hunters represent 4 percent of the adult US population). Because of their clout, they are able to shape the policies that affect the future of wildlife in this country, which is to the detriment of not only animals and their advocates but also to nature and wildlife lovers who enjoy visiting national parks and viewing animals in their natural habitats.

Gun advocates, like hunting advocates, work to promote legislation that favors hunting and conserving game species—so that they can be hunted—although some other species benefit as a side effect. Other groups that benefit financially from hunting are the manufacturers and sellers of ammunition and archery equipment, and the hunting guides, lodging providers, and taxidermists who service hunters. As the number of hunters in this country declines, these groups work harder to bring more people into hunting as well as to influence legislation that is favorable for their industry.

The gun industry, for example, spent $40 million lobbying the federal government from 1998 to 2004.[79] That includes a whopping $18 million from the Gun Owners of America and $11 million from the National Rifle Association (NRA). Hunting groups like Safari Club International (SCI), National Shooting Sports Foundation, and Ducks Unlimited spent an additional $2.5 million on federal lobbying.[80]

Some gun rights groups have pushed for legislation that benefits hunters, such as measures that would ensure hunter access to federal lands, provide federal funds for hunter education, reduce penalties for hunters who illegally bait, criminalize hunter "harassment," and more. For example, the NRA was instrumental in structuring the National Wildlife Refuge System Improvement Act of 1997, which states that hunting is a "priority use" of refuges. Due to the work of hunting and gun groups, every state now prohibits individuals from disturbing hunts by, for example, intentionally making noise to scare off animals. The gun lobby has also created other groups that provide cover for the pro-gun agenda, such as the Ballot Issues Coalition, a group that gives money to state campaigns to protect hunters' interests; the Public Land Shooting Sports Roundtable, which promotes shooting on state and federal land; and the National Wildlife Conservation Partners, which advises the president and Congress on issues related to wildlife and hunting.

Pro-hunting organizations include Safari Club International (which spent almost a million dollars on lobbying from 1998 to 2004), the National Shooting Sport Foundation (which spent $640,000 from 1998 to 2004), and the US Sportsmen's Alliance (which spent a half million dollars from 1998 to 2004), as well as "waterfowl conservation groups" like Ducks Unlimited and Delta Waterfowl.[81]

Safari Club International is the biggest player in terms of sport hunting advocacy. As a 501(c)(4) (lobbying) organization, SCI sponsors hunts and hunting competitions and provides trophy books and awards to exceptionally prolific hunters. SCI also lobbies on behalf of wealthy trophy hunters who are looking for rare animals to kill. For example, SCI representatives regularly attend CITES conventions in order to advocate for removing animals from the endangered species list. They have lobbied to weaken the Endangered Species Act and the Marine Mammal Protection Act, and in 1998 they successfully lobbied Congress to lift a ban on the import of polar bear trophies into the United States from Canada.

How does SCI support these important conservation activities? Because of its focus on rare trophy animals, it attracts a wealthy membership—40 percent of SCI members have an annual income more than $250,000, and the average annual income of one of its members is more than $200,000.[82] The group is known to have close ties with the Bush administration (the deputy director of the US Fish and Wildlife Service, Matt Hogan, was a former lobbyist for SCI, and SCI has lobbied to allow the import of endangered trophy animals into the United States).[83] It also receives taxpayer money from the US Fish and Wildlife Service via the African Elephant Conservation Act, and with this money funds Communal Areas Management Program for Indigenous Resources (CAMPFIRE), an elephant "conservation" program that sells the right to hunt African elephants for $10,000 apiece, in effect working to reinstate the legal ivory trade. CAMPFIRE's stated goals are to use the funds raised from hunting elephants to support African villagers, but it's difficult to miss the importance to SCI's members of the opportunity to legally kill elephants.[84] SCI also runs a charitable foundation known as Safari Club International Foundation, which focuses on wildlife conservation and hunter education.

Still not convinced that hunters wield considerable clout? Look no further than the Congressional Sportsmen's Foundation, a 501(c)(3) organization made up of hunting advocacy groups and outdoor industry manufacturers and suppliers. This organization advises Congress on pro-hunting issues through its affiliation with the Congressional Sportsmen's Caucus, which is made up of more than three hundred pro-hunting legislators. Finally, because most issues of interest to hunters come up on the state rather than the federal level, the National Assembly of Sportsmen's Caucuses is made up of more than fifteen hundred state legislators, who each are affiliated with one of the twenty-two state sportsmen's caucuses.

The political strength of the pro-hunting lobby is easy to see when election campaigns start heating up. While some politicians like Dick Cheney are fervent hunters, many are not. Yet every election cycle sees the carefully staged photo ops of candidates in camouflage, killing animals in order to demonstrate that they are friendly to the all-important hunting lobby—and perhaps to make themselves look stronger in the process.

THE FUTURE OF HUNTING

Hunting has been on a steady decline in the United States. The number of hunters over the age of sixteen has dropped from a little more than 14 million in 1996 to 12.5 million in 2006—a 10 percent decrease—and a correlating decrease can be seen in hunting-related revenue over the same period, even while a small minority of wealthy trophy hunters has become more powerful.[85] At the same time, the number of hunters is dwarfed by the number of people who participate in wildlife watching—71 million. That number is increasing. People who feed, photograph, and watch wildlife generate more than $45 million a year in revenue through all of their purchases, about twice that of hunters, who generate $22.7 million.[86]

Hunting's decline can be tracked to a number of social phenomena, such as the increasing movement of the population from rural areas to cities and suburbs; development that has turned once-public lands into private property; the federal government's sale of hundreds of thousands of acres of public land to raise money for education;[87] more private landowners disallowing hunting on their land;[88] the changing demographics of the population; the rising cost of hunting; and, as family values and dynamics change, hunting no longer being what it once was—a bonding experience between father and son.

Recruitment of Youths and Women

Historically, both in the United States and elsewhere, the vast majority of hunters have been men: 11.8 million US hunters are men, and only 1.2 million women hunt. Ninety-six percent of all hunters in the United States are white.[89] Hunting by women and nonwhite hunters has increased but is still an activity in which a very small portion of the population participates. The number of children hunting has also decreased, from 700,000 kids between the ages of sixteen and seventeen in 1996 to 584,000 in 2001.[90]

Faced with such diminishing numbers, hunting groups such as the National Wild Turkey Federation, the US Sportsmen's Alliance, and the National Shooting Sports Foundation are attempting to lower state minimum age hunting laws to attract more youth. Recent research points to a connection between adult hunting and having hunted as a child. More than 90 percent of today's adult hunters were initiated into hunting before the age of twenty.[91] In fact, if an individual has not learned to hunt by the age of twenty, there is a very low likelihood of hunting participation as an adult. Minimum age laws, then, are a definite barrier for hunting recruitment, and this fear is what propels legislators in states such as Wisconsin and Michigan to work on lowering age limits. Currently, only twenty states have laws that restrict most hunting for children under twelve. In October 2005, an eight-year-old girl killed the first black bear of Maryland's hunting season. One hunting publication even advocated reducing the amount of safety training for youths, stating that "mandatory prerequisite coursework and certification processes add more barriers that discourage some youths from hunting."[92]

Yet incidents do happen. According to the Wisconsin Department of Natural Resources, 29 percent of all hunting accidents involved kids between the ages of twelve and seventeen—more than any other age group. One particularly egregious case involved a thirteen-year-old, David Kingston, who was shot in the back by his grandfather in November 2005. According to newspaper accounts, the boy's relatives retrieved the deer who had been shot before seeking help for David. The boy's cousin even allegedly kicked David and threatened to duct-tape his mouth if he wasn't quiet.[93]

Besides legislation, hunting and shooting groups work with state agencies to sponsor youth recruitment hunts that are funded with tax-payer money, and many are aimed at very young children. Animals are brought in to be killed at close range to give the children a "win" they can be proud of. Alabama, for instance, offers youth dove hunts while Pennsylvania offers pheasant hunts for youth.[94]

The US Fish and Wildlife Service also sponsors grants that are given to groups targeting children as new hunters. Using $330,000 in taxpayer money, the Council for Wildlife Conservation and Education, Inc., an arm of the National Shooting Sports Foundation, produced three hunting videos for distribution to schools for grades four through twelve that emphasized hunting as a recreational pastime.[95] In nineteen states, public school districts offer hunting education classes in high schools; in fourteen of those states, instructors bring guns into the classroom.

Other federal funds are used to help hunting organizations and game agencies understand how to make children into hunters. A 2003 government-funded study, for instance, looked at the way that kids' perceptions of animals change throughout childhood and how they are affected by various factors in their lives. Young children, the study showed, typically view animals from a "moralistic and humanistic" perspective, which is not conducive to hunting. The challenge for game agencies, according to this study, is to change kids' views in ways that would favor hunting, such as through encouraging children to attend hunting or fishing events with family and friends, teaching them about ecological interdependence, or starting children off with "catch and release" type programs.[96]

Finally, there are also a great many programs aimed bringing women into the fold. Again, federal tax dollars are used to support these programs. Recent studies by the US Fish and Wildlife Service and the National Wild Turkey Federation focus on tailoring hunting activities to women by basing them on known factors that prevent women from getting involved. The Florida Fish and Wildlife Commission and the Maryland Department of Natural Resources, for example, offer "Becoming an Outdoors Woman" (BOW) programs that provide women the opportunity to hunt deer, turkey, hogs, and doves. Illinois offers bird hunting clinics for women and kids. South Carolina offers hunts exclusively for women and the disabled. On the private level, the NRA offers a program called "Women on Target," which aims to create more hunting opportunities for women by creating a safe, "women-only" atmosphere.

The funny thing about so much focus and money being spent on turning women into hunters is that, not only has hunting been historically a male activity, but also there are links between hunting animals and hunting women. Both feminist analysts as well as hunting advocacy materials have made this connection.[97] "Hunting for Bambi," an Internet hoax in which men could pay thousands of dollars to hunt naked women with paintballs, is perhaps the most obvious demonstration of the sexualization of hunting. Ecofeminist Marti Kheel writes of the hunting-sex connection, one of the most prevalent themes in the descriptions of hunters' experiences: "Both the hunt and the sexual act are premised on the notion of the buildup of tension; the orgasm and the kill provide the sought-after relief."[98] In a 2004 study in *Society & Animals*, the authors analyzed issues of *Traditional Bowhunter* and found a strong degree of sexualization of animals, women, and weapons in its ads, photos, and editorial content.[99]

CONCLUSION

Hunting has a long history in this country. It is tied to positive issues like conservation but is inextricably linked to the decimation of species, the genocide of the Native Americans, and the growth of one of the greediest, vainest types of animal abuse in this country today—the pastime of trophy hunters, who hunt rare and endangered animals in order to hang bodies on their walls and get listed in a book.

But hunting is by no means the only negative issue facing wildlife today. Wild animals are threatened by the introduction of new diseases, the exotic pet trade, and the loss of habitat due to commercial development, housing, oil, mining, and more.

As an example, some western states still have small populations of wild horses. These horses are descendents of the highly trained Spanish mounts, who the Spanish abandoned during the seventeenth and eighteenth centuries. They quickly reverted to their wild state and became the wild mustangs that are still seen in states like Colorado and New Mexico today. Sadly, thanks to the ever-encroaching demands of civilization, these beautiful horses are also increasingly rounded up and sold at auction, notwithstanding their supposed protection under the Wild Free-Roaming Horses and Burros Act of 1971.

The wild horses of the West are a sad example of the effect of hunting on this country. Even though wild horses are a potent symbol of freedom and the American West, they represent a breed that is unconquered and that must be brought under human control, even if that means eliminating them entirely. Additionally, many people have the idea that animals are only good if they are used for something, and, without being trained or used for some personal or commercial purpose, these animals are viewed as not good for anything.

And so it is with the rest of this country's wildlife. Coyotes, wolves, bison, and prairie dogs are seen as pests, not good for anything, and in fact, harmful to the economic interests of some people and industries. Thus, they must be eliminated. But game animals, on the other hand, are good for something: hunting. Thus, some must be selectively bred on game farms and stocked in fenced enclosures, and sport hunters pay big money to selectively kill them for pleasure. At least they are good for something. If they weren't, they'd be gone altogether.

What You Can Do

The following are a number of ways that readers can take action to stop the killing of animals for sport and profit.

- Educate people about the harm hunters cause to animals and the environment. Many animal welfare groups provide free leaflets and other informational packets that you can distribute.
- Vote. Hunters make up a small, but very powerful, American minority. Nonhunters need to vote on issues dealing with wildlife in their local and state elections. Be sure to contact your elected representatives.
- Utilize the democratic process to help wild animals by supporting or opposing legislation involving hunting or wildlife management. Attend state wildlife meetings and get involved in the decision-making process. Encourage your legislators to enact or enforce wildlife protection laws, and insist that non-hunters be equally represented on wildlife agency staffs. The number of humane wildlife watchers outnumbers hunters by nearly a five-to-one margin—there's no reason for hunting's disproportionate voice.
- Before you support a "wildlife" or "conservation" group, ask if it supports hunting. Many wildlife groups support hunting.
- If you own land, post "No Hunting" signs.
- Do what you can to ensure that wildlife is safe in your community by promoting the use of nonlethal control techniques.
- Report poachers in national parks to the National Parks and Conservation Association at 1-800-448-NPCA.

Chapter 4

THE FUR AND SKINS INDUSTRIES

Animals as Clothing

Perhaps ironically, the saving grace of fur-breeding is that most of the animals do not have to endure this confinement for long, since the majority are killed and pelted at the age of 7–8 months.[1]

—*The Mink* by Nigel Dunstone

It is interesting to note that, for example, the life span of a mink on the farm exceeds that of a mink in the wild, and the farmed mink is healthier and stronger than his wild counterpart.[2]

—Fur Information Council of America

INTRODUCTION

For many of us, fur is an anachronism, a passé symbol of the opulent consumerism and extravagant materialism of the 1980s. "Nobody wears fur anymore," we think, and for the few people who do, the animals are surely cared for better than they were two decades ago—hasn't the fur industry learned to take public concern seriously and clean up its act?

Indeed, fur sales have indeed dropped since the 1980s, and the industry still suffers from a well-deserved stigma. Yet the fur industry as well as the exotic skin industry have invested in slick marketing campaigns and have appealed to designers in order to increase sales of these products. On catwalks and in retail stores, fur and exotic skins are occupying the spotlight again. Luckily, while producers and manufacturers are enjoying a tepid renaissance with the fur fad in select venues, only a small percentage of celebrities and other consumers wear fur. And exotic skins are still primarily a very high-end luxury item worn by few. At the same time, little has changed for the animals whose skins are used to make the products. They still spend their lives in cramped, squalid conditions on misleadingly named "farms." They suffer terribly in traps. They can be slaughtered in the most grisly manner.

There are no federal legal protections for animals who experience the worst living conditions and slaughter on US fur farms, and there is little regulation regarding the ways that trappers can catch animals for the fur trade. Since the United States imports a great deal of its fur and skins, the countries that supply us with furs can have an even more appalling lack of regard for animal welfare. The fur and skin trade is increasingly globalized, and even domesticated animals such as cows and sheep used for textiles can suffer greatly.

FUR

Fur clothing has been worn by people around the world for millennia. But since the development of fabrics using plant and synthetic fibers, fur has become a luxury worn by a small minority of the population. As women in the Western world entered the workforce and gained economic independence in the twentieth century, middle-class women began to wear furs as well. In recent decades, however, the rise of the humane movement has shed light on the cruelties inherent in the fur industry. As a result, most people in the United States today don't think twice about not wearing fur. Yet, while the number of animals killed for fur has decreased, fur trim—used to accentuate clothing—

has become ubiquitous on runways and in department stores, with half a billion dollars in global sales. It seems that fur is now on everything: trim, hats, coats, gloves, furniture, purses, earmuffs, trinkets, blankets, bikinis, and more. There's even fur yarn for do-it-yourselfers.[3]

While consumers still have good reason to be horrified about the routine and shocking abuse endured by animals who are raised on mis-leadingly named fur "farms" or caught in traps, fur companies have exploited labeling loopholes and public trust to bring fur back into stores. The number of animals killed for fur trim is increasing in tandem with sales, and foxes, opossums, sables, otters, beavers, chin-chillas, minks, rabbits, raccoons, coyotes, lambs, dogs, cats, and other animals perish for trim. While products made of cat, dog, and seal are banned in the United States, dog and cat fur products have made their way into this country disguised as mislabeled or unlabeled products.

Animal welfare groups such as the Fur Free Alliance estimate that the fur industry kills more than 50 million animals each year. The number of animals used to make one fur coat varies according to

Lynx fur is highly prized by the fur industry.
(Photo by Erwin and Peggy Bauer, US Fish and Wildlife Service)

species: twelve to fifteen lynx, fifteen to twenty foxes, sixty to eighty mink, and so on.[4] China (and its deplorable lack of animal protection) is the largest exporter and the United States one of the top importers. According to the International Fur Trade Federation, 2003 global fur sales totaled $11.7 billion. The US fur industry's retail sales were $1.8 billion for the same year, and there were more than a hundred domestic fur garment manufacturers and nearly fourteen hundred fur stores.[5]

Ranches

Because of the overtrapping of fur-bearing animals from the seventeenth to the nineteenth century in this country, fur farming developed in the 1860s as a way to replace the wild animal for the fur trade. Later, these farms became more popular as the public learned about the horrors of trapping. Eighty-five percent of fur now comes from animals on fur farms.[6] Fur farms raise and kill minks, foxes, rabbits, bobcats, raccoons, sables, chinchillas, lynx, and more. Mink is the most commonly farmed animal on US fur farms—in 2002, 320 mink farms sold 2,506,819 pelts.[7]

A typical fur farm contains hundreds of animals in wire cages in open sheds. The cages are barren, with the exception of nesting boxes for some animals for part or all of the year. With no protection from bitter cold and intense heat, these animals can perish from hypothermia and heatstroke. Several animals can be confined inside each cage. For example, up to four foxes can be crammed inside cages that are only five square feet. And mink, who would naturally spend much of their time in the water, live their entire lives inside two-and-a-half-foot square cages with no access to swimming water. Some breeding animals live up to eight years in these conditions, which are nothing short of appalling. Cages are often filthy, with piles of feces accruing underneath. The waste attracts flies and other insects, and animals are often infested with parasites such as fleas and ticks. Dirty living conditions can cause bronchial and nasal infections, as well as mastitis, uterine infections, and mucosal inflammations.

The fur industry responds to the concerns of animal protection groups and the public by denying that such conditions exist. When shown undercover video of animals in fur farms, for instance, the industry has responded by maintaining that the videos are staged "snuff films" and that because the industry is regulated, no such abuse can exist.[8] Yet there are no federal regulations regarding the treatment of animals while on the farm or during their slaughter.

Fur farms may feed carnivorous animals slaughterhouse offal, thick ground-up sludge consisting of discarded body parts, organs, and expired meat, dairy, and eggs.[9] One Fur Commission USA video crows, "Just imagine that a glamorous full-length mink coat is made from the pelts of perhaps fifty mink that ate their way through five thousand pounds of leftovers!" and concludes, "Fish heads never looked so good!"[10] Contaminated feed can infect animals with bacterial diseases such as botulism and *Salmonella*, which can kill the animals who ingest the feed, as well as cause females to have stillbirths and abortions prior to full development of the fetus.[11] Producers may restrict food over the winter so that female breeding mink, for example, lose weight to become more fit for mating, increasing their breeding productivity.[12] Some fur farms restrict food so severely, the animals can lose one-third of their body weight, causing not only frustration, hunger, and increased aggression, but also increased premature mortality rates.[13]

Animals suffer from a number of diseases on fur farms. Adult mink, for example, can suffer from plasmacytosis, which is a fatal blood disease that takes a long time to kill its victim, and distemper, a viral disease causing vomiting, diarrhea, and sometimes death. Mink can also contract botulism, which causes vomiting, paralysis, and sometimes death, and their intestinal tracts may be attacked by viral enteritis. They may also have gastric lesions, ulcers, tooth decay, and kidney abnormalities.[14] Female breeding mink can live up to four years, and they commonly develop tumors, cysts, retinal degeneration, broken teeth, and cancer. Farmed foxes can suffer from distemper, encephalitis, parvoviruses, and infections of the urinary tract, uterus, and respiratory system. Parasitic infections can cause central nervous system diseases and mange. Inbreeding can cause a number of serious problems, including crippling nervous disorders and deformations. Some breeds can be more predisposed to developing diseases or sensory disabilities.

Intensive confinement on fur farms prevents the animals from engaging in virtually all of their natural behaviors, including swimming, digging, running, interacting socially, avoiding aggression or harassment, and hunting or foraging. This leads to a lifetime of intense frustration, which causes many animals to mutilate themselves, cannibalize their cage mates, or perform stereotypic behaviors such as compulsively pacing back and forth, bobbing their heads, or circling over and over. Some breeding animals may also kill their babies.

In the wild, mink are active, swimming and diving multiple times a day, using several nest sites, hunting, and exploring. One study found that farmed mink suffer from frustration as a result of being denied swimming opportunities. In fact, their stress response was virtually the same when they were denied access to swimming as it was when they

Red fox kits. Foxes are one of the most common animals ranched for fur. (Photo courtesy of US Fish and Wildlife Service)

were deprived of food.[15] Up to 80 percent of farmed mink compulsively bite their tails, and some of their tails become completely bald due to repeated biting.[16] Studies have documented stereotypic behaviors in up to 98.3 percent of farmed minks.[17]

Animals are ready for slaughter when they are about seven to ten months of age. Fur producers may kill animals in a variety of ways. They may break the necks of smaller animals such as mink, or they may electrocute animals such as foxes by inserting metal rods into their anuses and forcing them to bite an electrode. They may inject them with poison or pesticides; producers often kill chinchillas by injecting chloral hydrate into their abdomens, which causes muscle

Fox in a cage on a US fur farm.
(Photo courtesy of the Humane Society of the United States)

spasms, and the animals may gasp and cry out.[18] The American Veterinary Medical Association (AVMA) has characterized the use of chloral hydrate as "unacceptable in dogs, cats, and small mammals."[19] Yet the fur industry maintains that it follows strict guidelines established by the American Veterinary Medical Association. Animals may also be gassed; up to fifty can be put into a single "killing box" at once, and it is filled with carbon dioxide. Studies have documented animals trying to get out and gasping for air in these killing boxes.[20] And producers may also use carbon monoxide from vehicle exhaust pipes, creating a prolonged, agonizing death for animals who struggle to escape and suffer convulsions.

While there hasn't been much research in the United States regarding the environmental effects of fur farms, the millions of animals on fur farms produce a massive amount of manure, which can enter soil and nearby water sources. Nitrogen and phosphorus in the feces can kill aquatic life and contaminate groundwater.

Trapping

The history of fur trapping in the United States and Canada is linked to the colonization of North America and the exploration of the western half of the continent. Originally, Native Americans trapped beavers, foxes, bears, otters, bobcats, and other animals—both for their own use and in order to trade with European Americans—by using traditional methods like deadfalls, snares, and nets. Starting in the early 1600s, the French were the first explorers to work with native trappers, especially the Huron and Ottawa. They traded knives, beads, blankets, guns, and other items for pelts and meat. While some of the pelts stayed in North America, most were sent back to Europe for the fashion-conscious French (beaver was especially prized for hats). A number of serious wars erupted among Native American tribes over who was in control of the trade, hunting and trapping rights, and the growing scarcity of the beaver (thanks especially to the introduction of guns). These wars radically changed the allegiances and territories of many eastern tribes, creating large numbers of refugees and eventually allowing the British to conquer large sections of the continent. As the winners of the many conflicts, the Iroquois ended up siding with the British against the French.

By the middle of the eighteenth century, the fox had been decimated and the French traders pushed out the Native Americans. But the French subsequently lost their central role to English explorers and traders, and furs were sent to London instead of Paris. The British began to use alcohol as a medium of exchange, increasing the amount of alcoholism among native trappers. By the time of the Revolutionary War, the first of many smallpox epidemics broke out, killing large numbers of native peoples with whom the British were trading. Finally, after the War of 1812, the Americans began to dominate the continent and the fur trade by prohibiting foreign traders to do their business on US soil.

In the early decades of the nineteenth century, American "mountain men" began to explore the territories west of the Mississippi and displaced the native trappers. They sold their wares to the large fur companies like the Rocky Mountain Fur Company and the American Fur Company. The fur trade finally collapsed around 1850 due to the overexploitation of fur-bearing animals, the movement of Native Americans onto reservations, and changes in the European fashion scene, whose style-conscious aristocrats had declared fur hats unfashionable.

Today, while there are very few who still make a living entirely off trapping in the United States, according to the National Trappers Association, there are more than five hundred thousand licensed trappers. They trap animals both for the fur trade as well as for contracts with state wildlife departments for animal damage control, population control, or disease control purposes.[21]

Trappers kill about 4 million wild animals for their fur each year, including muskrats, minks, beavers, coyotes, opossums, foxes, and other animals. Fur trappers primarily use three kinds of devices to restrain or kill animals: steel-jaw leghold traps, conibear traps, and wire snares. Leghold traps are the most common. When an animal steps on and triggers the trap, its two metal jaws snap shut, trapping the animal by the paw or leg. Animals often sustain broken bones, deep lacerations, and severed tendons and ligaments. More injury occurs as the frightened and angry animals struggle to escape, breaking bones, knocking out teeth, and even gnawing off their own limbs. And while trappers' and furriers' lobbying groups maintain that the leghold trap, as well as other popular traps, are humane, the American Veterinary Medical Association's position on these traps is clear: "The AVMA considers the steel jaw leghold trap to be inhumane."[22] (It is not just inhumane when killing targeted animals; fur industry and trapping groups like the Fur Institute of Canada test new trap models on captive animals.)

Many trappers use wire snares, which is a wire noose that traps the animal and tightens around the neck, leg, or chest as the animal fights to get away. Snares are notorious for taking a long time to kill animals such as coyotes and foxes. Animals trapped in snares may die from strangulation, trauma as a result of non-neck captures, hypothermia, hyperthermia, and predation. Animals can pull the snares out of their anchor points in the ground, even though the snare has already encircled their necks. In one study, a male coyote suffered for at least a few weeks after escaping a snare, which was still embedded in the animal's neck at the time he was found and killed. The snare had cut through his neck and trachea, obstructing jugular veins and carotid arteries and preventing him from eating.[23]

Another popular trap is the conibear trap, whose purpose is to kill its target instantly by snapping shut around the animal's neck. For many animals caught in these traps, there is no quick death; these traps often crush the animal's chest or pelvis, causing a prolonged, agonizing death.

Some traps capture and kill animals underwater, such as the drowning sets designed to kill beavers, mink, and muskrats. Often using a steel-jaw leghold trap, drowning sets restrain animals underwater until they drown—sometimes taking up to fifteen minutes. Trappers may set conibear traps underwater as well. Most state laws require that trappers must check traps within certain time periods, which may be as long as seventy-two hours. Five states have no requirements, which means that trappers can leave animals languishing in traps for days on end. State wildlife departments rarely enforce these regulations, and since most trappers are part-time, they may check traps once a week or less.

The leghold trap is designed not to kill animals but to restrain them. During the time that the animals are in the traps, they can perish from blood loss, dehydration, or complications from injury. Others may be eaten by predators. Some animals chew off their trapped limbs and successfully escape, but those who do may die from infection, inability to hunt or escape predators, or blood loss. The industry, however, maintains that leghold traps represent state-of-the-art technology, even though they work in largely the same way that they did when they were first introduced to this country four hundred years ago. Many animals are still alive when trappers return. Trappers kill animals in ways that are horrific by anyone's standards—clubbing them, shooting them in the head, or standing on them as they slowly asphyxiate.

The fur industry maintains that trapping is not inhumane. Industry representatives and advocates say trapping is *necessary* in order to protect wild animals, such as mink and beaver, because their populations are so high now that if they were not trapped, disaster would result. Of course, both mink and beaver, as well as most of the other trapped fur animals, exist in far fewer numbers in the wild now than they did before the advent of fur trapping, making the industry's claims particularly specious.

Animals trapped for their fur aren't the only ones to suffer often excruciating deaths in traps. Millions of other animals perish every year as unintended targets, since the traps indiscriminately trap whomever triggers them. Birds of prey, songbirds, opossums, deer, and even companion dogs and cats also are mutilated or, in the trappers' words, they are merely "trash"—dead animals of no use.

Thankfully, trapping is a dying business in the United States. Mississippi's licensed fur trappers, for example, have dwindled to about three hundred, down from about five thousand in 1977. State wildlife officials attribute this decline to falling demand for fur products.[24] At the same time, trapping is virtually unregulated; only eight states have passed trapping legislation restricting or banning the use of steel-jaw leghold traps, for example. Although more than eighty-five countries have already banned their use, the federal government has yet to pass any legislation regulating or banning steel-jaw leghold traps.

The Fur Trade

The introduction of the fur trade in North America coincided with the arrival of the first European explorers on the East Coast of this continent, and was at its height between the seventeenth and nineteenth centuries, involving French, English, and American explorers and traders, and primarily Native American trappers. Until the colonization of North America, Russia had been the top provider of furs from animals, such as beavers, wolves, foxes, squirrels, martens, and hares, to European consumers. After colonization, the United States and Canada became the biggest suppliers of the world fur market.

The United States is one of the world's top fur producers, along with Russia, Canada, Denmark, and China. In 2002 the market value of pelts sold from US fur farms was more than $88 million.[25] Yet we import most of the fur sold in this country, much of it from China. And while treatment of animals on domestic fur farms is atrocious, the conditions in China are even worse.

China raises and kills millions of animals for fur every year, including dogs and cats. Chinese fur producers collect stray animals—those who were at one time beloved companions—and strangle, bleed, or club them to death. China is not only a major new fur producer, but because of increasing incomes, it has become a major consumer of fur products as well. Chinese have joined Russians and Europeans as the major wearers of fur products in the world.

A 2005 investigation into Chinese fur farms documented thousands of animals crammed into tiny, barren wire cages for their entire lives. And even worse, a large number of animals were still conscious when they were skinned, with some animals lifting their heads after their skin had been completely removed.[26]

Legislation and Changes in the Industry

Passed in response to a Humane Society of the United States (HSUS) investigation documenting the horrific conditions in Chinese fur production, the US Dog and Cat Protection Act of 2000 prohibits the import or export of dog and cat fur products. And the Fur Products Labeling Act of 1951 requires that furs are accurately labeled and sold using their accepted English names. However, this legislation allows retailers to sell fur trim products and clothing items that cost less than $150 without labeling them.

Another problem is mislabeling and false advertising. For example, a 2006 HSUS investigation revealed that major US retailers and designers were falsely advertising real fur as "faux." Testing revealed that coats whose trim was advertised as faux contained fur from domestic dogs, and others had fur from raccoon dogs, an Asian canine whose appearance resembles raccoons.[27] Millions of these animals are confined on Chinese fur farms, and they are treated barbarically. Grotesque undercover video documents them being skinned alive.[28]

A subsequent HSUS investigation revealed that dozens more retailers and designers—including Burlington Coat Factory, Bloomingdale's, J.C. Penney, Macy's, Saks Fifth Avenue, and brands Baby Phat, Andrew Marc, and MaxMara—were falsely labeling apparel whose trim was labeled "raccoon" or even "Finni Raccon" [sic] that in fact came from raccoon dogs. All of the coats tested were falsely advertised (some as faux) or labeled, unlabeled, or had a combination of false advertising and labeling problems.

In response to HSUS's investigation, Calvin Klein, Tommy Hilfiger, and Foot Locker pledged to go completely fur free, and other designers pulled the raccoon dog fur garments and promised to not use that type of fur again. Other retailers and designers took little action.

After learning of the investigation, J.C. Penney even had its employees cover the "raccoon" label with black marker and return the products to the shelves.[29]

The investigations spurred the introduction of the Dog and Cat Fur Prohibition Enforcement Act in 2007. If passed, it would require all fur garments to be labeled properly regardless of value, and it would ban the sale of raccoon dog fur.

The fur industry misleads consumers by using uncommon names for animals in an attempt to make fur more palatable, such as by using *tanuki* instead of raccoon dog. In addition, much cheap fur comes from China, and much of it could be from any animal—dog, cat, or endangered species. Since many enforcement officials are overworked or do not know what to look for, it's easy for prohibited items to slip past.

The United Kingdom and Austria have banned fur farms. Other countries have implemented welfare reforms that require, for instance, enriched living environments where the animals are allowed to climb, dig, nest, and swim. Despite the positive leadership of these countries, there is no federal law regulating the humane raising and killing of animals on fur farms.

The industry has indeed suffered thanks to public opposition to the methods used to produce fur. We know that American fur production has decreased since the 1980s: US mink farms produced 2.63 million pelts in 2005, down from more than 4.5 million in 1989.[30] Also, in 2005, there were 277 US mink farms, a decrease from 1,027 in 1988.[31] Finally, the number of companies producing fur goods in the United States dropped from a high of 503 to a low of 120 by 1998, and the number of workers employed by the industry dropped as well by 22 percent during this period.[32]

Fur sales dropped approximately 44 percent during the 1990s, but since the late 1990s, fur has been experiencing a resurgence.[33] According to the Fur Information Council of America (FICA), fur sales are on the rise, and the numbers of designers using fur has increased ten-fold in the last twenty years. The value of US mink pelt production is going back up. Fur sales figures for 2005 in the United

States were $1.82 billion, an increase of 80 percent since 1991, when the industry began gathering statistics.[34] Finally, more stores are carrying fur than ever before, according to the industry.[35] These alarming numbers may have to do with colder winters, income increases among the wealthiest sectors of the US economy, the increasing use of fur trim in clothing rather than full fur coats, and the increasing pervasiveness of fur on runways.

There is still no question that the public is concerned about the conditions in which animals raised for fur are confined and slaughtered. Most are less interested in wearing the visible symbols of excess that were popular in the 1980s. But public concern for the abuse inherent in fur production isn't the only reason the industry is suffering overall, despite its recent resurgence. A tremendous variety of faux furs is also available in every style and price range. There are haute couture faux fur choices, including full-length mink and fox styles that are completely synthetic but amazingly similar to animal fur. And more affordable faux fur jackets, coats, trimmed products, pillows, blankets, and furniture are easily found at nearly every retailer in the country.

SKINS

In addition to the more than 50 million animals killed each year for their fur, millions more are killed for their skins or hides. Whether by-products of the meat industry, such as cow leather, or "exotic" skins from endangered animals smuggled into the country, such as tigers, leopards, lizards, and snakes, hides and skins are big business in the United States. US consumption of animal skins plays an important role in the increasingly globalized wild animal trade as well. We export skins from animals such as alligators from domestic factory farms, and we import skins from other countries. Many of the skins that cross our border do so illicitly, as part of an illegal international trade in endangered animals that is fueling species eradication worldwide. Whether from domesticated or endangered animals, the skin trade is responsible for terrible abuses of individual animals, and it threatens entire species.

Leather

Leather is the most profitable co-product of US slaughterhouses, with 35 million cow hides generating $5 billion in exports and domestic sales each year.[36] Leather comes from animals used for meat, who spend their lives on factory farms in miserable conditions, endure painful mutilations, and suffer agonizing slaughter, as we've seen. Slaughterhouses sell the skins of cows raised for beef, dairy cows, veal calves, pigs, lambs, and deer. These skins are used for a multitude of goods, from shoes to clothing to furniture to car seats. Cowskin and sheepskin rugs are even dyed in artificial-looking colors or to resemble other animals such as leopards, tigers, or zebras.[37]

In addition to the cruelty involved in factory farming and slaughter, leather production has its own environmental problems and public health hazards. The tanning process uses a veritable broth of toxins to prevent skins from rotting, causing environmental problems and ensuring that the skins will take decades to biodegrade. Tanneries use chromium to tan leather, a known carcinogen that can cause convulsions, liver and kidney damage, ulcers, and even lung cancer.[38] In fact, the tanning of buffalo hides during the great buffalo extermination of the nineteenth century was a primary factor in the destruction of many forests and the pollution of many rivers on the East Coast, through the intensive stripping of the bark of the hemlock trees to produce tannin and the industrial runoff (which included lime, animal hair, and animal flesh) into rivers.[39] Chromium joins a long list of similarly hazardous airborne and solid pollutants from a typical tannery: arsenic, formaldehyde, sulfuric acid, chlorine, phosphoric acid, glycol ether EB, glycol ether PMA, toluene, methyl isobutyl ketone, methanol, xylol, manganese sulfate, ethylene glycol, zinc, copper, and lead. For every pound of leather, a pound of waste is produced, which can contaminate the air, water, and ground.[40]

The chemicals used in leather production affect nearly everyone in the supply chain. According to the National Institutes of Health, "Tanners and processors had increased risk of bladder, lung, and nasal cancer from leather dust, chromium, and other chemicals. Leather workers had increased risk for lymphoma and cancer of the nose, larynx, lung, and bladder. Boot and shoe manufacturers and repairers had increased risk for cancer of the buccal cavity."[41]

In Third World countries that slaughter cattle and produce leather for the international market, tanning is even more dangerous and is primarily carried out by the poor. Indeed, production of hides and skins has shifted to developing countries, which now produce more than 60 percent of the world's leather. These countries have lower labor costs and more lenient environmental regulations.[42] Animal welfare issues can be even worse than in the United States. For example, People for the Ethical Treatment of Animals' investigation of the Indian leather trade revealed that "spent" dairy cows were shipped hundreds of miles before being slaughtered with dull knives.[43]

Exotic Skins

Animals raised or poached for their skins suffer many of the same abuses as those in the fur industry—and in addition to the suffering resulting from inhumane treatment, the trade in exotic skins decimates wild populations and fuels smuggling for underground markets. Yet the substantial problems with exotic skins receive little attention, perhaps because for many people, it's easier to empathize with furry, "cute" animals instead of reptiles, birds, and fish. As a Barneys New York employee told the *New York Times*, "People tend to get outraged about the animals that are warm and fuzzy rather than about those which are less so, like snakes."[44] In addition, while cheap fur enjoyed for some time a heyday on the backs of average American consumers, exotic skins are typically the products of top luxury labels, and retailers command a high price that most consumers are not willing to pay.

Exotic skins include those from tigers, kangaroos, leopards, zebras, alligators, crocodiles, snakes, lizards, ostriches, fish, chickens, emus, stingrays, and even tigers and leopards. Manufacturers use them to make purses, coats, wallets, belts, vests, shoes, gloves, furniture, rugs, and other goods. These products are becoming more visible on runways and in stores; as a senior enforcement officer for the Convention on International Trade in Endangered Species explained in a London newspaper, "In the 1980s and 1990s the illegal skin trade virtually ceased to exist because it was not fashionable. . . . But we are seeing models going back into it and a consequent boom in the trade."[45]

In the United States and around the world, so-called farms and ranches raise animals such as alligators, crocodiles, snakes, ostriches, and others for exotic skin production. For example, American alligator farms often keep animals by the hundreds inside dark sheds.[46] For these animals who can live to be a hundred years old in the wild, slaughter is agonizing—workers kill them by clubbing them on the head, cutting them, and bleeding them to death. As one scientist explained in an article on the industry, "On a busy day, farmed alligators are simply skinned alive. They can survive like that for two hours. A wild rattlesnake fares worse. Even at the official slaughterhouses of Texas, Louisiana, and Oklahoma, its head is put on a meat hook and it is disemboweled before its skin is pulled off."[47]

In Australia, more than 3.8 million kangaroos are killed each year for their skins.[48] Companies such as Adidas use these for its soccer shoes sold in the United States, and they are also used for motorcycle gloves.

Illegal traffic in wild animals nets more than $10 billion a year— the third-largest source of illegal income after drugs and arms.[49] Indeed, the illicit wildlife trade is often associated with transnational drug, gun, and even human smuggling.[50] Drug smugglers have even been known to stuff wild animals with narcotics, and once they were over the border, they killed the animals and removed the drugs.

Like fur, there is little enforcement of trade rules for exotic skins. The same people charged with enforcing endangered species laws are the authorities responsible for monitoring drugs, human trafficking, and other smuggling—all legitimate and time-consuming problems, too. As a result, many officials are simply too busy to check whether shipments of fur or skins are labeled correctly. And some endangered animals, such as some species of reptiles, look so much like their non-endangered cousins that it is virtually impossible to tell the difference.

The wildlife trade, which also includes traffic in live animals, is second only to habitat destruction in terms of the most serious threat to species survival. Not only does poaching kill off entire populations of animals such as snakes and crocodiles, but it also introduces invasive species and kills "nontarget" animals, harming individual animals and threatening entire species.

Like the fur industry, the biggest insult of the skin industry is that millions of animals endure miserable lives and excruciating slaughter—all for fashion. Whether farmed or wild, animals used for their skins suffer terrible abuses for an antiquated, unnecessary industry, given the wide array of natural and synthetic alternatives available, like microfiber and pleather.

WOOL

Wool is another popular animal product that is common in clothing, furniture, rugs, and more. Humans have used wool for thousands of years, and the world's oldest wool cloth dates from 1500 BCE. In the United States, eighteenth-century American settlers kept flocks of sheep, and the first American wool-weaving factory was established in 1788 in Connecticut.

Australia and New Zealand are the world's largest wool producers, with flock sizes of approximately 120 million sheep and nearly 50 million sheep, respectively. Other wool-producing countries include China, South Africa, and Turkey. In some countries, flock sizes can be huge—as many as a hundred thousand animals, and sometimes more.

Although wool is one of the most common textiles in the United States, its domestic use has been decreasing in the past decades. In 1970, for example, consumption from US wool mills was more than 240 million pounds, but by 2003, that number had dropped to just under 49 million pounds.[51] During the same period, wool imports also decreased.

Australian wool accounts for nearly half of the wool used in clothing worldwide.[52] Merino sheep are the most common breed in Australia, and their characteristically wrinkled skin creates both greater amounts of wool and severe health problems. The animals may die from heat exhaustion or heatstroke in the summer, and urine and moisture collect in the folds of their skin, which attracts blowflies. The flies lay eggs, then maggots consume the animals' flesh, resulting in an agonizing condition known as fly-strike that can be fatal. In order to prevent fly-strike, Australian ranchers place lambs in restraints called "cradles" and use shears to slice large pieces of flesh from around their tails and legs—all without any kind of pain reliever. Not only does this procedure cause acute pain, but the wound can also take weeks to heal, causing more suffering. Bowing to pressure from animal protection advocates, the government has passed legislation that forces Australian wool producers to phase out the process, called *mulesing*, by 2010.

While mulesing is one of the wool industry's most egregious offenses, the shearing process is by no means kind to the animals, either. Full-time shearers can shear more than 350 animals each day, which means that animals often endure rough handling and broken skin.[53] Since shearing can be a substantial cost for producers, whose profit margins are small to begin with, some wool producers simply employ unskilled workers to perform the shearing, or they do it themselves. Sheep can die from exposure after premature shearing.

In addition, male sheep are typically castrated when they are still lambs, and producers also remove their tails—all without painkillers. The two most common methods for castration are the rubber ring method and the surgical method. In the first, a rubber band tightly squeezes the scrotum, causing the testicles to gradually atrophy and drop off. The second method involves slicing the scrotum and cutting or tearing the testicles to remove them. In order to remove the lamb tails, ranchers use a rubber ring method similar to that used for castration, or they may simply use a knife to remove the tail.

As sheep age and their wool production declines, they are sent to slaughter, and they suffer the same routine abuse during handling, transport, and slaughter as other farm animals. But for millions of even unluckier sheep, the end is worse. Each year, Australian wool producers send approximately 6 million live sheep to the Middle East for slaughter. The sheep are crammed on crowded multideck ships, which are not cleaned during the journey. Tens of thousands of animals die on the trip that can take up to three weeks. After arriving in countries such as Saudi Arabia, Jordan, Kuwait, and Bahrain, they endure further transport to slaughterhouses. Since many of these countries have little or no animal welfare standards, millions of sheep endure agonizing slaughter while fully conscious.

Contrary to popular belief, the *shearling* that is commonly found on coats and jackets is not wool, but another type of sheepskin that has become more popular in recent years. It comes from the skin of a sheep or a lamb who was shorn once before slaughter, but the wool is still attached to the skin.

THE FASHION INDUSTRY

While a number of businesses and designers no longer use fur and widespread fashionable alternatives to fur, skins, and other animal textiles abound, many retailers and designers still use objectionable animal products. For example, retailers such as Bebe, Neiman Marcus, Bloomingdale's, and Saks Fifth Avenue still promote fur sales. Designers such as Jean Paul Gaultier, Louis Vuitton, Christian Dior, and Yves Saint Laurent still use and promote fur. Gucci, Prada, and Versace have used seal fur for their international collections, despite the US ban on its sale.

In order to protect the economic interests of fur and leather producers, organizations such as Fur Information Council of America, International Fur Trade Federation, Leather Industry of America, Fur Takers of America, National Trappers Association, and Fur Commission USA work to promote fur sales, pass legislation, and portray fur production positively to the public and press. Even hunting organizations such as the US Sportsmen's Alliance actively oppose state legislative efforts to restrict trapping. Many of these organizations maintain that fur sales are up, and that fur is firmly back in mainstream fashion. Although fur collections are increasingly gathering attention at some fashion shows, some of the publicity can be credited to its controversial status.

In the mid-1990s, as the fur industry faced plummeting sales, fur companies and industry groups such as SAGA Furs and FICA began giving fur to fashion students, who typically have to pay for their own fabric in school. Groups also began sponsoring fur fashion design contests, trips, and internships. Not only did some students take advantage of saving money by working with the "donated" fur, but others saw using fur as a way to raise the price of their clothing, which made these novice designers appear more prestigious. These higher prices, as well as the contests and internships, were a way for some students to enter the design field. The fur industry has reaped some benefits with its clever strategy, because some of the students who began using fur are still designing with it today.

Yet at the same time, a growing list of high-profile designers such as Todd Oldham, Stella McCartney, Kenneth Cole, Ralph Lauren, Betsey Johnson, Marc Bouwer, and Jay McCarroll refuse to use fur. Tommy Hilfiger and Calvin Klein are ending their use of fur. Retail giants like Gap, H&M, Forever 21, Banana Republic, Wet Seal, and more have ended their sale of fur.

Throughout the fashion industry, synthetic alternatives to fur and skins have become more popular. Faux fur is available, from full-length coats to inexpensive trim, and it's an easy replacement for animal fur. The same is true of synthetic skins, and man-made fibers are even more comfortable and stylish than fabrics made from animals.

In addition, designers and retailers are increasingly marketing to people who do not wear other animal products. These companies are increasing availability of "vegan chic" products for not only vegans, but young, hip people who follow Hollywood trends and celebrities like Natalie Portman, Joaquin Phoenix, and Alicia Silverstone. One fashion retail consultant explained in the *New York Times*, "People are more conscious today of what they're wearing, why they're wearing it and how it affects the environment." Ignoring these issues, he continued, "is not sexy today."[54]

More and more hip boutiques and designers like Stella McCartney cater to people who want couture and luxury without the guilt. There are even professional image consultants who provide style advice to people who wish to be chic but cruelty free in their clothes, shoe, accessories, and cosmetics choices.[55] Even bargain retailers like Target, Payless, and H&M sell a tremendous array of designer knock-offs that are inexpensive, stylish, and faux. A Payless spokesperson noted in a *News & Observer* article that today's synthetic leathers are superior to previous alternatives, stating, "The technology has come a long way and we're taking advantage of it."[56]

As the industry moves away from using fur and skins, it's never been easier to make more compassionate—and fashionable—choices.

CONCLUSION

The best thing about the fur and skin industry is that it has not regained the profits that it enjoyed in the 1980s, thanks to the concern of American consumers over the rampant mistreatment of animals whom these industries exploit. Thanks to the plethora of synthetic alternatives— whether faux fur or snakeskin, pleather or microfiber, there is a tremendous array of materials that are not only humane but are also increasingly superior to animal-derived fabrics.

The fur industry says that what we wear is a matter of personal choice. But is it? We do not knowingly wear fluffy coats made out of puppy fur. And most Americans would never wear jackets made out of baby sealskin. We obviously do exercise moral judgment when choosing our fashions. Most Americans, once they know the cruelty involved in a product or practice, will choose not to buy these products because they don't want to support the industry.

Yet, for so many of the animals involved in the fur and skins industries, the routine cruelty inflicted on them would indeed be illegal and result in cruelty prosecutions if the victims were dogs or cats. And for that matter, many of the victims are dogs and cats, but they *are* raised and slaughtered in other countries that do not have the same laws or any welfare regulations at all.

One of the great tragedies of this industry is that animals suffer miserable existences and barbaric slaughter in order for us to wear a piece of ornamental trim or carry a gaudy new bag that will be out of fashion in the next season. But thanks to the growing availability of alternatives, animals do not have to be our slaves for fashion any longer.

What You Can Do

The following are a number of ways that readers can improve the lives of animals used for textiles.

- Don't purchase items made from fur. Whether clothing, shoes, accessories, or furniture, synthetic alternatives abound. Retail stores across the country as well as online stores stock an amazing and affordable array of products made from faux fur.
- Products with animal fur trim often do not indicate on the label that fur is part of the garment, so check labels carefully, and if you're in doubt, pass.
- It's also easy to purchase clothing, furniture, and more made from synthetic skins—pleather, microfiber, and others—so passing on products made from animal skins is not only simple, but fashionable and usually less expensive. Other fabric options abound, including acrylic and Primaloft.

Chapter 5
THE ANIMAL
EXPERIMENTATION
INDUSTRY
Animals as Tools

Currently, nine out of ten experimental drugs fail in clinical studies because we cannot accurately predict how they will behave in people based on laboratory and animal studies.[1]
> —Mike Leavitt, Health and Human Services Secretary

Science and research do not compel us to tolerate the kind of inhumanity which has been involved in the business of supplying stolen animals to laboratories or which is sometimes involved in the careless and callous handling of animals in some of our laboratories.[2]
> —President Lyndon B. Johnson, upon signing the
> Laboratory Animal Welfare Act in 1966

INTRODUCTION

Of all the animal industries discussed in this book, the use of animals for medical research is surely the most controversial. While it is clear that humans no longer need to eat or wear animals to survive, it is much more difficult to question the view that medical research depends on animals. Because of the pain and suffering often involved in biomedical research, however, questioning vivisection—or scientific research and testing on animals—was a catalyst for the modern American animal protection movement.

Part of why vivisection is still a life and death issue for so many is the way the animal research industry has typically framed the debate. Those who promote the use of animals in science pose the issue as a question of sacrificing animals to save humans, or, as industry groups put it, "Your child or the rat." If the choice really were between, as the argument goes, my child or the rat, everyone would want to see his or her children saved and would sacrifice animals to achieve that end.

But is that really the most accurate way to see the debate, and is that really the question that best sums it up? Or are there other ways of envisioning the issue that do not sacrifice either the child or the animal, but that allow for both to survive and thrive? Polls show that a high number of people want to see more alternatives to animal research, indicating that our feelings about animal research are not as simple as we are often led to believe. It might be better to ask: How can we save the child without sacrificing the rat? And if this can be done, why aren't we doing so already?

A look into the agendas of those promoting animal research may shed some light on the answer. Like many of the other industries we explore in this book, the product-testing and medical research industries are worth billions. A recent report shows that funding for medical research has doubled from $37 billion per year in 1994 to $94 billion in 2003,[3] with most of that funding coming from private funds through the medical industry and the government via the National Institutes of Health (NIH). The pharmaceutical industry is even better endowed—annual US drug industry revenues have topped $231 billion.[4]

Clearly, there are many billions of dollars at stake in regard to the ways that product and drug testing, as well as medical research, is conducted. And the extent of the money at stake gives us a sense of why the industry wants to continue with business as usual. Groups like Americans for Medical Progress and National Association for Biomedical Research, which both the medical and the pharmaceutical industries support, actively lobby on behalf of those industries to convince the public and policy makers that animal testing and animal research is necessary. But how necessary is it?

ANIMAL WELFARE ACT

President Lyndon Johnson signed the Laboratory Animal Welfare Act (LAWA) in 1966 to appease the public's outrage over the theft of pets for animal research. Now named the Animal Welfare Act (AWA), this law governs the transportation, housing, feeding, and veterinary care of warm-blooded animals in laboratories, as well as animals bred and transported for the pet industry and for those who are in zoos or circuses. However, since 1972 the USDA has defined "warm-blooded animal" to exclude mice and rats, the two most common animals used in research, as well as birds (animals raised for food have been excluded since the earliest days of the law). Since 1989 domestic animal protection groups have demanded that the USDA follow Congress' intent and protect all warm-blooded animals in laboratories. These groups have faced opponents such as the USDA, the National Association for Biomedical Research, and former Sen. Jesse Helms (R-NC), who succeeded in formalizing their exclusion through an amendment to the 2002 Farm Bill. The AWA now explicitly excludes "birds, rats of the genus *Rattus*, and mice of the genus *Mus*, bred for use in research, horses not used for research purposes and other farm animals."[5]

Laboratories that use covered animals—in other words, animals who are not rodents, birds, or farm animals—fall under the jurisdiction of the USDA, which handles licensing, inspection, and all other compliance and enforcement measures. Because the LAWA was originally crafted to address incidences of pet theft, the bulk of the bill in its early years mostly dealt with licensing issues for those who supply the animals to the labs as well as the labs themselves. In addition, labs funded by the National Institutes of Health must comply with NIH standards as well as AWA regulations. Because the AWA does not cover mice, birds, and rats, labs that do not receive government funding and that only use those animals are not accountable to any government agency at all. Because of the growing popularity of transgenic mice and rats—rodents who have had new genes inserted into their genetic code—the number of laboratories that fall into this category is rapidly increasing.

Congress has amended the AWA three times. In 1970 it was broadened to include animals used in the entertainment and pet industries. The 1970 amendment also included a requirement mandating the use of anesthetics and painkillers (in instances where they do not interfere with the experiment) as well as a requirement that all dealers have USDA licensing. In 1985, through an amendment to the Food Security Act known as the Improved Standards for Laboratory Animals Act, Congress amended the AWA again to require training for animal care staff. The amendment's purpose was to provide for better care and handling of covered animals, minimal exercise standards for dogs, environmental enrichment for primates, and improvements in housing conditions. Another provision of the new act was the requirement that facilities using covered animals must form Institutional Animal Care and Use Committees (IACUCs) to further oversee the treatment of animals at those institutions. In addition, it mandated that researchers demonstrate proof that they considered alternatives to painful or distressful research and prohibited multiple surgeries on the same animal. In 1990 Congress passed an amendment that mandated a five-day waiting period before municipal shelters could sell animals to research facilities, in order to prevent the immediate transfer of pets to laboratories before their guardians could claim them.[6]

The USDA, through APHIS, inspects research facilities on a semiannual basis. Facilities with a history of violations must be inspected as often as twice per year, while others are only inspected once every two to three years.[7] There are currently about seventy inspectors staffed to inspect more than a thousand research facilities and eight thousand or so dealers, exhibitors, carriers, and handlers.[8] The only other "oversight," albeit only at the internal level, for research facilities using covered animals is through the mandatory IACUC that each facility must establish. IACUCs must have at least three members, including a veterinarian, someone who is not a researcher, and someone who doesn't work for the institution. IACUC members review all proposals or protocols in which animals will be used and ensure compliance with government regulations. There is no explicit charge, however, to decide whether the proposal is scientifically worthy or whether animals are really necessary.

The AWA also mandates that researchers provide pain medication and anesthesia for covered animals—"if the experiment allows."[9] Unfortunately, since the researcher makes the decision as to whether anesthesia or pain medication is scientifically necessary, there is little mandate with respect to pain at all. Experiments that cause pain are subject to IACUC review, which sometimes mandates pain relief to be administered to an animal according to protocol. Additionally, the USDA can write up a facility that blatantly violates the pain relief provision, which could lead to, if the violation is not rectified, a fine, or, if the violation is severe, the loss of the USDA license.

Every year, the USDA puts out an annual report detailing the number of facilities the agency inspected, the number of reportable, or covered, animals at each facility, and how many animals were used in experiments involving no pain (approximately 615,000 in 2004), pain in which researchers used pain relief (approximately 400,000 in 2004), and pain for which "no drugs could be used for relief" (86,748 in 2004). Again, since these numbers do not include rats, mice, and birds (let alone amphibians, reptiles, and fish), who the USDA does not protect under the AWA, one can only guess at the numbers of these animals subjected to pain every year. Of those animals who the USDA does cover, guinea pigs and hamsters, the smallest and most "mouse-like" of all the reportable animals in 2004, endured the bulk of the painful experiments (23,772 and 43,299 animals, respectively).[10]

Types and Numbers of Animals

It is difficult to find exactly how many animals are in American laboratories today, because research and testing facilities don't have to
report the number of unprotected animals—i.e., mice, rats, birds, reptiles, or amphibians—even though they comprise 85 to 95 percent of
the total animals in labs each year.[11] According to the USDA,
inspected facilities used more than a million *reportable* warm-blooded
animals in research, testing, or experiments in 2004.[12] The number of
reportable animals in inspected facilities has dropped from 1.6 million
in 1973 to 1.1 million in 2004 (the number was at its highest—2.1 million—in both 1985 and 1992).[13] While this looks like good news for
laboratory animals, this may simply reflect the fact that laboratories
are replacing reportable animals with nonreportable animals, such as
mice and rats. By factoring in the estimated number of nonreportable

Mice are one of the most commonly used animals
in scientific research and product testing.
(Photo courtesy of People for the Ethical Treatment of Animals)

animals, we can estimate that 20 million or more animals altogether are used every year. Also, in 2004, the USDA inspected 1,079 research facilities, including nonprofit facilities such as universities and hospitals, testing laboratories that contract out to companies to develop products, commercial facilities and independent manufacturers, and government laboratories.[14]

Rodents are by far the most used group of animals in research because of their small size, quick reproductive cycles, and economic cheapness—prices start as low as $9 for a rat from Charles River Labs, as opposed to $850 for a macaque monkey from Primate Products, Inc., according to *Lab Animal*'s Buyers' Guide.[15] The fact that the USDA does not regulate their use is probably also another selling point. Genetically modified mice and rats are especially popular. Breeding companies can custom "create" these animals, allowing researchers to manipulate and study various aspects of gene function or expression, model diseases and genetic abnormalities, and more. "Knockout mice" (in whom researchers have "knocked out" a gene and replaced it with a new one, making them much more susceptible to disease) are also popular with researchers who use them to study cancer, heart disease, aging diseases, and to develop and test drugs. Overbreeding is inevitable when creating transgenic mice, and, as a result, facilities produce many more animals than necessary and kill millions of "throwaway rodents" every year.

Rabbits are the most common reportable animal in laboratories, with about 265,000 used in US labs in 2004.[16] They are popular because researchers can purchase them for as little as thirty dollars, they are easy to handle, and because of their short gestation periods, their reproductive cycles can be easily tracked. New Zealand rabbits, the most common breed used, have pink eyes that allow researchers to easily see ophthalmologic changes. Also, since their eyes are extremely sensitive and their tears don't easily wash out toxins, researchers are able to conduct tests in which caustic substances can be left on their eyes for days. It is easy to draw blood from their light-colored ears. Rabbits also produce antibodies that some researchers consider far

New Zealand rabbits are the most common rabbit in laboratories. (Photo courtesy of People for the Ethical Treatment of Animals)

superior to those of any other laboratory animal,[17] and their high fertility rate and unique reproductive system make them popular in reproductive and fertility studies. Indeed, the term "rabbit test" comes from the gonadotropin pregnancy test, in which researchers injected female rabbits with a woman's urine—and then killed them—in order to inspect the ovaries to tell if the woman was pregnant.[18] Researchers used rabbits to develop the rabies vaccine, as well as to study cancer therapies, eye infections, skin infections, high blood pressure, epilepsy, diabetes, and the effects of smoking and drug addiction.[19]

After rabbits, guinea pigs and hamsters are the next most common reportable animals in medical research. Guinea pigs have been popular for so long, in fact, that the term "guinea pig" arose years ago when referring to someone or something being used to try something new. Researchers used guinea pigs to research tuberculosis; to develop antibiotics, anticoagulants, replacement heart valves, and blood transfusions; and to study nutrition. Today, guinea pigs and hamsters are still commonly used for drug testing and research, as well as for infertility studies.

Medical researchers use farm animals such as sheep and pigs for heart disease and heart and valve replacement procedures. Pigs are common subjects of xenotransplantation experiments, in which researchers attempt to replace unhealthy human organs with animal organs. So far, scientists have successfully transplanted pig hearts and other organs into sheep, but they have not had similar success for humans, who have all died after receiving organs from pigs, baboons, and even chimpanzees.

Dogs are used next often in research and testing because they are easy to handle, one tragic drawback to being man's best friend. In 2004 US laboratories used about sixty-five thousand dogs for a variety

---

Bea

While out for an evening walk, author Kristin von Kreisler discovered a terrified, emaciated beagle on the side of the road. She rescued the little dog, thinking she would return her to her home, but she soon learned that the dog's "home" was an animal research laboratory. Unwilling to return the beagle to such a fate, Kristin decided to provide her with a real home.

In the early days of Bea's life with Kristin and her husband, John, the malnourished little beagle, now named Bea, was mute, pathologically fearful, and terrorized from her experience at the lab. She shook whenever approached, rolled on her back and urinated when in the company of men, and quaked with fear when visiting the veterinarian, who counseled Kristin that Bea may never get over her past and accept the love of people. But happily, after a couple of years, Bea not only grew fat and her coat glossy, but she also gradually lost much of her fear and learned to accept the love of her new guardians. Even more astounding, she learned to deal with the stress of visiting the "men in white coats" at the veterinarian. As Kristin says, she chose to be courageous.

Bea was not the only one to be transformed. Through knowing Bea and seeing how her experience in the lab transformed her, Kristin became an animal welfare advocate who is determined to spare other animals from a life in the lab.

After living in a lab, Bea spent the last fifteen years of her life surrounded by love. (Photo courtesy of Kristin Von Kreisler)

of projects, including toxicity tests, surgical teaching programs for medical students, and dental and heart experiments. They are also research subjects for testing veterinary drugs and pet foods. Dogs are even used by untrained salespeople in demonstrations of medical devices and products.[20] Their use is controversial for many because of their popularity as family pets, which perhaps explains why the number of canine research subjects has dropped 67 percent since 1973 compared to just a 31 percent drop in overall animal numbers of reportable species.[21]

In 2004 American research facilities used about fifty-five thousand nonhuman primates.[22] The most commonly used primates are monkeys, specifically macaques. Researchers have infected primates with syphilis, hepatitis, and other human viruses, used them in a variety of transplant surgeries, behavioral studies, and neurological studies, and subjected them to crash tests and other experiments in which their humanlike bodies suffer a variety of traumas. We've even sent chimpanzees into space on space shuttles.[23]

The use of chimpanzees is particularly controversial due to their intelligence and emotional and social complexity, their close genetic relationship with humans, and the fact that they are an endangered species. While countries such as the United Kingdom and New Zealand prohibit the use of apes in experimentation, about 1,300 chimpanzees are currently in US labs.[24] Some researchers claim that chimpanzees are a useful model for studying AIDS, but, unfortunately for those hoping for a cure for AIDS, chimpanzees infected with HIV typically don't become symptomatic. In 2007 the National Institutes of Health announced that it will stop breeding chimpanzees for research, citing financial reasons since care for one chimpanzee can reach $500,000 over her fifty-year life.[25]

While this is good news for chimpanzees, the overall use of primates in research may be on the rise, according to the Humane Society of the United States, which points to the increase in the number of National Primate Research Centers, a doubling of biomedical research funds, and new breeding colonies being established both in the United States and overseas, where these colonies will escape US government oversight.[26]

Once common high school dissection subjects, about 24,000 cats were research subjects in 2004, almost entirely in neurological research and vision studies. Some of the more notable examples include experiments in which researchers severed cats's spinal cords, sutured their eyes, forced them to endure lengthy sleep deprivation, and more. Not surprisingly, a great many of these experiments involved pain; in 2004, researchers used 378 cats in painful experiments without painkillers and more than 9,000 painful experiments where the animals received analgesics.[27] (In 2000 those numbers were higher, and half of all of the experiments conducted on cats involved pain or distress.) Like dogs, cats are easy to breed, obtain and handle, making them popular for these types of experiments, even when painful.

WHERE LAB ANIMALS COME FROM

"Laboratory animals," as we now know them, did not exist until the twentieth century. Americans have always categorized animals according to their utility value, and for most of American history they were considered farm animals, companion animals, or wild animals. Up until the mid-twentieth century, there was no laboratory animal category, and there were not companies that purpose-bred animals for research.

Prior to the 1960s, many of the animals who were used for testing, educational uses, military uses, or research were former pets who municipal animal shelters sold for research, often through dealers who acted as middlemen. "Pound seizure" refers to the practice of selling animals who would otherwise be euthanized. While it is much less common today to find shelters selling animals into research, three states —Minnesota, Oklahoma, and Utah—still *require* that publicly funded shelters do this, while other states allow it. From the 1940s to the 1960s, when pound seizure was a regular practice, laws mandating the surrender or sale of "surplus" pets to laboratories were passed at the behest of the National Society for Medical Research, now known as the National Association for Biomedical Research, the largest pro-vivisection lobbying organization in the country.[28]

As mentioned previously, Congress passed the Laboratory Animal Welfare Act in 1966 to alleviate public outrage over the horrendous conditions that many animals endured at the hands of dealers supplying laboratories. One *Life* magazine article in particular highlighted the gruesome and heartbreaking conditions on the property of one such dealer.[29] While the LAWA did not ban the practice of pound seizure, it did establish licensing and care requirements for the breeders and secondhand dealers who sold animals to research institutes.[30] These dealers, known as class B (or "random source") dealers, can legally acquire animals from animal shelters, auctions, other licensed dealers, or from "any person who did not breed and raise them on his/her premises."[31] Prior to the passage of the LAWA, dealers were not licensed or inspected and sold not only shelter animals to labs but also stolen animals, provided by "bunchers" who captured stray animals on the street. While it is still illegal for a class B dealer to obtain dogs and cats from people who found or stole them, this is still a common practice. Bunchers can answer "free to a good home" ads and sell the pets to dealers, and labs have been notoriously lax in examining paperwork documenting the source of the animals. Furthermore, the fact that dealers can still legally acquire animals from rural auctions or trade days (day-long flea markets) allows for illegally acquired animals to enter dealers' hands. Ten to twenty class B dealers across the country obtain up to eighteen thousand dogs and cats for research through these ads and markets each year.[32]

In an attempt to end the sale of pet animals into research, federal legislators introduced two bills in 1996—the Family Pet Protection Act of 1996 and the Pet Safety and Protection Act of 1996—that would have banned research facilities from acquiring animals from class B dealers. The biomedical research community aggressively fought these bills, claiming they would impede research, and they did not pass. The USDA's assistant secretary for marketing and regulatory programs, Michael Dunn, even testified on behalf of the Family Pet Protection Act, saying that class B dealers—who at that time supplied one-quarter of all animals sold into research—had inaccurate or falsified records for more than half of the dogs they sold.[33]

Congress introduced and voted down similar bills in subsequent years, and at the time of this writing, "Buck's Bill" is pending. Proposed in 2007, this would prohibit class B dealers from selling "random source" animals to labs. While only time will tell whether subsequent years will bring successful legislation to safeguard companion animals from research, the number of class B dealers who sell animals for research has dropped steadily in recent years to an all-time low, and many dealers are finally facing prosecution for their crimes.[34]

Today, most animals used for research come from companies that breed them specifically for this purpose. In 2004 there were 4,571 USDA-licensed class A and B dealers selling to animal researchers.[35]

A perusal through *Lab Animal* magazine's annual buyer's guide lists more than eighty companies selling amphibians, cats, dogs, ferrets, rabbits, rodents, primates, and farm animals, as well as supplies. By far, the most sellers and the most products are found in the rodent category, with various breeds of mice, rats, guinea pigs, and chinchillas available in a variety of strains such as inbred, outbred, mutant, hybrid, and transgenic.

The biggest and most well-known American suppliers include Ace Animals, Hilltop Lab Animals, Simonsen Laboratories, Taconic, Jackson Laboratory, Xenogen Biosciences, and Zivic Laboratories, which specialize in rodents; Animal Biotech and Archer Farms specialize in sheep and pigs; Rana Ranch Bullfrog Farm breeds frogs; the Buckshire Corporation, Primate Products, and Worldwide Primates breed and import primates; Harlan Sprague Dawley offers rodents, rabbits, cats, and dogs; Charles River Laboratories produces rodents, rabbits, and primates; and Covance Research Products produces dogs, rabbits, guinea pigs, and primates. Most of these companies provide not only "research models" (animals, in other words) but a variety of product development services, contract testing, and research services.

One of the earliest laboratory animal suppliers in the United States, and also one of the largest and most diversified, is Harlan Sprague Dawley, founded in 1931. Today, the supplier has about two dozen facilities around the world and provides not only 240 stocks and strains of animals but animal feed and several related products, as well.[36]

Jackson Laboratory is another early entrant into the field, founded in 1929 as a nonprofit research institution. In addition to supplying mice, creating new mouse strains on order, and providing other development research services to customers, Jackson Laboratory has been designated as one of twenty-one cancer centers to conduct basic cancer research by the National Cancer Institute.

The largest global supplier of animals for research is Charles River Laboratories. Besides supplying purpose-bred animals to facilities around the world, Charles River also provides drug development and testing services for pharmaceutical and biotech companies. The supplier manages the colony of approximately 250 chimpanzees at the Alamogordo Primate Facility in New Mexico, the nation's second-largest chimpanzee facility for the National Institutes of Health, under a ten-year, $42.8 million contract. Under the contract, Charles River is to provide for the animals' long-term care after their years of being used for biomedical research, with no "invasive research" to be conducted on them for the remainder of their lives. However, according to the contract, the chimpanzees must remain available for use in federally supported biomedical research.[37]

Charles River also used to run a rhesus monkey breeding colony in the Florida Keys that was the subject of considerable local controversy, thanks to the environmental destruction resulting from the operation. The monkeys ate the delicate mangrove trees, and their waste, which was released directly into the protected waters of the Florida Keys National Marine Sanctuary, polluted the waters.[38] The pharmaceutical giant Merck later bought the colony to use for its research.

Today, there are a dozen suppliers of primates to the biomedical community, but as the number of American suppliers has dwindled (partly due to the fact that many countries have banned the catching and export of primates for research purposes), demand has increased. In 2004 the eight national primate research centers (university-affiliated research centers and breeding facilities) underwent a $100-million expansion, and demand may still be greater than can be met with current populations.[39] The major suppliers of primates for American researchers are Alpha Genesis, Inc., Buckshire Corp, Harlan Bio-products, Highwater Farms, Mini-Mitter Company, Osage Research Primates, Primate Products, Inc., Rhenos LLC, Shared Enterprises, Three Springs Scientific, Inc., Worldwide Primates, Inc., and Zoologix, Inc.[40] These firms also constitute the major importers of wild-caught and colony-bred primates into the United States for any reason.[41] Covance, formerly Hazelton Research Products, has been a major supplier as well, and in 1989 officials discovered that several research monkeys at its Virginia facility were infected with the Ebola virus. The animals, who had been imported from the Philippines, were all euthanized to prevent the transmission of the disease to other animals or people.[42] Similar outbreaks occurred at Hazelton's Texas and Pennsylvania facilities in the 1990s as well. (These public health risks aren't limited to just primates. In August 2005 at least three mice carrying the deadly bubonic plague disappeared from a metropolitan New Jersey lab.)[43] On the other hand, many pharmaceutical and biotech companies run their own in-house monkey colonies, which eliminates the need to purchase or import new animals.[44]

Some research facilities still purchase random-source dogs and cats. *Lab Animal* lists several class B dealers (including Hodgins Kennels, Triple C Farms, MWI Veterinary Supply Company, Kiser Lake Kennels, and R&R Research) that still provide random-source dogs and/or cats for research purposes, but there is no way to know how many dogs and cats they provide annually.[45]

One reason why research facilities buy so few animals from class B dealers is that transgenic mice and rats are much more common and available than ever before. Supply houses create these animals by inserting the DNA of other animals into them in order to study gene function and human disease. Since 1989, when the US Patent Office issued the first patent for a genetically engineered animal, transgenic mice and rats have increased in popularity. Yet there is no way to know how many are born and used annually, since there are no regulations that govern their use or that require research facilities to report their use.

On the other hand, random-source dealers like Delta Biologicals still sell animals for dissection, including dead frogs, mink, fetal pigs, and rabbits. Carolina Biological Supply Company supplies live amphibians, reptiles, and other animals for classroom use, as well as dead cats, rabbits, frogs, fetal pigs, and other animals. Where do biological supply houses like Delta and Carolina get their animals? Fetal pigs, sheep, cow hearts, eyes, and other organs are slaughterhouse by-products, but cats, rabbits, and frogs typically arrive alive, where the supply house kills and preserves them in formaldehyde. Frogs and other amphibians as well as crawfish and worms are caught in the wild. Rabbits and mink usually arrive from fur farms, and cats are gathered by class B dealers or are shipped in from countries like Mexico and then killed for classroom use.

Finally, there are a couple of other ways that animals make their way into laboratories and classrooms that are of questionable means at best. For instance, racetracks have sold former racing greyhounds for research, and these animals have been found at private corporations as well as schools such as Colorado State University.[46]

One way that the entertainment industry and animal research are linked is through the fates of former circus chimpanzees. Because chimpanzees used for circuses, television, films, and in other forms of entertainment often become difficult to handle as they age, some become research subjects when they are no longer profitable or easy to control.

LIFE IN THE LAB

Many animals in laboratories spend their entire lives in isolation in metal cages, without toys, soft beds, or the barest of comforts. Rabbits, dogs, monkeys, apes, and rats are all highly social animals and, in the wild or in other domestic situations where they enjoy companionship, they spend much of their time grooming, communicating, and inter-acting with one another—behaviors that are impossible when these animals live in cages. More to the point, however, for an intelligent, feeling social creature to spend his or her life in a cage with no com-panionship or interaction with others, with little or no opportunity for exercise or play, and with limited and stressful interaction with humans, is not a life that anyone should have to endure. Yet, many mil-lions of animals have endured such living conditions, and many mil-lions more continue to do so. It is, after all, cheaper and easier to put an animal into a cage without toys or beds that require cleaning. It is cheaper and easier to disregard exercise that would take up valuable worker time, to keep them in smaller cages, and to prohibit them from interacting with companions. So what if the animals are frustrated, bored, depressed, or lonely? Who can say whether or not animals are able feel such emotions at all?

Thankfully, people who live with these kinds of animals know that their companion dogs, rats, and rabbits all demonstrate a very wide range of behaviors and emotions, and that the more stimulation, natural activities, companionship, and care an animal receives, the happier she is. Countless scientific studies that compare animal behavior in conventional laboratory settings to environments modified to better suit them demonstrate that stereotypic behaviors like rocking, pacing, staring, fur-chewing, or self-mutilation are common in the typical barren laboratory cage. These studies also show that their natural behavioral repertoire narrows considerably over time in lab environments.[47]

Environmental Enrichment

The term "environmental enrichment" refers to ways that animals in laboratories or other environments can have some of their behavioral needs met while living under these artificial conditions. The Animal Welfare Act mandates environmental enrichment for nonhuman primates, including modifying cages and other housing to allow monkeys and apes to pursue "normal" or species-typical behaviors and social interactions, rather than the stereotypical behaviors associated with bored, depressed, or psychologically damaged animals; examples include social housing, "inanimate enrichment items" like toys, and opportunities to forage for food. In addition, APHIS created standards that mandate exercise for dogs.

Examples of environmental enrichment for primates include housing monkeys and apes either in pairs or in groups; training primates to cooperate during certain procedures like blood drawing to limit the use of restraint methods; providing "foraging devices" that let animals find their own food; providing perches, swings, and shelves for climbing and swinging, as well as a variety of toys; and even, in a few cases, letting them watch television.

According to the USDA, five years after the regulations were in place, APHIS inspectors found that most facilities were not in compliance with the new regulations, which led to the drafting of more policies, some of which were not enacted.[48] Conditions have improved for primates in labs since these requirements were put into place. Yet, sadly, because the USDA maintains that the "psychological well-being" of the primates is difficult to define and impossible to measure, APHIS inspectors have no way of reporting whether or not the animals are happy. While anyone who lives with and cares for a companion animal could easily tell whether or not a friend was happy, unfortunately, this type of subjective measure is not acceptable for a laboratory environment. Instead, proposed measures to detect psychological well-being include everything from "longevity, growth rate, reproductive success, hair coat, and body condition" to "heart rate, blood pressure, body temperature, levels of serum cortisol and other hormones, and rates of lymphocyte proliferation or suppression" to, broadly, behavior.[49] It is ironic that well-intended government regulations that were intended to make life better for primates in labs cannot be deemed successful without, in many cases, yet more invasive procedures to measure the success of the regulations.

It is worth looking at a couple of the hundreds of studies addressing the effects of environmental enrichment on primates, such as the following:

> Individually housed subjects watched the videotapes more than socially housed subjects. When viewing time was averaged across all videotapes, the chimpanzees watched the monitor a mean of 38.4% of the time available. . . . Subjects habituated to repeated presentations of the videotapes, although the effect was small numerically. Although this type of enrichment did not extensively alter behavior, it did occupy a significant portion of the subjects' activity budget.[50]

In this case, the measure of whether the chimpanzees enjoyed the television was how much of their "activity budgets" were spent in front of it. Even more poignant is the following example:

Ice cubes are distributed across the floor, hidden in high plastic barrels (we call these igloos), tucked into corners of the cages, etc. As
the animals come out, the excitement of the hunt starts and continues
until the last ice cube is found. Hoarders clutch them to their chests,
. . . others fill their mouths and carry the cubes to the top of the cage,
where they lay them down and watch carefully as the cubes get
smaller and smaller. Still others have learned to skate through the
puddles, making mad dashes in order to slide further and further. No
detrimental effects have been found of providing the ice cubes.[51]

Thank heavens no detrimental effects were found to be associated
with providing ice cubes to the animals—otherwise, even this one
small enrichment, which seemed to provide the animals so much pleasure, might be removed.

Unfortunately, primates, and to a much lesser extent, dogs, are the
only animals the government requires to receive enrichment or exercise. This means that many other dogs and most rabbits, cats, guinea
pigs, mice, and rats still spend their entire lives in barren cages with
only food and water containers, and, when appropriate, a litterbox or
another method for containing urine and feces. Toys, blankets, companionship, and an environment that is more interesting than a cage
are nonexistent for most of these animals, with the exception of mice,
who typically are kept in groups.

Thanks to the 1985 amendment to the AWA, laboratories must
allow dogs limited exercise and socialization. However, animal scientists strenuously fought these provisions. They were able to have the
new provisions watered down after a group of scientists performed a
study demonstrating that dogs did not exercise more in larger cages
(i.e., cover greater distances when walking).[52] The study did not, it is
worth noting, compare dogs playing with humans or other dogs in
parks to lonely dogs pacing in small cages.

The USDA Animal Welfare Information Center even provides
resources for the voluntary enrichment of birds, cats, dogs, farm animals, ferrets, rabbits, and rodents.[53] The US Public Health Service's
Guide to the Care and Use of Laboratory Animals encourages

"enriching the environment as appropriate to the species."[54] Suggested examples include opportunities for foraging, egg laying, and flying for birds; elevated resting shelves, scratching posts, and the like for cats; social housing and the opportunity to interact positively with humans, chew toys, and exercise for dogs; social housing, the ability to forage and dig, and opportunities for exercise and play for rabbits; and finally, social housing for rodents, opportunities to search for their food, exercise, burrow, and chew, and even the ability to control their environment to some degree, such as by providing small houses that animals can hide in.

While the enrichment suggestions are different for each animal, it is interesting to note that for all species, the encouragement of social housing demonstrates the importance of living with and interacting positively with other animals, as opposed to existing alone. There is no way to know how many live in these "enriched" environments compared to those who live alone until their deaths, but we can assume the number is low, based on the costs and difficulties associated with providing social housing, toys, exercise, and the like. One positive aspect of enrichment programs is that hundreds of studies have demonstrated that animals living in environments that promote psychological well-being have better health, and they are in turn easier for workers to handle. Yet for some animals such as gerbils, the opposite is true: allowing them to live more naturally makes them less easy to handle. Other risks of environmental enrichment include the potential for harm to the animals (e.g., from fighting with other animals when living socially), negative behavioral changes if researchers move animals from social housing back to individual housing, and possible changes to the research data.[55] These risks mean that many researchers choose not to provide enrichment opportunities for their research animals, even when their university or facility typically provides them. And as a result, even simple improvements that would improve the welfare of these animals are simply not available.

THE SCIENTIFIC USE OF ANIMALS

The use of animals in scientific research has been traced as far back as the days of the ancient Greeks, who also practiced dissection and other techniques on living and dead human beings (mostly prisoners and slaves).[56] Human dissection was discontinued after the rise of Christianity in the Roman world, but it was practiced again during the Renaissance. Experimentation on animals became a standard part of medical research in the late eighteenth century, with wild animals, farm animals, and domestic cats and dogs being used as subjects. By the mid-nineteenth century, human dissection was largely replaced by animal experimentation, but it reappeared, infamously, under the authority of Nazi and Japanese scientists during World War II.

Medical Experimentation

Animals are used as research subjects in a wide range of studies, ranging from asthma to AIDS, cancer to diabetes, birth defects to biochemical weapons, organ transplants to heart problems, and antibiotics to vaccines. Early examples of animals being used in research include work on rabies, smallpox, anthrax, and rickets, and later, the effects of insulin, penicillin, anticoagulants, anesthesia, open-heart surgery, tranquilizers, chemotherapy, organ transplant surgery, laparoscopic surgery, and a variety of drugs.[57]

    While it's less morally uncomfortable to think of animal research as being geared toward finding cures for a host of human (and even animal) diseases, much of animal research is conducted in the field of experimental psychology, where animals are used as models not for human anatomy but for the human psyche. Animals are subjects in psychological research projects that cover such topics as depression, obesity, cigarette smoking, anxiety, social isolation, pain, bulimia, and hallucinations.[58] These studies are often particularly invasive, sometimes involving surgically manipulating the brain in order to gauge behavioral changes or changing aspects of the animal's environment in order to assess what the animal will do. One of the most infamous examples of the latter were psychologist Harry Harlow's "Mother Love" experiments in the 1950s; for these studies, Harlow took baby rhesus monkeys from their mothers and gave them artificial mother replacements, made from wood, wire, and cloth. Sometimes these maternal replacements were benign and provided the lonely babies with someone to hug when distressed, but at other times the "mothers" would shock or otherwise harm the babies when they tried to hug them. The results of this research (and of much other psychological research) demonstrated something that most everyone knew already: babies, when deprived of the love of a mother, would develop emotional and psychological problems that lasted throughout their lives.

But, putting aside much of the psychological research, we are still left with medical research that is critical to human life, right? The answer is not so simple.

Drug, Cosmetic, and Household Product Testing

Each year, thousands of new or updated household products—everything from shampoo to toothpaste to drugs for AIDS, cancer, and baldness, from floor cleaners and shoe polish to mascara and new drugs—are sold in the United States. Over the years, the majority of these products or their components have been tested on animals to find out if they could cause harm to humans.

The FDA, through the Federal Food, Drug, and Cosmetic Act, is responsible for assuring that cosmetics, drugs, medical devices, and other household products are safe for the public and properly labeled. With the exception of cosmetics, the act requires proof of the safety of these items before they can be sold to the public, and for some of those products—such as drugs, medical devices, and products containing certain chemicals—some animal testing is mandated. Drugs especially are typically tested on hundreds of animals before approval.[59] Further, the Environmental Protection Agency also requires that animal testing be conducted on a variety of chemicals to monitor their levels of toxicity. For products (or their ingredients) that have not been tested on animals, such as cosmetics and many household products, the FDA requires that they are labeled with a notice reading, "Warning: The safety of this product has not been determined."

Many cosmetic companies no longer test their products on animals—and many countries, including all European Union countries, have banned cosmetic testing entirely. These companies either use previously tested ingredients and avoid using new ingredients, or they use alternative methods for testing.[60] Other corporations continue to test their new products and ingredients on animals rather than risk the warning label. Cosmetic safety tests are primarily focused on toxicity and have historically included a variety of tests to measure how toxic either a finished product or one of its ingredients is to the skin, eyes, or the whole body.

Because of the current requirement that drug manufacturers test drugs on animals, pharmaceutical companies test all of their drugs and medical devices on animals before they can be released. Many drug companies maintain animal testing facilities to do this, while others outsource their testing to companies such as Covance, which is not only one of the largest lab animal suppliers in the world but also is one of the largest contract testing companies.

Preclinical drug testing (i.e., before human clinical trials) typically involves using metabolic tests to detect how the body absorbs the drug, tests that measure a drug's toxicity, and efficacy studies that test whether the drug works the way it should. Other studies may be required as well.

The most notorious of the toxicity tests is the LD50, or the Lethal Dose 50 test. This test measures the dose at which half of the animal subjects (usually one hundred) died from the ingestion or injection of the test substance. The LD50 test was routine in the development of cosmetics, household products, and drugs. It was also one of the cruelest forms of animal testing and caused enormous suffering. Thankfully, neither the FDA nor the EPA require the LD50 test anymore, and the Interagency Research Animal Committee has recommended that it no longer be used. Today, many testing facilities instead use a combination of existing chemical data, in vitro testing (testing that is done outside of a human or animal body, in a controlled laboratory environment, using real or artificial cells or tissues), and other types of toxicity tests to replace the LD50. Sadly, some drug companies still use the LD50, such as Allergen, the maker of Botox. Besides the fact that a number of animals lose their lives to test each batch of Botox, a product that temporarily reduces the appearance of facial wrinkles, the LD50 is notoriously unreliable—chemicals that are toxic in other animals very often don't cause problems in people, and vice versa.

Other infamous tests are the Draize Eye Irritancy Test and the Draize Skin Irritancy Test. These test the toxicity of chemicals to the eyes or the skin of an animal, usually a rabbit. In the case of the eye test, researchers restrain the rabbit in stocks that keep her eyes held open. The researcher applies a toxic substance to one eye, and the rabbit remains immobilized for a period of several days or weeks until the researchers are able to measure the amount of damage to the eye. The skin test involves shaving and sometimes scraping the rabbit's skin and applying the toxin to the exposed skin. Again, the animal is restrained until the level of damage is measurable.

Not only do these experiments cause suffering for animals, but undercover video taken by organizations such as PETA has documented egregious abuses at experimentation facilities, including lab workers swearing and yelling at animals, punching dogs in the face, roughly jamming feeding tubes into primates' noses, dissecting live animals, and more. Undercover footage such as this has prompted federal investigations and penalties for violations of the Animal Welfare Act.[61]

The US military also uses hundreds of thousands of animals to test the effects of biological, nuclear, and chemical weapons, as well as conventional warfare, combat trauma, infectious diseases, and more. Researchers subject animals to gunshots, burns, radiation, blasts, corrosive materials, diseases, decompression, and more. In 2001, the US Department of Defense (DoD) used 330,149 animals in experiments. Only 7 percent were reportable species under the AWA. Rodents comprised the majority of subjects, at 89 percent. Fish, amphibians, reptiles, and birds comprised just a little more than 7 percent. The DoD also used farm animals, rabbits, dogs, cats, primates, marine mammals, and other animals.[62] A quick perusal of the DoD Biomedical Research Database reveals that in 2004, taxpayers paid millions of dollars for animal research that investigated the effects of Ebola, mustard gas ($4 million for this experiment alone), gunshots, jet fuel toxicity, toxic fire gases, traumatic brain injury, and more.[63] At the same time, the military uses some of the most high-tech alternatives to animals, including computerized mannequins that can blink, breathe, and talk—simulating a wide range of combat trauma situations. The mannequins can either improve or die, depending on the care provided.[64]

Companies that test on animals do so not to protect the consumers or even to protect themselves from liability, but in order to continue making products that are toxic to humans, animals, and the environment. Often, test results that show that a product is toxic to humans do

---

Mama

One day Margo got a phone call from a woman who worked at the San Francisco Zoo. There was a laboratory rabbit and her baby whom a local medical facility had sold to the zoo for snake food, demonstrating the absolute cruelty of an industry that both exploits and typically kills rabbits for human needs, then, once the tests have concluded, exploits them for profit.

The zoo employee was a friend of rabbits, so she called House Rabbit Society, and Margo took Mama and Baby into her home. Mama and Baby were New Zealand rabbits—common lab and meat rabbits. Mama had a metal clip embedded in her ear that had to be removed surgically. Both lived with Margo, and later with her large group of foster rabbits, for two years. Mama never warmed up to humans and remained extremely hostile to people, but she loved her new life with others of her own kind.

Sadly, two years later Mama was infected with myxomatosis, a deadly viral disease that was used by the British in order to eliminate the rabbit overpopulation problem that they created when they imported rabbits to Australia for sport hunting. Baby survived, and she lived with Margo until she died on Christmas Day five years later.

Mama, who spent two years inside a lab before becoming a part of Margo's family, enjoying a carrot. (Photo by Margo DeMello)

not lead to the product being removed from the marketplace; instead, toxic household products are simply labeled to warn consumers of the danger. After all, animal testing does not necessarily result in a product that is safer or less harmful; it often results in a product that *may* be poisonous but that carries a label stating that fact in order to protect the company from liability. So each year, companies continue to produce thousands of new ingredients and products and to test them on millions of animals, yet the products are no safer because they had been tested on animals.

ALTERNATIVES TO ANIMAL RESEARCH AND TESTING

Animals are just one form of research model used to study medical questions. Others include computer simulations, in vitro tests, and epidemiological studies, all of which have been useful in studying genetic function, drug development, nutrition, psychology, disease, anatomy, and more. So, could these and other not-yet-developed methods completely replace the use of animals in medical research and product testing?

One goal of the Animal Welfare Act is the minimization of animal pain and distress via the use of alternatives to animal research and testing, and, thankfully, many organizations and researchers are indeed working on this. The Alternatives Research and Development Foundation, for example, provides grants to scientists developing alternatives. The Johns Hopkins Center for Alternatives to Animal Testing also works to develop alternatives in research and testing through collaborating with scientists, animal welfare groups, and the biomedical industry. The Institute for In Vitro Sciences is a nonprofit organization providing in vitro research and testing services, as well as training for other scientists in the use of alternative methods. Finally, the National Institute of Environmental Health Sciences established the Interagency Coordinating Committee on the Validation of Alternative Methods to develop and validate nonanimal testing methods. Today, hundreds of companies no longer use animal tests.

The AWA also requires that researchers consider alternatives to animal use when formulating their proposals and that they investigate all alternatives to the use of live animals before settling on the use of animals for their research project. Even with this mandate, millions of animals are still used as research subjects in this country. The development of or investigation into alternative methods, while encouraging, seems to be a second thought for many researchers.

Why aren't more alternatives being developed, and why aren't more researchers utilizing nonanimal methods in their research? It takes time, effort, and money to develop new methods, which interferes with the researcher's or the lab's agenda. Sometimes it's just a case of inertia. Changing methods, even when it would not be difficult or expensive, involves doing something new or different, and for scientists, like the rest of us, change is often hard.

Developing alternatives for animal testing and research is one part of what is known in the research community as the Three R's: reduction, refinement, and replacement.[65] Reduction means reducing the use of animals to get more results from fewer animals; refinement means minimizing animals' pain and distress and/or enhancing their well-being; and replacement means replacing animals with nonanimal methods.

Alternatives to animal use are numerous. They include clinical research and observation—in other words, testing drugs and therapies in a controlled experiment on consenting human populations. These must take place after animal testing and before a drug is released to the public. Microdosing involves giving human volunteers very small doses of drugs in order to test safety and efficacy. In epidemiological studies, entire populations are examined in order to study health trends, and they can, for example, link diseases like lung cancer to smoking. Genetic research can reveal which genes can lead to hereditary health problems. In vitro research uses cell and tissue cultures in a test-tube or a petri dish, and one of its uses is drug development. Post-market surveillance involves tracking drug side effects after the drug has been cleared by the FDA and is available to the general public. Human autopsies and noninvasive imaging technologies like CAT scans and MRIs allow the human body to be explored, and the use of human stem cells and tissues is useful in developing vaccines, for example. Artificial tissues are good tools for determining toxicity. And computer and mathematical models can simulate physiological processes and provide a way to chart the action of a toxin in cells and its effects on the whole body.

In vitro research is particularly valuable for testing diseases at the microscopic level, since that is the most fundamental level at which diseases manifest. A number of important in vitro products such as EpiDerm (an in vitro human skin model) and EpiOcular (an in vitro human corneal model) are being used to replace animal toxicity tests like the Draize tests; artificial tissues such as Corrositex are another excellent and inexpensive way of conducting toxicity tests.[66] Mattek Corporation, the makers of EpiDerm and EpiOcular, have also released other models derived from human cells that mimic the human trachea, the inner cheek, and even the vagina.

Unfortunately, the FDA does not require post-marketing drug surveillance, which would force scientists and the government to study further the side effects of drugs after their release. Sometimes this happens when patients suffer adverse effects or even die after taking the drugs. Skipping this step allows companies to remain ignorant of the side effects resulting from their drugs, since a popular medication can make millions of dollars each day it is on the shelves. For example, Merck, the maker of the anti-inflammatory drug Vioxx, tested the medication on mice and rats in several experiments. Yet, in 2004, the company withdrew Vioxx from the market. Why? As many as fifty-five thousand people died from heart attacks and strokes after taking Vioxx.[67] Since then, thousands of lawsuits have been filed against Merck for patient deaths and other damages, which demonstrates the dangers of relying on animal testing rather than clinical research.

While the FDA does mandate animal testing for drugs and other chemicals, some government agencies also support the development of nonanimal methods. In 1997, the National Institute of Environmental Health Sciences created the Interagency Coordinating Committee on the Validation of Alternative Methods (ICCVAM) as well as the National Toxicology Program Interagency Center for the Evaluation of Alternative Toxicological Methods (NICEATM). These were formed in order to "coordinate the development, validation, acceptance, and harmonization of alternative toxicological test methods throughout the US Federal Government."[68] In 2000 ICCVAM recommended that federal agencies stop using the Draize skin tests for measuring skin corrosion.

In 2001 the United States also signed onto the International Organization for Economic Cooperation and Development's decision to phase out the use of Lethal Dose 50 test, which could impact animal testing in the OECD's thirty member countries.

Indeed, Europe is far ahead of the United States in many issues related to lab animals. In June 2002, for instance, the European Union voted to ban immediately new cosmetics with ingredients that have been tested on animals if alternative testing methods exist, and, as of 2005, new cosmetics that have ingredients for which no alternative testing procedures exist are now banned. Also in 2001 the European Centre for the Validation of Alternative Methods (ECVAM) completed validation studies on three other alternative in vitro test methods for assessing skin corrosivity—EpiDerm, Episkin, and the Rat Skin TER Assay. In 2007 the European Centre for the Validation of Alternative Methods approved five more tests that render the use of mice and rabbits unnecessary, leading the way for cosmetic testing to be completely banned in the European Union.[69] Unfortunately, the US government has been very slow to validate alternative methods.

THE USE OF ANIMALS IN EDUCATION

Animals are also used in a variety of ways in our secondary and post-secondary educational system, most commonly for dissection.

The dissection of frogs, worms, cats, mink, rabbits, fetal pigs, and more in middle and high school biology classes has occurred in the United States for years, thanks in part to efforts of the dissection procurement industry and teachers' groups such as the National Association of Biology Teachers and the National Science Teachers Association. These groups maintain that animal dissection is necessary for biology instruction, and they actively fight any efforts to curtail the use of live or dead animals in the classroom.

The Humane Society of the United States and the World Society for the Protection of Animals estimate that 6 million animals are killed—many of them, such as frogs, are caught in the wild, and many, such as cats, are rounded up from animal shelters or countries like Mexico—for dissection in the United States alone every year. Capturing wild animals such as amphibians not only threatens dwindling populations, but the disposal of millions of formaldehyde-soaked specimens each year poses a threat to ecosystems.

State and local policies on dissection vary, but, for approximately three-quarters of public high school students, the dissection of a dead animal preserved in formaldehyde is a rite of passage.[70] For many, it is not a good one at all, given the level of trauma it causes for many students—some of whom are turned off from science altogether after participating in a dissection.[71] The tradition is also an unhealthy one, as formaldehyde presents health risks to teachers and students.

Because so many students have expressed concern over the dissection of animals in their schools, nine states and a number of school districts have passed "student choice laws" that allow high school students to opt out of dissection without jeopardizing their grades, while six other states (not to mention a number of countries) have opted for other policies that allow some form of student choice. Some choice laws, however, exclude certain animals like frogs, and others allow teachers to intervene and stop a student from opting out. Because most school districts do not provide options for students, students who object on moral or other grounds to the dissection of animals can risk receiving a failing grade.

Student choice laws, which are based on the First Amendment guarantee of religious freedom rather than on any humane motive (since many students object to animal dissection on religious grounds), allow students who morally object to the dissection of a live animal to instead follow an alternative lesson plan that covers the same material. Examples available today range from high tech (computer simulations, online dissections, CD-ROM, and video dissections) to low tech (slides, models, and charts), all of which are available for schools and teachers to purchase or can be borrowed from organizations like the Humane Society of the United States, Animalearn, and the National Anti-vivisection Society, all of which maintain large lending libraries. Even Carolina Biological Supply Company, the oldest and one of the largest biological supply houses in the country, sells video and computer simulations of dissections in addition to animal dissection kits. Recent studies have compared computer simulations to animal dissections and have deemed them as useful as and, in some cases, superior to actual dissection.[72]

Student science projects using animals are not limited to dissection. Some high school biology classes include components in which students conduct experiments on live animals, and student science fair projects involving animals, while less common than they once were, are still popular. Many of these are benign: one student measured whether dog fur or human hair grows faster by shaving a patch of hair on his head and on his dog and comparing results; another "tested" the neighborhood dogs to see what dog treats they preferred. Others have been much less so, allowing for unmitigated pain and even death for the animals used.

One particularly notorious example gained media attention in 2007. In order to enter a science fair, a high school student conducted animal research at the University of New Mexico that led the lab's research veterinarian to resign, calling the experiments "torture." The research involved hanging mice by their tails with tape, forcing mice to swim until they nearly drowned, terrifying pregnant mice, and subsequently electrically shocking their babies—all research that UNM officials defended. Luckily, the science fair rejected the experiment on ethical grounds.[73]

The National Science Teachers Association maintains that experimental procedures should not involve animals "if such procedures are likely to cause pain, induce nutritional deficiencies, or expose animals to parasites, hazardous/toxic chemicals, or radiation."[74] The Intel International Science and Engineering Fair, the largest student science fair, now prohibits projects that cause more than momentary pain or suffering or that kill the animals involved. Thankfully, this prohibits projects that at one time were quite common, such as toxicity studies

(studies in which students exposed animals to tobacco smoke were at one time extremely popular), behavioral experiments that induce helplessness or cause emotional distress, and studies that involve physical pain. However, students at the Intel fair can still use animals, and when animals do die, the experiment is terminated only if the procedure directly caused the death of the animal or if more than 30 percent of the animals died.[75] Because the Animal Welfare Act does not cover the use of animals at high schools or science fairs, we must rely on the educational and science fair organizations to create policies that are humane.

One area of study that has tremendous potential for a positive understanding of animals also has some potential ethical problems as well. Field studies, conducted in high school or college wildlife classes, involve students who may handle, trap, tag, or collar wild animals in order to study them. Some of these activities may also involve changing the composition of social groups by adding or subtracting members; playing back vocalizations in order to understand responses; manipulating the food supply; depositing scents; or even manipulating the gene pool. While studying wild animals in their native environments has generated a huge amount of the information about the social structure of wild animals, their intelligence, and their emotional expressions, these studies can also be carried out in such a way as to minimize disruption to the animals' lives. Biologist Marc Bekoff recommends that:

> A guiding principle should be that wild animals whom we are privileged to study should be respected, and when we are unsure about how our activities will influence the lives of the animals being studied, we should err on the side of the animals and not engage in these practices until we know the consequences of our acts.[76]

Finally, the use of animals in American medical and veterinary schools is another area in which thousands of animals die each year. Thankfully, this too is changing. According to the California Davis Center for Animal Alternatives, "The greatest advances for alternatives to animal research have been achieved in the area of education."[77] Just a generation ago, every medical school and veterinary school in the country used live animals to teach medical and veterinary students surgical techniques as well as subjects like physiology and pharmacology. These "dog labs" involved the anesthetizing, operating on, and killing of dogs the school typically acquired from local shelters. Many schools have switched to pigs, which is ethically no different but does not raise the same level of opposition from the general public.

As of this writing, only thirteen medical schools use live animals to train medical students, which may be illegal under the AWA, given its requirement to use alternatives when they are available. The fact that alternatives are readily available is clear, given the fact that only two of the top-twenty ranked American medical schools still use live animals. The remaining schools, including Dartmouth, Duke, Emory, Harvard, Stanford, and Yale, no longer use animals as teaching tools. These leading universities instead use patient simulators, human cadavers, surgical observations, and computer simulations.

The fact that so many medical schools have, during the past twenty years, stopped using animals in their courses is an enormously positive change. This movement occurred because medical students around the country expressed reservations about killing animals as part of their education, and many refused to participate in dog labs and other classes in which animals were killed. There is simply no reason why institutions like Johns Hopkins or the University of California at San Diego haven't made this change as well.

Veterinary schools have also typically sacrificed animals in order to teach veterinary students animal anatomy and surgical techniques. Today, two-thirds of US veterinary schools have changed their curriculum to allow students to opt out of live animal surgeries and other terminal procedures, but most still use live animals in their core courses and many in their elective courses. Students are also often expected to perform terminal surgeries.[78]

The move away from live animal labs in medical and veterinary schools demonstrates the efficacy of live animal alternatives, such as synthetic animal models, computer-linked mannequins, computer simulations, other types of surgical simulator tools, interactive DVDs, spay/neuter programs, and deceased companion animal body donation programs. The creation of alternatives to the use of live animals both in medical and veterinary schools does more than save the lives of those animals who would have been killed in classroom studies. Perhaps even more important, these alternatives can also substitute for the use of animals in much of biomedical research. The question is, then, why is medical research so slow to follow in the footsteps of medical schools?

GOOD SCIENCE OR BAD SCIENCE?

As a measure of the importance or irrelevance of animal research, advocates both for and against make competing claims about how much it has or has not played a part in the awarding of Nobel Prizes. According to an analysis conducted by the Humane Society of the United States, two-thirds of the Nobel Prizes awarded in the fields of physiology and medicine went to researchers who primarily or entirely used nonanimal-based methods for their research.[79] But the Foundation for Biomedical Research shows that the winners of seven of the last ten Nobel Prizes in medicine have relied at least in part on animal research. So, who's right? Perhaps we should wonder if determining whether animals have played an important role in Nobel Prize-winning work is the best question, or whether we should be asking when the awards for pioneering nonanimal-based technologies will generate similar prestige.

Animal researchers have made some discoveries through the use of animals, although anti-vivisectionists point out that most or all of these same discoveries could have been made without the use of animals. There are also numerous examples in which animals were very poor models for human health or anatomy, leading in some cases to tragic results where drugs (such as thalidomide, and more recently, Vioxx) caused severe health problems in humans, even after extensive animal testing. Sometimes, the FDA approves drugs even when they cause problems in animals, but clinical tests don't indicate human health issues. Conversely, drugs that show promise in human clinical trials are sometimes pulled back by the FDA when animals who are administered the drug develop side effects.[80]

Chimpanzees, as close as they are to humans genetically (they share more than 98 percent of our genes), are not even perfect human models. While most HIV researchers now think that HIV originated in primates as Simian Immunodeficiency Virus (or SIV), HIV in chimpanzees operates very differently than it does in humans. Chimpanzees infected with HIV for research purposes respond asymptomatically and show no signs of infection, and many chimpanzees even reject the HIV virus through their own natural immunity. For that reason, chimpanzees are probably not good subjects to test a potential HIV vaccine, since their natural immunity is not shared with most humans. Chimpanzees also don't get sick when infected with hepatitis B, although the hepatitis B vaccine was originally tested on chimpanzees. They also respond differently to hepatitis C than humans.

Xenotransplantation (or xenograft)—transplanting nonhuman animal organs into humans—research is another area in which researchers consider the use of animals to be critical for saving human lives. Because of the worldwide shortage of human organs available for transplant—more than ninety-two thousand Americans are currently awaiting an organ transplant and more than half will die while waiting—the result is a growing black market in organ sales as well as illegal harvesting of organs and tissues for transplant, some of which make recipients sick. While most organ donation advocacy groups focus on recruiting new donors or improving procurement practices in order to meet the growing demand, and some even propose incentives for organ donation, there is support in the biomedical community to focus instead on xenotransplantation.

Scientists have been working on xenotransplantation for decades. Yet, aside from the ethical concerns about creating "body part farms" where animals are raised in order to provide organs for humans, xenotransplantation has, from a medical perspective, been a total failure. Since 1964, when doctors transplanted a chimpanzee heart into a man, to 1984, when a baboon heart was transplanted into an infant, to 1994, when a pig's liver was transplanted into a woman, the result has been the same: in all cases, the patients died shortly after their surgeries.[81] This failure demonstrates that even the relatively small genetic differences between, say, chimpanzees and humans are actually quite large when it comes down to the ability of organs from one species to survive in the body of another species, even if they are closely related.

Animal researchers claim that the use of animals in medical science and product testing is critical to human health. Yet, opponents of animal experimentation, including a number of scientists and doctors, counter that it is wasteful, that animals are poor models for human disease, that clinical testing of drugs and vaccines often reveals side effects and problems not seen in the original animal testing, that the animals suffer needlessly, and that the use of animals in biomedical research diverts money away from nonanimal alternatives. Clinical research, for example, focuses directly on human patients but receives far less funding than animal research, according to a study in the *Journal of the American Medical Association*.[82]

In a recent article in the *British Medical Journal*, the authors examined twenty-five published reviews of animal experiments and focused especially on those that examined the effect the animal research had on the subsequent clinical research.[83] In a majority of the cases reviewed, the authors found that the animal data were either irrelevant or they conflicted with the results of the clinical trials. How could this be? The authors found a number of methodological problems with animal experiments and ultimately concluded that "the value of animal research into potential human treatments needs urgent rigorous evaluation" and that "systematic reviews can provide important insights into the validity of animal research."[84] So why isn't the medical community performing these reviews in order to demonstrate, once and for all, whether animal research is good or bad science?

FUNDING FOR ANIMAL RESEARCH

In order to fairly calculate whether or not animal research is ultimately good or bad for society (it's very rarely good for animals), we have to look at both the costs and the benefits. We know that animal research has yielded some benefits to humanity, although, by shifting toward nonanimal methods, we expect to continue to see humans benefit. Then again, there are several beneficiaries of animal research: the biomedical industry, including government, university, and private scientists; pharmaceutical firms; contract testing labs; lab animal, feed, and equipment suppliers; government agencies; biomedical advocacy groups; and even some health charities. All of these organizations benefit financially from animal research, and it is these benefits that shape the direction of biomedical research to a large extent.

Biomedical research is a multibillion-dollar industry with hefty operating costs: scientists' and technicians' salaries; the cost of purchasing millions of animals per year; the cost of feeding and maintaining all of those animals; the lab equipment and animal housing units; the cost of experiments and procedures; and the cost to dispose of the bodies. In addition to the millions of animals killed each year, the financial costs of animal research are certainly not trivial.

Who funds animal research? Since much animal research takes place at nonprofit organizations such as colleges and hospitals, it is heavily funded by the federal government via the National Institutes of Health, which, bottom line, means that taxpayers pay for it. A good portion of the NIH's $28-billion budget goes toward animal research.

The pharmaceutical industry is also a major player with respect to funding animal research and testing. The pharmaceutical companies that the Pharmaceutical Research and Manufacturers of America (PhRMA) represents spent $39 billion in 2005 on research and development, which uses animals in both the research and the preclinical testing stages. The industry as a whole spent more than $50 billion in both 2005 and 2006 on research and development.[85]

But the pharmaceutical industry doesn't just directly fund animal research. It also ensures that the legislative environment remains favorable to its interests through donations to congressional campaigns and lobbying efforts. In 2004 PhRMA, which represents every major US pharmaceutical company, gave more than $72 million in political contributions to federal legislators and millions more in state contributions, making it the tenth-largest lobbying organization in the country.[86] Another half dozen pharmaceutical companies are also among the top one hundred corporate donors, such as Monsanto ($22 million in 2004) and Procter & Gamble ($21 million in 2004), bringing the total of congressional contributions in 2004 to $121 million.[87] Thanks to these types of contributions, the industry can ensure that it will remain relatively unburdened by too many government regulations, that prescription drug prices remain high, that drugs from other countries not be imported to the United States to reduce costs to consumers, that pharmaceutical companies can easily advertise drugs to consumers without the burden of overregulation, and that patent protections will be extended so that generic drugs remain difficult for consumers to purchase. Of course, pharmaceutical companies, like so much of the biomedical industry, also need to ensure that their use of animals in research and development remains unhindered.

A third to a half of the thousands of industry lobbyists are former federal officials, and there is a revolving employment door between the FDA and the pharmaceutical industry. Biomedical companies also gave fees or stock options to at least 530 NIH scientists between 1999 and 2004.[88] Yet, even with all of this lobbying and with the billions of dollars in tax breaks and subsidies that the government provides to pharmaceutical companies, drug prices in the United States remain the highest in the world, and drug company profits are soaring.

By far, the biggest funders—and the largest beneficiaries—of animal research are the medical and biomedical organizations that lobby on behalf of animal research. The National Association for Biomedical Research (NABR), cofounded by the founder of Charles River Laboratories, is the largest national nonprofit organization dedicated to influencing public policy affecting animal research and ensuring that animal research is not threatened. With an annual income of almost $8 million, its membership is made up of more than three hundred universities, medical schools, hospitals, veterinary schools, pharmaceutical companies, and "other animal research-related firms." NABR spends $80,000 per year lobbying Congress in order to ensure that animal research is not threatened or burdened with additional regulations.[89] NABR also has a separate educational arm, the Foundation for Biomedical Research (FBR), with a budget of $2 million and more than $10 million in assets.[90] The FBR's aim is to win the public relations war with animal protection advocates by focusing on supposed benefits associated with animal research and alleging that animal protection advocates pose threats to public health and safety.

And while FBR is not a lobbying organization like NABR, it does ensure that its agenda of keeping animal research safe is successful. Both the 501(c)(3) Foundation for Biomedical Research and the 501(c)(6) National Association for Biomedical Research are headed by Frankie Trull, a registered lobbyist who runs Policy Directions, Inc., a Washington, DC, lobbying firm that specializes in biomedical research. According to its IRS Form 990, the nonprofit FBR even pays Policy Directions about $82,000 per year for "management services."[91]

Besides the Foundation for Biomedical Research, clients of Policy Directions include Procter & Gamble, lab animal suppliers Charles River Laboratories and Covance, fifteen of the major pharmaceutical companies including Merck and Eli Lilly, and a number of biotechnology firms. Policy Directions is one of the top one hundred lobbyists in Washington, with about a million dollars in annual income and nearly $7 million paid to congressional representatives and their campaigns from 1998 to 2004.[92]

Other big spenders with an interest in animal research include the American Medical Association, which earned more than $300 million in 2004 and spent $92 million on political contributions from 1998 to 2004;[93] Biotechnology Industry Organization, which earned $68 million in 2004 and spent $23 million in political campaigns from 1998 to 2004;[94] Animal Health Institute and its educational arm, Animal

Health Institute Foundation, which spent almost $600,000 in lobbying activities from 1998 to 2004;[95] and Americans for Medical Progress, primarily an educational organization, funded by the US Surgical Corporation.[96]

Health charities and government health organizations such as those that research and try to find cures for diseases like cancer, AIDS, and diabetes also often fund—and publicly defend—animal research, with millions of dollars more spent by these agencies every year to infect animals with human diseases that may or may not manifest themselves similarly in different species. Government health organizations like the National Cancer Institute often have a "mutually reinforcing industrial relationship" with lab animal suppliers and other elements of the research community.[97] For example, Jackson Laboratory, a supplier of inbred laboratory mice, got its initial success due to the awarding of a government contract to breed mice for cancer research in the 1950s.[98]

None of this elaborate corporate spending on political contributions, with the resulting positive legislation, would happen without the cooperation of legislators and other government officials. Besides the common practice of former legislators and other federal officials taking lucrative jobs either in the private industries that they used to vote on or regulate, or with lobbying companies that lobby their old colleagues, some benefit even while they are in office from their ties to the health and animal industries. According to the Center for Public Integrity, for example, 16 percent of current US legislators or their spouses have financial ties (i.e., they may work in the industry or serve on a board, or may own stock or other financial interests) to the health industry, including more than 7 percent having ties to the pharmaceutical industry.[99]

Because of the efforts of the biomedical industry, their lobbyists, and their supporters on Capitol Hill, taxpayers directly fund much animal research through NIH spending, the publicly funded National Cancer Institute, and other agencies, driving the various businesses that profit from animal research as well. Through the biomedical community, pharmaceutical industries, and health charities, and their generous contributions to political campaigns, these groups ensure that animal research will continue unabated for years. One interesting, and frightening, law that was passed in part through the intensive lobbying by the research community was a 2002 FDA rule change known as the Animal Efficacy Rule that allows some drugs, such as vaccines against bio-warfare agents, to be approved immediately after animal testing but without any clinical testing whatsoever.

What do the billions of lobbying dollars, combined with the legislative changes we discussed earlier, tell us? On the one hand, we see increasing levels of public concern about animal research and testing demonstrated through the history of animal welfare legislation and the greater protections afforded animals in labs. On the other hand, as the industry flexes its muscles through political contributions, government lobbying, and multimillion-dollar public relations campaigns, it has gained some important wins as well, such as the Helms Amendment to the 2002 Farm Bill that formally excluded rats, mice, and birds from AWA protection, demonstrating that the industry remains very threatened by increased protections for the animals it uses. And while it's clear that there will still be much money to be had for nonanimal research such as in vitro methods, post-marketing surveillance, and more clinical research, the current industries that profit from animal research—such as the lab animal breeders and dealers, the lab animal equipment suppliers, and the like—would likely suffer from such a shift.

THE BATTLE OVER ANIMAL RESEARCH

Animal researchers and the biomedical and pharmaceutical organizations that depend on animal research are engaged in an intense public relations battle with anti-vivisectionists—and oftentimes the public—on the morality and efficacy of animal research. While the animal researchers appear to be winning the battle, based on public opinion polls supporting the use of animals in research when respondents are given no alternatives to the use of animals, the tide may be turning.

Numbers of reportable animals used in research and product testing are going down (by about a half million in the United States since 1973, or by more than 50 percent during the same period),[100] but this reduction most likely masks an increase in the use of mice, rats, and other noncovered animals. This is a strong possibility given the rise in transgenic rodents, which itself creates an even larger ethical problem, since a very small number of transgenic animals meet the necessary criteria for inclusion in the research protocols. This means that researchers kill untold numbers of animals immediately after birth. Perhaps a more conclusive indication of a change in opinion is the fact that those same polls indicate a strong public interest in the use of animal alternatives. In addition, they show that the majority of the public only supports animal research when it definitively can lead to cures for life-threatening human illnesses, when there is no pain involved for the animal, and/or when no alternatives exist.[101] In other words, the public doesn't at all seem to follow the biomedical community's insistence on using animals in all cases, for any purpose. These are powerful indicators indeed, and as we've seen, the industry frames the debate as a polarized "your child or the rat" issue.

Certainly, some researchers are conducting studies in order to find a cure for life-threatening illnesses such as AIDS, cancer, or diabetes. But there is no way to know how much of current research addresses these purposes, nor whether that research will be successful.

While AWA regulations, as well as NIH guidelines, require that scientists use, when possible, pain-relieving drugs and anesthesia to alleviate pain and distress for the animals involved, we have seen that these regulations exclude 85 to 95 percent of the animals involved in painful and nonpainful experiments. Since researchers do not have to report these animals, there is no way to know how many suffer from pain. Furthermore, the fact that eighty-six thousand AWA-covered animals in the United States (about 5 to 6 percent of total reportable animals) undergo painful experiments without anesthesia or pain medication should give the public pause, since pain is one thing that gives the public discomfort across the board.

Laws mandating anesthesia during surgeries and analgesics for pain (when they will not harm the results of the experiment) reduce the suffering of some animals in laboratories, but a great many product safety tests and medical procedures—such as force-feeding or injecting known toxins into animals—are based upon pain. Researchers measure toxicity in these tests by quantifying the number of animals who suffer and die from them. Finally, what about the emotional pain caused by living a life in a cage, with no companionship or physical comforts, only to be removed from the cage to have one's blood drawn, to have one's temperature taken, or to undergo surgery? This, too, surely constitutes suffering.

Overwhelmingly, polls show that Americans and Europeans want to see more being done to increase the use of nonanimal alternatives in research and testing.[102] The public is uncomfortable with the idea that animals often suffer and die for human benefit, especially when it is becoming more and more clear that effective alternatives exist and are becoming more prevalent all the time. The public is also clear on pain and suffering: one poll indicated that support for animal research plummeted more than 40 percent when suffering goes from mild to severe.[103]

Finally, the public demands that medical research be effective. Scientists and government regulators must be able to apply reliably the results of these studies to humans. But if that's the case, why do so many drugs fail in clinical trials? If animal testing does not ensure that drugs are safe and work the way they are expected to, then what's the point? Not only because of the millions of animals killed each year, but also because of drug and product safety concerns, the public needs to be assured that animal research is a good use of taxpayer and private funds *and* that it will make the public safe. It isn't just animal protection advocates who are asking whether the animal tests are accurate for humans, or whether they are necessary, or whether they duplicate work that was already done—such as the countless studies performed over the last fifty years studying the effects of tobacco on the body— or whether they are wasteful. We all have heard horror stories about bureaucratic overspending common in government; we should not be surprised to learn that much of today's research and testing is replicating earlier work and still may not lead to safer products. The Environmental Protection Institute's High Production Volume (HPV) Challenge involves the retesting of substances like rat poison, gasoline, turpentine, lead, and propane. While we should be safe from these hazards, we also already know that many of these compounds are harmful. Does testing these substances on animals once again to prove that they are toxic really protect us or the environment?

Finally, what about the question of morality—is it ethical to conduct animal experimentation, even if it were effective, a good use of dollars, and didn't lead to extensive animal pain?

De-animalizing the Animal

For many scientists and the organizations that support them, this issue is handled simply through the "your child or the rat" question. As long as the debate is framed in such a simplistic manner, animal research advocates appear to win handily. But many people are increasingly discussing this issue. It's not just animal protection advocates on the one side, and animal researchers on the other. The intense debate about the morality of the issue involves a growing number of people, making the matter less easily settled.

One need only look at one of the biggest contradictions in the justification for animal research: animals must be seen as close enough to humans that the tests will result in meaningful results. No credible scientist working on human health issues would bother to test a drug on an animal if he didn't think the results could be applicable to humans. So we must grant the similarity of humans to not only chimpanzees but also to mice and rats in order for the tests to have validity. On the other hand, one of the ways that researchers have historically justified animal research is by distancing animals from humans. The argument states that because they aren't human, animals cannot reason, they cannot remember and anticipate pain, and they certainly don't enjoy the same legal and moral standing that humans do. This is a step up from the Cartesian model of animal consciousness that viewed animals as unconscious, unfeeling machines, but the underlying meaning is the same: Since animals are not humans, they don't feel the same, they can't register pain or loneliness or fear, and they don't warrant the same protections.

But how can animals be both similar enough to humans to use for product and drug testing, and different enough so that they are subjected to treatments that could never be done on humans? And, if we are similar enough that psychologists can study animals in order to understand human depression, why would those same researchers not recognize that intensive confinement, segregation from other animals, and lack of positive stimulation would result in an animal suffering from loneliness, sadness, anxiety, and even depression, just like humans would in similar circumstances? How do scientists justify this tension between difference and sameness?

Animals must be de-animalized, just as they are in modern agriculture, in order to justify all the things that are done to them in the lab. This is one reason, after all, that lab animal suppliers often don't use the term "animal" at all. The creatures who they sell are "research models." Models are not animals, and they certainly are not *specific* animals. And the distance must increase between researcher and animal to make the use of these animals acceptable.

Both biologist Lynda Birke and psychologist Kenneth Shapiro have discussed the animal/not animal dichotomy that is so prevalent in scientific thinking today.[104] Rats, who the public typically thought of as carriers of filth, first appeared in labs "from the wild" at the turn of the twentieth century. Researchers now use thousands of strains of rats for specific scientific purposes, moving them further away from any type of wild animal. Laboratory rats no longer represent disease, but the scientific progress against disease, a marvel of symbolic inversion. On the other hand, in order to justify the continuing research on millions of rodents each year, the public still needs to feel some abhorrence or ambivalence toward them. Our feelings for dogs and primates make using them for research more problematic. It is a narrow linguistic and conceptual rope that scientists and the public walk—moving back and forth between rat as animal and rat as scientific tool—but it is necessary in order to win the war of public sympathy.

While these different characterizations of the rat perfectly capture the public's ambivalence toward animal research and the work that scientists must do to alleviate that concern, rats are not the only animals who researchers de-animalize. Kenneth Shapiro also points out that animals are de-specified as well: they no longer represent their own species, but instead represent ours.[105] Rat no. 29474B is no longer a rat at all, or even an animal, but a human simulacrum. In order to justify using a rat—a species that split off from the human evolutionary line 87 million years ago—to mimic human biological functions, the rat can no longer be a rat at all.

Scientists, when referring to lab animals and scientific procedures, use a particular kind of language in order to create a distance between animal and researcher, object and subject. In the past and even sometimes today, animals in labs were not killed—they were "sacrificed." Animals in labs don't have names. They have numbers. They don't act, choose, or play a role in what happens to them. They are acted *upon*. In short, in the language of science, animals are objects and never subjects of their own lives. If they were granted subjectivity, it would be much more difficult to experiment on them—not because scientists are animal haters or lack compassion. After all, many scientists and laboratory workers have companion animals at home. But *those* animals are seen as individuals and are treated as such; it is only the animals in the lab who must be objectified. Scientists have been trained to be objective, above all, so treating their animal models with the same attention or concern provided to their companions would interfere with the work.[106]

Animals are de-individualized—simply members of groups of faceless, replaceable, nameless animals "sacrificed" each year. For animals such as inbred mice or rats who look virtually identical and who may not express suffering as visibly as other animals, the process of de-individualizing is even easier. And for many research models, what is important isn't even the animal but the anatomical part of the animal that is the focus of the research.

Lab Animal Workers

We've seen who benefits from animal research and who suffers from it. But there is another side to suffering in the industry: the laboratory workers who care for, and often have to kill, animals used in research. A number of recent studies have examined the stress experienced by workers who have to kill animals as part of their jobs, including shelter employees, laboratory workers, and veterinarians. These studies show that significant numbers of workers experience "perpetration-induced traumatic stress," or "moral stress," related to the killing of animals in their care. Sociologist Arnold Arluke calls this the "caring-killing paradox," in which many people who are drawn to work involving animals paradoxically also must participate in the animals' deaths.[107] Depression, substance abuse, and high blood pressure are a few of the health issues that some of these workers suffer.[108] In another study, Arluke found that while many laboratory technicians ended up in their occupations simply to make money or as a stepping-stone to another job, many others were attracted to the work because of their love of animals.[109] Not surprisingly, those who saw their work as just a job also saw animals as just part of their work, and in many cases, they viewed animals quite negatively. They specifically hated the way that the monkeys displayed their antipathy toward their treatment and conditions—by screaming, pulling, grabbing, fighting, and biting. It shouldn't surprise us to find out that these workers were unmoved by the death or suffering of the animals, and they did little to improve the well-being of their animals. Workers who took their jobs because of their affinity for animals, on the other hand, developed relationships with animals, spent their free time with them, advocated on behalf of them, and, because of their strong attachments to them, suffered greatly when they suffered or were killed.

Other researchers and workers are known to cope with the unsettling aspects of their work by compartmentalizing, or separating their scientific and commonsense responses to animals, which allows them to go home to their dog without feeling bad about what they just did to the dogs at the lab.[110] In a recent *Nature* study, one interviewed researcher asked, "How do you keep caring for the animals without

---

Tulip and "the Girls"

Until I became responsible for the husbandry needs of thousands of rodents, I had never known a rat or a mouse. As an undercover investigator for an international animal protection organization, I worked in the thick of the transgenic rodent "revolution" at the University of North Carolina at Chapel Hill (UNC). The Thurston-Bowles Building, where I was employed as a laboratory animal technician, was merely one of twelve animal buildings on UNC's campus, and it had approximately fifteen rooms housing racks upon racks of rows upon rows of Plexiglas shoebox cages filled with rats and mice.

I hate to admit it, but when I first learned that I would be working with rats and mice, I felt relieved, as I believed that seeing these species experimented upon would somehow be less upsetting than working with so-called higher species, like dogs, cats, or primates. I could not have been more wrong. I was surprised to discover that rats and mice have personalities every bit as unique as any of the dogs or cats we have at home, and that they are just as capable of suffering from hopelessness, stress, and pain.

In the six months that I worked undercover at UNC, I witnessed immense suffering. Using a hidden camera, I documented the following (and much more) on videotape: cages so severely overcrowded that animals died from suffocation; injured but live mice in the "Dead Animal Cooler," forced to eat the remains of others in order to survive; the slow deaths of rats in "binge drinking experiments," so that researchers could learn that binge drinking causes brain damage; animals denied veterinary care and euthanasia even with severe pain-causing injuries and illnesses; and experiments in which researchers used household scissors to cut the heads off of fully conscious baby rats, because skipping anesthesia saves time.

One day, soon after I began working in the lab, I told an experimenter that if she ever had mice who were healthy but had to be killed because they were not useful to her lab, I would be happy to adopt them. She motioned to a dozen cages housing nearly a hundred mice who were slated to be killed in the gas chamber that afternoon and told me to take my pick. I felt terribly guilty as I chose ten mice—all females, so they would not breed—to take home and treat like queens, knowing that the other mice had been born only to be killed.

The experimenter explained that her lab had injected the embryos of pregnant mice with a jellyfish gene, and that after the babies were delivered and weaned, she looked at them under a black light—if the mice glowed in the dark, the jellyfish gene had taken effect, and the mice had the genetic makeup necessary for her lab's experiments. If the mice did not glow, well, they were throwaways. The Girls, as I came to call my adopted mice, did not glow in the dark.

Lily, Iris, Daisy, Tulip, Petunia, Violet, and their sisters lived long, happy lives with me. They spent endless hours playing in their hammocks, igloos, and coconut cabanas in large cages and foraged for foods they had never seen before. Spinach, oats, apples, seeds, and nuts were staples, but they also ate a little bit of everything I had for dinner, with avocado (vegetarian) sushi being their all-time favorite.

I was amazed by the elephant-sized personalities of these tiny animals. Tulip, who was named for her bulbous figure, was used as a breeder in the lab and, as a result, she was the nurturing mother figure of the group. Like any good mother, Tulip kept the Girls in line, resulting in her nickname: Field Commander Turlington, Tulip. Petunia, a petite black mouse who was the most outgoing of the Girls, answered to her name and loved to ride around on my shoulder as I did housework. She was fearless and often came nose to nose with my dog without even flinching. Iris, a white mouse with a twin sister named Lily, liked to sit in my lap while I watched television at night.

Being the guardian of these tiny angels—and all that they represented to me—was very special after the horrors I witnessed in the lab, and I am so grateful I was given the opportunity to give them a loving "second life."

Story by Kate Turlington

being scorched by the fact that you are using them up?" Another one admitted, "Whenever you talk about the research, the stock answer is to say that we are curing cancer or saving premature babies. You don't talk about finding out what a bit of the brain does just because you are quite curious to know." [111]

Some researchers and research technicians definitely feel something for the animals used in research. In 1993, the University of Guelph in Canada held a unique memorial service to commemorate and honor the animals used in research, and the school has held similar events in subsequent years. And while other universities and even private animal testing or research facilities have since created their own memorials to the animals used at those facilities, most animal research institutes do not openly or otherwise acknowledge the lives or deaths of the millions of animals used annually.[112] There is no doubt that these types of tributes provide some satisfaction and an alleviation of some guilt for the workers who participate in them. Yet, ultimately, they provide a nice justification for biomedical research by asserting to the workers, students, and even the public that animals have made a great contribution to science—a contribution that, the argument goes, humans could surely not live without.

Tulip, rescued from a university animal lab, enjoys playing with her other mouse friends. (Photo by Tal Ronnen)

CONCLUSION: WHERE TO DRAW THE LINE?

Animal protection advocates are often accused of picking the most egregious of animal experiments to attract public sympathy (cases, by the way, that are easy to find by perusing any medical journal), in which animals are poisoned, electrocuted, intentionally crippled, and worse. But the medical research lobby engages in the same practices, highlighting the lifesaving drugs and procedures that have alleviated suffering, particularly for children, and downplaying all of the animals and money wasted on useless research.

That is why it is helpful to direct some of our attention toward the tens of billions of dollars spent annually in the United States alone on research that is neither essential, nor lifesaving, nor even new, but is commercially driven and motivated primarily by an interest in grant money for the researchers, income for the university, and/or profits for the affiliated industries. Four hundred thousand people die in this country every year from the effects of tobacco, yet researchers are still testing the effects on tobacco on animals, and companies like Phillip Morris use animals to test the toxicity of new cigarette products on health. Do we *need* a new, slightly less toxic but still poisonous cigarette?

It is clear that product testing no longer has to take place on animals given the alternatives developed in recent years, that dissection is not necessary in high school or even in medical and veterinary schools, and that much of medical experimentation could be eliminated by using existing and developing alternatives. So what is the problem? Why is there still such opposition to moving in this direction?

Some good for human and animal health has come from medical testing on animals. But it also must be acknowledged that even more good could come from tests on live human subjects, but this is never a reason to start doing this without consent. In fact, one of the rules governing the use of humans in any sort of experimental protocol is not only that the human subject must give informed consent and that the study must not just benefit humans in general, but there must be also some demonstrable benefit to *that* human in particular. Not only do animals not benefit from most of animal research and testing, but the individual animals whose lives are lost receive nothing positive in exchange.

Why do so many people feel that if we do *not* test on animals, we are letting people suffer and die from preventable or curable diseases? Philosopher Katherine Perlo writes: "You would not be accused of 'letting your child die' because you had refrained from killing another child to obtain an organ transplant." In other words, *not* supporting future animal experimentation does not equal letting children die, and it certainly doesn't equal killing them, as animal protection advocates are often accused. Perlo also points out that supporting animal testing and experimentation is the default action, whereas opposing them is seen as the aggressive anomaly, as dangerous as withholding a life-saving drug from a child.[113] Furthermore, just because most people would choose to save one's own child or companion animal over a neighbor's child or animal, this commonsense favoritism should not serve as a basis for social policy.

Matthew Scully, former speechwriter for President George W. Bush and author of *Dominion, the Power of Man, the Suffering of Animals, and the Call to Mercy*, argues that one concern about animal experimentation is that there is a moral continuity between humans and animals and that cruelty to animals will lead "inexorably to cruelty to humanity."[114] The easier it is for us to kill animals, according to Scully, the easier it is for us to move toward the killing of people who are considered expendable.

We think it works both ways: killing desensitizes us to the suffering of others, and it reduces our empathy or ability to feel the pain of others. Whether we are killing strangers in foreign wars to protect our interests or we are killing animals by the millions for research, the result is the same: an acceptance of suffering and death, as long as we think that there may be a benefit to us.

An end to the use of animals in product testing, military experiments, and education is a good goal. Even ultimately ending the use of animals in medical research can be achieved without sacrificing the lives of countless human (and animal) victims to illnesses or suffering. It is naive to suggest that this could or would happen overnight, but as a start, the government and the scientific community should develop and implement technologies and procedures as soon as possible to replace the use of all animals in our laboratories. Congress has already passed two pieces of legislation that express intent to develop alternatives: in 1993, Congress amended the Public Health Service Act to direct the NIH to conduct or support research that reduces, refines, or replaces animal tests. In 2000 Congress passed the ICCVAM Authorization Act that established ICCVAM as a permanent committee comprised of representatives of fifteen federal agencies. The committee's purpose is to develop recommendations, guidelines, and regulations that promote acceptance of toxicological tests that reduce, refine, or replace animal tests.

Most animal researchers, government labs, and private corporations that use animals maintain that they are committed to the Three R's: refinement, reduction, and replacement. But this "commitment" has not translated into many concrete changes; the profits to be made by animal research suppliers are simply too great. For others, changing methodologies and creating new procedures takes time and work, and without a strong incentive to do so, it is just as easy to stick with current methods.

We know, though, that with a real commitment from the scientific community, these changes can and will happen, without jeopardizing the health of our citizens. We also know that Americans overwhelmingly want to see us move away from a dependence on animal research and have been saying so for years. All it takes is a commitment.

What You Can Do

The following are a number of ways that readers can reduce the use of animals in medical research, education, and product testing.

- Buy products not tested on animals. Support companies that no longer test their products on animals by shopping exclusively for products from those companies. Send a message to those that still test by no longer buying their products. Every major anti-vivisection organization as well as many of the national animal protection organizations offer free brochures listing companies that do not test on animals.
- Educate your friends and family. Tell others about how easy it is for individuals to stop animal testing through smart shopping choices.
- Fight dissection in schools. If you are a parent, teacher, or student, you can find out whether your state offers alternatives to dissection, and you can promote those alternatives. If your state does not offer alternatives, or if you need help finding out about what alternatives are available, contact Animalearn at www .animalearn.org. This organization offers a huge amount of information and even has a lending library of items to use in the classroom.
- Donate to charities that don't fund animal research. If you want to support causes that help people who suffer from diseases such as AIDS or breast cancer, there are many charities that either conduct nonanimal research on those diseases or provide services to people living with the disease. To find out which charities don't support animal experimentation, visit www.humaneseal.org.
- Consider donating the body of a deceased companion animal to an Educational Memorial Program. Increasingly popular in veterinary schools, these programs teach anatomy, surgical methods, and more. They provide a humane, effective alternative to using live animals. For more information, visit www .educationalmemorial.org.
- Tell your congressional representative that you want to see legislation that calls for the reduction and replacement of animals in laboratories.

Chapter 1

THE PET INDUSTRY

Animals as Family

Pets provide us with unconditional love and affection. It makes
people feel good to be able to provide something for them in return.[1]
—Bob Vetere, American Pet Product
Manufacturers Association

A man who killed and charred his ex-girlfriend's cat was given six
months in jail and four years probation, with a condition he doesn't
own pets during those four years.[2]
—*Tahoe Daily Tribune*

INTRODUCTION

O f all the ways that humans use animals in modern society, the
treatment of animals as pets is seemingly the most benign. For
many domestic animals, this is certainly the case, and for many Americans, companion animals are a beloved part of the family. Indeed, more
Americans (63 percent, or 71 million households) live with a companion
animal than have children of their own. Americans spent $40.8 billion in

2006 on food, toys, clothing, travel paraphernalia, and more for their animals, and they spent even more on traveling with them, taking them to parks, special gyms, spas, and even luxury hotels.[3]

But for many millions of other dogs, cats, birds, rabbits, and other animals, life as pets or as animals involved in the pet industry is far from a life of luxury. From the factorylike conditions of many animal mills, to the horrors of unregulated transportation across the country and living in a pet store at the mercy of untrained store employees until their eventual sale to unscreened customers, young animals are at the mercy of people whose only concern is profit. Even after being purchased, many animals continue to suffer at the hands of their new "owners": living outside in all kinds of weather or permanently imprisoned in a cage or fishbowl, serving as guard dogs at the end of a chain, receiving little or no medical care, having no human or animal companionship, and far worse. For millions, life as a pet ends when the family decides they can no longer keep him and brings him to the local animal shelter to be, in many cases, euthanized. Tragically, this is the most merciful fate for many animals; thousands of other companions endure abandonment, being sold to laboratories, fighting in blood sports, or suffering other grisly fates.

If domestic animals like dogs and cats are those animals who receive, relatively speaking, the best care and treatment of any animals in modern society, how can we treat them so poorly? How can we simultaneously lavish extraordinary amounts of love, money, and care on our beloved companion animals, yet, at the same time, allow millions of those same animals to suffer and die?

That is the irony of the American pet industry. There is no doubt that the companion animal relationship can be one of the richest, most fulfilling ways that humans and animals can interact, bringing huge benefits to both person and animal. Yet the "production" of those animals, in a world already filled to capacity with domestic animals who either have no home or are living lives of abuse or neglect, is often driven by profit rather than concern for animal welfare. And this is one of the complex challenges that the animal protection movement faces: how to correct the gross injustices in the pet industry while still allowing for the possibility of the human–companion animal relationship?

THE PET INDUSTRY

The pet industry in the United States is a multibillion dollar industry. According to the American Pet Product Manufacturing Association (APPMA), Americans spent $2.1 billion purchasing animals during 2006—but this figure does not include the amounts earned by breeders who sell to pet stores or directly to the public, dealers who transport pets from breeders to pet stores, and others in the industry who profit from the sale of live animals. This adds up to more than 382 million dogs, cats, fish, birds, rabbits, reptiles, and other animals.[4] Industry groups like APPMA, the Pet Industry Joint Advisory Council, and specialty organizations like the American Kennel Club, the American Rabbit Breeders Association, the Cat Fanciers' Association, the National Pet Alliance, and the National Alternative Pet Association have a vested interest in ensuring that Americans continue to buy rather than adopt animals. They fight legislation that restricts the breeding, showing, or sale of purebred animals, as well as spay/neuter legislation aimed at halting the numbers of animals euthanized in our nation's shelters. This well-funded industry even fights legislation requiring that pet stores provide care information when selling an animal; after all, if pet stores provided that information, many people simply would not buy an animal once they saw how much work might be involved in caring for him.[5]

Thanks to the work of national animal protection organizations as well as the thousands of local humane associations and animal rescue groups, many Americans now realize that they can adopt rather than buy or breed companion animals, thus saving animals' lives as well as enriching their own. Because of these efforts, the pet industry has suffered financially. According to *Pet Age Magazine*, the percentage of pet stores selling live animals—36 percent in 2005—dropped to its lowest point since the magazine began collecting statistics, and it dropped 9 percent from the previous year. In addition, the sale of animals made up just 10 percent of pet store profits that same year (compared to 11 percent in 2003, 13 percent in 2002, and 17 percent in 2001), while profit margins on live animal sales have been steadily slipping as well.[6] But the pet industry remains a multibillion-dollar industry, and it will continue to ensure that breeders, dealers, and pet stores can continue to traffic in live animals without interference from government or animal welfare organizations.

In fact, the pet industry sees animal welfare organizations as its biggest enemy, spending millions of dollars fighting legislation aimed at improving the lives of domestic animals and attacking animal protection efforts for their infringement upon animal breeders' "rights." For instance, the Cat Fanciers' Association provides information on grassroots lobbying on its Web site in order to combat the "animal rights legislation that would severely limit the responsible breeding and showing of animals."[7] The American Kennel Club's position statements on breeding restrictions and population control emphasize the right of "responsible" breeders to continue to breed their animals as they see fit, unfettered by laws or by the interference of animal protection groups. The American Rabbit Breeders Association goes further in its position on the protection of its members' right to breed rabbits for any purpose—as companion animals, meat, fur, or for research. Its Web site even includes a page of listings of rabbit meat processors, including the processors' per-pound prices for "fryers." And the umbrella group for the entire pet industry, the Pet Industry Joint Advisory Council, in its position statement on puppy mills, blames animal welfare organizations for maligning the industry through their "inaccurate" and "misleading" focus on puppy mill puppies and reaffirms its position that pet stores are a legitimate source for the public to buy puppies.[8]

Other organizations protect the rights of "pet owners" rather than the industry at large. One such organization, the National Pet Alliance, works to "protect the rights of responsible pet owners" and fights "coercive legislation" such as mandatory spay/neuter laws (although they do support the sterilization of shelter dogs and cats).[9] The American Dog Owners Association works to "promote, protect, and defend responsible dog ownership."[10] Finally, the National Animal Interest Alliance opposes nearly all animal protection laws, including sterilization laws, prohibitions on keeping exotic animals as pets, and all other laws that "restrict the rights of responsible owners while doing little to enhance the well-being of the community or the animals covered."[11] What all of these groups have in common is a uniquely American focus on the "rights" of either an industry (animal breeders) or a class of people (animal "owners") to keep, breed, or use animals as they see fit, as long as it is "responsible" as defined by that organization. This argument speaks to the American love of individual freedoms while assuring us at the same time that, through the industry's voluntary compliance with a set of standards that they themselves have created, the animals' well-being will be ensured. But not a single pet industry group puts the rights of animals to live without harm or exploitation on the same level with the industry's right to exploit them. It is this distinction between industry groups and the animal protection groups that oppose them—the rights of the industry to maximize profits versus the rights of the animal to live without suffering—that result, in many ways, in the various forms of exploitation that follow in this chapter.

THE BREEDING AND SALE OF COMPANION ANIMALS

Domestic animals, including companion animals, are the result of controlled breeding for human purposes, a process that goes back many thousands of years. This process has shaped everything from the size, shape, and color of the animals who live with us to their temperaments and even their relationships with us. Because the purpose of breeding animals always has been to fill human needs rather than for the benefit of the animal, and because of the abusive conditions in which animal breeding often occurs (both in the pet industry as well as animal agribusiness), some critics have made a comparison between the breeding of animals and the forced breeding or rape of humans under the conditions of slavery, genocide, or imprisonment.[12] A look at the conditions in which animals are bred for the pet industry in this country may shed some light on these uncomfortable analogies.

Breeding Facilities

Most Americans are by now aware of the term "puppy mill," thanks to the work of a number of national and local animal protection organizations as well as media investigations conducted by national newspapers, magazines such as the *Atlantic Monthly*, and television shows such as *Dateline* and *Hard Copy*. Puppy mills are large, usually filthy facilities that are typically found in rural areas, where puppies are bred in large numbers and usually sold to pet stores via brokers. Operations that sell directly to the public aren't required to be licensed. Dogs in these facilities spend their entire lives in wire cages or dog runs. They are bred over and over again, producing litter after litter, until they are worn out. These puppies often develop health conditions due to the lack of medical care and proper treatment.

One ASPCA animal cruelty investigator described two particularly callous puppy mill operators who fed dead dogs to other dogs and amputated the leg of a pregnant dog with a handsaw in order to keep her alive long enough to give birth again. The investigator explained, "Most breeders learn how to keep their standards just above violating cruelty statutes, but the conditions are still unacceptable."[13]

Sounds bad, right? Most people would never want to buy a dog, or any other animal for that matter, if they knew they were bred in conditions such as these, and if they knew that their puppy's mother was most likely still living in a cage with no love, no medical care, and no exercise.

The problem with the term "puppy mill," however, is that no breeder identifies their facility as a puppy mill, and no pet store acknowledges that its puppies come from such a place. Any commercial animal breeding facility that grosses more than five hundred dollars per year, has more than three breeding females on the premises, and sells wholesale must have a USDA license and is subject to inspection from APHIS. However, there is a shortage of USDA inspectors—fewer than a hundred for more than 3,500 licensed pet breeders, 1,100 licensed dealers, and transporters, as well as every research facility and animal exhibit in the country. That's a total of more than 9,000 facilities in all. Furthermore, the conditions that the animals live in at licensed facilities must conform to the Animal Welfare Act, but the AWA does not define puppy mills, so inspectors do not seek out such facilities for extra scrutiny.[14] So, it's difficult for most people to know how many such facilities exist and whether the puppies sold at their local pet store, for instance, come from a puppy mill.[15]

Nearly all animals available at US pet stores come from commercial breeding facilities or mills. The HSUS estimates that in the United States, 2 to 4 million dogs are purchased from puppy mills each year.[16] Other types of breeders include hobby, show, backyard breeders, and "accidental" breeders, nearly all of whom are exempt from any federal, or, in most cases, state or local legislation. They typically sell their animals directly to the public via newspaper ads, the Internet, or similar means.

Commercial breeders, whom the USDA classifies as class A dealers, breed dogs, cats, rabbits, and other animals for wholesale trade. Facilities can range in size from small to large, many with more than a thousand animals on the property, and some selling multiple breeds and species of animals. Again, commercial facilities that gross more than five hundred dollars per year must have USDA licensing that complies with the Animal Welfare Act, which includes standards for space per animal, shelter, feeding, water, sanitation, and veterinary care.

Unfortunately, oversight is notoriously lax. Hearts United for Animals (HUA), a Pennsylvania animal welfare group, visited puppy-breeding operations after USDA inspections occurred, armed with the inspection reports for those facilities. HUA volunteers found serious violations in cage conditions, sanitation, and temperature of the kennels, for instance—violations that were not noted on the inspection reports.[17]

Wholesale breeders typically sell their animals to brokers or dealers, who transport them to the pet stores that will ultimately sell the animals. These same individuals also supply labs. Brokers and dealers charge fifty to two hundred dollars for puppies at the wholesale level, with those same puppies being sold at pet stores for anywhere from five hundred to two thousand dollars. Rabbits cost as little as three dollars at the wholesale level and twenty-five to thirty dollars at pet stores.

Conditions at large commercial facilities can range from good to terrible, if one's definition of "good" includes adult animals living in a cage for their entire lives. At the bottom end of the scale, there are hundreds of documented cases of dogs or rabbits living in filthy conditions, with matted fur, sores on legs and feet, various disorders (like parvo, kennel cough, hip dysplasia, deafness, cataracts, epilepsy, glaucoma, and tooth and mouth diseases), and in temperatures ranging from burning summer heat to subzero winter conditions. Some puppy mill dogs are surgically debarked.

Dogs and rabbits in large commercial facilities are routinely bred multiple times throughout the year, until the animals are worn out from so many births. Dogs are typically bred twice a year and can produce litters usually until six or seven years of age; the worse the conditions, the earlier she'll probably stop producing viable litters of substantial size. Other breeders, however, will keep breeding their dogs until the dogs eventually die.[18] A litter a year is the norm for cat breeders, but because cats will come into heat again about two months after their last litter is born, they can be bred more often. In operations focused more on profit, higher frequency litters will be the norm. Once litter frequency slows down, the animals meet their end. Rabbits, due to their famously high fertility, can technically be bred as frequently as twelve times a year, but the norm for most breeders is to breed their females four to six times per year. Rabbits can continue to give birth up until about six years of age, at which point either fertility starts to wane or they succumb to one of a number of reproductive cancers.

One 2006 inspection of a Maryland puppy mill revealed dozens of dogs and puppies crammed into a building with no access to fresh air.

Many dogs were covered with fly-infested open sores, eye infections, and an overpowering odor of urine and feces. Animal control inspectors assumed that the building had not been cleaned in a very long time. Water pans were filled with algae, and at least one pen had a half bushel of dried feces. Sadly, these conditions did not lead to a punishment against the owner of the kennel or even a loss of his license; instead, he was given twenty-four hours to get the dogs to a veterinarian and improve the food, water, and hygiene. Another site visited by inspectors that same week found puppies and dogs living in rabbit hutches, some with ears bloodied from being eaten by flies, others with bloody noses, no shavings or bedding of any kind, and again, no access to fresh air or sunshine, with no evidence of a cleaning for several days.[19] Sadly, while both kennels were licensed by the county, neither were licensed by the USDA.

The Breeding Process

Today, humans control virtually every aspect of the reproductive processes of domestic animals: whom they mate with, how often they mate, under what conditions the mating occurs, whether a mother can raise her own babies, where the offspring go after weaning, or even whether the animal will be permanently sterilized. On the other hand, if we were to give domestic animals, such as dogs or cats, free reign to mate with whomever they please, as often as they please, the overpopulation problem of companion animals would be even worse than it is today. Clearly, if we are to be responsible caretakers of our companions, humans need to exercise some level of control. Of course, the breeding process, as focused as it is on human gain, leaves much to be desired in terms of the treatment of animals.

From the language used to refer to animals used in breeding—"stock," "earning units," "bitches," "queens," "studs," "cocks," "bucks," and so on—it seems clear that the welfare or individuality of the animals is not the primary concern in a breeding operation, and that they are just necessary tools to create an end product.

Breeders choose their breeding "stock" in order to assure that the mothers can regularly produce and nurse a large litter or can produce healthy babies who conform to breed standards. Breeders choose "studs" based on physical attributes, with an eye toward complementing the attributes and correcting the "faults" of the mother. In some breeding operations, the breeder may own both the males and the females, while in others, the breeder will pay another breeder a "stud fee" to access a male's sperm. Stud fees can range for a dog from five hundred to two thousand dollars, and for a cat from one hundred to a thousand dollars, or the cost of a puppy or a kitten from the litter.

Depending on the animal, the male is placed with the female in order to mate; he may remain with her for multiple breeding sessions in order to ensure a pregnancy, but in most cases the breeder removes him after one to three days. In cases where the male is too far away to bring to the female, breeders may use artificial insemination, which involves either vaginally or surgically implanting the collected semen into the female, followed up by ultrasounds to detect pregnancy. As one veterinarian who maintains a Web site for dog breeders says, "Keep in mind that you are looking for a dog/bitch that will improve upon your dog. Think breed standards!"[20]

If this process sounds impersonal (if we were speaking of humans, we would call it dehumanizing), that's because it is. The goal of any breeder is to produce litters that will satisfy the breeder's objectives, whether it be "improving the breed," as hobby and show breeders claim, or making a profit, as is the case for all commercial breeders. The feelings and welfare of the animals in question are not just secondary; they don't factor in at all.

Different animals require different breeding techniques, of course. Rabbits, who are much cheaper to raise than cats or dogs, typically spend their lives in outdoor caged operations, where breeders have both males and females. Rabbit breeders often replace half of their breeding animals every year in order to ensure high production, killing those who are replaced.[21]

The raising of captive birds is a very different operation from the raising of mammals like dogs or cats, and this industry has its own problems. Most captive-raised birds sold in this country are advertised as "hand fed" or "hand raised." This means that after a parrot, for example, has laid a fertile egg, it is taken from the mother and incubated until the baby has hatched. Then the breeder hand raises the baby bird. Because the bird is raised without a mother, the baby develops docile behavior that is markedly different from the natural behavior of a wild animal. Indeed, birds raised by other birds would not end up as tame pets. Other breeders only hand-feed briefly and sell the unweaned babies for the purchaser to "finish off." This increases the breeder's profit margin and allows for a bond to develop between the new caretaker and the baby bird, but it can also cause emotional problems due to the lack of an adult bird role model.[22] Most bird lovers agree that hand raising a bird provides the best chance for creating a tame pet bird, even while it eliminates much of the bird's natural behaviors. A handful of states including Minnesota and California have attempted to prohibit the sale of unweaned birds at pet stores and bird marts. The Pet Industry Joint Advisory Council has opposed these efforts.

One new development in the domestic bird trade has been the development of "bird mills," large-scale bird breeding establishments like Kaytee Preferred Birds, a Florida-based establishment that raises thousands of birds per year in a factory farm–like environment for Petsmart. In addition to the confined, unhealthy conditions, many bird welfare advocates fear that without human socialization, the birds will grow up to be aggressive, adding to the already growing problem of abandoned birds.[23]

Parrot mill birds, whose offspring can sell for up to $2,500 at pet stores, never get to fly or experience anything that a wild macaw, conure, African gray, or Amazon would living in the wild. Instead, they spend years and years in empty wire cages, often with no sunlight or light of any kind and with nothing but a perch to sit on. They have no toys to play with and are not allowed to raise their own young, because the babies must be hand raised in order to fulfill the mandates of the pet parrot industry. Breeders may even leave toys or other distractions out of cages in an attempt to increase breeding.[24] Like other breeder animals, after their prime breeding years are over, worn-out breeder birds are sold or sometimes killed.

Kaytee's response to the bird community's concerns has been predictable. In a series of e-mails sent by Kaytee to bird groups and reprinted by bird behaviorist Sally Blanchard in the *Pet Bird Report*, Kaytee defended the company's practices, saying the birds' health is monitored by veterinarians and that Kaytee's facilities and transportation systems follow the highest standards of care.[25] Kaytee also mentioned that the preweaned chicks are shipped to Petsmart stores, where store clerks hand-feed them and teach customers how to feed the babies—despite the fact that most pet store clerks receive little training in animal care. Kaytee doesn't acknowledge the need for early socialization for birds—a necessity not only for the development and happiness of the bird but also to prevent a flood of birds being dropped back onto the market because their new guardians couldn't deal with their behavior. Because many birds like parrots and macaws live fifty or more years, the fact that there is a growing behavior-related abandonment problem is something that the bird industry should take seriously. According to the Avian Welfare Resource Center, thousands of birds are abandoned every year. As Blanchard states:

> I have been crusading for years to make bird breeders and buyers understand the significance of proper early socialization in the healthy emotional development of parrot chicks. This crusade is not that of "soft heart/soft head animal right's [*sic*] fanatics" but a clear message from thousands of knowledgeable people concerned about the welfare of parrots. The process of early socialization is an essential ingredient in the development of pet potential.[26]

Breeders of dogs, cats, rabbits, and birds routinely "cull" those babies who don't conform to breed standards, have genetic defects, or whom they otherwise deem unacceptable due to health, looks, size, or temperament. Other breeders cull when the litter is too large. Culling can mean selling the leftover offspring for a lower price, but generally it means killing. On the other hand, certain breed standards seem to *demand* the killing of unwanted babies. For instance, the American Boxer Club's code of ethics prohibits the sale by a club member of a boxer with a coat color not conforming to breed standards.[27] Because up to 20 percent of all boxers are born white, this has led to the routine killing of a huge number of white babies (although some members now give them away, a practice that used to be prohibited as well).[28] Other breeds such as Australian Shepherds have similar "defects"; the Australian Shepherd Club of America recommends immediate killing for the 25 percent of all puppies born white, because some may be born blind or deaf.[29]

How do breeders "cull" their animals? The Lop Rabbit Club of America recommended in their 1996 guidebook that breeders cull lop babies by smashing them against the floor and that they kill adults by carbon dioxide poisoning.[30] Some dog breeders ask their veterinarians to euthanize unwanted puppies, but many veterinarians will not euthanize a healthy animal. Even bird breeders cull their unwanted offspring, usually by carbon monoxide poisoning or ether.

For independent breeders, the expenses incurred in carefully breeding an animal can quickly outpace the costs, which can include stud fees, supplies, medicines, vaccinations, food, veterinary costs, registration costs, and of course the cost of the inevitable newborn deaths themselves, which, according to one breeder, average 25 percent per litter.[31] One has to wonder, given these high costs—the economic costs and the mortality costs alike—when will the costs be so high that they will outweigh the benefits?

Dealers and Brokers

Animal brokers, also known as class B dealers, import, buy, sell, or trade animals in the wholesale market. Brokers typically buy animals from breeders and sell them to pet stores. They must be licensed by the USDA to conduct business, and like class A dealers, they are subject to inspection. They ship baby animals by the crateload on airlines or, more commonly, by the truckload. The AWA regulates the conditions under which transportation occurs—animals must be a minimum age, healthy, transported in safe temperature-regulated containers, and picked up promptly upon arrival. But again, oversight is lax. Many animals die during transport (known as "shrinkage") from stress, lack of ventilation, or exposure to hot or freezing temperatures. Their deaths are accepted by the pet industry as a normal, albeit costly, part of doing business.

The Missouri-based Hunte Corporation is the largest broker of puppies in the United States, which sold 85,000 puppies of more than seventy different breeds and made $28 million in profit in 2002.[32] Hunte's public relations material claims that the puppies they purchase and resell are not from puppy mills but from USDA-licensed kennels—a false distinction at best. Furthermore, while Hunte Corporation does not itself run breeding facilities, it does own a number of breeding facilities that have been the subject of numerous complaints over the years. For example, in November of 2003, the Missouri Department of Natural Resources investigated Sunrise Puppies, a breeding kennel owned by Hunte. The department found ponds that were contaminated by the dead animals buried in trenches on the property.[33]

Given the fact that less than one hundred USDA/APHIS inspectors are responsible for inspecting more than nine thousand facilities of all kinds in this country, it's not surprising that problems like this escape notice. According to the USDA, inspectors reported 18,275 violations in 2004, covering both class A and class B dealers, with 282,823 animals affected.[34] The greatest number of violations by far involved facility cleanliness; other violations involved feeding, exercise, housing, and veterinary care. How does the USDA deal with these violations? It seldom gives warnings to facilities in violation of the Animal Welfare Act, and it rarely fines them. Facilities that the USDA actually fines ultimately pay only a fraction of the original fine. According to a USDA audit of APHIS, inspectors

. . . do not have the authority, under current legislation, to effectively enforce the requirements of the Animal Welfare Act. For instance, the agency cannot terminate or refuse to renew licenses or registrations in cases where serious or repeat violations occur (such as the use of animals in unnecessary experiments, or failure to treat diseases or wounds). In addition, APHIS cannot assess monetary penalties for violations unless the violator agrees to pay them, and penalties are often so low that violators merely regard them as part of the cost of doing business.[35]

Those in the animal business whose profits hinge upon producing, selling, or transporting the maximum number of animals at the lowest possible cost are certainly lucky that APHIS inspectors are as overworked, underfunded, and powerless as they are.

Pet Stores

Contrary to what most pet stores tell their customers about where they buy their puppies, birds, kittens, bunnies, and other small animals ("Individuals in your local community who breed registered animals and offer occasional litters" is how Petland's corporate Web site puts it), most large pet stores like Petco, Petsmart, and Petland purchase their animals from brokers who purchased the animals from large commercial breeders throughout the country.[36] In order to ensure that the animals are still extremely young at the time they arrive at the pet stores, brokers typically buy animals from breeders well before weaning age. This is another reason for "shrinkage," or the mortality rate among young animals destined for pet stores.

Once at the pet store, animals are dependent on the care of a typically young, untrained, underpaid, and transitory population of store clerks with little incentive to ensure that all animals have fresh water, much less that dead mice are removed from aquariums. Petco, a national pet supply store that sells birds and small animals, is so notorious for the poor care given to its animals that PETA maintained two Web sites that focused on the problems at many of Petco's stores, including one page that listed, by month and by store, every reported case of an animal suffering or dying—fifty cases were recorded in January 2005 alone. (In April 2005, however, Petco acquiesced to PETA's request to stop selling large birds such as parrots, cockatoos, and macaws. In return, PETA ended its "Petno" campaign against the company.)[37]

While some pet stores pay veterinarians to treat sick store animals, many stores do not. Employees routinely leave smaller animals like mice, fish, and rats to die, or they kill them, since the cost of those animals is too low to warrant any additional expenditures. On top of the obvious profit motive operating to prevent animals from getting the best treatment in pet stores, there is very little oversight of individual stores, leaving the animals, once again, under the protection of untrained workers. The federal Animal Welfare Act does not cover animals in pet stores unless the store sells exotic animals or resells animals to research facilities. It is up to the states or municipalities to provide something other than the industry's "voluntary standards," yet only twenty-six states and the District of Columbia provide any kind of protection at all.[38]

As mentioned earlier in this chapter, California is one state that requires pet stores to provide written care information with the animals they sell, but because of pet industry lobbying, stores only need to provide class-specific care instructions. As an example, instructions for macaws and parakeets—two very different animals with different needs—are the same. California is a minority in even this level of attention. Most states do not require that pet stores provide any information with the sale of an animal, and indeed, a customer is lucky to receive anything at all.

On the other hand, there are a couple of bills pending in state legislatures, that, if passed, would provide a much greater level of care for animals in pet stores than anywhere else in the country. For instance, there are bills pending in Massachusetts, Oregon, New Jersey, and Florida that would protect animals in a variety of ways, such as by providing for state inspections of pet stores, mandating veterinary care, establishing a hotline for reporting sick animals at pet stores, and mandating disclosure of breeder information to consumers. An Illinois bill passed in 2003 requires that pet stores provide a stimulating environment for animals, veterinary care, proper food, and sanitary conditions. A similar California bill would have established new procedures for caring for animals in pet stores, protected animals from abuse and neglect in pet stores, and placed limitations on the sale of certain animals. The governor vetoed it after heavy lobbying by the Pet Industry Joint Advisory Council and Petco.

The lack of customer education, combined with the total lack of purchaser screening, means that anyone can go into a pet store in any state and buy any animal they want, for any purpose, with no accountability whatsoever. Providing accountability, whether through screening before sales or carefully providing appropriate instructions with an animal, would reduce store profits.

The sale of all animals only accounted for an average of 10 percent of all pet store sales in 2005, and the percentage of pet supply stores not selling animals at all rose to 55 percent in that same year, an 11 percent increase over 2004.[39] Yet, for those stores that sell animals, puppies still represent a cash cow. In fact, the sale of puppies can account for as much as 70 percent of a pet store's profits in a given month because of the high prices that stores can charge. The Hunte Corporation encourages stores to carry the largest number of puppies they can hold; the more puppies they carry, the more they can sell.[40]

While large chains like Petland and countless smaller stores around the country continue to sell puppies, and most other chains still sell birds, reptiles, fish, or other small animals, the trend among retailers is to not sell animals. Since Pet Age began surveying stores in 2000, the percentage of sales attributed to live animal sales has dropped by 8 percent.[41] The industry attributes this trend to changes in market conditions and changes in consumer perceptions of animal sales, as well as to the influence of animal protection advocates.[42]

Pet Shows

Pet shows play an important part in the exploitation of companion animals, through their focus on purebreds with the resulting emphasis on breed standards and breeding. Dog, cat, and rabbit shows are sponsored by the major breed organizations, such as the American Kennel Club, the Cat Fanciers' Association, and the American Rabbit Breeders Association. These events promote the supposed benefits of breeding purebred animals. Mixed-breed animals or cosmetically imperfect animals are largely ignored. Additionally, competitive animal shows are sporting events of a kind, with animal entrants competing against each other to be the best in a category or class. For instance, the Westminster Kennel Club Dog Show, the oldest dog show in the United States, bills itself as "dedicated to the *sport* of purebred dogs" (emphasis is ours). In order to feed this relentless quest for perfection, breeders must continuously breed more and more "perfect" animals, which ultimately leads to the killing of countless others. For every grand champion, countless dogs or cats with incorrect colors, ears that aren't perky enough, or hair that is not silky enough are sold as pets or sometimes killed.

The increasing reliance on cosmetic surgery for dogs is another result of the focus on breed perfection. Certain breeds of dogs require, in order to conform to standards, docked tails (Australian shepherd, rottweiler, fox terrier, corgi, poodle, and schipperke) cropped ears (Great Dane and American pit bull terrier), or both (boxer, Doberman pinscher, miniature pinscher, and schnauzer). According to the American Kennel Club (AKC), these standards are "are acceptable practices integral to defining and preserving breed character and/or enhancing good health."[43] A veterinarian normally performs both ear cropping and tail docking a few weeks after birth. Although veterinarians did not provide pain medication for years, and some still do not, it is much more common today. Some veterinarians refuse to crop ears or dock tails altogether. On the other hand, some breeders continue to perform these surgeries themselves, sometimes using rubber bands for tail docking, which can result in infection and considerable pain.[44] Contrary to the AKC's claims, the historical reasons for tail docking (to keep working dogs' tails safe and clean while hunting) and ear cropping (to make certain dogs look more vicious and to protect ears of fighting dogs) are not valid today, and they are certainly not necessary for health reasons. Some dog behaviorists also worry that because dogs use their tails to communicate with other dogs, tail docking puts them at a disadvantage when socializing and may interfere with physical functions such as maintaining stability as well.[45]

Because of these concerns, a number of countries like Sweden, Norway, Switzerland, and Germany have now banned or restricted the procedures. As of this writing, Vermont's Senate passed a bill to ban ear cropping (and the House is set to consider it in 2007). California's proposed bill was stalled by the state's appropriations committee in 2005. The proposed ban has the support of the California Veterinary Medical Association and Association of Veterinarians for Animal Rights. The AKC opposes the bill because, according to an AKC spokesperson, it would be the first step toward "allowing the government to have more and more control over how responsible owners keep and enjoy their dogs."[46]

Finances behind the Industry

The pet industry is big business. Petco, with more than eight hundred stores, reported net sales of $541.5 million for the fourth quarter of 2005, up 10 percent from the previous year, and Petsmart reported net sales of $1 billion for the first quarter of 2006, up 10.7 percent from the previous year.[47] The puppy industry in Missouri alone is worth $40 million a year, while the industry in just one county in Pennsylvania is valued at about $4 million per year.[48]

While fewer pet supply stores sell animals now than at any time in the past, retailers that continue to sell animals are thriving. We've seen how breeders, dealers, and pet stores put profits above the welfare of animals in order to achieve these numbers. As large corporations continue to buy their animals—even birds—from large commercial kennels, costs can be curtailed, bringing up the bottom line. As smaller stores see the benefits that result from putting profits above welfare, they will buy their parrots, for example, from large commercial operations in order to compete.

But it's not just frugal business practices that produce such success. The government supports the pet industry through tax dollars and favorable legislation. Pet industry lobbying groups, as well as individuals associated with the largest pet stores, dealers, and breeders, contribute generously to a variety of federal, state, and local campaigns in order to assure industry-friendly legislation and, primarily, lack of oversight.

One example of the pet industry's ability to influence legislation was the Puppy Protection Act of 2002, which appeared as an amendment in that year's federal agriculture bill. The act would have provided for better standards of care and socialization for puppies bred in large commercial establishments. The American Kennel Club, the National Animal Interest Alliance, and the American Veterinary Medical Association opposed the bill. Due to a concerted effort by these groups, lawmakers stripped out the amendment and killed the act.

Another way that the pet industry benefits from a cozy relationship with our legislators is through government-sponsored loans. For example, the Hunte Corporation benefited from two USDA Rural Development loans, which totaled almost $4 million in 2000 and 2001,[49] both years that the USDA was responsible for inspecting Hunte's and its subsidiaries' facilities.

OVERPOPULATION

It is indisputable that there are legions of unwanted dogs, cats, and other animals who perish in our nation's shelters every year. According to the Humane Society of the United States, of the 6 to 8 million dogs and cats who enter animal shelters in this country every year, only 3 to 5 percent of cats and 25 to 30 percent of dogs are returned to their homes, and about half of all shelter animals are euthanized.[50] Most shelters do not keep statistics on the number of other abandoned or euthanized animals. In addition to these millions of animals, countless thousands of other loose and stray animals die from starvation, disease, or traffic accidents.

The loss of life and the suffering that this entails is enormous. The cost to taxpayers is also substantial. It costs taxpayers about $105 for an animal control officer to pick up a stray dog or cat, transport the animal to the shelter, provide food and water for the animal, euthanize the animal if not adopted or reunited with his family, and send the body to the landfill.[51] Animal control programs in this country alone cost $2 billion per year, and this does not count the millions that independent animal organizations spend to rescue and "re-home" animals.

Whether shelters euthanize 1 million or 15 million healthy former pets each year is not the point; the point is that any healthy animal who dies because there is no home for him is one animal too much. On that, most people who work with domestic animals, either through rescue, through breeding, or through other means, seem to agree. What the various stakeholders in the debate do not agree on, however, is who is to blame for the tragedy of animal overpopulation, and what can be done to stop it.

Breeders vs. Rescue Organizations

Rescue organizations and animal shelters that work on the front lines rescuing abandoned and unwanted animals collectively spend millions of dollars per year on everything from spaying/neutering and other medical costs, food and other animal maintenance costs, staff, and the countless other expenses involved in running an organization. While some organizations can afford to pay their staff members salaries, many cannot—they are staffed mostly or entirely by volunteers, who themselves fund a great deal of the work. Not surprisingly, rescuers and those involved with animal shelters and other welfare organizations see themselves fighting to save animals against a never-ending tide of breeders who breed too many animals, pet stores that sell animals to the public with no screening or education, and the general public that abandons animals. No matter how hard rescuers and animal advocates work, the animals just seem to keep coming, with no end in sight.

The breeders, pet stores, and pet industry groups, not surprisingly, have another take. The American Kennel Club, for example, says that the overpopulation problem is the result of irresponsible breeding and marketing, and owners who are unwilling to train and care for their animals—yet the AKC is against all restrictions on breeding. The Rabbit Education Society, a rabbit breeder advocacy group, does not recognize the term "overpopulation" as it applies to rabbits and places the responsibility on people who do not keep their animals. The Cat Fanciers' Association also contends that there is no overpopulation problem; the reason animals are euthanized is because of faulty shelter policies rather than too many animals.[52]

But the most common refrain is this: the problem with too many unwanted animals is not the production of those animals. It is that "irresponsible breeders" will sell animals without the proper education, combined with the fact that the public is not educated nor committed to training and keeping its animals.

Yet, if the problem lies squarely with the public and with "irresponsible" breeders, why do the breeder organizations and industry lobbying groups fight any attempt to either regulate breeders or to provide better education to the public? As we have seen, breeders and industry groups fight any legislation that would require the public to spay or neuter their animals, even if breeders are allowed special permits or dispensation. Finally, we have seen the industry fight to prevent the education of the public in matters of animal care or the necessity of spay/neuter, as the Pet Industry Joint Advisory Council does regularly. While some breeders like Marshall Pet Products have begun selling neutered and spayed animals in order to counter animal protection advocates' concerns about selling unaltered animals, this does not change the fact that the industry as a whole is still heavily opposed to spaying and neutering. Petland, for instance, filed a lawsuit in 2005 against the city of Athens, Ohio, to protest a 2004 law mandating that all dogs and cats older than six months must be spayed or neutered before being sold.[53] In 2004 the Pet Industry Joint Advisory Council helped defeat a California bill that would have prohibited the sale of unaltered (unneutered or unspayed) cats and dogs throughout the state. It's difficult to reconcile the public positions of many of these groups with the reality of their actions. While many say they care about the problem of unwanted animals being killed, their educational and lobbying dollars are spent fighting any attempts to solve the problem.

Solving the Problem

Animal welfare groups have attempted to solve the problem, either on a national level or in their own communities. Most welfare organizations agree that the problem is twofold: the continuous breeding and selling of animals when there are not enough homes for them, and the lack of education and commitment on the part of the general public. Therefore, solutions must include providing easily accessible, affordable sterilization for the general public, supplemented by humane education and breeding legislation.

At the University of California at Davis, the new Shelter Medicine Program is one positive development. It establishes standards for shelter animal care, trains veterinarians to provide shelter care, and works on solving some of the problems that bring animals into shelters in the first place, such as lack of spay/neuter and lack of awareness about animal behavior.[54]

Because the pet industry targets the general public as the consumers of their "products" (animals), the animal welfare community also must target the public in order to counteract the industry's misleading and harmful messages: purebred animals are best; rabbits and other small animals are easy "starter animals" and ideal for children; birds, rabbits, and other animals are happy living in cages for their entire lives; dogs can happily live outside in a backyard; birds can be inexpensively fed on a diet of seeds; or wild animals like snakes and iguanas are appropriate pets.

Informing the public that animals are a lifelong commitment—that they are intelligent, curious, sensitive creatures who depend on humans for their survival and happiness, and that people should never purchase animals on a whim or for a child—is a full-time job, especially in light of the dollars behind the industry and the seductive power of its message. When breeders and industry groups use the language of "rights," the message becomes even more powerful: Why shouldn't I have the right to own my own monkey? Why shouldn't I be allowed to keep my dog outside on a chain? Why shouldn't I have the right to breed my animals as often as I want?

The educational message of the animal welfare community is most strongly focused on the central message, however: Domestic animals should be spayed or neutered. This message is as simple as the math behind it. If the breeding of dogs, cats, rabbits, and other animals stops, even temporarily, the supply of domestic animals would dry up, and the epidemic of euthanasia in our nation's shelters would end. A fertile cat and her offspring can produce 420,000 cats over seven years, and a fertile dog and her offspring can produce 67,000 dogs over six years.[55] Still, not only must the solution include education about spay/neuter, but each community must provide affordable, accessible spay/neuter services to everyone. If people with low incomes cannot afford the $50 to $150 that is charged at most veterinary offices for spay/neuter, or if they do not have the means to transport their pet to the veterinarian, they will simply not be able to do it. Spay/neuter cannot be a luxury that only the middle class or the wealthy can afford. Spaying and neutering is a public health issue, like vaccinations, that the community should support: either we pay for the animals to be sterilized, or we pay animal control services to deal with the repercussions. Therefore, legislation must be written to provide funds for low-cost (or no-cost) spay/neuter.

Finally, the pet industry must also be restricted. Legislation is needed to mandate that all animals bred and sold, either by breeders or through pet stores, are spayed or neutered at the time of sale. One such bill was proposed in California, which would have mandated that retailers sell only sterilized cats and dogs; it died in the state legislature in 2004, after heavy lobbying by the Pet Industry Joint Advisory Council.

NEGLECT, ABUSE, AND MISTREATMENT

For most of us, companion animals are part of the family, and we would do anything to protect them. However, millions of other animals are not as fortunate, and cases of cruelty and neglect appear regularly in the news. While many of these high-profile cases attract media attention to a serious problem, the overwhelming majority of suffering animals receive no attention. Tragically, most do not survive, either facing death at the hands of their abusers or euthanasia at a veterinarian's office or an overcrowded shelter.

Of all animals, the majority of reported abuse cases involve companions, yet there are no solid numbers documenting the occurrence of animal cruelty and neglect. A recent Humane Society of the United States study of high-profile cases indicated that 57 percent involved intentional cruelty, and 43 percent involved extreme neglect.[56] The study revealed that the most commonly reported cruelty offenses involved shooting, animal fighting, torturing, and beating. Of neglected animals, 70 percent were malnourished and 30 percent suffered from starvation. Other animals suffered drowning, stabbing, or even being burnt alive.

Forty-two states and the District of Columbia have laws making certain types of animal cruelty felony offenses, thirty-six states prohibit the ownership of an animal for some point after being sentenced for abuse, and twenty-eight states require psychological counseling for certain cruelty offenses. Unfortunately, this means that nine states don't even consider the most heinous cruelty to be a felony, and misdemeanors typically only warrant a sentence of probation with a maximum six-month jail sentence in rare cases or a fine of up to a thousand dollars. Even for felony-level offenses, which can warrant a fine of up to $100,000 or a sentence of up to five years, perpetrators are very rarely prosecuted or sentenced to the fullest extent of the law—but at least these are steps in the right direction.

Hoarding

Although hoarding has only recently received attention as a serious issue, it is a common form of animal cruelty. It differs significantly from other abuse in the attitude and intent of the perpetrator. Hoarding usually involves individuals who do not provide adequate veterinary care, food, or shelter for the large numbers of animals they have collected. In most cases, hoarders believe that they have the animals' best interests in mind, and they cannot understand how their actions cause the animals to suffer—and suffer they do.

Hoarding cases may involve hundreds of animals. Disease, infection, starvation, and even death are commonplace. While a lack of sanitation and proper care contribute to these horrifying conditions for the animals, the psychological effects on the victims can also be tragic. As a result of their serious medical conditions and lack of socialization, many animals have little chance of finding a permanent home, and once rescued, they face euthanasia often at overcrowded shelters.

Journalist Susan Davis explores the complicated issues surrounding hoarding by focusing on a San Francisco Bay Area case that captured national media attention. In this case, a San Francisco woman purchased a home in the suburbs to house her dozen cats, whom she never sterilized because she felt it would have been "traumatic" for them. Within a few years, the population of cats jumped to almost two hundred. When the police finally entered the house, they found a horrific scene: feces, urine, trash, and dying, dead, and decomposed cats.[57] Ultimately, the local humane society removed all the cats from the home and euthanized all but twenty-eight. Sadly, the woman in this case, who authorities reportedly caught hoarding animals twice before, started collecting cats again at her house, as well as at her office.

The factors that make hoarding so complicated are twofold. First, the psychological condition of the hoarders—psychologists categorize it as addiction or obsessive compulsive disorder—leads them to rigorously defend and hide their actions, and it causes most of them to start collecting animals again as soon as they are able.[58] Second, law enforcement and animal control agencies look like the bad guys when they impound the animals, many of whom must be euthanized. Because hoarders truly feel that they are helping animals, even when their animals are actually suffering, the public can sympathize with their behavior. On top of that, there are no state regulations that define hoarding, making the job of arresting and prosecuting hoarders much harder.[59] Ultimately, society needs to take hoarding seriously, and courts must give hoarders strict sentences, including in many cases a ban on future ownership of animals and psychological counseling to ensure that hoarders don't re-offend.

Eileen was neglected and suffered before being rescued with about thirty other rabbits. (Photo by Erin Williams)

Backyard, Chained, and Caged Animals

Another tragic type of neglect is the plight of the "backyard pet," an animal who lives chained or caged outside, isolated from the family and facing health problems, injury, boredom, and behavioral problems. While the most frequently recognized victims are dogs, other animals including cats and rabbits also suffer from this type of neglect.

Many animals who live outside are at risk for injuries and disease. Animals are hit by cars, and encounters with urban wildlife can mean disaster, even for large dogs; conversely, roaming cats and dogs can kill wild birds and other small animals. Heatstroke, heartworms, rabies, and feline AIDS are common conditions for animals who live outside.

Dogs are social animals who need to live indoors with their pack—their human family. Because domestic dogs have been a part of human society for so long, their temperament is in many ways a reflection of their interaction with humans. They are dependent on us to a degree not seen in other animals. Bored and psychologically isolated, backyard dogs can react to stress by developing behavioral issues, including fearfulness, hyperactivity, aggression, excessive chewing, digging, barking, and whining.

Eileen with her friends Opie and Harry. (Photo by Han-Yu Loo)

Eileen

In May 2004, animal control offices and volunteers with House Rabbit Society and East Bay Animal Advocates (EBAA) rescued more than thirty rabbits who had been confined in a backyard in Hayward, California. Volunteers found food bowls that were empty, except for feces, and the available water was filthy, full of algae and waste. All of the rabbits had matted hair and were covered in dirt, urine, and feces. Signs of neglect were everywhere.

The rabbits were confined in an outdoor enclosure with machinery, cans of gasoline, and junk strewn around the property. Survivors were living among a huge number of rotting corpses and body parts. Most of the rabbits were suffering from significant medical problems, including tumors, open sores, shredded or half-eaten ears (from the constant fighting for food), eyes that were completely closed from infection, as well as sexually transmitted illnesses. Their diet consisted of bread, water, and whatever leftover food the homeowners threw to them, and the surviving rabbits had witnessed their babies being killed by neighborhood raccoons.

One of the first rabbits rescued was a filthy white rabbit named Eileen, who Christine Morrissey of EBAA pulled from the backyard. Eileen was pregnant and suffering from the *Encephalitozoon Cuniculi* virus as well as a virulent inner ear infection, which resulted in a head tilt and serious balance problems.

Since Eileen's rescue, she has been adopted by Karen Courtemanche, founder of Harvest Home Animal Sanctuary and the leader of the Hayward, California, rescue. Eileen's hair is now a glossy white, she has put on weight, and best of all, she has a new best friend named Opie. Eileen and Opie, along with Barney the dog, lounge in the kitchen and the breakfast nook throughout the day, and at night, they run through the rest of the house and watch television in the living room with the rest of the family.

Sadly, many domestic rabbits endure the same fate. Most families with rabbits keep them in outdoor cages or hutches. As a result they are susceptible to serious health problems such as heatstroke, mosquito-borne illnesses, painful sores from wire cage bottoms, and even maggot infestation. Like dogs, rabbits are social animals who crave companionship and affection, and their keen intelligence requires stimulation and attention—neither are available for a rabbit living in a backyard cage. Rabbits living loose in a yard are not as bored as caged rabbits, but they are no safer. They fall prey to many of the same conditions afflicting caged outdoor rabbits; they are also vulnerable to attack by domestic and wild animals, and they can easily dig under most fences to escape.

Left in this situation, many outdoor animals wander off or attempt to escape. While some of their efforts result in angry neighbors complaining about noise or property destruction, other situations may be much more serious. Left to run loose, dogs and cats get in fights with other neighborhood animals, contract deadly diseases more easily, and often get hit by cars. Others lose their way and never find home again. Animals who roam outdoors may also fall prey to dogfighting, which is an especially bloody practice. In one Arizona dogfighting case, detectives estimated that 50 percent of the 3,396 animals people reported missing may have been stolen by people involved in dogfighting.[60]

Loose cats and rabbits can quickly form stray, or feral, colonies, which cause a number of problems for the community, and ultimately, for the animals themselves. Cats living in colonies must kill birds and other small animals to survive. Rabbits living in feral colonies can cause environmental damage by grazing on golf courses, retirement communities, or college campuses. The results are almost always the wholesale killing of the rabbits.

Finally, stray animals can be easily stolen by "bunchers," people who collect stray animals to sell to class B animal dealers who resell them to research laboratories.

Tens of thousands of dogs live not just in the backyard for their entire lives, but at the end of a chain. For these dogs, a life spent inside a warm home with love and affection from humans is only a dream. Other dogs, who live chained as "guard dogs," are permanently confined to the yards of businesses like auto repair shops. These social, intelligent animals endure psychological trauma from isolation, emotional deprivation, and boredom. They can even develop repetitive, obsessive behaviors—pacing, tail chasing, and chewing.

They also often suffer physically from their prolonged containment. Animals can develop chronic illnesses as a result of exposure to extreme weather, as well as heatstroke and hypothermia. Dogs who live in confined areas must live among their own feces, which can cause infections as well as maggot infestation. They are also more susceptible to poisoning, as well as electrocution from digging up wiring.

Humans also suffer from keeping dogs outside. Each year, approximately 799,700 people require medical attention for dog bites.[61] Who are the most common animals to bite? Chained, unneutered male dogs. Cases of dogs biting people, especially children, have become more and more common, as children often approach chained dogs to pet or taunt them, and they are bitten and sometimes killed as a result. Chained dogs, due to their lack of human contact, are often unsocialized and aggressive, and they can be violent when approached. This leads to tragic results when they may maul children and are inevitably killed afterward. Groups such as Dogs Deserve Better educate the public about dog chaining and have had a number of legislative successes in municipalities across the country, including helping Connecticut pass the first state bill to ban the chaining of dogs. However, the AKC has opposed state legislation that would restrict or ban the chaining of dogs.[62]

Some states and cities are increasingly banning breeds of dogs that have been deemed dangerous, such as pit bulls, the breed most commonly targeted. While pit bull–type dogs and rottweilers were found to be involved in more than half of all fatal dog bites tracked in a recent nine-year period in the United States, more than twenty-five breeds of dogs have been known to kill a person.[63] Some people feel that if pit bulls are banned, other dogs like Dobermans will instead fall prey to dogfighters and those who breed and train dogs to be vicious. If pit bulls are unavailable, these breeders will simply turn to another easily trained and potentially aggressive dog. The solution instead should be to target those people who breed and sell dogs for fighting, and to strictly monitor or ban instances of dogs living outdoors, as pampered indoor animals rarely will be used for fighting or attack purposes.

Some municipalities have laws banning the chaining of dogs.
(Photo courtesy of People for the Ethical Treatment of Animals)

It is not surprising that chained dogs and dogs who are kept for "protection," fighting, or to intimidate others often spend their lives in inner cities plagued by violence, poverty, and despair, or in rural areas overwhelmed by poverty. Sociologists have shown that violence and poverty are thus correlated: the lower the income in a community, the higher the level of violence. The combination of suburbanization, pollution, decaying infrastructure, loss of jobs, drugs, gangs, and homelessness create a high level of misery for the residents of inner cities—human and nonhuman alike. The plight of rural communities with no means of employment, very few social services, and the highest levels of poverty in the country create similar levels of suffering. Animal welfare advocates and law enforcement officials concerned about problems with vicious dogs should also be aware of these connections while seeking a solution. Rather than just targeting a breed of dog, or even the way that dogs are treated, society should also look at the lack of education and opportunity that allows conditions to deteriorate so badly in many cities and rural areas.

Timber

Timber, a mixed-breed shepherd-malamute with a gentle personality and a love of naps on soft pillows, is a chain survivor. During this sad time in his past, the dog who didn't even have a name lived a solitary life on the end of a chain in a New Mexico backyard, because he dug holes in the grass. Animal advocate Viki Elkey, who lived next door to the lonely dog, visited the neighbor and tried to educate him about the need to walk and play with his dog. Viki tried repeatedly to convince the man that his dog deserved a better life than the one he was living. Sadly, the man continued to let "the black-and-white dog" languish at the end of a chain in an empty back yard.

After another year of boredom and solitude, the dog escaped and arrived at Viki's door with his entire neck ripped open from the chain. Viki called animal control, and an officer responded and brought the dog to a veterinarian to have his neck stitched up. Unfortunately, the dog's owner was allowed to reclaim him, although he was told to keep him off the chain. But the man wrapped the chain around the dog's neck—right on top of the stitches—and tethered him to the ramshackle dog shack. Because he refused to comply with the no-chaining order, the man received a subpoena to appear in court. He was so angry at having to go to court to face a penalty, the man agreed to relinquish the dog—now called Timber—to Viki. Thankfully, relinquishing the dog didn't get him out of trouble—he was at least still required to pay a fine.

Timber needed to make up for all the lost attention. His good-natured soul harbored no ill feelings toward humans, but he wasn't happy being in a backyard during the day, even without a chain. Viki reclaimed him from the rescue group that had placed him. Luckily, Viki's friend Danielle Bays, who had been closely following Timber's story, had just bought a house in Santa Fe with room for another dog and an office where she could work from home.

Timber now lives with Danielle, another dog named Ridley, and three cats. He sleeps on anything he wants, digs in the yard, plays with all the toys that Danielle gives him, and goes to a Santa Fe dog park. The dog park is Timber's favorite place—a large field where dogs run free without leashes is like a dream for a chain survivor. In 2005 Timber won a Milagro Award from Animal Protection of New Mexico for his courage in enduring and then escaping a life of misery, as well as his work since then in educating the public about the tragedy of chaining dogs. He attended the awards banquet, seated comfortably on two padded chairs and acting graciously camera shy as Viki hung the Milagro medallion loosely around his neck.

Timber was lucky enough to find a loving home after enduring a bleak existence at the end of a chain. (Photo by Danielle Bays)

While the plight of chained dogs is gaining attention, there is very little focus on animals who spend their lives in cages or tanks. Most small animals, birds, reptiles, and amphibians who live as companion animals spend much or all of their lives in small cages or tanks of inadequate size. While most people would not tolerate living with a free-running mouse—nor would it be safe for the mouse—there are alternatives to small store-bought cages and tanks. Larger enclosures—either custom made or purchased—provide more adequate living conditions for these animals with complex needs. Bird, reptile, and small animal rescue groups provide resources on how to build or buy sophisticated enclosures that allow the animals to perform their natural behaviors.

The Violence Connection

Law enforcement officials, humane organizations, and scholars have long known of the connection between violence toward animals and violence toward people. Cases of serial killers who started out their careers torturing animals are well documented. We see this especially among young killers, such as school shooters Eric Harris and Dylan Klebold of Littleton, Colorado, and other teenaged killers such as Kip Kinkel, Andrew Golden, Luke Woodham, and Michael Carneal. It has been documented that all of these boys tortured and mutilated animals, including cats, squirrels, cows, and dogs, before they turned their guns on parents, classmates, and teachers. Violence toward animals has been connected to a host of criminal behaviors, violent and nonviolent alike.[64]

As law enforcement officials, aided by the work of animal welfare organizations and scholars, recognize the connection between animal abuse and human violence, more programs exist to counsel and rehabilitate young abusers before their violence escalates. One national program is the National Cruelty Investigation School, which trains law enforcement officials how to conduct cruelty investigations, focusing on the link between animal cruelty and human violence. Many local agencies are following suit with their own special units.

Another well-documented connection is the link between violence toward animals and domestic violence. For instance, studies have found that between 71 percent and 85 percent of women who escaped their homes due to domestic violence reported that their partner had abused the family animals as well.[65] About 1.5 million women are victims of rape or physical assault by an intimate partner every year, and domestic violence is the most prevalent form of abuse for women in the United States today. This is a very real threat to women, children, and their animals. Abusers use violence, or threats of violence, against animal companions in order to exercise control over their partner. Killing or threatening to kill an animal reinforces a woman's isolation and lack of control over her own life, keeping her, in many cases, bound to her abusive partner.

Because most domestic violence shelters do not accept companion animals, even on a temporary basis, women who escape their abusers often must leave animals at home to be further victimized, or they must remain in their homes with their animals. Luckily, there are a few programs available to help women in these circumstances, such as the Companion Animal Rescue Effort (CARE) in New Mexico, which provides temporary foster care for the companion animals of abused women. In addition, more domestic violence shelters are working with local animal shelters to provide refuge for animal victims of domestic violence.

Animals and Empathy

A number of recent studies point to a correlation between positive attitudes toward companion animals and a more humane attitude toward other animals, and even some very preliminary studies are showing there is a link between positive attitudes toward animals and a more compassionate attitude toward people. Anthropologists James Serpell and Elizabeth Paul trace the evolution of animal keeping in the West and its association with attitudes toward fellow humans.[66] They point out, for example, that starting in the seventeenth century, many of the most

House Rabbit Society rescued Lucy after she was duct-taped to a piece of dynamite and thrown in a lake. She now lives with her companion, Benny. (Photo by Rachel Hess)

Lucy

At first glance, Lucky seems similar to most other rabbits. Petite and curious, she enjoys the company of people as well as her two rabbit companions, and she always welcomes a treat. What makes Lucky distinctive is that, despite surviving a horrible act of cruelty, she has not lost her trust in people.

In 2004 Lucky's owner, Nick, duct-taped her to a quarter-stick of dynamite and threw her into a California lake. The fuse did not detonate, and Nick and his friends retrieved her from the lake. Shockingly, the young people debated whether to relight the fuse. They also documented their efforts to blow her up, placing photos of the bedraggled and terrified rabbit online.

Soon afterward, a House Rabbit Society (HRS) rescue volunteer saw the images and alerted authorities. Officers rescued Lucky and released her into the care of the organization. After providing her with medical and foster care for three weeks, HRS adopted her to Rachel Hess, an experienced rabbit guardian. Now named Lucy, she lives with a permanent, loving family, including two other rabbits, Abigail and Benny, who play with her during the day and snuggle with her at night. Rachel notes that when she and her husband first adopted Lucy, she was the "beta" female bunny to Abigail's alpha bunny. But Lucy exerted herself and is now the alpha female. All three bunnies are still bonded and they cuddle and groom, but Lucy definitely is the lead bunny. She knows she is home, she is loved, and she has a permanent family.

---

enlightened humanitarians had an affinity for animals, and that scholars and philosophers dating back to the ancient Greeks thought eliminating violence toward animals would make humans more peaceful.[67]

In fact, during the eighteenth and nineteenth centuries when the commercial pet industry began to develop, many saw animal companionship as a way to cultivate middle-class virtues, like kindness and self-control, in young people. According to historian Katherine Grier, parents and moralists saw having a relationship with a companion animal as a way to instill positive virtues in a child, which she calls the "domestic ethic of kindness." She views this ethic as an integral part of reducing some of the casual violence toward animals that was prevalent at the time.[68] The idea that children can learn positive values by relating to animals is still with us today, as both humane organizations and pet industry promoters encourage parents to bring home an animal as a way to teach responsibility, kindness, and nurturing behavior to children.

Today, many scholars think that living with animals does in fact teach empathy and compassion.[69] However, at least one recent study challenges this notion, finding evidence that living with animals is *not* correlated with empathy and that living with cats is, in fact, *negatively* correlated![70]

EXOTIC ANIMALS AS PETS

Besides the problems plaguing more common animal companions, exotic "pets"—certain birds, reptiles, amphibians, and even tigers and monkeys—face bigger difficulties. They suffer from forced removal from their native habitats; trafficking to laboratories, zoos, and hunting operations; and inappropriate care and housing in captivity. Others are bred in captivity in conditions totally inappropriate to their needs. In addition, many of these animals pose dangers to their owners, either by diseases or injuries. A lack of legal protection for many of these animals perpetuates these issues.

The National Alternative Pet Association, a group of people advocating on behalf of people wishing to keep wild animals like snakes, lizards, prairie dogs, skunks, wallabies, llamas, monkeys, exotic cats, and hedgehogs, defines exotic pets as "unconventional" and claims that legislation prohibiting the ownership of such animals is discriminatory. But banning the possession of certain animals is not discrimination. Rather, bans provide protection for wild animals, domestic animals, and the public.

The Capture and Trafficking of Wild Animals

What exactly is an exotic pet, and how do they enter the pet market? "Exotic pet" is actually a euphemism for "wild animal." What transforms wild animals into exotic animals is simply capture and transport from their native environments by the exotic pet industry, into pet stores, auctions, or other venues for animal sales.[71] In most cases, animal traffickers catch and ship these animals, resulting in the deaths of millions in the process. Some victims of the illegal trade in endangered species wind up at exotic animal auctions. Here, they face fates as ill-treated spectacles in roadside and mainstream zoos, prey animals in canned hunts, and experimentation subjects in laboratories. The trade in exotic animals is pervasive, with an estimated ten to fifteen thousand big cats like tigers and lions living in the United States alone—more than are left in the wild. Of those, 10 percent are in legitimate zoos, and the rest live in backyards or in roadside zoos and circuses.[72] This trade is also big business: tiger cubs are available online for anywhere from nine hundred to seven thousand dollars apiece, and a baby chimpanzee can cost as much as fifty thousand dollars. There are about fifteen thousand pet primates in the United States.[73]

Convention on International Trade in
Endangered Species of Wild Fauna and Flora

While some of the trade in wild animals in this country is legal, much of it is illegal, depending on the population status of the species in question. Endangered animals are protected by CITES, the Convention on International Trade in Endangered Species of Wild Fauna and Flora, a voluntary international agreement between governments that regulates such trade. According to CITES, the international wildlife trade is a multibillion-dollar industry with traders dealing in hundreds of millions of plants and animals, as well as the products derived from them;[74] approximately a quarter of this trade is illegal. CITES-protected animals include such diverse species as lemurs, whales, dolphins, sea turtles, bears, kangaroos, sloths, porcupines, and elephants—roughly five thousand species total. CITES works by controlling the trade of these species through a licensing system that member governments administer. Unfortunately, CITES' focus is relatively narrow, covering only international trade, which allows traders to easily exploit animals within their own borders and does not at all address consumer demand for exotic species. According to one study, without adequate field protection of species within their borders, CITES' protection is largely inadequate.[75]

Parrots are an example of a CITES-covered bird. While parrots have been in human homes for so long that most of us no longer think of them as exotics, they are still caught in the wild in great numbers, leading to the decimation of many species.[76] While CITES is intended to protect most parrots, and the US domestic bird breeding industry is thriving, the smuggling of parrots caught in the wild continues. This trade results in high mortality rates, up to 30 to 50 percent for many species.[77] Legal and illegal traders alike ship these animals via commercial airlines; since airline guidelines for shipping live animals are currently voluntary, with no penalty for noncompliance, a high mortality rate is the result.

Animals CITES does not protect, such as nonendangered species and species that dealers catch and trade within their own countries, may be legally or illegally traded. Typically, US state wildlife divisions define animals who are legal to trade, and they may include painted turtles, garter snakes, and African pygmy hedgehogs. Illegal animals may include native animals such as raccoons, certain types of deer, opossums, and wild pigs, as well as CITES-protected animals.

Even native-caught animals such as turtles fare poorly in the wild animal trade. Because the costs of acquiring these animals are so low, traders have little to no investment in ensuring that the animals make it safely to the pet stores or auctions, resulting in a high number of deaths.

These rescued jaguars, former exotic pets, lived out the remainder of their lives with each other at Wildlife Rescue and Rehabilitation in Texas. (Photo courtesy of Wildlife Rescue and Rehabilitation)

Impact on Native Species and Cultures

There are few studies that look at the impact of the legal trade of wild animals on populations in source countries, even though governments that allow the exporting of CITES-covered animals must issue such findings. CITES does not cover many animals currently traded, thus there are no requirements at all to gauge whether the trade is sustainable. However, most conservationists would agree that there is a limit on how many animals can leave a country without destroying native

Jaguar

Back in 1983, Wildlife Rescue and Rehabilitation (WRR) was called in to rescue a young female jaguar who had escaped the confines of a dog run in a San Antonio backyard. She was being held as a pet. Since she was only six months old, when the opportunity presented itself, she would climb out the top of the cement-floored kennel and explore the backyard. On this particular day, she decided to venture a little farther and see the neighborhood. The police were called, then WRR was called, and after making a complete fool of myself by grabbing the only part of her I could get a firm grip on, she proceeded to drag me about the block as if she were the kite and I her tail. WRR did not prevail when the authorities insisted that we give her back to her owner. There were no laws against the keeping of wildlife within the city limits at that time.

But the next time we received the call and once again retrieved the large, spotted cat, there was something different about her. She was much more subdued; her spirit had been broken, and so had her nose. It is common for the unscrupulous individuals who sell and breed wild animals to instruct those who purchase them as pets, especially big cats, to beat them in the face with a length of rubber hose to discipline and control them. This young female had been beaten so badly that her entire nose and nasal cavities were caved in and bleeding. This time, when the authorities suggested we send her back and when her owner threatened us with legal action, we promised him that we would file cruelty charges for what he had done to her. He went away, and the beautiful young jaguar stayed with us. She began a considerably happier life here at WRR. In time she mended, in body and spirit. She was bright and energetic and loved to climb trees and lie in the tall grass sunning herself.

The female jaguar had been at WRR for about one year when we were called to assist an animal protection group on the East Coast that was working to close a roadside zoo and find sanctuary for the animals held there. There was one male jaguar who was scheduled to go to a overseas zoo, and they were trying to stop the move and needed a sanctuary to agree to take him. I agreed, and in only a few weeks the male was on his way to Texas, where he eventually bonded with the female. They made a loving, devoted couple. The two jaguars lived together at the Wildlife Rescue Sanctuary for many years. They both died in 2005 of old age, within two months of each other.

—Story by Lynn Cuny, founder and executive director,
Wildlife Rescue and Rehabilitation, Kendalia, Texas,
www.wildlife-rescue.org

populations, and that current trade levels are, for many populations, unsustainable. CITES' ability to protect certain species, ironically, has in some cases harmed other species, as those species may be traded in increasing numbers to make up for the difficulty of acquiring the original target species.[78] Furthermore, it is not just the number of animals taken that harms the native population. It is also the methods used to collect animals. Many traders catch animals by destroying their habitats, and others catch baby animals by killing the parents.

Native cultures are also affected when dealers remove wild animals for international trade, leading some nations to ban the export of live animals. Namibia, for example, banned the export of wild animals in 2001 to ensure that the native cultures could continue to hunt the animals for their own subsistence as well as to protect the ecotourism industry in that country. While some individual catchers in the source countries benefit from the wildlife trade by capturing animals, the profit is insignificant when compared to the cultural loss of native species.[79] It is clear that the major beneficiaries in the international trade in wildlife are not the cultures or people in the source countries, but the pet industry in consumer countries like the United States.

Living in Captivity

Because exotic animals are wild animals, it is no surprise that they suffer when living in captivity. After having survived the trauma of capture, the removal from family (especially for the young animals whom the pet trade favors) and the transport in a frightening, usually overcrowded environment, many animals simply do not survive the continuous stress of the pet store and the trip to a new home.

If they make it to their new home, most wild animals do not fare much better. About 80 to 90 percent of captive exotics such as reptiles do not receive proper veterinary care, and about 90 percent of wild "pets" die in their first two years of captivity.[80] Since most new caretakers are unaware of their complex physical and nutritional needs, many captives develop medical problems that are difficult to treat even when they do receive care. Veterinary care for exotic animals, if it is even available, is typically more expensive than the cost of care for domestics.[81] To make matters worse, while most guardians lack basic knowledge about physiological needs, their ability to provide social and emotional support for wild animals is even worse. Because so few people understand wild animal behavior, their responses to normal behavior such as biting is to further confine, punish, or even surgically "correct" the animal. The majority of captive wild animals live miserable existences, neglected in cramped tanks or cages and devoid of social contact with their own species.

Risk to Humans

Normal behavior for many adult wild animals involves territoriality, sexual behaviors, and aggression. Once the cute baby monkey becomes a demanding, sometimes unpredictable adult, many caregivers neglect, punish, or abandon the animal because they fear the very real potential of injury. Every year we read about family tigers tearing off children's arms, lions mauling their caretakers, and countless other stories of captive raccoons, skunks, bears, and other animals harming or killing people.

Wild animals also may bring with them diseases communicable to other animals or people. Recent examples of such zoonotic diseases include tularemia, monkeypox, rabbit hemorrhagic disease, rabies, ringworm, leptospirosis, hepatitis, and more. *Salmonella* is one of the most common examples, with ninety thousand people becoming infected from captive reptiles each year. Each new disease outbreak inevitably results in large numbers of animals being killed by public health officials or frightened owners.

The Fate of Some Wild Pets: Turning Them Loose

What happens to exotic pets once little Johnny has been bitten, or Linda Sue contracts *Salmonella*? Many people take the easy way out and simply release their former pet into the neighborhood park or another spot they deem "wildlife friendly." If these animals are lucky enough to survive in their new surroundings (which will most likely be unsuited to their physical needs), they can cause serious damage to the environment. Nonnative animals like turtles, frogs, and snakes will compete with native species for resources, and in some cases they have overtaken native species completely. Nonnatives can also bring diseases and prey on local wild and domestic animals. This is one of the reasons why California and Hawaii continue to prohibit the keeping of ferrets as companions. Others find their way into local shelters, which are rarely equipped to handle a tiger or a boa constrictor. Because of the ease with which people can acquire exotic animals, and the lowered costs due to Internet sales, wild animals are becoming more and more commonplace at animal shelters, compounding the existing problems with housing, caring for, and adopting all of the dogs, cats, and other animals still inundating our city and county facilities.[82]

The Fate of Others: Roadside Zoos and Canned Hunting Operations

Even more disturbing is the fate of other exotic animals. Because finding a good home for snakes, tigers, or lemurs is easier said than done, many owners turn to zoos, which generally do not accept such animals. The few sanctuaries that exist for wild animals, especially large ones, are often overcrowded and underfunded. In addition, local animal shelters are ill equipped to handle anything other than the occasional raccoon. So, what can be done for an unwanted wild animal? Richard Farinato of the Humane Society of the United States writes:

> The business of exotics can be viewed as a large circular pathway on which an animal or a species travels. Spaced along this circle are institutions or entities such as zoos and other exhibits, circuses, animal trainers, pet shops, animal dealers, importers, auctions, hobby and commercial breeders, rescues, and sanctuaries.[83]

After a person buys an exotic baby animal from a breeder or a pet store, and the animal reaches maturity and behaves in a natural but threatening way, he may decide to surrender the animal. After exhausting the normal avenues, the owner may resell the animal back to the breeder, who can turn the animal into a breeder (which is the fate of many birds) or who may resell the animal again. In many cases, the animals will be bred again, contributing to the continuation of the wild pet trade in this country.

Others look for new homes for their former pets by advertising in magazines like *Animal Finders' Guide*, a source used by animal dealers and brokers to buy and sell exotic animals. As we saw in Chapter 3, these animals may make their way to exotic animal game farms that breed animals to be pets, food, or hunting targets, or they may be sent to roadside zoos or petting zoos.

Legal Protection

Wild animals living in homes have little legal protection in this country. The Animal Welfare Act, for example, only protects animals in the custody of USDA licensees, such as research facilities, zoos, and dealers; it does not protect wild animals in private homes. Sometimes, disease outbreaks or the latest child mauling may result in new legislation that restricts the keeping of wild animals. Examples include a monkeypox threat in 2003, which resulted in a federal ban on the import and transport of African rodents and prairie dogs; a 2005 outbreak of *Salmonella* that resulted in a number of localities prohibiting the sale or promotional giveaway of turtles; and a rash of wild animal maulings that led to New York's new ban on the keeping of dangerous animals in 2002. In 2006 the Senate approved the Captive Primate Safety Act, which, if passed by the House, would end the primate pet trade. While Congress enacted the Captive Wildlife Safety Act in 2003 to end the trade in big cats, it did not specifically prohibit the keeping of these animals as pets. They can still be found in thousands of homes across the country.

Twenty-six states have some kind of restriction on the private keeping of large exotic animals, and twenty-two states require licenses or some other sort of regulation. But no state wholly bans the keeping of wild animals, and three states have no regulations at all. Georgia and California currently have the most comprehensive wild animal laws on the books. Other states, such as North Carolina, Ohio, Oregon, Texas, West Virginia, Iowa, Washington, Indiana, and Missouri, are considering legislation that would ban the keeping of certain kinds of wild animals as pets.

Ultimately, we may have to wait for more tragic illnesses or maulings before more laws protecting these animals and the public are enacted, given the large financial stakes involved on the part of the wild pet trade. Even then, we may only expect to see the keeping of dangerous animals like big cats prohibited.[84]

CONCLUSION: THE TREATMENT OF COMPANION ANIMALS

The love we receive from companion animals is extremely valuable, as millions of people who live with animals as part of their families can attest. According to a large and growing body of sociological and psychological research, companion animals provide humans with a variety of benefits, from decreasing blood pressure and cholesterol levels and increasing opportunities for exercise and socialization to decreasing loneliness. Even the National Institutes of Health and the Centers for Disease Control and Prevention have weighed in on the health benefits of living with a companion animal.[85] Both authors of this book could not imagine our lives without our animal families, and we could never calculate the immeasurable degree to which they have improved and influenced our lives.

In the summer of 2006, the Chinese government engaged in a campaign of clubbing, hanging, and shooting to death tens of thousands of family dogs as a response to an outbreak of rabies. What was remarkable about the many stories concerning this atrocity is not just the unspeakable cruelty and horror, but the response of the Chinese citizens, who mobilized to stop the killings and put themselves at risk in a politically repressive society.[86] This response is a testament to the power of companion animals to transform our lives and our collective responsibility to ensure safe, loving homes for them.

We have to ask ourselves: How does society repay the millions of dogs, cats, birds, rabbits, and other animals who enhance our lives to such a great extent? Certainly, millions of Americans cherish their companions as family members, buying them the best food, toys, beds, and other necessities as well as luxuries. We shower our animal friends with affection and attention, and many guardians include pets in their wills. For those millions of companion animals who sleep on soft beds, nestled between their human partners, and wake up to a day of snacks, toys, games, and naps, this form of "dominance" is probably benign, and most likely quite welcome—as it certainly is for the humans who benefit from their companionship. But the millions of animals who are surrendered to animal shelters every year, the countless other abandoned animals, and the thousands of cases involving animal cruelty or abuse point to a different segment of the population that does not see animals the way that so many of us do. Human dominance causes suffering for all those animals who lead lives of solitude, hunger, cold, and want; who suffer at the end of a chain or in a desolate cage or a backyard; who spend years giving birth to litter upon litter until they are worn out. Similarly, the wholesale exploitation of the pet industry, with its relentless focus on maximizing profits at the expense of animal welfare, shows a lack of regard for the animals on whose backs they reap their profits.

We've looked at the enormous price paid by millions of animals who are relinquished at animal shelters each year. We've seen the fate suffered by the majority of these animals who are euthanized due to no fault of their own, because there are still too many animals being produced in this country with no thought about the consequences. The cost to the animals is enormous, and the cost to society is both financial and spiritual—how do we calculate the effects? Animal shelter workers, not surprisingly, bear the brunt of this trauma; many enter the profession because of their love for animals, and many are involved, in one way or another, in killing those animals—many of whom they've developed an attachment to—on a daily basis.[87]

What can be done to improve the treatment of our companion animals and to discourage the exploitation that is implicit within the industry that breeds and sells them? For many animal advocates, the solution lies in providing basic protections to companion (as well as other) animals that would preclude the kinds of abuse and exploitation so common today. Others call for a change in the status of companion animals as property and a change in the nature of the relationship that bonds them to us.

The change should begin with legislation to increase penalties for animal abuse, to mandate spay/neuter of companion animals and restrict the nonstop breeding of companion animals, and to prevent the pet trade from exploiting wild animals. But clearly, as people who welcome animals into our homes and participate as consumers in the multibillion-dollar pet industry, we need to reassess our position on animals. If we love them as much as we say we do, and as much as the billions of dollars that we spend on pet supplies indicate, then we need to take action. Like any group of consumers, we can control the industry that supplies us by making it clear that we will no longer support the suffering of animals through the pet trade as it exists now.

What You Can Do

The following are a number of ways that readers can improve the lives of companion animals and reverse some of the suffering caused by the pet industry.

- Adopt a pet. If you are interested in bringing a companion animal into your family, visit your local animal shelter, humane society, or local rescue group. You can find dogs, cats, birds, rabbits, guinea pigs, and all manner of domestic animals in need of a home.

- Make an informed decision. Research the proper care of companion animals before bringing one home. If you already live with an animal, consult some of the organizations referenced on pp. 405–407 to find out more about their needs.
- Provide excellent care. When we bring an animal home, we are committing to their lifelong care. That means top-quality food, fun toys, soft bedding, clean conditions, lots of exercise and attention, regular veterinary care, and plenty of love.
- Provide appropriate habitats. Domesticated companion animals are not "made" to live outdoors. Dogs, cats, rabbits, and most other companion animals prefer living in a house with human companionship, where they will be safe from harm, and the human family benefits the most from this type of arrangement.
- Provide companionship. Most companion animals thrive when they are able to have the companionship of another member of their species, as long as the animals are spayed and neutered and are introduced to each other with care.
- Spay/neuter. Most companion mammals can and should be spayed or neutered, both to prevent more unwanted births and also for health and behavior reasons.
- Buy cruelty-free products. Many household products and cosmetics were tested on animals, including companion animals like dogs, rabbits, rats, and mice. Only purchase items that have not been tested on animals.
- Volunteer. People of all ages can volunteer to help animals. Animal shelters need volunteers to clean cages, socialize animals, walk dogs, talk to the general public, and more. If you are too young to volunteer at a shelter, you can still donate blankets, collect donations at your school, or even help an elderly neighbor to care for their animals.
- Watch for abuse. Keep an eye out for animal abuse, neglect, or

cruelty. If you see something, report it to your local animal control or police department.

- Know your resources. Put together a list of your community's animal resources, including the wildlife rehabilitation agency, animal control, the local rescue groups (including different kinds of breed and species rescue), and emergency veterinarians, so you will be prepared to make a call if need be.
- Animal emergency kits. Put together an animal emergency kit in the case of a natural or other disaster: include food, water, leashes, bowls, carriers, and any information that would be needed if you had to evacuate yourself and your animals. Also prepare an emergency travel kit to keep in your car, which should include a leash, food, an animal carrier, and a blanket in case you come across an injured animal. (Check www.humanesociety.org for more information on putting together emergency supplies.)
- Join an organization. There are groups for people concerned about animals of every age group in every community, as well as online. This is a great way to meet new friends and share resources with like-minded people.

Chapter 7

THE ENTERTAINMENT INDUSTRY

Animals as Amusement

I think that while the loss of the large Indian rhinoceroses is greatly to be deplored, yet, in my opinion, the three young ones that survive will be of more benefit to the world at large than would the forty rhinoceroses running wild in the jungles of Nepal, and seen only at rare intervals by a few ignorant natives.[1]
　　　　　—William Hornaday, director of the Bronx Zoo, 1902

INTRODUCTION

Americans love animals. We love watching them eat, play, interact with one another, and even sleep. We also love touching them and being as close to them as possible. If we're not watching our own animals, we're bird-watching, whale-watching, photographing wildlife, scuba diving, snorkeling, or watching Animal Planet and Webcam footage from zoos and animal sanctuaries.

One reason modern Americans are so captivated by animals today is their disappearance from our lives. In our postindustrial world, companion animals remain the only form of physical connection that

Americans have with animals. Since animal agriculture now takes place behind the closed doors of huge factories and most Americans live either in cities or suburbs, interacting with noncompanion animals has effectively become a thing of the past for the great majority of us. Thus, the proliferation of animals in films and on television allows many of us to see animals who we would never generally get the chance to see. But long before television and film, Westerners had devised ways of seeing and connecting with wild animals through zoos and circuses, which brought wild animals into domestic enclosures for urban dwellers to see.

But simply having a fascination and a desire to watch animals—especially wild ones—is not enough to explain the other ways people use and have used animals as entertainment, such as circuses, marine mammal parks, dog or horse racing, animal fighting, and rodeos. What is it that draws so many people to entertainment venues in which animals are not just present but are forced to perform sometimes dangerous stunts for our pleasure? How is it that many people find amusing the prospect of seeing large wild animals like elephants, chimpanzees, and tigers dressed up like children, forced to perform tricks or made to behave in ways that belie their intelligence, strength, and wildness?

Whether it is through the billions of tourist dollars spent at zoos and wildlife parks per year, the proliferation of the modern ecotourism and wildlife safari trade, whale-watching, bird-watching, or the enormous popularity of Animal Planet television shows like *Animal Cops* and *Meerkat Manor*, we see that the public craves seeing animals. Whether we observe animals from the comfort of our couches during *The Dog Whisperer* or we travel thousands of miles to Australia, Africa, or Antarctica to watch koalas, lions, or penguins, it is clear that this trend will continue. But there is one question we should ask: Is all this attention good or bad for the animals? Certainly, documentaries that focus on the plight of wild animals and their loss of habitat seem good for animals—educating the public on the ways in which animals are imperiled and what we can do about it seems to only have positive consequences. Likewise, shows that focus on animal rescuers, animal trainers who use animal-friendly methods, and many of the other ways that we can watch animals on television and sometimes in film seem to be beneficial.

On the other hand, many of the other ways in which humans can see and even interact with dolphins, elephants, bulls, horses, or other wild and domesticated animals don't necessarily provide those animals with any benefits. Circuses, rodeos, and marine mammal parks not only force animals to perform in ways that are unnatural for them and keep many of their animals confined in situations that are sometimes very intensive, but they also don't seem to benefit the "stars" of the shows at all.

In this chapter, we will look at the various venues in which humans can watch animals in order to examine the conditions in which the animals live, the possible benefit or harm to them, and the motivations of the people who derive pleasure from watching them. We focus on both wild and domesticated animals, as both are used for entertainment in a number of ways. Typically, the wilder and more exotic the animal, the more pleasure most of us get from simply watching the animal or observing their performances or tricks in circuses and marine parks. In some ways, watching a very wild or exotic animal act like a human is even more interesting than watching a domesticated animal—already much like us—do humanlike tricks. But domestic animals, because of their proximity to many of us, typically must perform—whether racing, fighting, or many of the activities found in the rodeo—since watching a domesticated horse, rooster, or cow in a zoo would not fit most people's idea of entertainment.

Ultimately, animals, whether domesticated or wild, are heavily featured in human entertainment both because of our pleasure in watching them and because animals, as sociologist Adrian Franklin points out, are both like us and different from us; they can be interpreted by us in a variety of ways, both to represent difference and otherness and to represent sameness and family.[2] As we'll see when looking at the ways animals are used for entertainment in this society, both interpretations prevail.

GOVERNMENT OVERSIGHT

The Animal Welfare Act covers most forms of entertainment that use animals. Congress passed the AWA in 1966 and amended it four times over the next twenty-five years. Its purpose is, among other things, to protect animals who are exhibited to the public, excluding livestock, fish, rodents, birds, amphibians, and reptiles.

Nearly everyone involved in the handling, transport, sale or transfer, and display of covered animals in the entertainment industry must be either licensed or registered with the USDA, and APHIS inspectors make periodic visits to all licensees to ensure that regulations are followed. As with animals in the pet and vivisection industries, the AWA provides regulations and standards with respect to handling, housing, feeding, sanitation, ventilation, veterinary care, and transportation of covered animals.

Most animal exhibitors purchase their animals through class A dealers (breeders who breed and sell their own animals) or class B dealers (who purchase animals from random sources); both must have USDA licensing. The USDA also requires that brokers who sell or trade animals, as well as those operating animal auctions, possess licensing. Exotic animal dealers who deal in animals from other countries or domestically raised exotic animals must have a different kind of license. Wild animal dealers who sell wild animals from the United States to other countries must have yet another kind of license.

Exhibiting animals to the public or having animals perform requires an exhibitor license, whether the show is a traveling show such as a circus or a stationary venue such as a zoo. The license is mandatory whether or not the public views the animals in person, remotely, or on television or film. Exceptions to this include whale-watching tours or other events in which people view animals in their natural environment, private collections of exotic animals, horse shows, animal racing, and most rodeos. There are currently more than 2,500 USDA-licensed animal exhibitors in the United States.[3]

Besides the standards of care that the AWA mandates for animal exhibitors, they must also keep accurate records of their animals including what veterinary care they receive, and they must ensure that the public is safe from the animals. Performing animals must also have rest periods between shows that are as long as the time in which they performed.

The AWA prohibits animal fighting events like dogfights, raccoon or bearbaiting, and cockfights, except in Louisiana where cockfights are, at this writing, still allowed (although legislation is currently pending in the Louisiana state house and senate to ban it, and most observers expect that this will happen by the end of 2007). In this case, the AWA provides no protection for birds in cockfighting operations because regulation falls under state laws.

Not only does the AWA exclude rodeos and horse racing, but the Horse Protection Act, which provides limited protection for horses in other types of events, also excludes these activities. Horse racing and dog racing are only covered by state laws and are enforced by each state that allows them, via the state's gaming and racing commissions. Rodeos are overseen by the Professional Rodeo Cowboys Association, a nonprofit organization that sets out rules regulating the sport as well as animal care. A number of states and localities outlaw certain rodeo practices or require, for instance, a veterinarian to be on site.

Marine mammal parks are not only covered by the Animal Welfare Act and are thus subject to inspections by APHIS, but they are also under the oversight of the National Marine Fisheries Service. These parks must follow regulations laid out under the Endangered Species Act, the Marine Mammal Protection Act, and the Convention on International Trade in Endangered Species of Wild Flora and Fauna.

ZOOS

More than 135 million people visit hundreds of zoos and marine parks in the United States every year and collectively spend millions of dollars, although media reports show that zoo attendance is declining.[4]

The Association of Zoos and Aquariums and the Zoological Association of America accredit about two hundred US zoos, and the World Association of Zoos and Aquariums accredits about two hundred zoos of some ten thousand total zoos around the world as well.

History of the Zoo

People have kept animals in captivity for thousands of years, long before the concept of "zoo" ever existed—as creatures of worship, as part of gladiatorial contests in the Roman Empire, for activities like bearbaiting and bullfighting in medieval Europe, and more. Wealthy elites in ancient Egypt, Greece, China, and Rome, and later in medieval and Renaissance Europe, also kept exotic animals. The keeping of these animals—such as giraffes, monkeys, elephants, and lions—in these early collections demonstrated either the wealth of the individuals or the wealth of the empire, as well as a mastery of nature through the ability to contain "ferocious" animals. The animals themselves were often gifts from the leaders of other kingdoms or states. By the late seventeenth century, private menageries, as they were called, were status symbols for wealthy Europeans, and commoners were not able to view them.

The history of modern Western zoos both reflects and departs from the centuries-long view that they were demonstrations of state power. But the history of modern zoos also reveals a close connection to big-game hunting and colonialism, as well as an unseemly link to the freak show acts that later evolved into modern circuses.

Ancient and early European exotic animal collections were not meant for public consumption; the idea of zoos for the public to visit and see wild animals and the idea of zoos as anything more than oddities or amusements really didn't develop until the eighteenth century. At this point, word spread about the collections of wild animals held by kings and other wealthy leaders, and citizens in England, France, and Germany clamored to see the exotic animals brought back from foreign lands.[5]

One way that commoners were able to see these animals was in the form of traveling entertainers, who in the mid-nineteenth century also offered minstrel acts like juggling, singing, poetry recitals, and human oddities shows. The purpose of these shows was spectacle—animals lived in small cages (when they weren't held by chains) alongside "freaks" and native peoples captured from colonial lands.

The first "zoological garden," the Ménagerie du Jardin des Plantes, opened in Paris in 1794, followed by the London Zoo in 1828, Amsterdam's Royal Society of Zoology in 1838, and similar zoological gardens in other European capitals. One of the first public zoos with an emphasis on science was the collection at Paris's Muséum National d'Histoire Naturelle that opened in 1793.[6]

Zoological gardens were different from both private menageries as well as traveling shows. Here, animals were available for viewing as people walked and looked at plants, rather than just standing in one spot and observing them in cages. In addition, where menageries were disordered collections of random animals, zoos were ordered collections, often organized by continent or taxonomic label. Like modern zoos, these early zoos competed for the best and most exotic animals and displays. And like the ancient collections, they were a place to put all the animals African and Asian rulers sent as gifts.

As time went on, people became more familiar with exotic wonders like native peoples and wild foreign animals, opening the door to making displays in the French and English zoos that were more decorative, and later, more educational. The architects of these zoos did not yet focus on conditions for the animals and their welfare, however.

The early French zoos were the first to propose the idea that zoos could advance the study of natural history, and they slowly began to emphasize education. This new development coincided with the rise of scientific ideas about animal nature that, not coincidentally, supported practices of animal confinement.[7] The idea that menageries could further scientific knowledge became popular at this time and spread throughout Europe.

Nineteenth-century zoos were still focused on the upper classes, charging entry fees that the poor couldn't afford.[8] The poor, instead, satisfied themselves with animal attractions like animal fighting, bear-baiting, and racing, all of which Northern European countries later prohibited—not because of concerns about cruelty to animals but as a way to control the poor. While the zoos of this time period promoted an educational message, they were still largely about entertainment; a chimpanzee tea party was the main attraction at the London Zoo from the 1920s to the 1970s, and similar tea parties were common at other zoos throughout the twentieth century.[9]

The history of American zoos is somewhat different. The first American zoos were the Central Park Zoo in New York, founded in 1860, and the Philadelphia Zoo, opened in 1874. These zoos, as well as other early American zoos, developed during the time when the first public parks were being devised and constructed, and indeed, many of the early zoos were built in parks. Attendance was free to the public as a way of drawing in the middle class and the poor and providing them with an educational, uplifting experience.[10] (As we saw with the history of hunting in the United States, this was part of the American democratic backlash against European elitism.) American zoos, however, also got many of their first exotic animals as gifts from foreign heads of state.

Early European zoos, like the traveling displays, showed their animals in small, barred cages. Some zoos, however, created elaborate displays like Bristol Zoo's Monkey Temple, an open-air "Indian temple" that humans had supposedly abandoned and the jungle had taken over. Monkey Temple was an early attempt to confine animals—in this case, rhesus macaques—in a "naturalistic" enclosure without bars or wires, where visitors could enjoy the animals behaving normally. The design was also based on a motif common to zoos in the nineteenth and early twentieth centuries, which echoed not only the jungle environments from which the animals supposedly came but also the exotic cultures with which the animals were associated.[11] (The connection between exotic cultures and peoples and exotic animals was made explicitly clear when Carl Hagenbeck, an animal dealer who supplied European zoos in addition to having famous clients such as P. T. Barnum, imported two young Cameroonian boys to keep a captured baby gorilla company at his zoo in Austria in 1910—the implication being that African boys and African apes were closely connected.[12] In 1906 the Bronx Zoo exhibited an African pygmy man with the chimpanzees until the city's African American community protested.)

It wasn't until the early twentieth century that Carl Hagenback, who founded the Hamburg Zoo in 1907, created a new style of animal enclosure using concrete moats, sunken fences, and other design aspects to both confine animals but also allow the public to have an unimpeded view of them. These new, easy-to-replicate "naturalistic" designs soon became the standard zoo-enclosure style. Hagenbeck was also one of the first people in the exotic animal business to propose that animals in captivity needed fresh air in order to thrive.[13] Large numbers of premature animal deaths plagued early European zoos, due to both the stresses of the animals' capture and transport as well as the inappropriate conditions. For example, the average life expectancy for an animal in the early years of the London Zoo was two years. But the ultimate focus of these changes was not to improve the animals' lives. Zoo animals were still bored and lived mostly solitary lives. The new enclosures were created to make the public enjoy visiting zoos more, since zoos now had to compete with more modern forms of entertainment and needed to do something to attract more customers.

Even today, the modern approach to zoo enclosure design known as "landscape immersion" is to replicate the animals' environments as closely as possible by using concrete forms to simulate rocks and other natural objects and to connect visitors with the habitat. The goal is to make visitors happier—indeed, studies show that visitors don't like seeing animals behind bars because it reduces their own viewing pleasure.[14]

As anthropologists Bob Mullan and Garry Marvin point out, by improving living conditions, or, by providing them "with a better stage and with more complex scenery and props to make the illusion more satisfactory," visitors will feel satisfied with the treatment of the animals and thus feel that the captivity of animals in zoos is morally acceptable.[15] A recent study demonstrated that zoo-goers view naturalistic enclosures as providing the best welfare for the animals.[16] That this public attitude is good for the animals is questionable; while larger, more naturalistic enclosures are inarguably better for the animals' happiness than living in the small cages common in the early part of the twentieth century, these naturalistic enclosures also serve the purpose of lulling the public into believing that the animals' welfare is best served within this environment rather than in the wild.

These naturalistic enclosures allow animals to express more of their natural or "wild" behaviors, as opposed to the stereotypical behaviors associated with animals in captivity. But is the goal to allow animals to live a more natural and thus happy life, or is it to provide zoo visitors with a better experience? Visitors consistently report that they enjoy watching animals engage in natural behaviors more than they enjoy watching them pace, rock, or exhibit other behaviors indicating stress or depression.

Naturalistic enclosures vary considerably. However, none truly replicate an animal's natural habitat. Since visitors pay to see the animals, enclosures that allow the animals to keep out of human sight or sleep during the daytime are unpopular. Because zoo employees need to regulate animals' diets, enclosures that allow for natural food foraging would be unpractical. Human convenience and pleasure thus win out over any real desire to keep animals happy. Finally, as philosopher Ralph Acampora points out, no matter how authentic the enclosure, the whole point of a zoo is to allow the public to view the animals, a situation that very rarely occurs in the wild, rendering the animals' behavior unnatural.[17]

Where Zoo Animals Came From

The second wave of British colonialism, starting in the nineteenth century, created new sources for animals, especially in the African and Indian colonies, and a bigger market in Europe for these newly acquired animals began to emerge. Understanding the effects of zoos on animals around the world involves looking at how they have historically acquired animals.

Carl Hagenbeck, whose influence on the design of zoo enclosures we mentioned earlier, was one of the most famous animal traders in the world. Working with European hunters throughout the colonial world who captured baby animals after killing their parents, traders who paid African and Asians for collecting animals, as well as naturalists and photographers who collected live animals, Hagenbeck purchased animals and sold them to the growing number of zoological gardens, circuses, wildlife shows, and other venues.[18] During the mid-nineteenth century, he bought and sold thousands of lions, hundreds of tigers, bears, elephants, giraffes, antelopes, and many other animals. During this same time, thanks to the stress of not just capture but transport across Africa or India to Europe, anywhere from one- to two-thirds of the animals died en route.[19] Zoos and circuses purchased their animals from the same dealers who controlled the animal trade,

African lions are commonly kept in zoos and as exotic pets in the United States. (Photo by Ken Stansell, US Fish and Wildlife Service)

and they often traded animals back and forth with each other, demonstrating the links between these two forms of entertainment venue.[20]

The collectors—themselves big-game hunters—who Hagenbeck and others like him hired, wrote extensively about their excursions. Notably, many left "kill diaries" in which they boasted in excruciating detail of their kills and of the baby animals who mourned at the sides of their dead mothers until they were snatched away, put into cages or tied or chained up, and transported to Europe. Because most social animals like gorillas, chimpanzees, elephants, and hippos guard their young, collectors had to kill the adults (sometimes the females, but often the entire herd) when capturing their babies.

Zoo historian Nigel Rothfels writes that for some of the animal catchers, killing the parents was necessary, whereas for others, such as animal catcher and elephant hunter Hans Dominik, the killing appeared to be the main motive, given his eager and detailed accounts of the bloody expeditions. It was Dominik's idea to kill an entire herd of adult elephants in order to procure a baby for the Berlin Zoological Gardens; in that 1898 expedition in Cameroon, he ended up, after killing every single adult, catching seven calves. One died immediately of suffocation due to the way he was confined, one died of his wounds from the attack, and two died during transport, leaving only three left for the zoo. According to Rothfels, "Dominik's story is about killing and the conspicuous display of power."[21] One nineteenth-century photo shows another animal catcher/hunter, Hans Schomburgk, riding a bicycle on top of the body of a dead elephant.

While apparently not too many tears were shed in the zoo world over the mass killing of animals in order to procure specimens, William Hornaday, director of the Bronx Zoo, was worried about the negative press that might come from the public learning about how many animals were killed in order to provide for exhibition. He wrote to Hagenbeck, regarding the killing of forty Indian rhinoceroses in order to catch four juveniles: "If that should get into the newspapers, either here or in London, there would be things published in condemnation of the whole business of capturing wild animals for exhibitions."[22]

Rothfels also notes the colonial context of power in which these animals were caught, whereby native peoples, native animals, and the land of the colonial territories were all seen and valued based on their importance for the colonial powers. Collectors used native men, sometimes as slaves, to help catch animals (when they weren't forced to work in factories and on plantations). They were chained as a method of control and beaten or shot as punishment. In many cases, collectors treated African and East Indian men as badly as the animals. This tells us something about the way that the use of colonial power was aimed equally at beings who were deemed undeserving of any type of respect. The trade in wild animals emphasized social inequalities, since certain peoples (African, Asian, and later Central and South American) provided the resources and labor that other groups such as Europeans, and later, North Americans, used for profit. This connection is clearer when we note that Carl Hagenbeck also imported humans from the colonies—many of whom died of European diseases—to display at his zoo in Austria and in traveling attractions, particularly after his animal-dealing business began to fail.[23] As we've seen, the wild animal trade was responsible for the growth of European and later American zoos during this period. In fact, the number of US zoos expanded from four to more than a hundred from 1880 to 1930.[24] Later, as we'll see, wild animal traders like Hagenbeck were also instrumental in the growth of circuses and other animal attractions.

After the end of the colonial era, animals for zoos continued to be captured in the wild. It wasn't until the signing of CITES (Convention on International Trade in Endangered Species of Wild Flora and Fauna) and the passage of the Endangered Species Act in 1973 that wild imports began to decline in the United States. However, then as now, unscrupulous dealers can fake certificates of entry to say that the animals are captive bred, and customs officials are not trained in the identification of exotic animals.[25] Finally, some animals arrive at zoos today via other means. Chimpanzee babies, for instance, have made it to zoos and other entertainment venues as a result of the bushmeat trade. As we shall see, the irony today is that after hundreds of years of zoos benefiting from the large-scale destruction of African and Indian wildlife, zoos now claim that they are in the business of saving these same animals.

Zoos Today

Starting in the 1970s, a growing debate about animal protection meant that people started to question the ethics of exhibiting wild animals in what many regarded as restrictive, cruel enclosures. At the same time, Congress expanded the Animal Welfare Act to include standards of care for animals in exhibits. More recently, a 1995 Roper Center for Public Opinion Research poll, for example, showed that 69 percent of Americans are concerned about the treatment of animals at zoos, aquariums, and wild animal parks.[26]

Since that time, many zoos across the world have responded to criticism by hiring veterinarians and other scientists, increasing the environmental enrichment for zoo animals, declaring that they are educational institutions, and claiming they are important sites for con-

Polar bear and cubs. These animals are common in zoos around the world. (Photo by Steve Amstrup, US Fish and Wildlife Service)

servation. (Of course, roadside zoos—which are condemned by animal welfare advocates and legitimate zoo personnel alike—don't even attempt to portray an educational or conservation message but instead are modern equivalents of the medieval traveling menageries and freak shows.) The mission of zoos is now supposedly not about entertainment but about helping the species. But is this true?

Many zoos now use environmental enrichment to reduce boredom and stress and to increase species-specific behaviors. For some zoos this means environmental complexity (such as trees, structures, jungle gyms, etc.) that can increase the ability of the animals to exercise; feeding enrichment in which the animals have to work for their food; the addition of new objects to allow animals to investigate or play; and social housing. But sometimes this simply means giving a gorilla a tire or a ball, or putting a group of unrelated animals together into an enclosure rather than keeping together an animal's kin group during his or her life. (This is particularly difficult to do when zoos need to manage populations by selling off animals.)

One of the reasons people visit zoos is to escape from urban environments and to be able to view and even interact with wild animals, something that has long been missing from the urban or suburban lifestyle. That's why even reputable zoos complement their educational message with exhibits and events that allow the public to ride, touch, feed, or get very close to animals. Visitors also like to see animals move. They become bored when animals are sleeping, even when they are nocturnal and should not be awake in the daytime. This leads to zoo patrons yelling at animals or pounding or tapping on enclosure windows. And even when zoo visitors do not react negatively to the animals, studies have shown that simply their presence is associated with behavioral changes in these animals—especially primates—that are indicative of stress.[27]

Research has shown that the average visitor spends thirty seconds to two minutes per enclosure—for example, forty-four seconds is the average time spent in front of a reptile enclosure at the National Zoo in Washington, DC.[28] Most visitors don't read the labels attached to these enclosures, which indicates that there's very little educational information being conveyed. Social ecologist Stephen Kellert's research has indicated that zoo-goers remain poorly educated about animals and their plight. In fact, after visiting the zoo, for many the major message is that humans are superior to other animals, according to Kellert's research.[29] In a recent study of Lincoln Park Zoo ape house visitors, researchers discovered that people ignored signs, complained when apes were resting, and fabricated answers to children's questions.[30]

The message that zoos promote most in defense of their activities is conservation. Some zoos use the term "arks" to emphasize their role in conserving species whose habitats were destroyed or that are on the brink of extinction thanks to overhunting or other problems. In addition, many zoos play a part in breeding rare and endangered species. Others, such as the San Diego Zoo, create research programs that focus on creating sustainable populations, conserving wildlife habitats, improving animal health, and even collecting endangered species' DNA data. Some zoos have released zoo-raised endangered animals into the wild. All of these are worthy causes.

But it's difficult to imagine that zoos, with a hundred-year history of wildlife destruction in order to acquire animals who would then live for only a couple of years in captivity, should be society's institution responsible for preserving thousands of species. Even habitat conservation and reintroduction programs can do only so much when thousands of acres of rainforest are being paved over or burned every day. Habitats continue to disappear to make room for development, cattle grazing, cropland, and more. Sport hunters continue to kill rare and endangered animals for trophies. And as humans continue to threaten habitats and entire species, it makes little sense to invest much hope in captive-breeding programs and the like when the root problems of species extinction continue to flourish. Perhaps most important to note, the majority of animals in zoos are not even endangered.

It will be a long time before our society and the rest of the world end the exploitive relationship with the planet's remaining wild areas. Captive-breeding programs constitute quick fixes, but they are difficult to manage. A large number of animals are critical to maintaining a diverse gene pool and healthy population, and as a result, programs often need animals from the wild in order to provide genetic diversity. Other species either don't breed well or don't breed at all in captivity. Pandas, for instance, who only number between 700 and 1,600 animals in the wild, are notoriously hard to breed, and zoos and panda conservation groups have so far seen around only one hundred successful panda births since these programs started. It was only in 2006 that the very first captive panda was reintroduced into a Chinese forest, after a three-year "training period."[31] Sadly, he was found dead of an apparent fall in 2007.

Most zoos are not good models for captive-breeding and species conservation. Those that have captive-breeding programs often simply use them to create more zoo animals, and they play no role in ensuring that wild animals can survive in their native habitats. People around the world are confronting the very real problems of habitat loss and species extinction on a scale unparalleled in human history—and if this trend continues, a few remaining individuals in captivity will be but a pathetic reminder of what once existed.

Ecotourism and the creation of wildlife preserves could be two ways to preserve habitats and to allow animals to live unmolested in their natural environment. By allowing limited ecotourism, tourists (unfortunately, only those who can afford it) could visit these places, and their expenditures could help fund efforts. It's worth noting that ecotourism can be hard on the environment as well, given how many more resources Westerners are accustomed to consuming.

Where Zoo Animals Go

What happens when a zoo animal gets old? It seems like an odd question, because one would assume that the animals would be allowed to live out their lives in the zoo environment with the animals with whom they've spent their lives. Sadly, while this is true for some popular and well-loved animals, the fate of most zoo animals is very different.

Zoos ship animals around the country many times throughout their lives. They manage populations in a way that is cost effective, keeps the right balance of animals for the zoo's mission, brings in visitors, and provides for breeding opportunities. This means that zoos will buy, sell, and borrow animals, sometimes temporarily and sometimes permanently, and remove animals from familiar environments and animals. Pandas, for instance, who are one of the rarest animals both in the wild and in zoos, are highly sought after by zoos that can afford them. Zoos must pay the Chinese government millions of dollars to acquire one, even on loan. Yet pandas increase zoo attendance whenever they arrive, so many zoos pay the money and pandas move from zoo to zoo.[32]

So what do zoos do when they have "surplus" animals? According to Dr. Albert H. Lewandowski, the chief veterinarian for the Cleveland Metroparks Zoo, surplus animals represent 1 to 2 percent of all zoo animals, and most zoos don't have space for them.[33] That means zoos must dispose of these old, sick, or just no-longer-useful animals. In the best cases, zoos find sanctuaries or other places where animals will be "retired." Sometimes, zoos euthanize animals and often sell animals through dealers and brokers to a variety of locations, including roadside zoos, private homes, exotic meat farms, research laboratories, the entertainment industry, and canned hunting operations.[34] The fact that zoos can and do consign their surplus animals to fates like these seems particularly ironic, given modern zoos' focus on captive breeding to save endangered species.

Thankfully, the American Zoo and Aquarium Association, the major US zoo accrediting agency, now prohibits member zoos from selling surplus animals to canned hunting operations or any other nonaccredited facilities. Unfortunately, this means that with fewer places to use to dispose of surplus animals, zoos resort to killing them. And nonaccredited zoos, which include most roadside zoos, petting zoos, and the like, don't need to abide by these rules at all. This means that after animals are no longer useful to roadside zoos, they sell these surplus animals to dealers who then ship them to private collectors, hunting ranches, or worse. For example, in 2006, country music singer

Troy Lee Gentry was indicted on federal charges from killing a tame bear named Cubby in 2004. The charges alleged that he had killed the bear while the animal was trapped in a pen. Gentry bought the bear for $4,650 from Minnesota Wildlife Connection, a private wildlife preserve that offers wildlife photography opportunities.[35]

The only real solution, if zoos were even to continue doing business, would be to strategically plan their "collections" so that all births and purchases were well planned out, creating no surplus animals, and further, that they only bring in animals to effectively further the goal of species or habitat conservation.

Marine Mammal Parks

Marine mammal parks and swim-with-dolphin programs differ from most zoos in that they make animals perform for the public rather than promoting their observation in their enclosures. Like the zoo industry, marine mammal park advocates state that keeping marine mammals like whales, dolphins, seals, and sea lions captive provides education to the public, allows scientists to gain information about the animals, and aids world conservation efforts. How would keeping animals in small pools and making them perform tricks in front of children do all this?

Sponsors of marine mammal parks, like zoos and other venues in which people can view wildlife, believe that entertaining the public with wild animals and educating them about their lives makes the public care more for those animals, and if the public cares, perhaps it will also support conservation efforts. By including lectures and exhibits on the lives of marine mammals and their natural habitats, as well as the importance of marine conservation, the parks mix educational messages with the fun of watching these playful animals. Dolphins, like pandas or other particularly cute animals, are especially effective at conveying this message because of their perceived friendliness, playfulness, and even the way their jaw line looks like a human smile. While zoos and marine parks encourage visitors to have an emotional connection to animals, by making them behave in humanlike ways, they also attempt to turn the public's fuzzy connection to these animals into an interest in conservation and an obligation to ensure that these animals survive in the wild. A 1995 Roper Center for Public Opinion Research poll, for example, reported that 90 percent of respondents believe that public display facilities provide a valuable means of educating the public.[36] However, no studies have measured the influence of these "educational programs" on people's behavior, especially as it relates to conservation.

Marine mammal parks also focus on learning about the animals themselves, employing scientists of all types to study the behavior, biology, and anatomy of the animals in the hopes of using that knowledge to extend their lives in the wild. Of course that knowledge may not be totally applicable to wild animals since the subjects are captive animals who often exhibit stereotypic behaviors associated with captivity. Like many zoos' captive breeding programs, this is more of a stopgap measure, given the massive human threats to dolphins, whales, and other animals from legal and illegal hunting, pollution, habitat loss, and more.

Finally, like zoos, marine mammal parks that have captive-breeding programs promote their efforts to ensure the continuation of endangered species. Certainly the captive breeding of dolphins, for instance, has reduced the need to remove dolphins from the wild for use in marine mammal parks, but so far no captive-born dolphins have been released to help wild populations sustain themselves. Less than 10 percent of zoos and marine parks are involved in conservation programs.[37]

But marine animal parks convey another message—that animals exist to entertain us, with their tricks, games, and pretend smiles. How much are people really learning, and wouldn't documentary films taken of animals in the wild combined with field trips to wildlife locations provide a better message? Displaying captive gorillas and tigers for hundreds of years has not helped to conserve these species that totter on the brink of extinction.

Marine mammals are, like other displayed animals, covered under the Animal Welfare Act, which provides standards for care and mandates that APHIS inspectors conduct annual inspections. Agencies such as the National Marine Fisheries Service (NMFS), which issues permits mandated by the Marine Mammal Protection Act and in conjunction with the Marine Mammal Commission, also oversee marine mammal parks and their practices involving catching, importing, transferring, and breeding marine mammals. Finally, a CITES permit is also required for importing a marine mammal listed under CITES into the United States. Swim-with-dolphin programs must also be licensed by the USDA, but the AWA provides no standards regulating the operation of these programs.

That's a lot of oversight, and it must mean that marine mammals are extremely well cared for, right?

The bad news is that the AWA regulations for the care of marine mammals are no better, and are in many cases worse, than they are for animals used in the pet and vivisection industries. A bottlenose dolphin, for example, is only required to have a twenty-four by twenty-four by six foot tank.[38] Standards are not as specific as they should be for the various species of marine mammals, all of whom require different types of food, space, water conditions, and more. The NMFS depends on parks to supply information on births, deaths, and transport, and oftentimes the parks simply do not furnish the information.

Even if the standards were much more exacting, however, is keeping wild dolphins, whales, and other animals in a captive environment cruel?

Michael Hutchins, director of conservation and science at the American Zoo and Aquarium Association, has stated that there is a "lack of appropriate medical screening, quarantine, pest control and sanitary procedures.... There's a clear pattern of preventable mortality as a result of factors controlled by zoo managers, exposures to toxins, extreme temperatures, injuries due to inappropriate social structure, starvation, poor nutrition, poor water quality, etc."[39]

In the wild, many species of marine mammals travel as many as one hundred miles per day and live in large, complicated social groups that fish or hunt for their own food and dive to extremely deep depths.

Killer whale pod. Killer whales, or orcas, live in the wild in groups of six to forty whales. (Photo courtesy of US Fish and Wildlife Service)

None of these conditions can be met in a concrete pool, no matter how expansive. As a result of the stresses and boredom of confinement, marine mammals can exhibit stereotypic behaviors such as aggressiveness, repetitive motions, obsessive chewing, and more. Their health suffers, too. They can suffer and die from reactions to chemicals such as chlorine in the water, poor water quality, bacterial infections, pneumonia, cardiac arrest, lesions, eye problems, ulcers, abscesses, and more.

Though some marine mammals can live longer in captivity now that conditions have improved, many do not. A 2004 investigation conducted by the *South Florida Sun-Sentinel* revealed, "More than 3,850 sea lions, seals, dolphins and whales have died under human care, many of them young. Of nearly 3,000 whose ages could be determined, a quarter died before they reached 1, half by the age of 7." The investigation also revealed that of the animals who had a cause of death listed, one in five died from avoidable causes including poisoning, consuming foreign objects, transit stress, and capture shock.[40]

The NMFS's public response to the investigation? "We've never really had the time and energy to do this sort of analysis," stated Steve Leathery, the head of the agency's marine mammal permitting office.[41]

The two oldest whales in captivity, Corky and Lolita, live at Sea World in San Diego and at the Miami Seaquarium, respectively. Better known by her stage name of Shamu, Corky was captured from the wild in 1969, when she was about five years old. She is only the latest whale to assume the Shamu moniker. The original Shamu was also captured and her mother killed by a harpoon in the process. She perished decades ago, as have her replacements. Corky spends much of her time endlessly circling her tank. Lolita has been in captivity since 1970.

The NMFS has not authorized a new permit for the catching of marine mammals for display since 1989 because of sufficient numbers of existing and breeding captive animals. Although it doesn't mean that the practice has been prohibited, at least the capture has lessened.

Catching marine mammals involves killing many other animals. Prior to 1989, the NMFS approved the vast majority of all permits, so it was hardly discriminating. The NMFS—which used to issue permits to the tuna industry to kill dolphins—is a branch of the Department of Commerce, making its allegiance to the animals somewhat questionable. Other nations—most notably Japan—continue to catch dolphins during bloody hunts for scientific research as well as for display in local marine parks. Marine parks that import wild-caught dolphins support captures such as the notorious dolphin drives in Japanese towns such as Futo and Taiji. Here, tens of thousands of dolphins not chosen for captivity are slaughtered for meat. Fishermen trap and kill these animals by frightening them into coves, spearing them, and cutting their throats. Gruesome footage reveals the water literally turning red with the blood of thousands of animals.[42]

The Public Reaction to Zoos and Marine Mammal Parks

Surveys show that zoo-goers react to animals in zoos with fear, awe, sadness, nostalgia, and unease about their captivity, and, as mentioned previously, that most do not take an educational message home with them. Instead, they have their own sense of human superiority over animals reinforced.[43]

So, while Americans and others go to zoos and marine mammal parks for entertainment, and because they have some fondness for animals, it's difficult to see the benefits to either the individual animals who must endure captivity, the species that are supposedly being saved, or even the visitors who come away with such mixed feelings.[44]

The concept of zoos is full of contradictions, or, as human-animal studies scholar Jonathan Burt puts it, they "are often places out of joint." [45] They offer visitors a chance to escape the city and journey into "nature," yet there is nothing natural about keeping penguins, tigers, or elephants in a city zoo. They are often housed indoors, with climate control to keep the animals alive, whether in a small, barred enclosure or in a large naturalistic setting made of fiberglass and concrete rocks.[46] Zoos are about conservation, yet this is a recent, and somewhat profit-driven, change. The history of Western zoos is tied to the destruction of wildlife around the world and is still involved in the capture of wild animals and the deaths of surplus animals—all in the name of conservation. Zoos are about education, yet some animals evidently have more educational value than others; pandas and other animals who are easy to anthropomorphize and who have the round furry bodies and big round eyes and who draw people to them are the most highly sought after, and they receive the most visitors.[47] People visit zoos because they love animals, yet even while they feel guilty about the conditions in which the animals live, self-interest (the desire to see or touch the animals) wins out, keeping zoos in perpetual business. It is strange that our love of animals and our ability to anthropomorphize at least some of them doesn't then allow us to empathize with them in order to end their captivity. Yet zoos still, as Nigel Rothfels puts it, disappoint. People don't just want to *see* animals; they want to *connect* with them, a condition that is impossible, given the structural limitations of the zoo. So even though zoos are for people and not for animals, we are still left unsatisfied.

CIRCUSES

The circus is a classic form of American family entertainment, as American as baseball and apple pie. For 150 years, Americans have been visiting the big top to be entertained by clowns, trapeze artists, acrobats, and a variety of animal acts. Who would not enjoy such wholesome entertainment?

Evidently, a great many people.

Circus attendance has dropped since the 1970s due to the rise of alternative forms of entertainment, as well as growing public concerns regarding the mistreatment of animals. To understand what the issues are with respect to circuses, we need to look at the history of the American circus as well as circus practices today.

History of the Circus

While circuses as we know them today are an American invention, they have their roots in two different historical phenomena: Roman public exhibitions and medieval European traveling shows.

Ancient Romans enjoyed attending a variety of public games and festivals, including horse and chariot races, gladiator competitions, and other human-animal events held in open-air arenas. The first such entertainment venue in Rome was the Circus Maximus, but these attractions, while popular, did not migrate to other parts of Europe. Instead, European elites entertained themselves with hunting, feasts, music, poetry, and athletic competitions, and, as discussed earlier, they owned private animal collections known as menageries. Commoners also entertained themselves with animal activities, but since they were excluded from hunting, they instead enjoyed bearbaiting (where a pack of dogs attacks an imported bear), cockfighting, as well as sports, plays, fortune-telling, magic acts, and traveling minstrel shows of all kinds. As people began to learn of the existence of exotic animals in European capitals, these animals began to join the traveling acts, along with the physically and mentally disabled, and beginning around the eighteenth century, native peoples. Traveling acts such as these were popular for centuries in Europe. At the end of the eighteenth century, they moved to the United States in the form of "dime museums." During the same time, Britain developed early versions of stationary circuses that combined equestrian activities with other entertainment in spaces such as the London Hippodrome.

American dime museums were started by men who called themselves scientists and ostensibly viewed these venues as educational, or more properly, educational through entertainment. In 1840 P. T. Barnum became the proprietor of the American Museum, bringing wild animal acts to prominence. These early dime museums exhibited animals alongside people with disabilities, tattooed people, native people, and "gaffes," or manufactured fakes like the Fijian mermaid, a mummified creation made up of the parts of multiple animals that was intended to resemble a mythological creature. Since people had never before seen any of these curiosities, managers and showmen were able to concoct bizarre explanations for their origins. These stories were morally and socially uplifting as well as educational. These exhibits told tales of cannibalism, savagery, and the man/"beast" connection seen then in both native people and the disabled. They left customers —white, civilized, and healthy—feeling not only good about themselves but good about the natural order and their place in it. At the end of the nineteenth century, the dime museum began to decline, but the acts themselves moved into newly developing venues like circuses— the rural version of the dime museum. By the 1840s the dime museum part of the circus finally became the circus sideshow, and P. T. Barnum, founder of the American Museum, went on to found P. T. Barnum's Museum, Menagerie, and Circus.

In the early days, circuses were relatively small affairs. Starting in the 1920s, more animals and more acts were added, and circuses grew into the large tent shows that we know today, capable of holding thousands of visitors for each show.

It's interesting to note that P. T. Barnum, founder of the first American circus, specialized originally in the display of freaks, only later moving on to animal acts. His first attraction was a blind, mostly paralyzed slave he purchased for $1,000 in 1835. He claimed that she was 161 years old and had served as George Washington's maid, and she brought in $750 per week. Later, after opening what would become Ringling Brothers and Barnum & Bailey Circus, his first major animal act was Jumbo, an elephant whom he purchased from the London Zoo in 1882 for $10,000.

Jumbo, like many of the other exotic animals used in circuses, was caught as a baby by the animal collector/hunters discussed in the previous section. Hans Schomburgk captured Jumbo in the Sudan in 1861, writing of the elephant's mother's death: "She collapsed in the rear and gave me the opportunity to jump quickly sideways and bring to bear a deadly shot, after which she immediately died. Obeying the laws of nature, the young animal remained standing beside its mother. . . . Until my men arrived, I observed how the pitful little baby continuously ran about its mother while hitting her with his trunk as if he wanted to wake her and make their escape."[48] After his mother's death, Jumbo was transported to Dar es Salaam, where he was used as a sandwich-sign carrier announcing concerts and events. His owner then sold him to a collector in Germany, and he was displayed in Carl Hagenbeck's Animal Park and later in the London Zoo. Jumbo died just three years after joining Barnum's circus, when he was killed by a train.

The story of Jumbo illustrates the vast importance of elephants to early circuses as well as those still operating today. Many circuses had multiple elephants, as expensive as they were; the Forepaugh-Barnum show in 1900, for example, had sixty elephants.[49] Jumbo's story also personifies the cruelty of the wild animal trade that furnished the elephants, tigers, and lions to the circus. It also demonstrates the often short life that a circus animal experienced, a situation that has not changed much today.

The circus continued to evolve in the United States during the twentieth century. Wild animal acts in which a trainer with a whip subdued dangerous animals began to become popular after the turn of the century. Even Carl Hagenbeck, famed animal dealer and zoo innovator, got into the act, creating traveling European circuses modeled after American circuses.[50]

Circuses Today

Most circuses still contain a mix of human and animal acts, although circuses no longer showcase human oddities (with a few exceptions, such as the popular freak show act Jim Rose Circus). Animal acts include old-fashioned equestrian events, wild animal acts, and a variety of trained elephant acts, which continue to remain the biggest crowd-pleasers and the biggest moneymakers for modern circuses.

Circus-goers can watch the trainer demonstrate his control over a dangerous wild animal through stunts by placing his head in a lion's mouth or by wrestling with a 350-pound tiger. Clyde Beatty, for instance, became famous in the 1930s for his acts that involved forcing big cats to perform tricks in a cage while he used a whip, a chair, and a gun to subdue them. These acts included lions, tigers, polar bears, leopards, dogs, wolves, and bears. The most well-known animal acts included elephants, and trainers forced them to stand on their front legs or on small podiums, carry circus performers or objects, balance on each other, and other tricks. Currently there are 675 elephants in the United States, and 125 of those are in circuses.[51]

How are the animals trained in these circuses? We know that during the early days of the circus, trainers threatened, whipped, and beat animals in order to get them to perform. Sadly, that is still the case in many circuses today. Former circus employees and undercover videos indicate that circus personnel may use food deprivation, intimidation, and various forms of physical and emotional punishment to train animals to perform tricks. Circuses like Ringling Brothers claim that their training methods are based on a loving bond between animal and trainer, yet undercover video footage shows elephants being whipped and shoved with bull hooks—a fireplace pokerlike tool used to control behavior—and electric prods.[52]

Even worse perhaps than the demeaning routines and the often abusive training are the conditions in which elephants and other circus animals must live. They are caged or "picketed" (which means chaining one front and one rear leg to a cable or chain) for most of their lives when they are not performing. Circus animals live a wholly unnatural life, and many respond to life in captivity by demonstrating stereotypic behaviors like weaving and rocking, which are associated with captivity-related stress.

Unfortunately, this stress manifests itself not only in these behaviors, but also in the illnesses and eventually the deaths of circus elephants. It also results in the numerous attacks in which elephants have lashed out at trainers or caregivers, sometimes killing them. In the United States alone, there have been twenty-eight deaths due to elephant attacks since 1983. These attacks virtually always result in the elephants being killed. Sadly, elephant attacks don't just happen at circuses or zoos; a former zoo elephant named Winky in 2006 killed a caregiver at an elephant sanctuary, demonstrating that even with excellent care, elephants are not suited for captivity.

Animals in zoos and circuses can pose a danger to the public, as well. In 2006 a Florida zoo director killed a rare two-hundred-pound tiger after she had escaped from her holding cell, which a handler had left unlatched.[53] In 2003 Roy Horn of the Las Vegas entertainment duo Siegfried and Roy was infamously mauled by his captive white tiger. There are countless documented cases of animals biting, kicking, and fatally trampling trainers; injuring onlookers; escaping and causing multi-car accidents; and stampeding through crowds and causing evacuations. Indeed, animals who lash out, escape, or simply act like wild animals risk being killed. Yet some captive animals have also helped people, such as the gorilla Binti at Chicago's Brookfield Zoo. She achieved fame in 1996 for gently picking up and cradling a boy who had fallen into the enclosure. She then brought him to the keeper's door for help.

What's more, facilities that allow people to interact with wild animals can present a public safety risk. Although the AWA requires private wild animal parks to put barriers between visitors and big cats, some operations allow people to touch these animals—and as a result, thirteen people have died from big cat attacks since 1990. About seven hundred private USDA licensees keep about five thousand big cats, either as pets or in private wildlife parks.[54]

A 2006 International Fund for Animal Welfare investigation revealed that even at USDA-licensed wild animal exhibits, operators fed big cats rotten meat, animals lived among "vermin and grossly inadequate sewage disposal," and most allowed interaction between people and big cats.[55]

It's not just animal protection groups that are concerned about the treatment of animals in circuses. Because circuses operate under the jurisdiction of the USDA, they undergo inspections by APHIS officers; Ringling Brothers and other major circuses have had their animal care practices investigated numerous times, resulting in formal complaints and citations, and tens of thousands of dollars in fines, settlements, and, in the case of Ringling Brothers, donations that the circus was required to make. Over a five year period from 1998 to 2003, the USDA conducted nine investigations into Ringling Brothers' activities.[56] In 2006, the agency opened four new investigations into Ringling Brothers' animal care, two of which involved deaths of young elephants at a captive breeding center.[57] Unfortunately, prosecutions are rare even when videotape documents the abuse, and the cozy relationship between Ringling Brothers and the USDA (Ringling Brothers gives seminars to USDA employees at their breeding center and is allowed to have their lawyers accompany APHIS inspectors on inspections at their facilities) results, more often than not, in cases being closed, even when the inspectors recommended that charges be made.[58]

Ringling Brothers is facing a lawsuit by a coalition of animal protection organizations that maintain the circus has violated the Endangered Species Act through its treatment of elephants.

Historically, all of the animals found in circus shows were captured from the wild. This is thankfully no longer the case for many animals, although many of the older elephants and other animals in modern circuses were born in the wild to parents who were shot to death in order to catch them. Ringling Brothers, in fact, opened in 1995 the Center for Elephant Conservation, an elephant captive-breeding program in Florida. This center has so far bred twenty Asian elephants, all of whom are used to supply Ringling's two touring units with elephant "performers," of whom there allegedly are currently sixty-one.[59] That's certainly great news for the circus industry, and it also means that Ringling no longer has to kill wild elephants in order to acquire them. (Even at this "conservation center," there allegedly has been abuse of the elephants. According to USDA records, workers forcibly wean babies from their mothers by using rope to separate the young from their mothers' sides.)[60] Unfortunately, other circuses around the world continue to capture wild elephants for their own operations by buying elephants from dealers who pay poachers to catch them. But it is odd that Ringling considers the captive breeding of elephants for use in the circus as an example of elephant conservation, even though it has not returned any of the elephants it has bred to the wild.[61] While the circus claims that some of its ticket sales go to conservation efforts, it does not reveal how much. Many conservationists and prominent critics such as biologist Marc Bekoff dismiss Ringling's other claims, such as the idea that scientists could use sperm from its captive males to impregnate wild elephants—especially since the million dollars it spends each year to breed circus performers could help elephants much more effectively if it addressed habitat preservation efforts.

Ringling Brothers and the rest of the circus industry routinely oppose laws that would prohibit or limit the use of animals in circuses, or that mandate more humane methods of care or would prohibit cruel training methods such as the use of the bull hook.[62] Representatives for Feld Entertainment, Ringling's parent company, testified against a 2006 California bill that would have limited the number of hours that circus elephants could be chained, mandated a minimum number of acres for each captive elephant, and banned the use of bull hooks.[63] To their credit, Ringling Brothers did support the passage of the Elephant Conservation Act in 1997, which provides financial rewards to local populations that help conserve elephant populations. On the other hand, activists claim that Feld Entertainment supports reopening the ivory trade, a charge Ringling denies. Ringling spokesperson Barbara Pflughaupt, however, noted that funds raised from ivory sales would benefit conservation, and Feld donated $7,000 to former Rep. Richard Pombo in 2003, one of Congress's most active elephant-hunting proponents.[64] In addition, Ringling Brothers spent $840,000 from 1998 to 2004 on lobbying the federal government and $180,000—its biggest sum yet—in 2004 alone on lobbying activities.[65]

The Captive Elephant Accident Prevention Act of 1999, had it passed, would have criminalized the use of elephants in circuses and other traveling shows or for rides. Predictably, the circus industry testified and maintained that the bill was based not only on inaccurate information about elephant treatment at circuses but was also simply "special interest legislation designed to promote the philosophy of a special interest group that is out of step with the views of the average American."[66]

Today, of course, circus lovers who don't want to participate in the cruelties described above can attend circuses that don't use animals,

Barbara, a former circus elephant, lived at the Elephant Sanctuary until her death in 2001. (Photo courtesy of the Elephant Sanctuary)

Barbara

Barbara was a female Asian elephant who was born in 1966 in the wilds of Southeast Asia. In 1968, when Barbara was two years old, she was captured by native elephant trainers known as *mahouts*. The mahouts, riding atop their trained elephants, captured Barbara by walking into the herd and dropping ropes around her neck and legs. With a trained elephant on either side, Barbara was dragged from her jungle home. She was taken to an elephant "work camp," where elephants move trees for the logging industry.

During the first few weeks at the logging camp, Barbara was tied to a tree, and her movement was severely limited. She was completely dependent on the mahouts for food, water, and medical treatment. Once Barbara learned to tolerate life in captivity, she was loaded into a wooden crate and sent by ship to the United States. Barbara arrived in Florida along with seven other elephants who would be her family for the next twenty-four years.

A circus purchased Barbara and the other elephants. For several months trainers taught the elephants a variety of tricks, including standing on their hind legs, lying down, and holding one another's tails. Learning the tricks was not difficult, but it was stressful and unnatural. For the next twelve years, Barbara and her new family performed in traveling circuses throughout the United States.

By fourteen she was of breeding age. Other members of her family were already pregnant when the herd was retired to a breeding facility in Florida. Sometime during this transition from performing to breeding, Barbara began to lose weight. Over the next twelve years Barbara struggled with this weight-loss condition. Several baby elephants were born during this time, but none to Barbara.

In November 1995, Barbara and her family were once again moved, this time to the Ringling Brothers, Barnum and Bailey Circus breeding compound. Ringling Brothers refused to allow Barbara to accompany the other elephants. Due to her emaciated appearance, Barbara was separated from her family and forced to live in solitary confinement, where she quickly became severely depressed.

On April 25, 1996, two thousand pounds underweight, Barbara was permanently relocated to the Elephant Sanctuary in Tennessee. She became the second resident of the nation's only natural-habitat refuge for Asian elephants. Barbara and Tarra, the sanctuary's first resident, became immediate friends, and, until Barbara's death five years later, they remained side by side, grazing the pastures and cooling themselves in the spring-fed stream.

—Story provided by the Elephant Sanctuary, www.elephants.com

such as the immensely popular Cirque du Soleil—one of a number of circuses within the Cirque Nouveau movement—or Chinese acrobat performances. Even modern traveling circus sideshows cater to folks with less mainstream tastes. Countries such as Sweden, Austria, Costa Rica, India, Finland, and Singapore have banned animal circuses. And twenty-seven US municipalities have passed measures banning circuses that use exotic animals.

RODEOS

The rodeo is a historical legacy from the days of the frontiersman and the American cowboy, combining traditions borrowed from nineteenth-century cattle ranching with more modern activities. Working cowboys held contests to see who was the best calf roper or who could best "break" wild horses into saddle horses, and these informal contests eventually formed the rodeo.

Another influence was the Wild West shows popular at the turn of the century, such as Buffalo Bill's Wild West Show and Exhibition. These shows combined reenactments of historical cowboy scenes with shooting and racing competitions, and they involved the use of horses and cattle, as well as Native Americans. Finally, modern rodeos are influenced by the Spanish and Mexican *vaqueros*, who worked with cattle in the Southwest.

Veterinarian and rodeo scholar Elizabeth Lawrence called rodeos ritual events, which serve to "express, reaffirm, and perpetuate certain values and attitudes characteristic of the cattle herders' way of life."[67] In this interpretation, the rodeo borrows the main themes from the cowboy's life and exaggerates them through performances with horses, who are viewed as the cowboy's primary work partners.

Rodeos include two types of competitions: roughstock events and timed events. Most also give an award for best "all-around cowboy."

Roughstock events involve the cowboy riding a bull or a bucking bronc in order to demonstrate his dominance over the animal. For instance, bareback riding is an event in which the cowboy subjugates a "wild horse," riding him bareback. It is a dangerous sport, both for the riders—bareback riders suffer more injuries than all other rodeo cowboys—and for the animals, who endure the pain of the bucking strap, a leather belt that is tightened around the animals' flank and that can cause painful, bloody sores. Timed events, on the other hand, are those that involve riders using horses to perform traditional cowboy tasks in a set amount of time. There are also additional events such as barrel racing (in which a rider on a horse races around barrels) and trick and clown performances, many of which include horses.

Traditionally, roughstock competitions used wild mustangs, because the subjugation of the wild Spanish mustang was a part of the cowboy's life during frontier days and symbolized the conquering of the American West. Successful cowboys were able to catch wild horses and not only subdue them, but eventually also tame them to the extent that they could be trained even for specialty activities like cattle roping and dressage, a form of training that results in an orchestrated performance. Saddle-bronc riding is similar to bareback riding, except that the cowboy uses a saddle, but the horse still wears a bucking strap. In both riding styles (as well as in the case of bull riding, which has no traditional origin, but rodeos still use it to demonstrate the cowboy's fearlessness), the rider must remain on the animal for at least eight seconds while using only one hand.[68] Bronc riding is the centerpiece of a rodeo performance.

Because there are few wild horses left, broncs are now purposely bred to jump, kick, and flip around their riders. So, while the sport is supposed to be symbolic of the conquering of the wild horse by man, the modern way the sport is carried out—selectively breeding domesticated broncs to look and act wild, so that they can be ridden and subdued for show—represents a powerful irony.[69] In addition, today, many broncs are former saddle horses who "went bad," or started to buck riders off. Since broncs are not confined in a pen or stall for most of the year, in that sense at least, it is less inhumane than other types of horse events, where horses have very little freedom to roam.[70]

The timed events such as calf roping not only demonstrate the cowboy's ability to rope the calf but also how well the cowboy's horse has been trained. This particular task is a difficult one for the horse to learn, as he must move backward, pull against the rope, stand firm without moving, and perform other difficult tasks. In calf roping, the cowboy must compete against the clock and rope his calf as quickly as possible. Steer wrestling is a similar event in which the cowboy, known as a "bulldogger," wrestles a steer to the ground as quickly as he can by grasping the animal's horn while still hanging on to his moving horse. Team roping is another timed event that involves two cowboys riding two horses. They first chase the steer, rope him around either his horns, head, or neck, then rope both of his hind legs, throwing him on the ground in the process.

All of these events are dangerous to the riders—which only adds to their appeal and the size of the prize that riders can win—but they're also dangerous to the horses, bulls, and calves. Who oversees rodeos to ensure the safety of the animals? Sadly, no government entity oversees the hundreds of professional and amateur rodeo events that take place every year. Instead, the Professional Rodeo Cowboys Association (PRCA) sets up standards that rodeos sponsored by the association (but not amateur rodeos or rodeos sanctioned by other organizations) and its ten thousand members must abide by. The sixty animal care regulations include a mandate that veterinarians be present for every performance; that animals can't be transported for a period of more than twenty-four hours without food and water; that team-roped steer are protected by horn wraps; that cattle in timed events aren't used two years in a row; that spurs on boots be dulled; and that animals be inspected for health prior to events.[71]

So, is there a problem with rodeos from the standpoint of animal cruelty? There must be a reason why virtually every national animal protection organization in the United States opposes rodeos. It doesn't take an expert to see the obvious pain and fear involved in a great many rodeo activities, but most especially those that involve steer or calf roping, in which calves and steers are moving at speeds of up to thirty miles an hour, then are dragged to a stop and thrown on the ground by a horse and a rider moving at the same dangerous speed. Broken necks are a common—and fatal—result.

Bucking contests such as bareback riding, saddle-bronc riding, and bull riding are also contests in which mostly tame animals are encouraged to buck by the application of a bucking strap, also known as a flank strap, sometimes with burrs stuck underneath it to cause extra irritation. Performers also use electric prods (according to rules, "as little as possible,") to cause the animal to buck. Spurs, even though they must now be "dull," still cause pain when stuck into an animal's side, again causing bucking. PRCA claims that bucking straps do not cause animals to buck, but that they only cause an animal who is already bucking to "kick high with its back feet."[72]

Finally, constant traveling is stressful on any animal, even with requirements that the animals have food and water once every twenty-four hours. Rodeo animals are transported in trailers, some of which are double-decker, and the PRCA says these are "specially designed for their protection."[73] Yet, transporting animals from rodeo to rodeo can cause injuries from fighting in as well as riding in the trailers.

Rodeo advocates claim, as do others whose livelihoods depend on the use of these animals for profit, that their animals are healthy and happy and that they could not perform well if they were not. However, rodeo animals are sent to slaughter when they are no longer useful, and untrained animals such as cattle are particularly expendable.

ANIMAL RACING

Animal racing has been around for thousands of years. The ancient Greeks and Romans, for instance, famously held chariot races using horses. Greyhound racing, the oldest and most popular of dog races, has its origins in "coursing," an ancient activity in which hunters used hounds to chase and bring down animals such as hares, foxes, and deer. Betting has accompanied dog and horse racing for thousands of years, thus providing profit not only to those people involved in breeding, training, or racing the animals but also to the general public. People attend horse races around the country and dog races in fifteen states, both for the thrill of the race as well as the hope of winning.

Horse Racing

Horse racing is most commonly practiced in the form of thoroughbred racing, where wealthy owners of finely bred horses hire trainers and jockeys to race them. Horses race are held in the United States on a variety of tracks and at a variety of distances, usually from nine hundred meters to a mile and a half per race.

Thoroughbred breeding and horse racing is a multibillion dollar industry. Training a thoroughbred can cost $22,000 per year, stud fees for top stallions can start at $25,000 and go up to $500,000, and top racing horses can cost up to $10 million. Add to those amounts the money made from gambling bets, tourist expenditures, the "purse" awarded to the owner of the winning horse (which now exceeds $1 million for the top races), and other related income, and horse racing is big money. In 1991 Alabama alone estimated its racing industry to be worth $80 million per year, and Maryland's racing industry may bring in an astounding $1 billion per year.[74] So it's not surprising that those with a vested interest in racing and gambling will do everything in their power to preserve their economic interests, and it's also no surprise to learn that the horses who bring in all this money are not protected under any federal legislation.[75] Instead, they are "regulated" by each state's racing or gaming commissions, whose concern lies largely with ensuring that the gambling takes place legally and that nothing is done behind the scenes to throw a race.

While on the one hand, handlers devote exacting attention to ensure the well-being of the top-ranked horses, the same cannot be said for those horses who are not so successful. Minimum living and training standards must certainly be met, but the practice of racing itself is rife with dangers to the horse: it is common for them to fall or fracture their bones while racing or training, which are often fatal conditions for horses. Sometimes, injured horses are illegally drugged so that they will race despite an injury. Other common injuries are those to ligaments or muscles as well as joint sprains, and many race horses are also susceptible to a disease called exercise-induced pulmonary hemorrhage.[76] Even top, well-cared-for horses suffer mightily for a sport in which all but a very few benefit. Barbaro, the winner of the 2006 Kentucky Derby and a favorite to win the Preakness Stakes, broke his leg during the Preakness. He received the best medical attention, but sadly, was euthanized because of the extent of his injuries in early 2007. Yet, Barbaro's accident and death became newsworthy to many who don't even follow horse racing, illustrating the public's concern for racing horses. It also demonstrates the cruelties of a sport that occasionally requires sacrifices resulting from the continuous and strenuous training required of a winning horse. Even after Barbaro's death, his genes are worth millions and his owners and trainers will surely capitalize on them, using them to create countless future racing stars.[77]

What happens when a racing horse's career is over? A winning stallion like Barbaro will usually be put up to stud when he is retired, and the most successful horses can hope to live a life of leisure once retired. But thousands of horses, most of whom will never win a race, are bred each year. Most horses will see their careers end after just a season or two and will be sold at auction—sometimes to people who want them as pets, sometimes to businesses like horseback-riding outfits, and sometimes to slaughter. Indeed, the winner of the 1986 Kentucky Derby, Ferdinand, was reportedly slaughtered in Japan for pet food.[78] In 2006 three foreign-owned slaughterhouses in Illinois and Texas killed 100,800 American horses, exporting their meat to Europe.[79] The Texas slaughterhouses closed, and in 2007, Illinois Governor Rod Blagojevich signed a bill prohibiting the slaughter of horses for human consumption, closing the nation's last remaining horse slaughterhouse.

Greyhound Racing

Dog racing, like horse racing, is a physically challenging sport with few real stars and more losers than winners. But dog racing has a far darker side that concerns the treatment of the dogs and their disposition, which is one reason why it only occurs on forty-six tracks in fifteen states today.

Traditionally, handlers trained greyhounds by encouraging them to race after a live rabbit or hare; today, the only legal way to train racing greyhounds is via an artificial lure that looks like a rabbit. The Greyhound Association of America, one of the two main greyhound-racing advocacy organizations, claims that "industry members who violate this practice may be expelled from the sport for life."[80] However, as recently as 2002, a greyhound breeder was caught using at least 180 living and dead domestic rabbits to train his dogs.[81] Sadly, this was no isolated occurrence, given the number of other reports of similar cruelties.

Like horse racing, greyhound racing is associated with gambling and takes place at the same tracks on which horses are raced and with the infrastructure in place for gambling. It is a less-lucrative industry than horse racing, but it has the potential to bring in big dollars: 3.5 million fans bet $3.5 billion in 1992, the year the sport was at its peak.[82] Since then, attendance has been down thanks to the unsavory reputation of the sport and the wide public concern about the mistreatment of the dogs, but revenue still tops $1 billion a year. The racing industry and especially the track owners give thousands of dollars to politicians in states where the legislatures have considered banning the sport; this tactic has served them well in states like Massachusetts and Rhode Island, both of which tried unsuccessfully to ban dog racing.

In a world in which millions of companion dogs are still euthanized every year for no other reason but there are too many of them, the breeding in the greyhound industry is certainly a cause for concern. More than 1,500 breeding "farms" breed nearly 30,000 dogs every year for this cruel sport.[83] They are located even in states where greyhound racing is illegal.

Breeding greyhounds live like so many other dogs bred in puppy mills for the commercial pet industry: stacked in kennels either outdoors or in barns, with no exercise, no toys, no love, and no life outside the cage. Even racing dogs live in small kennels during their life off the track; sometimes as many as a thousand dogs live at each track. Because there is so little regulation about the care of racing dogs, most racetracks have their own rules regarding dog welfare.

Because greyhounds are so much cheaper to breed and train than thoroughbreds, they are much more expendable. As the former director of the National Greyhound Association, Gary Guccione, noted, "There's no practical way to control how many are being bred. . . . The expense of getting into the greyhound business is much less than other forms of racing. This makes people want to breed a lot to get that one litter that has the champion in it."[84] Furthermore, gambling makes greyhound owners much more interested in the short-term investment potential of their dogs rather than in their lifelong care. Injuries are rampant in the industry, including broken legs, necks, and heart attacks. Some dogs are drugged in order to perform, and kennel cough is common due to the close living conditions. Veterinary care is

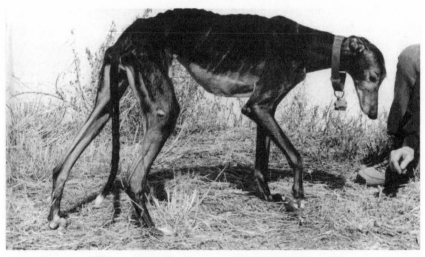

An emaciated Fever right after her rescue by Greyhound Companions of New Mexico. (Photo courtesy of Greyhound Companions of New Mexico)

minimal for animals who are only expected to live for, at most, a couple years.

But perhaps nothing is more horrific in the greyhound industry than what happens to a dog when his or her career is over. While racing dogs' lifespans are more than twelve years, they stop racing after three to five years. Some dogs are returned to the breeding farms on which they were born, spending the rest of their lives in small ken-

---

Fever

On February 18, 2000, Fever's previous adopter surrendered her to Greyhound Companions of New Mexico. Weighing only twenty-eight pounds and resembling a corpse, neither words nor photos can depict the grave condition of this pitiful greyhound. Trembling from weakness and the below-freezing temperature, Fever struggled to stand while her adopter casually recounted the story of how and when she obtained this six-and-a-half-year-old greyhound and why she was surrendering her to me.

The woman had adopted Fever from a Texas greyhound adoption group in August 1998. A year and a half later, this once-lively retired racer was succumbing to what appeared to be the final stages of starvation and prolonged confinement in a crate.

After overcoming the initial shock of seeing an animal so close to death from starvation, I rushed her home to shampoo her and replace the collar that harbored the same stench as she, likely from dried fecal matter and/or vomit. I made arrangements for immediate veterinary care, which was essential for her survival.

Over the next few months, Fever improved dramatically, going from twenty-eight to sixty-two pounds and developing a love for shoes, stuffed animals, car rides, and meals. Meanwhile, Greyhound Companions of New Mexico, along with the district attorney's office, pursued animal cruelty charges against the woman who had abused Fever. Indicted by the grand jury, the woman later entered a plea of no contest to extreme cruelty to animals. Her sentencing included psychological counseling, community service, and supervised probation for one year.

Fever was bred for one purpose: to race and make money for the people who invested money in her. Most greyhounds begin life at breeding farms tucked away in rural areas. These remote farms are often the burial grounds for the greyhounds who will never qualify for any racetrack. The burial sites are also the final resting place for the racers who are too slow or too broken to continue competing, and no adoption group has room for them.

Many greyhounds are killed before they are ever raced, and most will not make it to the age of three due to injuries or other disqualifying traits. Fever was unusual because she raced until she was four years old. But once she stopped earning her keep at the racing kennel, she was replaced by younger, faster dogs. Luckily, a greyhound rescue group in Texas rescued her. Otherwise, she would have likely been loaded onto a "kill truck" or sent "back to the breeding farm," which is a euphemism for a bullet to the head. Breeding is not an option for racers who aren't highly successful, as they likely will not produce winners. Losing greyhounds are also sold or given away to hunters, illegal racers, or even medical researchers.

On October 20, 2004, Fever lost her battle with escalating health problems and died at the age of eleven. Fever had four years and eight months in her second home, where she lived free from the neglect and abuse she suffered at the hands of her first adopter, following a life of hardship at the racetrack. In spite of the injustices she endured, she remained gentle, affectionate, and kind to all the people and animals she encountered.

Fever's story should serve as a reminder that adoption is not always a happy ending for retired racing greyhounds. Hopefully, this will stir the conscience of all who think adoption is the answer to problems inherent within the dog-racing industry. The termination of breeding greyhounds for the purpose of racing is the ultimate protection for these dogs. Adoption is not the solution; abolishing racing is.

—Judy Paulsen for Greyhound Companions of New Mexico

nels as breeders. Owners or track operators kill some dogs outright. While neither the National Greyhound Association nor the Greyhound Racing Association of America include information about this common practice on the "animal welfare" pages of their Web sites, in 2002 the bodies of three thousand greyhounds were found at the home of a former security guard at an Alabama racetrack, who was paid ten dollars apiece to "retire" them.[85]

Fever enjoying her well-deserved life of luxury.
(Photo courtesy of Greyhound Companions of New Mexico)

The good and the bad news about greyhound racing is that there is an enormous number of US greyhound rescue groups that will take former racing greyhounds, rehabilitate them, and find them adoptive homes. This is good news because these groups place thousands of animals who would otherwise suffer horrific deaths into good homes every year. The bad news is that the presence of these selfless people allows greyhound breeders, trainers, owners, and racers to continue to breed thousands more dogs every year, dogs who they will dispose of in a very short time. They will be able to boast of the adoptions as if they themselves were to thank for this one small bit of mercy. On the other hand, some "rescue groups" have been caught over the years selling their rescued greyhounds into biomedical research via class B dealers. This is perhaps the saddest end that these animals can experience in an industry that profits from suffering.

BLOOD SPORTS

Blood sports such as dogfighting and cockfighting are illegal in nearly every state, yet, in isolated rural areas and even inner cities, these activities are growing in popularity. In addition, coursing, the competitive racing of dogs to catch and kill rabbits, is allowed in some states. While most of us wouldn't consider attending any blood sports, these criminal and barbaric activities still harm millions of animals each year.

Dogfighting involves placing two viciously "trained" dogs in an enclosure, where they fight until one is too injured to continue and quits the fight due to extreme pain or severe exhaustion, or until one dies. Some dogfighters use performance-enhancing drugs as well.

At a dogfight, more than a hundred people may place bets up to fifty thousand dollars. The underground dogfighting industry is huge, with millions of dollars involved in selling, breeding, training, fighting, and betting on the dogs. Some top dogs are worth tens of thousands of dollars. And there's even more that goes on at dogfights than the abuse and illegal gambling. Drugs are commonplace at fights, and gang activity is often involved as well, especially at the inner-city fights that are increasing in popularity.

Oftentimes, organized and violent crime goes hand-in-hand with both cockfighting and dogfighting. For example, in August 2006, two intruders broke into the home of a high-profile dogfighter and pit bull breeder and killed him. Thomas Weigner bled to death after his attackers attempted to torture him and force him to reveal where he had hidden the hundred thousand dollars he had won at recent dogfight. Authorities discovered that Weigner had about three hundred pit bulls tied to stakes or confined in small pens.[86]

Photos of dogs who have survived dogfights show pit bulls with faces scarred so badly they often cannot see—assuming they still have eyes. Injuries include ripped ears, scars, ripped mouths and noses, crushed sinuses, tissue damage, and broken bones. Deaths are usually attributable to these injuries, massive blood loss, and sometimes exhaustion. While rules generally state that a fight ends when a dog gives up or refuses to engage the other dog, some fights can last hours and end only when one dog dies an agonizing death.[87] Seriously injured survivors may die days later from blood loss or infection, or their owners may kill them if they do not wish to keep a dog who loses.

Though dogfighting is illegal in every state and a felony in forty-eight states, it is growing in popularity. About 250,000 dogs—mostly pit bulls—are victims every year. It's estimated that at least 40,000 people across the country either own or breed pit bulls for fighting, and it's difficult for police to monitor criminal activity because dogfighters are so secretive. One investigator told the *Fort Worth Star-Telegram*, "This dogfighting deal is right under our noses. It's a big deal . . . probably as big as the underworld drug business. It's everywhere."[88]

Of the dogs lucky enough to be rescued from dogfighting rings, most are too aggressive to be adopted into new homes. Kennels breed dogs for an artificially high level of dog aggression, which puts other neighborhood companion animals at extreme risk. Indeed, the breeding process itself can even be dangerous for the dogs, and breeders may use a "rape box" to restrain female dogs from attacking males during breeding. As a result of their training and breeding, the great majority of rescued dogs face euthanasia at shelters.

Cockfighting involves placing two specially bred and trained "gamecocks" together in a pit and betting on the winner. Cockfighters, or "cockers," usually attach razor-sharp knives or ice pick–like gaffs to the birds' legs to injure and mutilate opponents. Birds often suffer from lacerations, eye injuries, punctured lungs, and broken bones. Like dogfights, cockfights often end in death, although some animals are forced to fight again and again.

Cockfighters cut the comb (the red comblike structure on top of the head) and wattle (the red pouchlike material at the front of the throat) off the birds, and they often give the birds drugs such as steroids, strychnine, or amphetamines to increase aggression, slow blood loss, and increase chances of winning. Like pit bulls, roosters found by enforcement officers during busts are invariably euthanized.

Hundreds of people can attend a fight, and they can erupt into violence even outside of the pit. High-stakes betting and weapons are commonplace at cockfights, and like dogfighting, the practice is connected to the illicit drug trade. Arguments at cockfights can result in human injuries, and fatal shootings are not uncommon.[89]

Cockfighting is illegal in every state but Louisiana and a felony in thirty-three states. As of this writing, Louisiana's Senate and House were expected to agree on a bill banning cockfighting. However, many states only prosecute cockfighting criminals with misdemeanor charges, and in states such as Texas, it is not illegal to attend a cockfight. In addition, in New Mexico where the practice was banned in early 2007, cockfighters have pledged to continue to practice their sport, the new law notwithstanding. In 2007 President George W. Bush signed a bill that made it a felony to buy, sell, or transport animals across state lines for the purpose of fighting. The bill also made it a felony to buy, sell, or transport weapons used in cockfighting.

Coursing is a blood sport in which people race dogs to catch and kill wild rabbits. While coursing is no longer common in the United States, open-field coursing is still practiced in some states in the West. This involves allowing greyhounds and other sight hounds to chase and catch jackrabbits in an open field. After participants locate the rabbits, they flush them out of their hiding spots so that they are out in the open. Then they release two or three dogs who chase the rabbits. Judges award points to the dogs based on their performance, including their aggressive pursuit and how many times they make a rabbit change direction. The rabbits who do not manage to escape are killed by the dogs inflicting back and neck injuries, punctured organs, and chest injuries. According to one recent television investigation, rabbits suffer a "slow, terrible death," with tug-of-wars between the dogs going on for a minute and forty-five seconds.[90] While many states have banned coursing, it is still legal in a few states such as California and Wyoming.[91]

FILM AND TELEVISION

People have used animal imagery for thousands of years. Representing animals in art, myth, literature, folktales, and architecture is a way that humans have conveyed complicated ideas and thoughts about both humanity and the animal kingdom. So we should not be surprised to find that with modern technologies such as photography, television, or film, animals are represented as well.

Art historian John Berger suggests that the prevalence of animal images in modern society substitutes for a lost direct relationship with animals.[92] This may very well be true and could account for the increasing popularity of nature films and television shows about animals, especially wild animals. But what are the effects of all of this animal imagery around us?

Archaeologist and film historian Jonathan Burt shows that how we see animals and how we think about them has changed thanks to the way that we see them on film.[93] We know that many films, television shows, or advertising campaigns involving animals often result in an explosion of adoptions or purchases of the animals depicted—and later, abandonment of those same animals. Such was the case for dalmatians following the live-action version of Disney's *101 Dalmatians*, Chihuahuas following the Taco Bell television commercials, and Jack Russell terriers due to the popularity of the television show *Frasier*. Other films might have an effect on how we view controversial animal issues, such as increased interest in vegetarianism following the films *Babe* or *Chicken Run* or heightened concerns about the keeping of captive whales following *Free Willy*.

But what about the real animals used in the fictional television programs and films, or in television commercials? The Animal Welfare Act regulates the use of performing animals on television or in film. As such, the USDA oversees the use of these animals, but as with the other industries regulated in this fashion, inspections are infrequent, standards of care are minimal, and laws are loosely enforced. In addition, movies that are shot outside the United States do not have to obey

American laws and will not get penalized if, for instance, animals are killed on set.

There is another side to Hollywood's use of animals on film—where the animals come from, and in what conditions they live when they are not on the set. While many domestic animals in movies or on TV today no doubt are well-loved companions whose guardians want to make them stars, many other domestic and wild animals are owned by animal trainers who keep them in kennels between productions. Some of these trainers no doubt provide exemplary conditions for their animals, and those that use exclusively domestic animals often adopt them from animal shelters. However, not all of them provide adequate care. While these trainers must have USDA licensing as animal exhibitors, we have seen that this does not ensure good welfare. Because there is no real oversight for private trainers who train wild and domestic animals for film and television, it's difficult to know how humanely the animals are trained. But given the intelligence, short attention span, and willfulness of a variety of wild animals, negative reinforcement is certainly one method used in order to achieve an obedient, well-trained animal. Primatologist Sarah Baeckler, for example, worked as a trainer with chimpanzees, and she saw animals being hit by other trainers when they did not perform correctly.[94] Training methods used to train elephants in circuses and zoos such as the bull hook are also used by those who train elephants for film and television.

The origins and keeping of wild animals for performances is more troubling. Wild animal actors are purchased from the same dealers who supply zoos, circuses, private collectors, and game farms, and many are taken from the wild, using the same unscrupulous methods discussed earlier in this chapter. Some trainers will acquire an animal for use in a single production, then turn around and sell the animal back to the dealer for other uses. Other times, trainers will breed or contract with a breeder to produce multiple animals to be used for one project; once that project is over, the surplus animals must be sold. For example, dozens of mountain lion cubs specifically bred for *Benji the Hunted* were immediately sold after the production through *Animal Finders' Guide*. As the

Performing Animal Welfare Society points out, the movie *Babe*, which had such an effect on the public with its positive message about farm animals, used more than nine hundred animals for the production, all of whom had to be placed after the film; while some may have been placed into private homes as companions, others no doubt were sold to farms and eventually slaughtered for food.[95]

Some animal training companies, like Hollywood Animals, rent out animal actors (including elephants, lions, tigers, bears, leopards, and panthers, as well as domestic animals) for use at private parties, promotional events, as well as in film. Other companies, such as Have Trunk, Will Travel, which provides elephants for films, television, weddings, and parties, promote themselves as conservationist organizations by breeding elephants "to ensure that our grandchildren will have the chance to see and appreciate these amazing animals."[96]

It will be a sad day indeed when we have to rely on companies like Have Trunk, Will Travel to provide the last possible opportunity for us to see elephants.

CONCLUSION

Americans crave animals in their lives. For many people, beloved companion animals don't completely fill that need. As the continued existence of zoos and circuses as well as use of animals in television, film, and more demonstrate, many of us seek out wild animals, even when that means we will support industries that cause harm to those very same animals.

Sometimes, it's difficult to see the harm when entertainment venues such as circuses, marine mammal parks, and even zoos hide their morally unpleasant dealings behind a façade of glitzy performances or even conservation rhetoric, creating an uncertain ambivalence for many people who are uncomfortable without knowing quite why. What's wrong with visiting the zoo, or the circus, or a marine mammal park, or even the rodeo?

One example of the downside of the entertainment industry's animal use is Mikey, a chimpanzee entered into the 2006 World Series of Poker by his owner and PokerShare.com. His participation in the contest was a marketing stunt intended to earn enough money to defray the costs of keeping him in a private home.[97] What's so wrong with a chimpanzee playing poker? Is it the way that this intelligent, complex animal was degraded by sitting in a chair, wearing children's clothing, pretending to play cards while he stuffed poker chips in his mouth? Is it the fact that Mikey could have been "trained" using punishments such as food deprivation or beatings at one time in his life? Or is it instead the possibility that Mikey could have been taken as a baby from his home in West Africa? Or maybe it's the possibility that as Mikey grows older, and less easy to handle, he will be sold to an animal dealer who will in turn sell him to someplace much worse?

In the end, it's all of those reasons. Mikey should be living in Africa with his kin, traveling with his fellow chimps, foraging for food, battling over status, grooming his friends, and even dying in the wild. No one has a right to take him away from that life and to turn him into something he's not—especially for profit and pleasure.

Other times, it's clearer that there's something wrong with the way we interact with animals outside of our homes. Blood sports, for instance, which are almost completely illegal in the United States, involve pitting two or more animals against each other in a fight to the death, as in cockfighting, dogfighting, or coursing. The fact that cockfighting and dogfighting are still widely practiced is a poor statement about the morals of some of our fellow citizens.

While the routine deaths of thousands of dogs and a fewer number of horses per year in the racing industries should be enough to give most sports fans pause, these industries continue to make billions of dollars of profit for racing enthusiasts every year.

It appears that until the time comes when we no longer have a desire to use wild as well as domestic animals for profit and pleasure, animals will continue to suffer. Perhaps we can learn to expand the already rich variety of programs and films available that show wild animals in their own habitats, such as the poignant and remarkable *March of the Penguins*, as well as the incredibly realistic computer-generated animation and animatronics that allow us to view all manner of animals without interfering in an animal's life.

In 2006 family films like *Charlotte's Web*, *Hoot*, *Happy Feet*, and *Open Season* grabbed moviegoers' attention with animal-friendly messages, while *Fast Food Nation* informed millions of slaughter-house cruelties. At the same time, the number of Americans who enjoy watching wildlife in animals' natural habitats reached more than 70 million, demonstrating a growing willingness to connect with animals on their own turf and on their own terms.

There is nothing better than meeting real animals. A growing number of sanctuaries provide opportunities to develop a relationship with both wild and domestic animals. Hundreds of wildlife sanctuaries across the country provide a second chance to countless injured and orphaned wild animals. And a growing number of farm animal sanctuaries give people a chance to get to know all manner of friendly, happy animals.

Not only can we still interact with animals, but we can learn from them, too. All we have to do is listen the right way. Both people as well as animals could be better for it.

What You Can Do

The following are a number of ways that readers can improve the lives of animals used for entertainment.

- Seek out entertainment activities that don't exploit animals.
- When you see films advertised with wild animal "actors," write to the producers to let them know why you will not go to see their film.
- On the other hand, send letters of thanks to studios that produce films with computer-generated versions of animals.
- When you see wild animals used in television commercials,

write to the companies behind the ads and tell them you will not
buy their products or use their services.

- Watch animal friendly movies and television shows with your
family. Shows like Animal Planet's *Animal Cops*, *Animal Miracles*, *Emergency Vets*, and *Wildlife Journal* are great ways to
watch wild animals in their native environments as well as
people and animals working together.

- In order to enjoy wild animals, snorkel, take a bird-watching
trip, go whale-watching, or start hiking. It's good for you, and
you may get to see some animals!

- If you or your family want to feel a connection with animals,
visit or volunteer at a local shelter or animal sanctuary. Taking a
dog for a walk at a shelter or socializing animals who are up for
adoption will bring happiness to their lives. Rescue organizations always need help with animal care and even fostering animals who are temporarily in need of a home. Wildlife sanctuaries need help providing care to rescued animals. Farm animal
sanctuaries across the country are open for tours and visits. All
are incredibly positive experiences.

- Get active in your local community. Cities such as Pittsburgh,
Fort Wayne, and Pasadena have prohibited rodeos, and cities in
fifteen states have banned the exhibition of wild animals for
entertainment. Contact the organizations listed at the end of this
book to find out how your city can join the list.

Conclusion

A NEW RELATIONSHIP
WITH ANIMALS

What makes humans especially obnoxious is our tendency to believe in our absolute superiority over all creatures. We alone, of all species, have come up with religions and philosophies that declare us uniquely deserving of global hegemony. Yet one by one, our 'unique' human traits have turned out to be shared: Chimpanzees have culture; dolphins make art (in the form of bubble patterns); female vampire bats share food with their friends; male baboons will die to defend their troop; rats have recently demonstrated a capability for reflection that resembles consciousness. We are animals, and they are us.[1]

—Author Barbara Ehrenreich

The task of the [animal protection] movement is to offer such people imaginative but practical options for what to do next after they have been revolted by a glimpse of the lives factory animals live and the deaths they die. People need to see that there are alternatives to supporting the animal-products industry, that these alternatives need not involve any sacrifice in health or nutrition, that there is no reason why these alternatives need be costly, and furthermore that what are commonly called sacrifices are not sacrifices at all—that the only sacrifices in the whole picture, in fact, are being made by non-human animals.[2]

—J. M. Coetzee, Nobel Prize laureate for Literature

I n this book, we've tried to show how animals are exploited, particularly in the United States. We've also attempted to demonstrate why that exploitation *matters*. Most people care about animals and don't want to see animals abused. That's why we have laws in every US state that prohibit animal cruelty.

But as we've seen, even with all of our laws, and even with a nation of caring people, we still tolerate—and many of us unwittingly participate in—an unprecedented degree of animal cruelty. How can this be so?

Hidden Suffering, Corporate Profits

Perhaps the biggest reason why society tolerates routine abuse of animals is that for the most part, these abuses are hidden. The industries that supply meat, eggs, and milk, as well as fur, skins, and other animal products do the dirty work behind closed doors. Most of us will never see the insides of factory farms, slaughterhouses, or cosmetic-testing labs. Even in the animal entertainment industry, we never see the lives of the elephants and the tigers once the circus tent is drawn to a close after the performance. And we certainly never saw the baby elephants nuzzling the bodies of their dead mothers before the animal catcher dragged them away for the sake of our amusement. If we did— if we saw the things that occur in order to bring us our bacon, eggs, kangaroo skin shoes, or dolphin shows, many of us would no longer buy or support these products and activities.

Animal behaviorist James Serpell notes that many traditional societies exercise a kind of detachment when dealing with the animals they raise.[3] For instance, native Polynesians kept some dogs as pets but raised other dogs for meat. In order to account for what seems to us to be a logical inconsistency, these Polynesians did not interact with or relate to the dogs intended for slaughter; they remained detached from them so that they would not be bothered by their fate. Clearly, we have adopted the same technique.

We also "verbally conceal" animal exploitation by using euphemisms to describe processes that we would rather not know about.[4] "Veal," "beef," "pork," and "sacrifice" are all words that obscure violence. In addition, lobbyists for the animal industries as well as professional wildlife managers put a positive spin on their desire to use animals for research, or their desire to kill wolves in order to protect farm animals, or their desire to hunt. Most of us accept these statements without questioning them, because it is easier to believe than to know the truth behind the myths.

This sort of detachment is easy, given the ways that animal abuse is hidden from our eyes. Yet, once the curtain is drawn back, Americans take note. When pigs or cows escape on the way to slaughter, it makes the news and people sympathize with these animals and their fight to escape death.

Not only do we cause animals to suffer, we also rob them of pleasure and their ability to pursue their own interests. As ethologist Jonathan Balcombe states, "If we recognize animals' capacity for pleasure, then we may conclude that it's wrong to deprive them of it."[5]

We've seen that the lives of animals, such as chickens, for example, can be profoundly different at a sanctuary than at a factory farm. Left to her own devices, a hen will scratch about in the dirt looking for food, build a nest to protect her young, roost with her companions, dust bathe, enjoy the warmth of the sun, and with good health, live more than a decade. On a factory egg farm, the same animal's eighteen-month lifetime would be filled with more suffering than we can even imagine. Crammed into a tiny wire cage, she would be unable to even walk or spread her wings, never feel the earth beneath her feet or sunlight on her wings, dust bathe, or even perch. She may be one of the animals who become trapped on the cage wires, perishing within inches of food and water. She may end up rotting under her cage mates' feet. Or, if she lives until her productivity wanes, she may be stuffed into an open pit for composting and left to suffocate.

The Moral Standing of Animals

Where did humans get the idea that animals do not deserve significant moral consideration? In the West, the idea comes from a combination of classical Greek and biblical texts involving the Great Chain of Being, in which God created all of life according to a hierarchy of higher and lower beings, with men on the top, underneath God, and animals below humanity.[6] The low moral standing given to animals was expanded by the writings of St. Thomas Aquinas, a thirteenth-century theologian who maintained that the world is divided into persons and nonpersons, and that nonpersons essentially are things that can be used in any way to serve the interests of persons. In this sense, animals exist to serve us by providing food, fur, skin, or labor. These ideas were furthered by the philosopher René Descartes, who argued in the seventeenth century that nonhuman animals are organic machines who are incapable of consciousness and whose behavior is simply a response to external stimuli, not a result of any sort of feeling or thinking.

These ideas serve the interest of industries that depend on the exploitation of animals for their profits. By maintaining the notion that humans are somehow inherently superior to animals, it allows the industries we've discussed to regard animals as objects, raw resources, or merchandise—all of which have an important economic value. While consumers have access to cheap meat and leather products, for example, these cheap products come with a hidden price. That price is paid in animal suffering, environmental destruction, worker exploitation, health risks associated with animal consumption, and the lowering of our own moral standards by accepting such widespread misery.

Both religious and secular authorities have long held a huge stake in maintaining this myth and have fiercely fought any challenges to it. On the other hand, in the eighteenth century, philosopher Jeremy Bentham assigned moral consideration to the ability of animals to suffer, famously stating, "The question is not 'Can they reason?' nor 'Can they talk?' but 'Can they suffer?'" With the introduction of Darwinism in the late nineteenth century, the idea emerged that humans and animals alike were not *created* and were certainly not created separately, but evolved to their present states by natural selection. The Great Chain of Being began to lose ground, and today, many more of us believe animal interests are worthy of our concern.

Crumbling Barriers

More recently, there has been a tremendous wealth of research indicating that animals and people are much more similar than we had previously believed. Research done on captive and wild chimpanzees, our closest relatives, has revealed that chimps outperform people in some memory tasks. They also hunt in groups, create and use tools, and exhibit signs of self-awareness, altruism, empathy, deception, and social learning—signs of culture and self-awareness.[7] They also demonstrate the ability to master and use complex language.[8]

A few decades ago, scientists and many laypeople alike dismissed the idea of animals possessing enough similarity to humans to warrant serious moral consideration. According to one evolutionary psychologist, "Fifty years ago, we knew next to nothing about chimpanzees. You could not have predicted the richness and complexity of chimp culture that we know now."[9]

It's not just chimpanzees who we now accept as being self-aware. Elephants and dolphins have also revealed awareness of themselves in experiments with mirrors.[10] N'kisi, a captive African grey parrot, not only has a vocabulary of 950 words, but he also cracks jokes and invents words and phrases for new ideas.[11] Even rats are able to reflect on what they do or do not know—a complex way of thinking. Prior to recent research, it was thought that only humans and other primates possessed this ability.[12] Rats even laugh while playing. Researchers who tickled rats found that they emit ultrasonic "chirps" of pleasure.

In experiments, they chase after the tickling hand and react to tickling like a child, chirping before the hand even reaches them.[13]

Animals are sentient. It's tough to find anyone who disagrees. And now there is a preponderance of evidence that animals have emotions and the capacity to feel pleasure as well as suffer. People are captivated by the idea that animals can have rich emotional lives, as we can see simply by looking at the sales figures for books like the best-selling *When Elephants Weep* and any number of books about keeping companion animals happy.

Indeed, those of us who share our lives with companion animals like dogs cherish their intelligence, playfulness, and affection for us. We would do nearly anything to protect them from harm, yet at the same time, countless dogs just like our family members languish in puppy mills and labs. Some are even killed for their fur to adorn our coats.

And what of animals who, like pigs, possess the same level of intelligence as dogs? *Dominion* author Matthew Scully points out the moral similarity between confining a dog and a pig in a gestation crate: "Your dog, a being of intelligence and emotional capacities entirely comparable to those of a pig, would beg and wail and whimper and finally fall silent into a state of complete brokenness. And anyone who inflicted such tortures on that animal, no matter what excuses might be offered, would be guilty of a felony. If the creatures are comparable, and the conditions identical, and the suffering equal, how can the one be 'standard practice' and the other a crime?"[14]

Not only are Americans uncomfortable with confining dogs in cages, but we don't want factory farms cramming pigs, chickens, and veal calves in cages, as demonstrated by the snowballing movement away from these inhumane confinement devices. We're realizing that there is a moral equivalent of abusing animals who we love and animals who we don't know.

One by one, the arbitrary barriers we have erected between humans and other animals are crumbling. The ability of animals to suffer is now accepted, virtually without exception. Americans know that animals should not be subjected to unnecessary pain and exploitation. It's simply a matter of common decency to allow animals to live free from harm.

Freedom and Animal Protection

For years, the fur industry has used the rhetoric of freedom to justify the slaughter of millions of animals each year for human vanity. Freedom of choice, freedom of religion, freedom of speech: freedom is one of America's most central values. So it's no surprise that the fur, meat, vivisection, and entertainment industries use the rhetoric of freedom in their outreach campaigns.

While the industries portray these issues as *your* freedom to eat a chicken drumstick or enjoy a circus or wear a fur coat, they are spending millions of dollars a year in advertising, lobbying, and campaign contributions in order to preserve *their* freedom to profit off of animals.

Even when very few people benefit from a particular practice that harms animals, we see that the major animal industries and their supporters line up to support it. As Matthew Scully points out in his description of the 1990 congressional ban against "crush videos," a few dozen members of Congress voted against the ban, not because they derive sexual pleasure from watching women in stilettos crush small animals to death, but because they most likely realized that taking any stance on animal cruelty is a slippery slope: once you acknowledge the extreme cruelty of one practice, what is to keep you from recognizing it in other practices as well, practices that may benefit you directly?[15] No one wants to argue that people's freedom of choice is being hampered by the prohibition on animal snuff films like this, yet every victory for animals, no matter how small, and every prohibition against cruelty, no matter how ghastly, is a clear threat to animal abusers.

The opposite is true as well: If it's okay to confine billions of animals per year into ugly warehouses and deprive them of every single minute of pleasure in order to slaughter them a few weeks or months after their births, then why shouldn't we allow and excuse every other type of atrocity in our society?

The spin campaigns of the animal exploiters are highly effective, because even those who don't profit from animal exploitation defend it due to the fear that they will lose their own choices by granting protection to animals. Scully also points out how fervently people condemn animal advocates for decrying cruel practices like fur farming or the production of foie gras, yet those same people will just as passionately defend their inalienable right to eat or wear whatever luxuries they choose. Because, after all, the freedom to eat a bit of fatty liver is worth fighting for, but the attempt to free animals from suffering is so utterly trivial as to be unworthy of discussion.[16]

A good example of this involves the 2006 ban on the sale of foie gras in Chicago. After the city council voted nearly unanimously to pass the ban, Mayor Richard M. Daley was quoted in the *Chicago Sun-Times* as stating, "We have children getting killed by gang leaders and dope dealers. We have real issues here in this city. . . . Let's get some priorities."[17] Yet in August 2006, Mayor Daley signed a proclamation that September 16, 2006, was "Official Tom Petty Day" for the City of Chicago.[18] And although Daley claimed that the foie gras discussion was "silly" and that it distracted the city from other priorities, in 2007 he instigated a measure to repeal the ban—revisiting the issue and pulling the council from other matters.

Environmental Devastation, Human Inequality, and Animals

If we look at the lives of people on this planet, we can't help but notice the growing inequality of income and wealth between the rich and the poor. Because wealthy countries overconsume and waste energy, raw materials, and manufactured goods, the poor must engage in practices that are harmful to the planet just to survive and that don't end up benefiting them in the long run. Each year, the world's small farmers lose topsoil and soil fertility because of overuse, urbanization and suburbanization, the plowing of marginal lands, and salinization from irrigation. Factory farms and the agricultural operations that support them pollute water with pesticides, herbicides, fertilizers, and animal wastes. Because third world governments, many at the behest of US corporations, encourage people to settle in forests and clear the land for farming and ranching, indigenous people who once lived on those lands lose their ways of life and cultures forever. Thanks to animal agriculture, identified by the United Nations as the largest contributor to global warming, we are seeing the possibly irreversible results in climate change.

Whether it's factory farming, the exotic animal pet trade, hunting of endangered species, or a legion of other kinds of animal exploitation, there are very real consequences to both the environment and other people. One of the goals of this book is to make the connections more explicit among animal exploitation, human rights issues, and environmental problems. Animal welfare is not only consistent with social justice and environmental concerns, but in many cases, caring about animals actually furthers advancements on these important issues. These movements have so much in common, and so much to fight for.

Compassion and Freedom of Choice

Perhaps when we realize that our food, clothing, entertainment, and other choices affect animals, the planet, and other people, we might be moved to make choices based not only on what *we are free to do*, but what would be good to do. French anthropologist Claude Lévi-Strauss famously wrote that animals are "good to think." He was discussing how the choices that different cultures make with respect to what animals they eat and which animals are taboo doesn't have anything to do with the inherent edibility of the animal (whether or not they are "good to eat"); rather, it has to do with how we think about that animal, and which animals best help that culture express its worldview.

What would our world be like if the foods that we chose were also good for the animals, the planet, and our fellow human beings? What if we chose to eat something that would demonstrate our compassion and caring for the planet and our fellow people?

The realization that we might in fact have that choice—and that those who work to protect animals aren't in fact taking away our freedom of choice—is exhilarating indeed. Given what we now know about the lives of the animals from whom we take so much—the playfulness of pigs, the family values of elephants, and the personal relationships of cows—it's difficult to see how we can continue to make these choices. How do we allow pigs to live, separated from their kin and confined on a hard concrete floor in a small stall in a windowless warehouse, when we know how much they enjoy grunting to their friends, napping in a soft bed, splashing in a pond, and eating apples?

We do have choices. We have the choice to eat foods that don't support the institutionalized cruelty of factory farms. We don't have to hunt to put trophies on our walls. We have the choice to purchase cruelty-free household products and cosmetics. We can choose to buy clothes and shoes that are not made of animal products, and we can just as easily choose to entertain ourselves in ways that don't exploit animals. We can continue to share our lives with animals in ways that benefit both animals and humans.

We are confident that most people, when given these choices, would at least want to pick the route that involves significantly less animal suffering. We know that most Americans have good hearts; they are sickened and alarmed by every new story about animal cruelty that makes it into the press, and all of us want to be decent and kind. We want to make good choices and to teach our children how to live their lives in a way that benefits society. But until society is able to see through corporate spin, our choices are limited indeed.

Recent Advancements and a Better Future

Just in the eight months between the time that we completed the first draft of this book and finished our final edits, there has been remarkable progress for animals. In November 2006, Arizona residents voted overwhelmingly to ban abusive gestation crates and veal crates. In a similar election landslide, Michigan voters approved a measure that will protect doves from being hunted. In early 2007 the nation's largest pig and veal producers, Smithfield Foods and Strauss Veal, announced that they are phasing out the use of gestation crates and veal crates, respectively. The United Nations issued a report acknowledging that animal agribusiness is the primary cause of global warming. The federal government issued a report indicating that the number of hunters is plummeting at the same time that the number of people who humanely observe wildlife outnumbers hunters nearly six to one. The National Institutes of Health announced that it will no longer breed chimpanzees for research. Duke University joined the overwhelming majority of US medical schools that no longer use live animals in their undergraduate curricula. Several high-profile designers, including Kenneth Cole and Calvin Klein, implemented fur-free policies. The US horse slaughter industry went virtually extinct. As of this writing, President George W. Bush signed a federal animal fighting bill; New Mexico banned cockfighting, and Louisiana's governor is expected to sign a bill banning it as well; Oregon's governor signed a bill banning gestation crates; and a report from the prestigious National Research Council called for in vitro methods to reduce and possibly eliminate animal-based toxicity testing.

We are changing the way we treat animals. While industries are abusing animals on a massive scale, we are making advancements at an unprecedented rate. This is due to the hard work of countless animal protection advocates, but more important, it is because our American conscience is awakening to the consequences of our choices regarding the lives of animals. Not only are people becoming aware of the ways in which animals suffer, but they know that this suffering *matters*.

There have never been more cruelty-free products and activities available to people who care about animals, and there has never been a better time to make genuinely simple changes in our lives to reduce animal suffering. It's remarkably easy to extend a bit of mercy to those who are defenseless.

Americans care about animals. They are a part of our history, and they are a part of our lives. Most people have shown remarkable compassion for some animals in their lives, such as companion animals. Rather than choosing to express our good feelings about animals in only one way, with just *some* animals, and tolerating the wholesale suffering of billions of other animals, we can just as easily allow *all* animals to benefit from our compassion. The choice is up to us.

ENDNOTES

NOTES TO CHAPTER 1

1. Joseph Cardinal Ratzinger, Peter Seewald, and Henry Taylor, *God and the World: A Conversation with Peter Seewald* (San Francisco: Ignatius, 2002), p. 78.

2. http://www.animalowners.org/intro.html.

3. USDA National Agricultural Statistics Service, "Poultry Slaughter: 2006 Annual Summary," Feburary 2007, http://usda.mannlib.cornell.edu/usda/nass/PoulSlauSu//2000s/2007/PoulSlauSu-02-28-2007.pdf (accessed May 31, 2007).

4. David J. Wolfson and Mariann Sullivan, "Foxes in the Hen House, Animals, Agribusiness, and the Law: A Modern American Fable," in *Animal Rights: Current Debates and New Directions*, ed. Cass R. Sunstein and Martha C. Nussbaum (Oxford: Oxford University Press), p. 206.

5. Jonathan Balcombe, *Pleasurable Kingdom* (New York: Macmillian, 2006), p. 226.

6. "Exploring *Dominion*: Matthew Scully on Animals—A Q&A by Kathryn Jean Lopez," December 3, 2002, http://www.matthewscully.com/lopez_scully.htm (accessed May 31, 2007).

7. Matthew Scully, "A Sunless Hell," *Arizona Republic*, February 19, 2006.

NOTES TO CHAPTER 2

1. Statement of Senator Byrd, in David J. Wolfson and Mariann Sullivan, "Foxes in the Hen House, Animals, Agribusiness, and the Law: A Modern American Fable," in *Animal Rights: Current Debates and New Directions*, ed. Cass R. Sunstein and Martha C. Nussbaum (Oxford: Oxford University Press), p. 217.

2. Yvonne Vizzier Thaxton, "In Perspective," *Poultry* 12, no. 2 (April/May): 5.

3. John Zogby et al., "Nationwide Views on the Treatment of Farm Animals," submitted to the Animal Welfare Trust, October 22, 2003.

4. USDA Agricultural Research Service, "FY-2005 Annual Report, Manure and By-Product Utilization National Program," http://www.ars.usda .gov/research/programs/programs.htm?np_code=206&docid=13337 (accessed July 27, 2006).

5. Bernard Rollin, "Farm Factories," *Christian Century*, December 19, 2001, http://www.religiononline.org/showarticle.asp?title=2194 (accessed June 6, 2007).

6. Worldwatch Institute, "Meat: Now, It's Not Personal!" *World Watch Magazine*, July/August 2004, pp. 12–20, www.worldwatch.org/pubs/ mag/2004/174 (accessed March 8, 2006).

7. B. R. Myers, "If Pigs Could Swim: Why Our Farm Animals Would Be Better Off on the Other Side of the Atlantic," *Atlantic Monthly*, September 2005.

8. USDA Cooperative State Research, Education and Extension Service, http://www.csrees.usda.gov/qlinks/extension.html (accessed September 13, 2006).

9. Wolfson and Sullivan, "Foxes in the Hen House, Animals, Agribusiness, and the Law."

10. Myers, "If Pigs Could Swim."

11. Kevin Garcia, "Charges Likely in Pigs' Deaths," *Brownsville Herald*, August 6, 2006.

12. Scientific Committee on Animal Health and Animal Welfare, "The Welfare of Animals during Transport 3," report for the European Commission, adopted by the European Commission, March 30, 2004.

13. Wayne Parry, "Live Turkeys Fall Off Truck in New Jersey," Associated Press, November 18, 2005.

14. Wolfson and Sullivan, "Foxes in the Hen House, Animals, Agribusiness, and the Law."

15. Donald McNeil Jr., "KFC Supplier Accused of Animal Cruelty," *New York Times*, July 20, 2004.

16. J. Raloff, "Hormones: Here's the Beef," *Science News Online* 161, no. 1 (January 5, 2002): 10.

17. Karen Kaplan, "Meat, Milk from Cloned Animals OK'd," *Los Angeles Times*, December 24, 2006.

18. C. Doering, "Groups Say FDA Should Ban Sale of Food from Clones," Reuters, October 12, 2006.

19. D. N. Wells, "Animal Cloning: Problems and Prospects," *Revue Scientifique et Technique* (International Office of Epizootics) 24 (1): 251–64. See also HSUS, "An HSUS Report: Welfare Issues with Genetic Engineering and Cloning of Farm Animals," http://tinyurl.com/38hxhf (accessed May 5, 2007).

20. HSUS, "An HSUS Report: Welfare Issues with Genetic Engineering and Cloning of Farm Animals."

21. "Safe as Milk?" editorial, *New York Times*, January 6, 2007.

22. USDA Agricultural Statistics Service, "Poultry Slaughter: 2006 Annual Summary," February 2007, http://tinyurl.com/2ath5j (accessed June 7, 2007).

23. Jennifer Viegas, "Chickens Worry about the Future," *Discovery News*, July 15, 2005.

24. R. Weiss, "Bird Brains Get Some New Names, and New Respect," *Washington Post*, February 1, 2005, p. A10.

25. Michael Specter, "The Extremist," *New Yorker*, April 14, 2003.

26. Tom Wyatt, "High Temps Fry 35,000 Chickens," *Post-Tribune* (Merrillville, IN), August 3, 2006.

27. J. Webster, *Animal Welfare: A Cool Eye towards Eden* (Cambridge, MA: Blackwell, 1995), p. 156.

28. National Chicken Council, "US Broiler Production," current as of June 8, 2006, http://www.nationalchickencouncil.org/statistics/stat_detail.cfm?id=4 (accessed August 31, 2006).

29. Mary Hendrickson and William Heffernan, "Concentration of Agricultural Markets," University of Missouri Department of Rural Sociology study commissioned by National Farmers Union, April 2007, http://www.nfu.org/wp-content/2007-heffernanreport.pdf (accessed May 5, 2007).

30. "Feed Marketing," *Feedstuffs*, September 14, 2005, p. 5.

31. "Zogby Poll on American Attitudes toward the Egg Industry," September 15–18, 2000, http://www.isecruelty.com/poll.php (accessed September 13, 2006).

32. Ian J. Duncan, "Welfare Problems of Meat-Type Chickens," Farmed Animal Well-Being Conference at the University of California–Davis, June 28–29, 2001.

33. Ted Shelsby, "For Maryland's Poultry Industry, the Egg Came First," *Baltimore Sun*, August 13, 2006.

34. Gary Thornton and Terrence O'Keefe, "Housing and Equipment Survey," *WATT Poultry USA* (June 2001): 38–47.

35. Alicia Karapetian, "Food Experts Say Bigger Birds Aren't Always Better," *Meating Place*, January 25, 2007.

36. Duncan, "Welfare Problems of Meat-Type Chickens."

37. B. Barlett, "Performance Problems in Growing Broilers," *Poultry Digest* (1988). See also R. J. Julian, "Evaluating the Impact of Metabolic Disorders on the Welfare of Broilers," in *Measuring and Auditing Broiler Welfare*, ed. C. A. Weeks and A. Butterworth (Cambridge, MA: CABI, 2004), pp. 51–59.

38. Temple Grandin and Catherine Johnson, *Animals in Translation* (New York: Harcourt, 2005), pp. 270–71.

39. I. Estevez, "Poultry Welfare Issues," *Poultry Digest Online* 3, no. 2 (2002). See also HSUS, "An HSUS Report: The Welfare of Animals in the Egg Industry," http://www.hsus.org/web-files/PDF/farm/welfare_egg.pdf (accessed October 10, 2006).

40. N. G. Gregory and L. J. Wilkins, "Broken Bones in Chickens: Effects of Stunning and Processing in Broilers," *British Poultry Science* 31 (1990): 53–58.

41. USDA National Agricultural Statistics Service, "Chickens and Eggs: 2006 Summary," February 2007, http://usda.mannlib.cornell.edu/usda/current/ChickEgg/ChickEgg-02-27-2007.pdf (accessed June 6, 2007).

42. C. J. Savory, K. Maros, and S. M. Rutter, "Assessment of Hunger in Growing Broiler Breeders in Relation to a Commercial Restricted Feeding Program," *Animal Welfare* 2 (1993): 131–52.

43. United Egg Producers, *United Egg Producers Animal Husbandry Guidelines for US Egg-Laying Flockers* (Alpharetta, GA: United Egg Producers, 2006), available online at http://www.uepcertified.com/docs/2006_UEPanimal_welfare_guidelines.pdf (accessed June 6, 2007). See also USDA National Agricultural Statistics Services, "Chickens and Eggs."

44. D. Fraser, J. Mench, and S. Millman, "Farm Animals and Their Welfare in 2000," in *State of the Animals 2001* (Washington, DC: Humane Society Press, 2001), p. 90.

45. United Egg Producers, *United Egg Producers Animal Husbandry Guidelines for US Egg-Laying Flockers.*

46. "Feed Savings Could Justify Beak Trimming," *Poultry Digest* 3 (1993): 6. See also J. Mench, "The Welfare of Poultry in Modern Production Systems," *Poultry Science Review* 4 (1992): 112.

47. United Egg Producers, *United Egg Producers Animal Husbandry Guidelines for US Egg-Laying Flockers.*

48. Richard Piersol, "Humane Society Tags Michael Foods Egg Farm," *Lincoln Journal Star*, June 13, 2006.

49. G. Cherian, "Fatty Liver Hemorrhagic Syndrome in Laying Hens: An Investigation into the Role of Dietary Fatty Acids," USDA Current Research Information System (CRIS).

50. A. B. Webster, "Welfare Implications of Avian Osteoporosis," *Poultry Science* 83 (2004): 184–92. G. Parkinson, "Osteoporosis and Bone Fractures in the Laying Hen," Progress Report of Work at the Victorian Institute of Animal Science, Attwood, Victoria, Australia, 1993.

51. Ian J. Duncan, "The Pros and Cons of Cages," *World's Poultry Science Journal* 57 (2001): 385. See also M. Baxter, "The Welfare Problems of Laying Hens in Battery Cages," *Veterinary Record* 134 (1994): 618.

52. Letter from Ian J. Duncan to Dr. Nancy Halpern, New Jersey Department of Agriculture, June 25, 2003.

53. Todd Frankel, "Charges Cloud Egg Factory's Expansion Plans in Neosho," *St. Louis Post-Dispatch*, October 2, 2005.

54. Tobias Young, "Recycling Chickens," *Press Democrat* (Santa Rosa, CA), November 22, 2006.

55. USDA National Agricultural Statistics Service, "Poultry Slaughter: 2006 Annual Summary."

56. Mary Hendrickson and William Heffernan, "Concentration of Agricultural Markets."

57. P. S. Ferket, "Tom Weights Up 7 Percent," *WATT Poultry USA* (July 2004): 32–42.

58. P. M. Hocking, R. Bernard, and M. H. Maxwell, "Assessment of Pain during Locomotion and the Welfare of Adult Male Turkeys with Destructive Cartilage Loss of the Hip Joint," *British Poultry Science* 40, pp. 30–34.

59. USDA Agricultural Research Service, "Spotting Top-Notch Toms," *Agriculture Research*, July 1998.

60. SCAHAW (Scientific Committee on Animal Health and Animal Welfare), "Welfare Aspects of the Production of Foie Gras in Ducks and Geese," December 1998, http://ec.europa.eu/food/animal/welfare/international/out17 _en.pdf (accessed June 7, 2007).

61. "Pâté Problems Raise Fowl Abuse Issues," CBS 4 News, March 6, 2006.

62. Steven Greenhouse, "No Days Off at Foie Gras Farm," *New York Times*, April 2, 2001, p. B1.

63. SCAHAW, "Welfare Aspects of the Production of Foie Gras in Ducks and Geese."

64. Greenhouse, "No Days Off at Foie Gras Farm."

65. Lee Klein, "Foie Wars," *Miami Times*, July 14, 2006.

66. S. Held et al., "Cognition Studies with Pigs: Livestock Cognition and Its Implications for Production," *Journal of Animal Science* 80 (2002): E10–E17.

67. USDA National Agricultural Statistics Service, "Livestock Slaughter: 2006 Annual Summary," March 2007, http://usda.mannlib.cornell .edu/usda/current/LiveSlauSu/LiveSlauSu-03-02-2007.pdf (accessed June 6, 2007).

68. D. Wright, "Was Your Meat Smarter than Your Pet? Research Suggests Farm Animals Are Surprisingly Intelligent," ABC News, May 22, 2005.

69. J. J. McGlone, "Alternative Sow Housing Systems: Driven by Legislation, Regulation, Free Trade, and Free Market Systems (but Not Science)," Annual Meeting of the Manitoba Pork Producers, Winnipeg, Manitoba, Canada, January 2001.

70. J. Vansickle, "Quality Assurance Program Launched," *National Hog Farmer*, February 15, 2002.

71. Temple Grandin, "Solving Return-to-Sensibility Problems after Electrical Stunning in Commercial Pork Slaughter Plants," *Journal of the American Veterinary Medical Association* 219, no. 5 (September 1, 2001): 608–11.

72. Hendrickson and Heffernan, "Concentration of Agricultural Markets."

73. USDA National Agricultural Statistics Service, "Quarterly Hogs and Pigs: 2006," March 30, 2007, http://usda.mannlib.cornell.edu/usda/ current/HogsPigs/HogsPigs-03-30-2007.pdf (accessed June 7, 2007). Also

see J. L. Barnett et al., "A Review of the Welfare Issues for Sows and Piglets in Relation to Housing," in "Welfare of Sows Housed in Stalls during Gestation," livestock update, ed. M. J. Estienne and A. F. Harper, Virginia Cooperative Extension (April 2003), http://www.ext.vt.edu/news/periodicals/livestock/aps-03–04/ aps-221.html (accessed October 11, 2006).

74. Temple Grandin, remarks given in New York, January 9, 2006. Audio available at http://tinyurl.com/yuv4we.

75. N. Johnson, "Swine of the Times: The Making of the Modern Pig," *Harper's*, May 2006.

76. Scientific Veterinary Committee, Animal Welfare section, "The Welfare of Intensively Kept Pigs," for the European Commission, http://ec.europa.eu/food/fs/sc/oldcomm4/out17_en.pdf (accessed June 6, 2007).

77. Statement by Smithfield Foods CEO in a Smithfield press release, January 25, 2007, available at http://www.smithfieldfoods.com/Investor/Press/press_view.asp?ID=394 (accessed May 5, 2007).

78. J. Leake, "The Secret Life of Moody Cows," *Sunday Times* (London), February 27, 2005.

79. USDA National Agriculture Statistics Service, "Livestock Slaughter: 2006 Annual Summary"; USDA National Agricultural Statistics Service, "Livestock Slaughter: 2005 Annual Summary," March 2006, http://usda.mannlib.cornell.edu/reports/nassr/livestock/pls-bban/lsan0306.pdf (accessed June 6, 2007).

80. Ibid.

81. D. M. Broom, "Effects of Dairy Cattle Breeding and Production Methods on Animal Welfare," *Proc. 21 World Buiatrics Congress, 1–7* (Punta del Este, Uruguay: World Association for Buiatrics, 2001).

82. C. J. Booth et al., "Effect of Lameness on Culling in Dairy Cows," *Journal of Dairy Science* 87 (2004): 4115–22.

83. Olivia Munoz, "Heat Causes Pileup of Livestock Carcasses," Associated Press, July 26, 2006.

84. "Milk Production," January 16, 2006.

85. USDA National Agricultural Statistics Service, "Livestock Slaughter: 2006 Annual Summary."

86. Hendrickson and Heffernan, "Concentration of Agricultural Markets."

87. USDA, "Feedlot '99, Part 1: Baseline Reference of Feedlot Management Practices, 1999," Veterinary Services, National Animal Health Monitoring System, May 2000, p. 38.

88. USDA National Agricultural Statistics Service, "Nonambulatory Cattle and Calves," May 2005.

89. J. Warrick, "They Die Piece by Piece," *Washington Post*, April 10, 2001, p. A1.

90. Ibid.

91. Donald McNeil Jr., "Videos Cited in Calling Kosher Slaughterhouse Inhumane," *New York Times*, December 1, 2004.

92. Office of International Affairs, *Microlivestock: Little-Known Small Animals with a Promising Economic Future* (Washington, DC: National Academy Press, 2000), p. 179.

93. Anne Kruger, "Of Rabbits and Rules: Boulevard Woman, County, Tangle over Splitting Lot," *San Diego Union Tribune*, July 19, 2005.

94. Susan E. Davis and Margo DeMello, *Stories Rabbits Tell* (New York: Lantern Books, 2003).

95. J. M. Hirsch, "Diet: Don't Laugh, but Rabbits Are Scarce; Producers Can't Ship Bunny Meat Fast Enough," *Charleston Gazette*, August 8, 2005.

96. Randy Kennedy, "The Way We Eat: Rabbit Is Rich," *New York Times*, March 12, 2006.

97. Hirsch, "Diet."

98. Jo Ellen O'Hara, "Another White Meat: It May Not Please Some, but Rabbit Is Finding Its Way to Tables in the 21st Century," *Birmingham News*, June 21, 2006.

99. United Nations Food and Agriculture Organization (UN FAO), *The Rabbit: Husbandry, Health, and Production*, Rome, 1997, http://tinyurl.com/yt2ygy (accessed June 7, 2007). See also J. McNitt et al., *Rabbit Production*, 8th ed. (Danville, IL: Interstate Printers, 1996).

100. UN FAO, *The Rabbit*, p. 104.

101. Davis and DeMello, *Stories Rabbits Tell*.

102. Ibid.

103. Ibid.

104. B. Blair, "Bunny Wins Barbecue Taste Test," *Republic*, July 15, 2006.

105. American Pet Product Manufacturing Association, "Industry Statistics and Trends," http://www.appma.org/press_industrytrends.asp (accessed September 2, 2006).

106. R. Bshary, W. Wickler, and H. Fricke, "Fish Cognition: A Primate's Eye View," *Animal Cognition* 5 (2002): 1–13.

107. T. Hastein, "Animal Welfare Issues relating to Aquaculture," *Pro-*

ceedings of the Global Conference on Animal Welfare: An OIE Initiative (February 2004): 219–27.

108. World Organization for Animal Health, *Proceedings of the Global Conference on Animal Welfare*, pp. 23–25.

109. "Seafood Faces Collapse by 2048," *CNN.com*, http://www.cnn.com/2006/TECH/science/11/02/seafood.crisis.ap/index.html (accessed May 3, 2007).

110. National Research Council, "Ecosystem-Based Fishery Management," in *America's Living Oceans: Charting a Course for Sea Change*, Pew Oceans Commission (Arlington, VA: Pew Oceans Commission, 2003), p. 35. Available online at http://www.pewtrusts.org/pdf/env_pew_oceans_final_report.pdf (accessed June 4, 2007).

111. "World Fisheries in Crisis," *Environmental News Network*, July 10, 1998.

112. Pew Oceans Commission, *America's Living Oceans*, p. 41.

113. T. Hastein et al., "Science-Based Assessment of Welfare: Aquatic Animals," *Revue Scientifique et Technique* 24, no. 2 (2005): 537.

114. World Organization for Animal Health, *Proceedings of the Global Conference on Animal Welfare*, pp. 23–25.

115. Anne Platt McGinn, "Rocking the Boat: Conserving Fisheries and Protecting Jobs," *Worldwatch*, June 1998, p. 12.

116. "World Fisheries in Crisis," *Environmental News Network*.

117. UN FAO, "Overfishing: A Threat to Marine Biodiversity," http://www.un.org/events/tenstories/story.asp?storyID=800 (accessed September 26, 2006).

118. Biello David, "Overfishing Could Take Seafood off the Menu by 2048," *Scientific American* (November 2, 2006), http://www.sciam.com/article.cfm?articleID=AAFCC579-E7F2-99DF-33CF444CDD8F7AAF (accessed May 3, 2007).

119. P. K. Dayton, S. Thrush, and F. C. Coleman, "Ecological Effects of Fishing in Marine Ecosystems of the United States," in *America's Living Oceans*, p. 43.

120. D. L. Alverson, "Discarding Practices and Unobserved Fishing Mortality in Marine Fisheries: An Update," Washington SeaGrant Program, Seattle, 1998. See also D. L. Alverson et al., "A Global Assessment of Fisheries Bycatch and Discards," FAO Fisheries technical paper no. 339, in *America's Living Oceans*, p. 5.

121. Dayton, Thrush, and Coleman, "Ecological Effects of Fishing in Marine Ecosystems of the United States."

122. Erica B. Goldman, "Scraping the Seabed Raw: Trawling Nets Rip Up Undersea Habitat," ABC News, December 30, 1999.

123. David Adam, "Time Running Out to Curb Effects of Deep Sea Pollution, Warns UN," *Guardian*, July 17, 2006.

124. UN FAO, "Overfishing: A Threat to Marine Biodiversity."

125. Goldman, "Scraping the Seabed Raw."

126. UN FAO, "Nearly Half of All Fish Eaten Today Farmed, Not Caught," September 4, 2006, http://www.fao.org/newsroom/en/news/2006/1000383/index.html (accessed September 30, 2006).

127. Rebecca Goldburg and Tracy Triplett, "Murky Waters: Environmental Effects of Aquaculture in the US," *Environmental Defense Fund*, p. 7.

128. Rosamond L. Naylor et al., "Effect of Aquaculture on World Fish Supplies," *Nature* 405, no. 29 (June 2000): 1018–19.

129. Ibid.

130. P. Lymbery, "In Too Deep: Why Fish Farming Needs Urgent Welfare Reform," 2002, p. 4, available at http://www.ciwf.org/publications/reports/in_too_deep_2001.pdf (accessed October 11, 2006).

131. World Organization for Animal Health, *Proceedings of the Global Conference on Animal Welfare*, pp. 23–25.

132. P. Lymbery, "Welfare of Intensively Farmed Fish: A Report for Compassion in World Farming Trust," 2001, p. 10.

133. T. Hastein et al., "Science-Based Assessment of Welfare," p. 536.

134. World Organization for Animal Health, *Proceedings of the Global Conference on Animal Welfare*, pp. 23–25.

135. Goldburg and Triplett, "Murky Waters," p. 43.

136. A. E. Wall, "Ethical Considerations in the Handling and Slaughter of Farmed Fish," in *Farmed Fish Quality*, ed. S. C. Kestin and P. D. Wariss (Oxford: Fishing News Books, 2000), pp. 108–15.

137. Lymbery, "Welfare of Intensively Farmed Fish," p. 7.

138. P. Southgate and T. Wall, "Welfare of Farmed Fish at Slaughter," *Practice* 23, no. 5 (2001): 277–84.

139. B. Roth, A. Imsland, and D. Moeller, "Effect of Electric Field Strength and Current Duration on Stunning and Injuries in Market-Sized Atlantic Salmon Held in Seawater," *North American Journal of Aquaculture* 65, nos. 8–13 (2003): 10.

140. National Research Council, "Genetic Status of Atlantic Salmon in Maine: Interim Report for Committee on Atlantic Salmon in Maine," in *America's Living Oceans*.

141. Naylor et al., "Effect of Aquaculture on World Fish Supplies," pp. 1020–21.

142. Goldburg and Triplett, "Murky Waters," p. 7.

143. Ibid.

144. R. W. Hardy, "Urban Legends and Fish Nutrition," *Aquaculture Magazine* 26, no. 6, pp. 47–50.

145. Brendan I. Koerner, "Shrimp Factor," *Slate.com*, January 13, 2006.

146. Goldburg and Triplett, "Murky Waters," p. 44.

147. Sharon Cohen, "Slaughterhouses of 2006 a Different Kind of 'Jungle,'" Associated Press, April 23, 2006.

148. US GAO, "Safety in the Meat and Poultry Industry, while Improving, Could Be Further Strengthened," report to ranking minority member, Committee on Health, Education, Labor, and Pensions, US Senate, January 2005, p. 1; US Department of Labor, Bureau of Labor Statistics, *Occupational Outlook Handbook, 2006–2007*, available online at http://www.bls.gov/oco/ocos219.htm#earnings (accessed August 3, 2006).

149. N. Popper, "In Iowa Meat Plant, Kosher 'Jungle' Breeds Fear, Injury, Short Pay," *Forward*, May 26, 2006.

150. US Department of Labor, Bureau of Statistics, "Highest Incidence Rates of Total Nonfatal Occupational Injury and Illness Cases, Private Industry, 2004," p. 1.

151. US Department of Labor, Bureau of Statistics, http://www.bls.gov/oco/cg/cgs011.htm (accessed August 3, 2006).

152. US GAO, "Safety in the Meat and Poultry Industry," pp. 5–6.

153. "Blood, Sweat, and Fear: Workers' Rights in US Meat and Poultry Plants," Human Rights Watch release, January 2005. See also Eric Scholosser, *Fast Food Nation* (New York: Houghton Mifflin, 2002).

154. D. Silver, "Safe Keeping," *National Provisioner*, April 2006.

155. "Blood, Sweat, and Fear," Human Rights Watch.

156. US GAO, "Safety in the Meat and Poultry Industry," p. 7.

157. Schlosser, *Fast Food Nation*, p. 181.

158. B. Herbert, "Where the Hogs Come First," *New York Times*, June 15, 2006.

159. US Department of Labor, Bureau of Statistics, "Highest Incidence

Rates of Total Nonfatal Occupational Injury and Illness Cases, Private Industry, 2004," p. 1.

160. National Center for Appropriate Technology, "CAFOs . . . They're a Gas!" http://www.ncat.org/nutrients/hypoxia/cafosgas.htm (accessed April 26, 2006).

161. S. Kirkhorn, "Community and Environmental Health Effects of Concentrated Animal Feeding Operations," *Minnesota Medicine* 85 (October 2002).

162. A. Chapin et al., "Airborne Multidrug-Resistant Bacteria Isolated from a Concentrated Swine Feeding Operation," *Environmental Health Perspectives* 113, no. 2, pp. 137–42.

163. "Father, Son Die in Manure Pond at Dairy," Associated Press, March 8, 2006.

164. R. Clarren, "Got Guilt?" *Salon.com*, August 27, 2004,

165. US GAO, "Safety in the Meat and Poultry Industry," p. 3.

166. Ibid., p. 16.

167. David Barboza, "Meatpackers' Profits Hinge on Pool of Immigrant Labor," *New York Times*, December 21, 2001.

168. "Raid on DeCoster Egg Farm Nets Illegal Immigrants," Associated Press, June 22, 2006.

169. Greenhouse, "No Days Off at Foie Gras Farm."

170. US Food Safety and Inspection Service, "Compliance Guideline for Controlling *Salmonella* in Poultry," August 2006, http://www.fsis.usda .gov/PDF/Compliance_Guideline_Controlling_Salmonella_Poultry.pdf. (accessed May 5, 2007).

171. Andrew Bridges, "Officials Track *E. coli* Strain to Calif.," Associated Press, January 12, 2007.

172. USDA National Agriculture Statistics Service, "Livestock Slaughter: 2006 Annual Summary."

173. Charles Abbott, "USDA Admits Skipped Meat Plant Checks for Thirty Years," Reuters, March 29, 2007.

174. US GAO, "Federal Agencies Need to Better Focus Efforts to Address Risk to Humans from Antibiotic Use in Animals," April 2004, p. 17.

175. "Of Birds and Bacteria," *Consumer Reports*, January 2003, http:// www.consumerreports.org/cro/food/chicken-safety-103/overview/index.htm (accessed August 5, 2006).

176. US GAO, "Federal Agencies Need to Better Focus Efforts to Address Risk to Humans from Antibiotic Use in Animals," p. 11.

177. Margaret Mellon, Charles Benbrook, and Karen Lutz Benbrook, "Hogging It: Estimates of Antimicrobial Abuse in Livestock," *Union of Concerned Scientists*, January 2001, p. xi.

178. Ibid., p. xiii.

179. Kirkhorn, "Community and Environmental Health Effects of Concentrated Animal Feeding Operations."

180. US GAO, "Federal Agencies Need to Better Focus Efforts to Address Risk to Humans from Antibiotic Use in Animals," p. 18.

181. "Not Chicken Feed," *Columbus Dispatch*, April 28, 2007.

182. "Keep Antibiotics Working: Antibiotic Resistance—An Emerging Public Health Crisis," http://www.keepantibioticsworking.com/new/resources_library.cfm?refID=36366 (accessed August 5, 2006).

183. Denise Grady, "WHO Finds Use of Antibiotics in Animal Feed Can Be Reduced," *New York Times*, August 14, 2003.

184. Rick Weiss, "FDA Rules Override Warnings about Drug," *Washington Post,* March 4, 2007, p. A1.

185. S. Kirkhorn, "Community and Environmental Health Effects of Concentrated Animal Feed Operations."

186. American Public Health Association, "Precautionary Moratorium on New Concentrated Animal Feed Operations," http://www.apha.org/legislative/policy/2003/2003-007.pdf (accessed July 27, 2006).

187. Amy R. Sapkota et al., "What Do We Feed to Food Production Animals? A Review of Animal Feed Ingredients and Their Potential Impacts on Human Health," *Environmental Health Perspectives*, February 8, 2007, p. 43.

188. Union of Concerned Scientists, "They Eat What? The Reality of Feed at Animal Factories." http://www.ucsusa.org/food_and_environment/sustainable_food/they-eat-what.html (accessed May 3, 2007).

189. Libby Quaid, "Agriculture Department to Reduce Mad Cow Testing by about 90 Percent," Associated Press, July 21, 2006.

190. Reuters, "New UN Pandemic Czar Warns Flu Could Alter World," *Canadian Press*, October 3, 2005.

191. A. El Amin, "World Bank Outlines Economic Effects of Bird Flu," *Food Production Daily*, July 12, 2006.

192. USDA Agricultural Research Service, "FY-2005, Annual Report, Manure and By-Product Utilization National Program," p. 206.

193. D. Morgan et al., "Farm Program Pays $1.3 Billion to People Who Don't Farm," *Washington Post*, July 2, 2006.

194. Eric Schlosser, "Order the Fish," *Vanity Fair,* November 2004.

195. Mark Floegel, "Corporate Pigs and Other Tales of Agribusiness: The Dirt on Factory Farms," *Multinational Monitor* 21, nos. 7–8 (July/August 2000).

196. S. M. Wilson et al., "Environmental Injustice and the Mississippi Hog Industry," *Environmental Health Perspectives* 110, supp. 2: 195–201.

197. Eric Schlosser, "The Cow Jumped over the USDA," *New York Times*, January 2, 2004.

198. M. Dorning and A. Martin, "Farm Lobby's Power Has Deep Roots," *Chicago Tribune*, June 4, 2006.

199. Libby Quaid, "Report: USDA Only Pretended to Do Probes," Associated Press, January 18, 2006.

200. Morgan et al., "Farm Program Pays $1.3 Billion to People Who Don't Farm."

201. Libby Quaid, "Small Farms Miss Out on Fed Money," Associated Press, October 10, 2006.

202. Morgan et al., "Farm Program Pays $1.3 Billion to People Who Don't Farm."

203. Dorning and Martin, "Farm Lobby's Power Has Deep Roots."

204. USDA Forest Service Range Management, "FY-2005, Grazing Statistical Summary," April 2006, p. iii.

205. "Subsidized Cow Chow," *Economist*, March 7, 2002.

206. Michael Pollan, "The Way We Live Now: You Are What You Grow," *New York Times Magazine*, April 22, 2007.

207. "Harper's Index," *Harper's*, April 2001, p. 17.

208. Thad Williamson, "The Real Y2K Crisis: Global Economic Inequality," *Dollars and Sense* 227, January/February 2000. See also Sandra Postel, "Carry Capacity: Earth's Bottom Line," *Challenge* 37, March/April 1994.

209. Paul Ehrlich et al., "No Middle Way on the Environment," *Atlantic Monthly* 280, December 1997.

210. Henning Steinfeld et al., "Livestock's Long Shadow" (Rome: UN FAO, 2006), available online at http://www.virtualcentre.org/en/library/key_pub/longshed/a0701e/A0701E00.pdf (accessed June 7, 2007).

211. UN FAO data available at http://faostat.fao.org/site/410/Desktop Default.aspx?PageID=410 (accessed June 7, 2007).

212. US EPA, National Pollutant Discharge Elimination System Permit

Regulation and Effluent Limitation Guidelines and Standards for Concentrated Animal Feeding Operations (CAFOs), Final Rule, 68 Fed. Reg. 7176, 7180 (February 12, 2003).

213. Floegel, "Corporate Pigs and Other Tales of Agribusiness."

214. S. Parker, "Finger-Lickin' Bad: How Poultry Producers Are Ravaging the Rural South," *Grist Magazine*, February 21, 2006, http://www.grist.org/news/maindish/2006/02/21/parker/index.html?source=weekly (accessed March 6, 2006).

215. "Environmental Impacts of Animal Feeding Operations," EPA Office of Water Standards and Applied Sciences Division, December 31, 1998, http://www.epa.gov/waterscience/guide/feedlots/envimpct.pdf (accessed June 7, 2007).

216. Jeremy Rifkin, "The World's Problems on a Plate," *Guardian*, May 17, 2002, http://www.guardian.co.uk/comment/story/0,3604,717044,00.html (accessed June 8, 2007).

217. Lucas Reijnders and Sam Soret, "Quantification of the Environmental Impact of Different Dietary Protein Choices," *American Journal of Clinical Nutrition* 78, no. 3 (September 2003): 665S.

218. Ibid, p. 664S.

219. Michael Pollan, "Power Steer," *New York Times Magazine*, March 2003.

220. Richard Manning, "The Oil We Eat," *Harper's*, February 2004.

221. Ed Ayers, "Will We Still Eat Meat?" *Time*, November 6, 1999.

222. "United States Leads World Meat Stampede," Worldwatch Institute, http://www.worldwatch.org/press/news/1998/07/02 (accessed June 7, 2007).

223. United States EPA, Revised National Pollutant Discharge Elimination System Permit Regulation and Effluent Limitation Guidelines for Concentrated Animal Feeding Operations in Response to Waterkeeper Decision, Proposed Rule, 71 Fed. Reg. 2006, p. 37,774.

224. Michael Jacobson, *Six Arguments for a Greener Diet* (Washington, DC: Center for Science in the Public Interest, 2006), p. 89.

225. David Molden, ed., *Water for Food, Water for Life: A Comprehensive Assessment of Water Management in Agriculture* (London: Earthscan, 2007).

226. Amanda Griscom Little, "Big Ag's Big Stink," *Salon.com*, July 7, 2006.

227. Ted Williams, "Assembly Line Swine," *Audubon Magazine*, March/April 1998, p. 27.

228. United States Department of Justice, "Tyson Pleads Guilty to Twenty Felonies and Agrees to Pay $7.5 Million for Clean Water Act Violations," http://www.usdoj.gov/opa/pr/2003/June/03_enrd_383.htm (accessed August 6, 2006).

229. Joe Baird, "Egg Farm to Shell Out $105,000 over Spill," *Salt Lake Tribune*, August 26, 2006.

230. EPA and USDA, Draft Unified National Strategy for Animal Feeding Operation, September 11, 1998.

231. Pew Oceans Commission, *America's Living Oceans*, p. vi.

232. Peter S. Goodman, "Permitting a Pattern of Pollution," *Washington Post*, August 2, 1999, p. A1.

233. Peter S. Goodman, "An Unsavory By-Product: Runoff and Pollution," *Washington Post*, August 2, 1999, p. A1.

234. "State Fines Foie Gras Plant for Manure Cesspool," *North Country Gazette*, March 7, 2007.

235. Confined Livestock Air Quality Committee of the USDA Agricultural Air Quality Task Force, Air Quality Research and Technology Transfer White Paper and Recommendations for Concentrated Animal Feeding Operations, Washington, DC, July 12, 2000, p. 7.

236. Gregory C. Pratt, "Dispersion Modeling Analysis of Air Emissions from Feedlots in Nine Townships in West-Central Minnesota," Air Quality Division, Minnesota Pollution Control Agency, St. Paul, Minnesota, May 26, 1998.

237. P. Viney et al., "Atmospheric Ammonia/Nitrogen Compounds Emissions and Characterization," *Proceedings from Workshop on Atmospheric Nitrogen Compounds*, March 1997.

238. EPA, Region 9. Animal Waste Management Fact Sheet: "What's the Problem?" http://www.epa.gov/region09/cross_pr/animalwaste/problem.html (accessed June 7, 2007).

239. "Cows Rival Cars as Smog Producers," *Fresno Bee*, December 15, 2002.

240. US Department of Justice, "Ohio's Largest Egg Producer Agrees to Dramatic Air Pollution Reductions from Three Giant Facilities," press release, February 23, 2004, http://www.usdoj.gov/opa/pr/2004/February/04_enrd_105.htm (accessed June 7, 2007).

241. Eshel Gordon and Martin Pamela, "Diet, Energy, and Global Warming," *Earth Interactions* 10 (2006).

242. Steinfeld et al., "Livestock's Long Shadow."

243. Ayers, "Will We Still Eat Meat?"

244. Steinfeld et al., "Livestock's Long Shadow."

245. *Livestock Development: Implications for Rural Poverty, the Environment, and Global Food Security* (Washington, DC: World Bank, 2001), p. 36.

246. Steinfeld et al., "Livestock's Long Shadow."

247. D. E. Johnson et al., "The Potential Contribution of Beef Cattle Methane to Global Warming: Background Information and Perspectives," in *Cattle on the Land: Environmental Sensitivity of Beef Production*, ed. F. M. Byers (College Station, TX: Texas A & M University Press), pp. 29–33.

248. Steinfeld et al., "Livestock's Long Shadow."

249. Ibid.

250. Reed F. Noss, "Cows and Conservation Biology," *Conservation Biology* 8 (September 1994): 613–16.

251. T. L. Fleischner, "Ecological Costs of Livestock Grazing in Western North America," *Conservation Biology* 8 (1994): 629–44.

252. David Sheridan, "Western Rangelands: Overgrazed and Undermanaged," *Environment* 23 (4): 44–51.

253. Edward O. Wilson, "Vanishing before Our Eyes," *Time*, April/May 2000.

254. D. Kaimonitz, "Livestock and Deforestation in Central America," EPTD discussion paper, IFPRI Washington, DC, and IICA Coronado, Costa Rica, 1995. Available at http://www.fao.org/ag/aga/lspa/LXEHTML/policy/ch2a.htm (accessed June 8, 2007).

255. Ayers, "Will We Still Eat Meat?"

256. USDA Forest Service, *Rangeland Reform '94 Final Environmental Impact Statement* (Washington, DC: USDI-BLM, 1995), p. 26.

257. D. S. Wilcove et al., "Quantifying Threats to Imperiled Species in the United States: Assessing the Relative Importance of Habitat Destruction, Alien Species, Pollution, Overexploitation, and Disease," *BioScience* 48, no. 8: 610.

258. *Livestock Development*, pp. 14–15.

NOTES TO CHAPTER 3

1. Associated Press, "Assembly OKs Eight-Year-Old Deer Hunters," *Chronotype Rice Lake Online*, August 13, 2006.

2. National Shooting Sports Foundation, "Families Afield," http:// www.nssf.org/programs/FamiliesAfield.cfm?AoI=hunting (accessed August 23, 2006).

3. US Fish and Wildlife Service, "National Survey of Fishing, Hunting, and Wildlife-Associated Recreation," May 2007, http://library.fws .gov/nat_survey2006.pdf (accessed June 4, 2007).

4. A 1998 survey of Americans showed that, while 93 percent of the public supported subsistence hunting by Native Americans and 67 percent of the public supported hunting for meat, only 42 percent supported sport hunting. See T. Heberlein and T. Willebrand, "Attitudes toward Hunting across Time and Continents: The United States and Sweden," *Game and Wildlife* 15, no. 3 (1998): 1071–80.

5. Edward Steinhart, "The Imperial Hunt in Colonial Kenya, ca. 1880–1909," in *Animals in Human Histories*, ed. Mary Hennigner-Voss (Rochester, NY: University of Rochester Press, 2002).

6. Ibid.

7. Daniel Justin Herman, "Hunting Democracy," *Montana: The Magazine of Western History,* Autumn 2005.

8. Ibid.

9. Andrew Isenberg, "The Wild and the Tamed: Indians, Euroamericans, and the Destruction of the Bison" in *Animals in Human Histories*, ed. Mary Henninger-Voss (Rochester, NY: University of Rochester Press, 2002).

10. Ibid.

11. Andrew Isenberg, "The Moral Ecology of Wildlife," in *Representing Animals*, ed. Nigel Rothfels (Bloomington: University of Indiana Press, 2002).

12. J. A. Tober, *Who Owns the Wildlife? The Political Economy of Conservation in Nineteenth-Century America* (Westport, CT: Greenwood, 1981).

13. US Fish and Wildlife Service, "National Survey of Fishing, Hunting, and Wildlife-Associated Recreation," 2001.

14. James Swan, *In Defense of Hunting* (San Francisco: Harper, 1994).

15. Christina Larson, "The Death of Hunting," *Washington Monthly*, January 9, 2006.

16. US Fish and Wildlife Service, "National Survey of Fishing, Hunting, and Wildlife-Associated Recreation," 2001.

17. Ibid.

18. See also Mark Damien Duda and Kira Young, "American Attitudes toward Scientific Wildlife Management and Human Use of Fish and Wildlife: Implications for Effective Public Relations and Communications Strategies," paper delivered at the North American Wildlife and Natural Resources Conference, 1998, http://www.responsivemanagement.com/download/reports/AmericanAttitudes.pdf (accessed June 5, 2007); Bruce Matthews, "Hunting and Outdoor Education," *Coalition for Education in the Outdoors Newsletter*, Winter/Spring 1991.

19. Matthew Scully, *Dominion: The Power of Man, the Suffering of Animals, and the Call to Mercy* (New York: St. Martin's, 2002).

20. Jim Posewitz, *Beyond Fair Chase: The Ethic and Tradition of Hunting* (Helena, MT: Falcon, 1994).

21. Tim Ingold, "From Trust to Domination: An Alternative History of Human-Animal Relations" in *Animals and Human Societies: Changing Perspectives*, ed. Aubrey Manning and James Serpell (London: Routledge, 1994).

22. Ibid.

23. Isenberg, "The Wild and the Tamed."

24. Joe Roman and Stephen Palumbi, "Whales before Whaling in the North Atlantic," *Science* 25 (July 2003).

25. International Whaling Commission, "Scientific Permit Whaling," http://www.iwcoffice.org/conservation/permits.htm (accessed June 5, 2007).

26. International Whaling Commission, "Aboriginal Subsistence Whaling," http://www.iwcoffice.org/conservation/aboriginal.htm (accessed June 5, 2007).

27. John Roach, "Majority Votes to Legalize Whaling," *National Geographic News*, June 19, 2006.

28. "Call for Shark Net Rethink after Whale Death," *ABC News Online*, August 2, 2005.

29. Associated Press, "Canadian Seal Hunt Begins amid Protests," *USA Today*, March 25, 2006, http://www.usatoday.com/news/world/2006-03-25-seal-hunt_x.htm (accessed June 5, 2007).

30. Doug Struck, "Warming Thins Herd for Canada's Seal Hunt," *Washington Post,* April 4, 2007.

31. David Usborne, "Climate Change: Canada's Cruel Harvest," *Independent*, April 2, 2007.

32. A 2005 survey commissioned by the International Fund for Animal Welfare found that 69 percent of Canadians opposed commercial seal hunting and that 78 percent found that clubbing seals was inherently cruel. Also, 79 percent felt that even if eliminating the seal fur industry caused job loss to some, it was justifiable. Finally, 63 percent of Canadians surveyed felt that seal hunting damages Canada's international reputation. Environics Research poll conducted for International Fund for Animal Welfare, "Survey on Canadian Attitudes toward the Seal Hunt," September 2005.

33. D. D. Dolton and R. D. Rau, "Mourning Dove Population Status, 2004." US Fish and Wildlife Service, http://www.fws.gov/migratorybirds/reports/status04/Dove.pdf (accessed June 5, 2007), p. 18.

34. Ibid., p. 8.

35. Matthew Brown, "Coyote Killing Contest in Montana Prompts Howls from Animal Rights Groups, Hunters," Associated Press, January 11, 2007.

36. Wall Hanger Farms, http://www.wallhangerfarms.com (accessed May 15, 2007).

37. "2003 Hunting Survey," *Field and Stream*, http://fieldandstream.com/fieldstream/hunting/article/0,13199,45217,00.html.

38. In 2003 the Bush administration made a proposal that would allow trophy hunters to kill and import into the United States their trophies of endangered animals, arguing that the fees paid by big-game hunters would be used by poor third-world nations to help conserve their wildlife. This proposed change, known ironically as an "enhancement-of-survival policy," was tabled thanks to public outrage but could be reintroduced at any time. Shankar Vedantam, "US May Expand Access to Endangered Species," *Washington Post*, October 11, 2003.

39. Scully, *Dominion.*

40. Bushveld Safaris, http://www.bushveldsafari.com (accessed October 10, 2006).

41. US Fish and Wildlife Service, "National Survey of Fishing, Hunting, and Wildlife-Associated Recreation," 2001.

42. Grand Slam Club Ovis, "Dan Duncan: 2005 Conklin Award Winner," http://www.wildsheep.org/Conklin/Conklin_2005_Duncan.htm (accessed June 5, 2007).

43. Reuters, "Cost to Hunt a Yak: $40,000?" *CNN.com*, August 9, 2006.

44. Marc Kaufman, "Big-Game Hunting Brings Big Tax Breaks," *Washington Post*, April 5, 2005, p. A1.

45. Zachary Goldfarb, "Pension Bill Also Curbs Hunters' Tax Break," *Washington Post*, August 5, 2006, p. A4.

46. Linda Goldston, "Zoo Animals to Go," *San Jose Mercury News*, December 14, 1999.

47. Kelly Niki, "'No-Win' Deal Would Extend Canned Hunts," *Fort Wayne Journal Gazette*, August 27, 2006.

48. *Field and Stream*, "The 2003 Hunting Survey."

49. See http://www.usahuntingsupplies.com/detail.aspx?ID=3265 (accessed June 5, 2007). The Bear Buster Bear Baiter Buffet was available for $779.95 at the time of this writing.

50. According to *Field and Stream*'s "2003 Hunting Survey," 65 percent of hunters oppose hunting in enclosures or fenced-in ranches.

51. Rebekah Scott, "Cheney in Region for a Day of Small-Game Hunting," *Pittsburgh Post-Gazette*, December 9, 2003.

52. Marjorie Hershey, "Strangers on the Range: Exotic Animals Add Spice to Texas's Ranch Economy," fiscal notes, Office of the Comptroller, State of Texas, April 1998.

53. Elizabeth Cary Mungall and William J. Sheffield, *Exotics on the Range: The Texas Example* (College Station: Texas A & M University Press, 1994).

54. Marjorie Hershey, "Strangers on the Range."

55. Susan Combs, "Fiscal Notes," Window on State Government, Texas Comptroller of Public Accounts, April 1998, http://www.cpa.state .tx.us/comptrol/fnotes/fn9804/fna.html (accessed August 26, 2006).

56. Ibid.

57. Mike Di Paola, "How Boom Boom the Rhino Escaped Dodgy Fate, Retired to Arizona," Bloomberg, December 12, 2006.

58. James Schlett, "Humane Society Seeks Animal Auction Probe," *Daily Gazette* (Sarasota Springs, NY), October 25, 2006.

59. Di Paola, "How Boom Boom the Rhino Escaped Dodgy Fate, Retired to Arizona."

60. Schlett, "Humane Society Seeks Animal Auction Probe."

61. Dan Higgins, "Catskill Rhinos Head West to Find Sanctuary," *Albany Times Union*, November 16, 2006; Di Paola, "How Boom Boom the Rhino Escaped Dodgy Fate, Retired to Arizona."

62. Victoria Edwards, *Dealing in Diversity: America's Market for Nature Conservation* (Cambridge: Cambridge University Press, 1995).

63. Courtney Dillard, "Civil Disobedience: A Case Study in Factors of Effectiveness," *Society and Animals* 10, no. 1 (March 2002).

64. Jonathan Pauli and Steven Buskirk, "Recreational Shooting of Prairie Dogs: A Portal for Lead Entering Wildlife Food Chains," *Journal of Wildlife Management* 71, no. 1: 103.

65. "Report of the Nontoxic Shot Advisory Committee," submitted to Minnesota Department of Natural Resources Fish and Wildlife Division, December 12, 2006, p. 1.

66. Brown, "Coyote Killing Contest in Montana Prompts Howls from Animal Rights Groups, Hunters."

67. US Fish and Wildlife Service, "Who We Are," mission statement, http://www.fws.gov/who (accessed June 5, 2007).

68. US Fish and Wildlife Service, "US Fish and Wildlife Service Proposes New Hunting and Fishing Programs on National Wildlife Refuges," press release, http://www.fws.gov/news/NewsReleases/showNews.cfm?newsId =ACABDE25-A9D2-2F0C-6122A1AE40ECCCE9 (accessed May 8, 2007).

69. Helene Lawson, "Controlling the Wilderness: The Work of Wilderness Officers," *Society & Animals* 11, no. 4 (2003).

70. Stephen Eliason, "Illegal Hunting and Angling: The Neutralization of Wildlife Law Violations," *Society & Animals* 11, no. 3 (2003).

71. Ibid.

72. Isenberg, "The Moral Ecology of Wildlife."

73. Ibid.

74. Animal Protection of New Mexico, "Animal Damage Control in New Mexico," 2003, http://www.apnm.org/campaigns/ADC/adc2003.pdf (accessed May 8, 2007).

75. Elisabeth Jennings, "Wildlife Disservices" in *A Primer on Animal Rights*, ed. Kim Stallwood (New York: Lantern Books, 2002).

76. Jody Emel, "Are You Man Enough, Big and Bad Enough? Wolf Eradication in the US" in *Animal Geographies: Place, Politics and Identity in the Nature-Culture Borderlands*, ed. J. Wolch and J. Emel (London: Verso, 1998).

77. Margaret Hair, "Outdoorsmen Convinced of Global Warming for Real," Knight Ridder/Tribune, June 11, 2006.

78. Bettina Boxall, "Foe of Endangered Species Act on Defensive over Abramoff," *Los Angeles Times*, February 14, 2006.

79. Center for Public Integrity, http://www.publicintegrity.org/lobby/profile.aspx?act=industries&in=43 (accessed July 25, 2006).

80. Ibid.

81. Ibid.

82. Advertising rate card for Safari Club International's publications, *Safari Times and Safari Magazine*, www.safariclub.org/sitelink/index.cfm?ContentID=159 (accessed August 26, 2006).

83. SourceWatch, "Matthew J. Hogan," http://www.sourcewatch.org/index.php?title=Matthew_J._Hogan (accessed May 8, 2007).

84. Adam Roberts, "Will It Ever End?" *AWI Quarterly* 46 (Winter 1997): 10–11.

85. US Fish and Wildlife Service, "National Survey of Fishing, Hunting, and Wildlife-Associated Recreation."

86. Ibid.

87. Bob Marshall, "For Sale: Your Hunting Heritage," *Field and Stream*, April 2006.

88. Christina Larson, "The Death of Hunting," *Washington Monthly*, January 9, 2006.

89. US Fish and Wildlife Service, "National Survey of Fishing, Hunting, and Wildlife-Associated Recreation," 2001.

90. Ibid.

91. M. D. Duda and K. C. Young, *Factors Related to Hunting and Fishing Participation in the United States* (Harrisonburg, VA: Responsive Management, 1993–1995).

92. National Wild Turkey Federation, US Sportsmen's Alliance, National Shooting Sports Foundation, "Families Afield: An Initiative for the Future of Hunting," http://www.nwtf.org/images/Families_Afield.pdf (accessed July 20, 2006).

93. Oliver Mackson, "Cousin Kicked Boy as He Lay Shot, Dying," *Times Herald-Record* (Hudson Valley, NY), February 10, 2006.

94. Pennsylvania Game Commission, "2006 Legislative Annual Report," http://www.pgc.state.pa.us/pgc/cwp/view.asp?A=520&Q=171272 (accessed May 15, 2007); National Sports Shooting Foundation, "Alabama Receives $26,000 Grant from Hunting Heritage Partnership," September 12, 2003, http://www.nssf.org/news/PR_idx.cfm?PRloc=news/HHP/03PR/&PR=AL.htm (accessed May 15, 2007).

95. Michael Markarian and Norm Phelps, "Hunters Set Their Sights on

Children," in *A Primer on Animal Rights*, ed. Kim Stallwood (New York: Lantern Books, 2002).

96. International Hunter Education Association, "Factors Related to Hunting and Fishing Participation among the Nation's Youth: Phase 1—A Review of the Literature" (Harrisonburg, VA: Responsive Management, 2003).

97. See Carol Adams, "Woman Battering and Harm to Animals," and Marti Kheel, "License to Kill: An Ecofeminist Critique of Hunters' Discourse," both in *Animals & Women: Feminist Theoretical Explorations,* ed. C. Adams and J. Donovan (Durham, NC: Duke University Press, 1995).

98. Kheel, "License to Kill," p. 91.

99. Linda Kalof, Amy Fitzgerald, and Lori Baralt, "Animals, Women, and Weapons: Blurred Sexual Boundaries in the Discourse of Sport Hunting," *Society & Animals* 12, no. 3 (2004).

NOTES TO CHAPTER 4

1. Nigel Dunstone, *The Mink* (London: T. & A. D. Poyser Ltd., 1993).

2. FICA, "Faqs," http://www.fur.org/poen_faqs.cfm (accessed May 8, 2007).

3. Fur Yarn Web site, http://furyarn.com/main/ (accessed May 8, 2007).

4. Fur Free Alliance, "Facts about the Fur Trade," http://infurmation.com/facts.php (accessed May 12, 2007).

5. International Fur Trade Federation, "Fast Facts," http://www.iftf.com/iftf_3_2_2.php (accessed August 12, 2006).

6. Ibid.

7. USDA National Agricultural Statistics Service, "Other Animals and Animal Products—Inventory and Number Sold: 2002 and 1997," http://www.nass.usda.gov/census/census02/volume1/us/st99_1_030_032.pdf (accessed August 10, 2006).

8. FICA, "Faqs."

9. "Super Duper Recyclers: How Farmers Turn Waste into Beauty," *FCUSA Commentary*, October 28, 1999, revised October 2006. Available online at http://www.furcommission.com/news/newsE68.htm (accessed October 12, 2006). Hans Henrik Dietz et al., "Outbreak of *Salmonella*

Dublin-Associated Abortion in Danish Fur Farms," *Canadian Veterinary Journal* 47, no. 12 (December 2006): 1201.

10. Fur Commission USA, "Chow Time," http://www.furcommission .com/video/Chow.htm (accessed October 12, 2006).

11. Dietz et al., "Outbreak of *Salmonella* Dublin-Associated Abortion in Danish Fur Farms."

12. European Commission Scientific Committee on Animal Health and Animal Welfare, "The Welfare of Animals Kept for Fur Production," report adopted December 12–13, 2001, p. 57. Available at http://ec.europa .eu/food/fs/sc/scah/out67_en.pdf (accessed June 6, 2007).

13. Ibid., p. 107.

14. Ibid., pp. 104–105.

15. Mason Georgia et al., "Frustrations of Fur-Farmed Mink," *Nature* 410 (March 2001): 35.

16. USDA APHIS, "Animals Used in Research," 2004, http://www .aphis.usda.gov/ac/awreports/awreport2004.pdf (accessed May 17, 2007).

17. Ibid., p. 106.

18. Ibid., p. 69.

19. American Veterinary Medicine Association, "Guidelines for Humane Euthanasia of Animals," *2000 Report of the AVMA Panel on Euthanasia*, 2001, p. 11.

20. European Commission Scientific Committee on Animal Health and Animal Welfare, "The Welfare of Animals Kept for Fur Production," p. 67.

21. See National Trappers Association, http://www.nationaltrappers .com/index.html. Other sources suggest that this number may be inflated, such as Mark Henricks, "Trappers: A Rare Breed in Business These Days," *Startup Journal, Wall Street Journal* Center for Entrepeneurs, 2003, http:// www.startupjournal.com/columnists/startuplifestyle/20031211-lifestyle.html (accessed May 8, 2007).

22. American Veterinary Medical Association, "AVMA Positions Address Animal Welfare Concerns," *AVMA News*, July 15, 2001, http://www .avma.org/onlnews/javma/jul01/s071501e.asp (accessed August 7, 2006).

23. Pierre-Yves Daoust and Peter H. Nicholson, "Severe Chronic Neck Injury Caused by a Snare in a Coyote, *Canis latrans*," *Canadian Field-Naturalist* 118, no. 2, April/June 2004, p. 243.

24. Ricky Flynt, "Fur Trapping in Miss.: Past, Present, and Future," *Mississippi Wildlife, Fisheries, and Parks: Wildlife Issues*, Fall/Winter 2001.

25. USDA National Agricultural Statistics Service, "Selected Characteristics of Farms by North American Industry Classification System: 2002," http://www.nass.usda.gov/census/census02/volume1/us/st99_1_050_050.pdf (accessed August 10, 2006).

26. Yi Hsieh et al., "Fun Fur? A Report on the Chinese Fur Industry," Care for the Wild International report, http://www.careforthewild.com/files/furreport05.pdf (accessed August 12, 2006).

27. Kasie Hunt, "Is Your Coat Fur Fake, or Is It Fido?" Associated Press, February 23, 2007.

28. HSUS, "Investigations," http://www.hsus.org/furfree/campaigns/investigations/investigations.html (accessed June 6, 2007).

29. Hunt, "Is Your Coat Fur Fake, or Is It Fido?"

30. USDA National Agricultural Statistics Service, "Mink," July 14, 2006, http://usda.mannlib.cornell.edu/usda/current/Mink/Mink-07-14-2006.pdf (accessed August 12, 2006).

31. Ibid.

32. Fur Goods, "Industry Summary," http://www.allbusiness.com/apparel-other-finished-products-made/fur-goods-fur/3779328-2.html (accessed May 15, 2007).

33. Ibid.

34. FICA, "Faqs."

35. Ibid.

36. USDA Agricultural Research Service, "Tanning Research Update," http://www.ars.usda.gov/is/AR/archive/nov98/tan1198.htm (accessed August 10, 2006).

37. *Los Angeles Times*, "Rugs: Take a Walk on the Wild Side," February 8, 2007, http://www.dallasnews.com/sharedcontent/dws/fea/home/shopping/stories/DN-NHG_skinrugs_0209liv.ART.State.Edition1.38f4eb3.html (accessed June 6, 2007).

38. Agency for Toxic Substances and Disease Registry, Centers for Disease Control and Prevention, "ToxFAQs for Chromium," http://www.atsdr.cdc.gov/tfacts7.html (accessed August 10, 2006).

39. Andrew Isenberg, "The Wild and the Tamed: Indians, Euroamericans, and the Destruction of the Bison," *Animals in Human Histories*, ed. Mary Henninger-Voss (Rochester, NY: University of Rochester Press, 2002).

40. USDA Agricultural Research Service, "Tanning Research Update."

41. Specialized Information Services, National Institutes of Health,

"Occupational Exposure to Hazardous Agents," http://hazmap.nlm.nih.gov/cgibin/hazmap_generic?tbl=TblIndustries&id=141 (accessed August 13, 2006).

42. Intergovernmental Group on Meat (Subgroup on Hides and Skins), UN FAO, "Hides and Skins and Skins and Leather Commodity Profile and Strategy for Development," Committee on Commodity Problems, seventh session, June 4–6, 2001.

43. PETA, "The Horror behind the Global Leather Trade," http://getactive.peta.org/campaign/US_indian_leather?qp_source=usindianleathergen (June 6, 2007).

44. David Coleman, "Next Front: Protecting Animals That Aren't So Cute," *New York Times*, February 2, 1997.

45. Jeremy Lovell, "Wild Animal Slaughter Surges for Fashion's Sake," Reuters, November 28, 2003.

46. Edith Stanley, "Chicken Again? These Gators Get a Steady Diet of Dead Fowl," *Los Angeles Times*, June 10, 2001.

47. Sue Reid, "Getting Under Their Skin," *Sunday Times* (London), February 16, 1997.

48. Australian Government, Department of the Environment and Heritage, "Commercial Kangaroo Harvest Quotas in 2006," http://www.deh.gov.au/biodiversity/trade-use/wild-harvest/kangaroo/quota/2006.html (accessed August 10, 2006).

49. "Global Illegal Wildlife Trade Worth $10 Billion," Reuters, July 31, 2006.

50. National Geographic Society and National Public Radio, "Southeast Asia's Illegal Wildlife Trade," *Radio Expeditions*, November 3–5, 2003, http://www.npr.org/programs/re/archivesdate/2003/nov/wildlife/index.html (accessed May 8, 2007).

51. USDA Economic Research Service, "US Mill Consumption of Raw Wool, Scoured Basis, Annual, 1970–2005," http://usda.mannlib.cornell.edu/usda/ers/89004/table31usmillconsumptionofrawwool.xls (accessed August 13, 2006).

52. National Farmers' Federation, "NFF Fact Sheet—Mulesing," http://www.nff.org.au/pages/policies_printfiles/NR%20152b-04.pdf (accessed August 12, 2006).

53. "Shearing Alternatives under the Spotlight," *Country-Wide Northern* (New Zealand), November 1, 2004.

54. Ruth La Ferla, "Uncruel Beauty," *New York Times*, January 11, 2007, http://www.nytimes.com/2007/01/11/fashion/11VEGAN.htm?page wanted=2&8dpc&_r=2.

55. Debbi Kickham, "Don't Be Cruel," *Boston Globe*, April 5, 2007, http://www.boston.com/yourlife/fashion/articles/2007/04/05/dont_be_cruel/ (accessed June 6, 2007).

56. Samantha Thompson Smith, "Style Goes Vegan," *News & Observer*, April 16, 2007, http://www.newsobserver.com/976/story/564665 .html (accessed June 6, 2007).

NOTES TO CHAPTER 5

1. FDA, "FDA Issues Advice to Make Earliest Stages of Clinical Drug Development More Efficient," FDA press release, January 12, 2006.

2. American Presidency Project, "Remarks Upon Signing the Animal Welfare Bill," August 24, 1966, http://www.presidency.ucsb.edu/ws/index .php?pid=27796 (accessed May 17, 2007).

3. Moses Hamilton et al., "Financial Anatomy of Biomedical Research," *Journal of the American Medical Association* 294 (2005): 1333–42.

4. David Willman, "The National Institutes of Health: Public Servant or Private Marketer?" *Los Angeles Times*, December 22, 2004.

5. From Subtitle D, Animal Welfare, from the Helms Amendment to the 2002 Farm Bill.

6. "Animal Welfare Act and Regulations," http://www.nal.usda.gov/ awic/legislat/usdaleg1.htm (accessed May 17, 2007).

7. USDA APHIS, "Animal Care: A New Era in Animal Welfare," February 2002, http://www.aphis.usda.gov/lpa/pubs/fsheet_faq_notice/fs _awnewera.html (accessed May 21, 2007).

8. "Compliance Inspections," June 2005, http://www.aphis.usda .gov/lpa/pubs/fsheet_faq_notice/fs_awinspect.html (accessed May 17, 2007).

9. USDA APHIS, "Animal Welfare Act," January 2002, http://www .aphis.usda.gov/lpa/pubs/awact.html (accessed May 17, 2007).

10. USDA APHIS, "Animals Used in Research," 2004, http://www .aphis.usda.gov/ac/awreports/awreport2004.pdf (accessed May 17, 2007).

11. US Congress, Office of Technology Assessment, *Alternatives to*

Animal Use in Research, Testing and Education (Washington, DC: US Government Printing Office, 1986), p. 5.

12. USDA APHIS, "Animals Used in Research."

13. Ibid.

14. USDA APHIS, "Animals Used in Research."

15. See *Lab Animal* online, http://guide.labanimal.com/guide/index.html (accessed September 15, 2006).

16. Ibid.

17. Susan E. Davis and Margo DeMello, *Stories Rabbits Tell: A Natural and Cultural History of a Misunderstood Creature* (New York: Lantern Books, 2003).

18. Ibid.

19. Ibid.

20. Sarah Treffinger, "Humane Society Urges Ban on Animal Demos," *Cleveland Plain Dealer,* January 16, 2007.

21. USDA, "Animals Used in Research."

22. Ibid.

23. Tara Gray, "A Brief History of Animals in Space," http://history.nasa.gov/animals.html (accessed October 12, 2006).

24. HSUS, "Chimpanzees in Research Fact Sheet," http://www.hsus.org/animals_in_research/chimps_deserve_better/chimpanzees_in_research_fact.html (accessed May 24, 2007).

25. Will Dunham, "US Stops Breeding Chimps for Research," Reuters, May 24, 2007.

26. HSUS, "An Introduction to Primate Issues," http://www.hsus.org/animals_in_research/general_information_on_animal_research/an_introduction_to_primate_issues.html (accessed May 24, 2007).

27. USDA APHIS, "Animals Used in Research."

28. John Parascandola, "Physiology, Propaganda, and Pound Animals: Medical Research and Animal Welfare in Mid-Twentieth Century America," *Journal of the History of Medicine and Allied Sciences*, February 2007.

29. "Concentration Camp for Dogs," *LIFE,* February 4, 1966.

30. As long as they generated more than five hundred dollars in annual sales.

31. USDA APHIS, "Random Source Dog and Cat Inspection Dealer," http://www.aphis.usda.gov/ac/dealer/randomsource.pdf (accessed May 17, 2007).

32. Kimberly Hefling, "Congress Tackles Animal Research Rules," Associated Press, May 14, 2007.

33. "Pet Protection Legislation Considered by House Subcommittee" *Animal Welfare Institute Quarterly* 45, nos. 2–3 (Spring/Summer 1996).

34. *Animal Welfare Institute Quarterly* 49, no. 4 (Fall 2000) cites the number at fifteen, whereas *Animals in Print* from May 4, 2004, reports there are twenty-seven class B dealers remaining.

35. USDA APHIS, "Fiscal Year 2004 Animal Welfare Act Inspections," http://www.aphis.usda.gov/ac/awreports/awreport2004.pdf (accessed October 12, 2006).

36. Harlan Sprague Dawley, Inc., "About Harlan," http://www.harlan.com/aboutharlan.asp (accessed May 24, 2007).

37. "NIH Chimpanzee Management Program (ChiMP) for Biomedical Research Chimpanzees," June 2001, http://www.ncrr.nih.gov/compmed/Chimp19-June-01.asp.

38. Natalie Pawelski, "Monkeys Raised for Research Wreak Havoc in Florida Keys," *CNN.com*, July 10, 1998, http://www.cnn.com/TECH/science/9807/10/monkey.island/ (accessed October 12, 2006).

39. Carolyn Marshall, "Monkeys for Research: Much Coveted, and Hard to Come By," *New York Times*, April 6, 2004.

40. From Primate Resource Referral Service, "Annual Resource Guide," http://www.wanprc.org/prrs/arg.asp#SUPPLIERS (accessed May 23, 2007).

41. Many or most primates shipped to the United States are acquired legally, but there have been well-documented cases of illegally caught primates being shipped to US suppliers such as Worldwide Primates. From Kathleen Uribe, "Primates and Trade," *TED Case Studies* 3, no. 1 (January 1994). Because of the regulations and negative publicity associated with breeding primates in the United States, a number of companies have looked overseas to find primates, supporting breeding colonies of monkeys in places like Indonesia, China, and Puerto Rico.

42. One result of the Ebola monkey crisis was the shutting down of Hazelton; a second result was that US air carriers stopped shipping wild primates from overseas.

43. "Plague-Infected Lab Mice Missing in New Jersey," Associated Press, September 15, 2005.

44. Marshall, "Monkeys for Research."

45. *"Lab Animal* Buyers' Guide 2004," *Lab Animal,* http://guide.labanimal.com/guide/product34.jsp?a=1&b=50140 (accessed October 12, 2006).

46. Dan Luzadder, "Greyhounds Make Terminal Run to CSU," *Rocky Mountain News,* June 7, 1998.

47. See "Environmental Enrichment Information Resources for Laboratory Animals: 1965–1995," *AWIC Resource Series* 2 (September 1995), for a complete bibliography on environmental enrichment.

48. "Environmental Enrichment for Nonhuman Primates Resource Guide," *AWIC Resource Guide* 32, July 2006, http://www.nal.usda.gov/awic/pubs/Primates2006/Primates.htm#user (accessed June 4, 2007).

49. USDA APHIS, "Final Report on Environmental Enhancement to Promote the Psychological Well-Being of Nonhuman Primates," July 15, 1999, http://www.nal.usda.gov/awic/enrichment/Enviromental_Enhancement_NonHuman_Primates.htm#promote (accessed June 4, 2007).

50. Mollie Bloomsmith and S. P. Lambeth, "Videotapes as Enrichment for Captive Chimpanzees *(Pan troglodytes),*" *Zoo Biology* 19 (2000): 541–51.

51. J. Fritz and S. Howell, "The Disappearing Ice Cube," *Laboratory Primate Newsletter* 32, no. 1 (1993): 8.

52. Larry Carbone, *What Animals Want: Expertise and Advocacy in Laboratory Animal Welfare Policy* (New York: Oxford University Press, 2004).

53. "Environmental Enrichment Information Resources for Laboratory Animals: 1965–1995," *AWIC Resource Guide.*

54. Institute of Laboratory Animal Resources, *Guide for the Care and Use of Laboratory Animals* (Washington, DC: National Academy Press, 1996).

55. Kathryn Bayne, "Potential for Unintended Consequences of Environmental Enrichment for Laboratory Animals and Research Results," *Institute for Laboratory Animal Research Journal* 46, no. 2 (2005).

56. H. Von Staden, "The Discovery of the Body: Human Dissection and Its Cultural Contexts in Ancient Greece," *Yale Journal of Biological Medicine* 65, no. 3 (May/June 1992): 223–41.

57. Americans for Medical Progress, "Everyday Wonders," http://www.amprogress.org/site/c.jrLUK0PDLoF/b.1086431/k.ACC8/EVERYDAY_WONDERS.htm (accessed May 24, 2007).

58. Kenneth Shapiro, "A Rodent for Your Thoughts: The Social Con-

struction of Animal Models," in *Animals in Human Histories*, ed. Mary Henninger-Voss (Rochester, NY: University of Rochester Press, 2002).

59. Anna Wilde Mathews, "Recent Cases Point to the Limitations of Animal Drug Tests," *Wall Street Journal*, March 30, 2007, p. B1.

60. Some companies, like the Body Shop, while purchasing ingredients that have been tested on animals, will only purchase ingredients tested prior to 1990, in order to discourage the continuation of animal testing.

61. Alan Scher Zagier, "Mo. Animal Research Lab Agrees to Settle Federal Complaint," Associated Press, March 23, 2007.

62. "Department of Defense Animal Care and Use Programs 2001," http://www.dtic.mil/biosys/downloads/fy01_report.pdf (accessed August 27, 2006), pp. 1–7.

63. Department of Defense Biomedical Research Database, http://www.dtic.mil/biosys/org/brd/index.htm (accessed August 27, 2006).

64. "Army Medics Train in Warlike Conditions," MSNBC, November 27, 2006, http://www.msnbc.msn.com/id/15916641/site/3000001/from/RS.4/ (accessed May 26, 2007).

65. William Russell and Rex Burch, *The Principles Of Humane Experimental Technique* (London: Methuen, 1959).

66. Kathy Keville, "Compassionate Cosmetics," *Better Nutrition* 64, no. 6 (June 1, 2002): 58.

67. Alexandra Marks, "How Drug-Approval Woes Crept Up on the FDA," *Christian Science Monitor*, November 26, 2004; or see Gardiner Harris, "FDA Failing in Drug Safety, Officials Assert," *New York Times*, November 19, 2004.

68. US FDA Center for Food Safety and Applied Nutrition, statement on animal testing, revised May 3, 1999, June 9, 2005, and April 5, 2006.

69. "Europe Set to Outlaw Cosmetic Testing on Live Animals," *Evening Standard*, April 28, 2007.

70. Jonathan Balcolmbe, *The Use of Animals in Higher Education: Problems, Alternatives and Recommendations* (Washington, DC: Humane Society Press, 2000).

71. Theo Capaldo, "The Psychological Effect on Students of Using Animals in Ways that They See as Ethically, Morally, and Religiously Wrong," Ethical Science and Education Coalition, 2001, http://www.neavs.org/esec/student_concerns/sc_psychological_effect_tcapaldo.htm (accessed May 17, 2007).

72. Ibid.

73. Jim Ludwick, "Good Science or Torture? Experiments at UNM Laboratory Draw Fire," *Albuquerque Journal*, May 20, 2007.

74. National Science Teachers Association, "Responsible Use of Live Animals and Dissection in the Science Classroom," position statement, June 2005, http://www.nsta.org/positionstatement&psid=44 (accessed October 12, 2006).

75. "ISEF Rules: Vertebrate Animals," http://www.sciserv.org/isef/rules/rules10.asp (accessed October 12, 2006).

76. Marc Bekoff, *Minding Animals: Awareness, Emotions and Heart* (Oxford: Oxford University Press, 2002), p. 171.

77. UC Davis Center for Animal Alternatives, Information Resources for Animal Welfare and Alternatives: Higher Education, http://www.vetmed.ucdavis.edu/Animal_Alternatives/highered.htm (accessed October 12, 2006).

78. Comparison of Alternatives Offered by Veterinary Schools, Association of Veterinarians for Animal Rights, http://www.avar.org/pdf/vtech/chart_av_school.pdf (accessed October 12, 2006).

79. M. L. Stephens, "The Significance of Alternative Techniques in Biomedical Research: An Analysis of Nobel Prize Awards," in *Advances in Animal Welfare Science 1986/1987*, ed. M. W. Fox and L. D. Mickley (Boston, MA: Martinus Nijhof), pp. 19–31.

80. Mathews, "Recent Cases Point to the Limitations of Animal Drug Tests."

81. Lynda Birke and Mike Michael, "The Heart of the Matter: Animal Bodies, Ethics, and Species Boundaries," *Society & Animals* 6, no. 3 (1998).

82. A. N. Schechter and R. A. Retting, "Funding Priorities for Medical Research," *Journal of the American Medical Association* 288, no. 7 (2002): 832.

83. Pandora Pound et al., "Where Is the Evidence that Animal Research Benefits Humans?" *British Medical Journal* 328 (February 28, 2004): 514–17.

84. Ibid.

85. "Pharmaceutical Industry: Growth Slowdown Calls for New R&D Strategies," *Pharmaceutical Business Review Online*, http://www.pharmaceutical-business-review.com/article_researchwire.asp?guid=DBEA503A-0DD4-44DA-8E6D-476665B11691 (accessed May 24, 2007); Billy Tauzin, "A Research-Based Pharmaceutical Sector Built to Meet the

Challenges of the 21st Century," remarks before the National Venture Capital Association, http://www.phrma.org/about_phrma/straight_talk_from_billy _tauzin/a_research-based_pharmaceutical_sector_built_to_meet_the _challenges_of_the_21st_century/ (accessed October 26, 2006).

86. Center for Public Integrity, "Pharmaceutical Research & Manufacturers of America," http://www.publicintegrity.org/lobby/profile.aspx?act =clients&year=2003&cl=L002495 (accessed May 24, 2007).

87. M. Asif Ismail, "Drug Lobby Second to None: How the Pharmaceutical Industry Gets Its Way in Washington," Center for Public Integrity report, July 7, 2005.

88. David Willman, "The National Institutes of Health: Public Servant or Private Marketer?"

89. Center for Public Integrity, "National Association for Biomedical Research," http://www.publicintegrity.org/lobby/profile.aspx?act=clients &year=2003&cl=L016973 (accessed May 24, 2007).

90. http://www.guidestar.org/pqShowGsReport.do?npoId=449182 (accessed May 24, 2007).

91. http://www.guidestar.org/FinDocuments/2005/042/746/ 2005-042746997-028996ce-9.pdf (accessed May 24, 2007).

92. Center for Public Integrity, "Policy Directions Inc.," http://www .publicintegrity.org/lobby/profile.aspx?act=firms&year=2003&lo=L002522 (accessed May 24, 2007).

93. Financial information from Guidestar.org, http://www.guidestar .org/FinDocuments/2004/360/727/2004-360727175-01eb476c-9.pdf (accessed May 24, 2007). Lobbying information from Center for Public Integrity, http://www.publicintegrity.org/lobby/profile.aspx?act=clients &year=2003&cl=L000382 (accessed May 24, 2007).

94. Lobbying information from Center for Public Integrity, http:// www.publicintegrity.org/lobby/profile.aspx?act=clients&year=2003&cl =L000763 (accessed May 24, 2007). Financial information from Guidestar, http://www.guidestar.org/FinDocuments/2004/521/224/2004-521224577-01 f8c4ac-9.pdf (accessed May 24, 2007).

95. Center for Public Integrity, "Animal Health Institute," http://www .publicintegrity.org/lobby/profile.aspx?act=clients&year=2003&cl =L000524 (accessed May 24, 2007).

96. Jill Howard Church, "The Business of Animal Research" in *A Primer on Animal Rights*, ed. Kim Stallwood (New York: Lantern Books, 2002).

97. Karen Rader, *Making Mice: Standardizing Animals for American Biomedical Research, 1900–1955* (Princeton, NJ: Princeton University Press, 2004).

98. Ibid.

99. Center for Public Integrity, "Industry Ties," http://www.publicintegrity.org/oi/db.aspx?act=ind&cycle=2002&sub=2&linkid=H (accessed October 12, 2006).

100. Brenda Goodman, "Pepsi and Coke Agree to Stop Financing Research that Uses Animals," *New York Times*, May 31, 2007, http://www.nytimes.com/2007/05/31/business/31testing-web.html?ref=business (accessed May 31, 2007).

101. National Research Council, *Science, Medicine, and Animals* (Washington, DC: National Research Council of the National Academies, 2004); S. Plous, "Proceedings for Pain Management and Humane Endpoints: Opinion Research on Animal Experimentation: Areas of Support and Concern," 2006, http://altweb.jhsph.edu/meetings/pain/plous.htm (accessed October 26, 2006).

102. Ibid. See also Mori poll, "Use of Animals in Medical Research, Survey 2005," December 2, 2005, http://www.ipsos-mori.com/polls/2005/cmp.shtml (accessed October 26, 2006).

103. Penn, Schoen, and Berland Associates, Inc., "Opinion Poll on Pain and Distress in Research," poll conducted for the HSUS, http://www.hsus.org/animals_in_research/pain_distress/opinion_poll_on_pain_and_distress_in_research.html (accessed October 12, 2006).

104. Lynda Birke, "Who—or What—Are the Rats (and Mice) in the Laboratory?" *Society & Animals* 11, no. 3 (2003): 207–24; Kenneth Shapiro, "A Rodent for Your Thoughts."

105. Shapiro, "A Rodent for Your Thoughts."

106. Lynda Birke, *Feminism, Animals, and Science: The Naming of the Shrew* (Buckingham: Open University Press, 1994).

107. Arnold Arluke and Clinton Sanders, *Regarding Animals* (Philadelphia: Temple University Press, 1996).

108. Arnold Arluke, "Trapped in a Guilt Cage." *New Science* 134, no. 1815 (1992): 33–35; Hal Herzog, "Ethical Aspects of Relationships between Humans and Research Animals," *Institute for Laboratory Animal Research Journal* 43, no. 1 (2002): 27–32; Vanessa Rohlf and Pauleen Bennett, "Perpetration Induced Traumatic Stress in Persons Who Euthanize Animals in Surgeries, Animal Shelters, and Laboratories," *Society & Animals* 13, no. 3 (2005): 201–20.

109. Arnold Arluke, "Systems of Meanings in Primate Labs" in *Regarding Animals,* ed. Arnold Arluke and Clinton Sanders (Philadelphia: Temple University Press, 1996).

110. Bernard Rollin, *The Unheeded Cry: Animal Consciousness, Animal Pain, and Science* (Oxford: Oxford University Press, 1989).

111. Emma Marris, "Animal Research: Grey Matters," *Nature,* December 13, 2006, http://www.nature.com/news/2006/061211/full/444808a .html (accessed May 30, 2007).

112. Susan Iliff, "An Additional 'R': Remembering the Animals," *Institute for Laboratory Animal Research Journal* 43, no. 1, (2002).

113. Katherine Perlo, "'Would You Let Your Child Die Rather Than Experiment on Animals?' A Comparative Questions Approach," *Society & Animals* 11, no. 1 (2003): 51–68.

114. Matthew Scully, *Dominion: The Power of Man, the Suffering of Animals, and the Call to Mercy* (New York: St. Martin's, 2002).

NOTES TO CHAPTER 6

1. "Americans Spend Big on Pet Projects," *Business Journal,* April 28, 2004.

2. William Ferchland, "Man Who Killed Ex-Girlfriend's Cat Sentenced to Six Months in Jail," *Tahoe Daily Tribune,* March 11, 2005.

3. American Pet Product Manufacturing Association, "2007–2008 APPMA National Pet Owner's Survey," http://www.appma.org/press _industrytrends.asp (accessed May 31, 2007).

4. Ibid.

5. Senate Bill 1357, which mandated that pet stores in California provide care information with the sale of animals, did pass in 2002 but not without extensive lobbying by the pet industry. In fact, thanks to the work of the Pet Industry Joint Advisory Council, the bill was so heavily gutted that, in its final form, stores would only have to provide care information for a "class" of animal, such as a reptile, rather than a species, such as a turtle or a snake, and penalties for failing to provide even that simple requirement are close to nonexistent.

6. "2006–2007 Retailer Report," *Pet Age,* http://www.petage.com/ pdf/0607retreport.pdf (accessed May 31, 2007).

7. Cat Fanciers' Association, "Unraveling the Mysteries of Grass Roots Lobbying," http://www.cfa.org/articles/legislative/grass-roots-lobbying .html (accessed May 31, 2007).

8. Pet Industry Joint Advisory Council, "Pet Stores, Puppies and 'Puppy Mills,'" http://www.pijac.org/files/public/PUPPIES.pdf (accessed June 5, 2007).

9. National Pet Alliance, "Helping Our Companion Animals Today," http://www.fanciers.com/npa/ (accessed May 31, 2007).

10. American Dog Owners Association, http://www.adoa.org (accessed May 31, 2007).

11. National Animal Interest Alliance, "NAIA Policy Statement: Pet Ownership," http://www.naiaonline.org/body/articles/archives/policy_pets .htm (accessed May 31, 2007).

12. Although none of these books look explicitly at the pet industry, Marjorie Spiegel's *The Dreaded Comparison* (New York: Mirror Books, 1996), Carol Adams's *The Sexual Politics of Meat* (New York: Continuum, 1990), and Charles Patterson's *Eternal Treblinka: Our Treatment of Animals and the Holocaust* (New York: Lantern Books, 2002) offer compelling arguments about the connections between our treatment of animals, including their forced breeding, and the treatment of slaves, women, and Holocaust victims.

13. Eric Olson, "States Attempt Crackdown on Puppy Mills," Associated Press, June 3, 2007.

14. The AWA, enacted in 1970, covers warm-blooded animals sold in the wholesale pet trade, as well as those sold and raised for research, zoos, and circuses, but the act does not cover, for example, pet stores or dog shows.

15. In May 2005 Sen. Rick Santorum (R-PA) introduced the Pet Animal Welfare Statute (PAWS), which would amend the AWA to provide greater federal oversight of puppy mills and other breeding facilities that don't just sell wholesale animals to dealers and brokers (already covered under the AWA). It would also provide federal inspection for those breeders who sell directly to the public, such as Internet sellers or pet stores that breed or import their own animals. Unfortunately, the bill (the second that Santorum has introduced) never made it out of committee thanks to the opposition of the major breeding organizations, as well as the entire pet industry.

16. Olson, "States Attempt Crackdown on Puppy Mills."

17. HUA, "Prisoners of Greed: Puppy Mills Breed Misery," http:// www.prisonersofgreed.org/USDA.html (accessed May 31, 2007).

18. See Fido, "When to Stop Breeding Dog: Last Pregnancy," http://

www.seefido.com/dog-breeding/html/when_to_stop_breeding_dog_la.htm (accessed May 31, 2007).

19. Renée Shreve, "Surprise Inspections Reveal 'Puppy Mill' Conditions at Two GC Kennels," *Republican Newspaper* (Garrett County, MD), August 17, 2006.

20. T. J. Dunn Jr. and Ginger Saari, "Dog Breeding: What Is Involved in Getting into the Business," http://www.thepetcenter.com/gen/dbb.html (accessed May 31, 2007).

21. Susan E. Davis and Margo DeMello, *Stories Rabbits Tell: A Natural and Cultural History of a Misunderstood Creature* (New York: Lantern Books, 2003).

22. "The Problem," http://www.birdadoption.org/problem.htm (accessed May 31, 2007).

23. Ibid. One unintended consequence of the surplus of unsocialized birds is the trend of people who turn to breeding their birds who, after maturity, have gotten "aggressive," meaning displaying normal birdlike behaviors, so that they can once again have a dependent and sweet baby bird, at least until the new bird reaches maturity.

24. Mira Tweti, "'Factory Farming' Approach Takes Toll," *News Tribune* (Tacoma, WA), December 18, 2005.

25. Sally Blanchard, "Kaytee Preferred Birds and PetsMart: Partners in the Avi-Industry—Is This Plan for the Birds?" *Pet Bird Report* 47, May 2000.

26. Ibid.

27. American Boxer Club, "Code of Ethics," http://americanboxerclub .org/ethics.html (accessed May 31, 2007).

28. Katherine Nevius, "Here It Is in Black and White," editorial article, http:// www.boxerunderground.com/feb_bu_99/knevius.htm (accessed May 24, 2007).

29. Australian Shepherd Club of America, "Facts You Should Know before Breeding Australian Shepherds," http://www.asca.org/Facts +Breeding/default.htm (accessed May 31, 2007).

30. David Pett, editor's comment in "Culling for Quality" by Lana Gore in *Lop Rabbit Club of America Guidebook*, 5th ed. (Hornbrook, CA: Lop Rabbit Club of America, 1996), p. 70.

31. Jane Johnson, "Costs," http://www.learntobreed.com/costs.html (accessed May 31, 2007).

32. John Ford, "Hunte Corp. Honored for Success," *Neosho* (MO) *Daily News*, August 4, 2001.

33. Michelle Pippin, "Hunte Violates DNR Regulations," *Neosho* (MO) *Daily News*, November 25, 2003.

34. USDA APHIS, "Violation Summary," July 26, 2005, http://www .aphis.usda.gov/ac/violations/2004violations.pdf (accessed May 31, 2007).

35. Taken from Rep. George Brown's comments regarding the USDA inspector general's January 1995 report, "APHIS Enforcement of the Animal Welfare Act," http://thomas.loc.gov/cgi-bin/query/z?r104:E14JN5-171 (accessed May 24, 2007).

36. Petland, "Pet Welfare Questions: Where Do Petland Puppies Come From?" http://www.petland.com/AboutPetland/PetWelfareQuestions1.htm (accessed June 5, 2007).

37. In 2004 Petco launched a "Think Adoption First" initiative that promoted adoption to its customers, even though the stores continue to sell rabbits, birds, rats, mice, and ferrets. While this campaign sounds wonderful on the surface, many animal welfare organizations see it as a cynical ploy to seem adoption friendly while still being able to profit off of the sale of animals.

38. This is in marked contrast to the 2005 Animal Welfare Bill passed in the United Kingdom, which provides a great degree of protection to animals sold in pet stores throughout England and Wales and mandates a standard of care for pet guardians throughout the nation.

39. "2006–2007 Retailer Report," *Pet Age.*

40. Jerry Doyle, "'Tis the Season: An Effective Puppy Program Is Important Not Only during the Busy Holiday Season but throughout the Year," *Pet Business*, December 2004, p. 58.

41. "2004–2005 Retailer Report," *Pet Age*, http://www.petage.com/ pdf/0405retreport.pdf (accessed May 31, 2007).

42. Jeff Siegel, "No More Doggies in the Window?" *Pet Age*, April 2006.

43. From the AKC's position statement on ear cropping, tail docking, and dew claw removal. See AKC, "Canine Legislation Position Statements," http://www.akc.org/canine_legislation/position_statements.cfm#earcropping (accessed May 24, 2007).

44. G. J. Noonan, J. S. Rand, and J. K Blackshaw, "Tail Docking in Dogs: A Sample of Attitudes of Veterinarians and Dog Breeders in Queensland" *Australian Veterinary Journal* 73 (1996); Linda P. Michels, "A Tale of Tails," 1999, http://www.amrottclub.org/tale%20of%20tails.htm (accessed June 7, 2007).

45. Robert Wansborough, "Cosmetic Tail Docking of Dogs' Tails," *Australian Veterinary Journal* 74, no. 1 (July 1996).

46. Cynthia Hubert, "Dog Cropping Bill Causes Uproar," *Sacramento Bee*, March 15, 2005.

47. "In Other News," *Pet Age*, June 2006; "In Other News," *Pet Age*, August 2006.

48. Laura Italiano, "4.4 Million Dollar Puppy Mill Scandal," *New York Post*, September 22, 1996.

49. John Ford, "Hunte Corp. Honored for Success."

50. HSUS, "HSUS Pet Overpopulation Estimates," http://www.hsus.org/pets/issues_affecting_our_pets/pet_overpopulation_and_ownership_statistics/hsus_pet_overpopulation_estimates.html (accessed September 30, 2006).

51. G. Handy, *Animal Control Management* (Washington, DC: ICMA, 2001).

52. Anna Sadler, "Pet Overpopulation: A Self-Fulfilling Prophecy?" *Cat Fanciers' Almanac*, September 1994.

53. "Petland Protests City Law," *Pet Age*, June 2005.

54. Lisa Lapin, "New Leash on Life," *UC Davis Magazine*, Fall 2004, pp. 25–27.

55. HSUS, "HSUS Pet Overpopulation Estimates."

56. HSUS, First Strike Campaign, "2003 Report of Animal Cruelty Cases," HSUS, 2003.

57. Susan E. Davis, "Prosecuting Animal Hoarders Is Like Herding Cats," *California Lawyer*, September 2002.

58. Ibid.

59. Ibid.

60. Maryann Mott, "US Dog Fighting Rings Stealing Pets for Bait," *National Geographic News*, February 18, 2004.

61. CDC, "Nonfatal Dog Bite—Related Injuries Treated in Hospital Emergency Departments—United States, 2001," *MMWR* 52, no. 26 (2003): 605–10.

62. "American Kennel Club News Article: Introduction of Tethering Bills in Multiple States," April 3, 2007, http://www.akc.org/news/blocks/print_article.cfm?article_id=3177 (accessed June 8, 2007).

63. Jeffrey Sacks et al., "Breeds of Dogs Involved in Fatal Human Attacks in the United States between 1979 and 1998," *Journal of the Amer-*

ican *Veterinary Medical Association* 217, no. 6 (September 15, 2000), http://www.cdc.gov/ncipc/duip/dogbreeds.pdf (accessed May 31, 2007).

64. Arnold Arluke, "Physical Cruelty towards Animals in Massachusetts, 1975–1996," *Society & Animals* 5 (1997): 195–204. See also Frank Ascione, "Children Who Are Cruel to Animals: A Review of Research and Implications for Developmental Psychopathology," *Anthrozoos* 6 (1993): 226–47.

65. Frank Ascione, "Domestic Violence and Cruelty to Animals," paper presented at the Fourth International Conference on Family Violence, Durham, NH, 1995; Frank Ascione et al., "The Abuse of Animals and Domestic Violence: A National Survey of Shelters for Women Who Are Battered," *Society & Animals* 5 (1997): 205–18; Frank Ascione, "Battered Women's Reports of Their Partners' and Their Children's Cruelty to Animals," *Journal of Emotional Abuse* 1 (1998): 119–33.

66. A survey of 354 college students shows that childhood pet ownership is strongly positively correlated with concern toward animals in general and with the practice of some form of ethical food avoidance, as well as membership in animal welfare organizations. See James Serpell and Elizabeth Paul, "Pets and the Development of Positive Attitudes to Animals" in *Animals and Human Society: Changing Perspectives*, ed. A. Manning and J. Serpell (London: Routledge, 1994).

67. Serpell and Paul quote Pythagoras, who was said to have written, "As long as man continues to be the ruthless destroyer of lower living beings, he will never know health or peace. For as long as men massacre animals, they will kill each other."

68. Katherine Grier, "'The Eden of Home: Changing Understandings of Cruelty and Kindness to Animals in Middle-Class American Households, 1820–1900" in *Animals in Human Histories*, ed. Mary Henninger-Voss (Rochester, NY: University of Rochester Press, 2002).

69. Frank Ascione, "Enhancing Children's Attitudes about the Humane Treatment of Animals: Generalization to Human-Directed Empathy," *Anthrozoos* 5, no. 3 (1992): 176–91. See also Gail Melson, "Studying Children's Attachment to Their Pets: A Conceptual and Methodological Review," *Anthrozoos* 4, no. 2 (1991): 91–99.

70. Beth Daly and L. L. Morton, "Children with Pets Do Not Show a Higher Empathy: A Challenge to Current Views," *Anthrozoos* 16, no. 4 (2003): 298–314.

71. Or, in some cases, the captive breeding of nondomesticated animals.

72. Beth Preiss, "What's the Matter with Kansas?" HSUS, August 26, 2005, http://www.hsus.org/wildlife/wildlife_news/whats_the_matter_with _kansas.html (accessed May 31, 2007).

73. Gerard Shields, "Primate Pet Trade Targeted," *Advocate*, June 3, 2007.

74. CITES, "What Is CITES?" http://www.cites.org/eng/disc/what .shtml (accessed May 24, 2007).

75. Michael Sas-Rolfes, "Assessing CITES: Four Case Studies" in *Endangered Species, Threatened Convention: The Past, Present and Future of CITES*, ed. Jon Hutton and Barnabas Dickson (London: Earthscan, 2000).

76. Scott Norris, "Sick as a Parrot," *New Scientist* 170, no. 2294. See also R. Low, "The Wild Parrot Trade: Stop It!" *PsittaScene* 53 (2002).

77. HSUS, "Live Cargo," http://www.hsus.org/wildlife/issues_facing _wildlife/wildlife_trade/live_cargo.html (accessed May 31, 2007).

78. Dilys Roe et al., "Making a Killing or Making a Living: Wildlife Trade, Trade Controls, and Rural Livelihoods," *Biodiversity and Livelihoods Issues* 6, March 2002, http://www.traffic.org/livelihoods/index.html (accessed May 31, 2007).

79. Ibid.

80. HSUS, "Reptiles as Pets: Hazardous to Your Health—and Theirs," http://www.hsus.org/pets/issues_affecting_our_pets/Reptiles_as_Pets.html (accessed May 31, 2007).

81. Additionally, the National Alternative Pet Association says that because many exotic pets are illegal, owners are afraid to bring them to the veterinarian for care, which is another reason why these animals suffer through the pet trade. See "Why Laws Prohibiting Exotic Animals Do Not Work," http://www.altpet.net/badlaw.html (accessed May 24, 2007).

82. Kris Axtman, "After Exotic Pets Are Rescued, What Next?" *Christian Science Monitor*, July 26, 2006.

83. Richard Farinato, "The Whims and Dangers of the Exotic Pet Market," http://www.hsus.org/wildlife/issues_facing_wildlife/should_wild _animals_be_kept_as_pets/the_whims_and_dangers_of_the_exotic_pets _market.html (accessed May 24, 2007).

84. A federal bill that prohibits the interstate pet trade in big cats became law in 2003, but it would not restrict the thousands of legal licensees who are allowed to keep or breed big cats.

85. National Institutes of Health, "The Health Benefits of Pets," National Institutes of Health OMAR Workshop, September 10–11, 1987, http://consensus.nih.gov/1987/1987HealthBenefitsPetsta003html.htm (accessed May 31, 2007). CDC, "Health Benefits of Pets," http://www.cdc.gov/healthypets/health_benefits.htm (accessed May 31, 2007).

86. Howard W. French, "Chinese Outcry: Doesn't a Dog Have Rights?" *New York Times*, August 9, 2006.

87. Arnold Arluke, "Managing Emotions in an Animal Shelter" in *Animals and Human Society: Changing Perspectives*, ed. A. Manning and J. Serpell (London: Routledge, 1994).

NOTES TO CHAPTER 7

1. Nigel Rothfels, "Catching Animals," in *Animals in Human Histories*, ed. Mary Henninger-Voss (Rochester, NY: University of Rochester Press, 2002), p. 203.

2. Adrian Franklin, *Animals and Modern Cultures: A Sociology of Human-Animal Relations in Modernity* (London: Sage Publications, 1999).

3. USDA, "Licensed Animal Exhibitors," http://www.aphis.usda.gov/ac/publications/reports/C_cert_holders.pdf (accessed June 3, 2007).

4. Elizabeth Hanson, *Animal Attractions: Nature on Display in American Zoos* (Princeton, NJ: Princeton University Press, 2002).

5. Franklin, *Animals and Modern Cultures*.

6. Richard W. Burkhardt, "Constructing the Zoo: Science, Society and Animal Nature at the Paris Menagerie, 1794–1838," in *Animals in Human Histories*, ed. Mary Henninger-Voss (Rochester, NY: University of Rochester Press, 2002).

7. Kay Anderson, "Animals, Science and Spectacle in the City," in *Animal Geographies: Place, Politics and Identity in the Nature-Culture Borderlands*, ed. J. Wolch and J. Emel (London: Verso, 1998).

8. Franklin, *Animals and Modern Cultures*.

9. Ibid.

10. Hanson, *Animal Attractions*.

11. Andrew Shapland, "Where Have All the Monkeys Gone? The Changing Nature of the Monkey Temple at Bristol Zoo," *Anthrozoos* 17, no. 3 (2004).

12. Garry Marvin and Bob Mullan, *Zoo Culture* (London: Weidenfeld and Nicolson, 1987).

13. Jonathan Burt, "Violent Health and the Moving Image: The London Zoo and Monkey Hill," in *Animals in Human Histories*, ed. Mary Henninger-Voss (Rochester, NY: University of Rochester Press, 2002).

14. See Chilla Bulbeck, *Facing the Wild: Ecotourism, Conservation, and Animal Encounters* (London: Earthscan, 2005).

15. Marvin and Mullan, *Zoo Culture*.

16. V. A. Melfi, W. McCormick, and A. Gibbs, "A Preliminary Assessment of How Zoo Visitors Evaluate Animal Welfare according to Enclosure Style and the Expression of Behavior," *Anthrozoos* 17, no. 2 (2004).

17. Ralph Acampora, "Zoos and Eyes: Contesting Captivity and Seeking Successor Practices," *Society & Animals* 13, no. 1 (2005): 69–88.

18. Rothfels, "Catching Animals."

19. Ibid.

20. Hanson, *Animal Attractions*.

21. Rothfels, "Catching Animals."

22. Ibid., p. 203.

23. Nigel Rothfels, *Savages and Beasts: The Birth of the Modern Zoo* (Baltimore: Johns Hopkins University Press, 2002).

24. Hanson, *Animal Attractions*.

25. Marvin and Mullan, *Zoo Culture*.

26. Roper Starch Worldwide, "Public Attitudes toward Zoos, Aquariums, and Animal Theme Parks," May 1995.

27. G. Hosey, "Zoo Animals and Their Audiences: What Is the Visitor Effect?" *Animal Welfare* 9, no. 4 (2000): 343–57.

28. Marvin and Mullan, *Zoo Culture*.

29. S. Kellert, *Kinship to Mastery: Biophilia in Human Evolution and Development* (Washington DC: Island, 1997).

30. James Janega, "That Researcher in the Ape House? She Was Studying You," *Chicago Tribune*, April 27, 2007.

31. Associated Press, "China Releases Panda Bred in Captivity," *MSNBC.com*, April 28, 2006, http://www.msnbc.msn.com/id/12517347/ (accessed May 29, 2007).

32. Rusty Dornin, "US Zoos Go Panda Crazy because of Crowd-Drawing Appeal," *CNN.com*, June 2, 2000, http://archives.cnn.com/2000/NATURE/06/02/panda.mania/index.html (accessed May 29, 2007).

33. "Zoo Survival Plan Calls for Fewer Animals and Improved Quality of Life," American Veterinary Medical Association press release, October 11, 2002.

34. Linda Goldston, "Zoo Animals to Go," *San Jose Mercury News*, December 14, 1999.

35. John Reinan, "Country Star Charged with Killing Tame Bear in Pen," *Minneapolis Star Tribune*, August 16, 2006.

36. Roper Starch Worldwide, "Public Attitudes toward Zoos, Aquariums, and Animal Theme Parks."

37. Naomi Rose, Richard Farinato, and Susan Sherwin, *The Case against Marine Mammals in Captivity* (Washington, DC: Humane Society of the United States, 2006).

38. AWA Regulations, Subpart E—Marine Mammals.

39. Sally Kestin, "Sickness and Death Can Plague Marine Mammals at Parks," *South Florida Sun-Sentinel*, May 16, 2004.

40. Ibid.

41. Ibid.

42. David McNeill, "Bloodbath: Japan's Dolphin Cull Gets Under Way," *Independent*, January 6, 2007.

43. Anderson, "Animals, Science and Spectacle in the City"; S. Kellert, *Kinship to Mastery*.

44. Not everyone enjoys zoos, however. Studies have shown that African Americans visit zoos much less often than whites, even when the zoos are located within a city. Some zoo personnel have speculated that perhaps it is because they empathize with the animals in the cages. Mullan and Marvin, *Zoo Culture*.

45. Burt, "Violent Health and the Moving Image."

46. Hanson, *Animal Attractions*.

47. Mullan and Marvin, *Zoo Culture*.

48. Rothfels, "Catching Animals."

49. Hanson, *Animal Attractions*.

50. Rothfels, *Savages and Beasts*.

51. Ted Friend, "Circuses and Circus Elephants," in *Encyclopedia of Animal Rights and Animal Welfare*, ed. Marc Bekoff (Westport, CT: Greenwood, 1998).

52. Bruce Read, Ringling Brothers FAQ, http://www.feldentertainment.com/pr/aca/FAQ1.htm (accessed September 26, 2006); Jennifer Santiago,

"Allegations of Severe Elephant Abuse against Ringling Brothers Circus," CBS 4, Miami–Ft. Lauderdale, January 4, 2006, http://cbs4.com/video/?id =11749@wfor.dayport.com (accessed June 8, 2007).

53. Associated Press, "Handler Blamed in Zoo Tiger Shooting," August 27, 2006.

54. Mark Clayton, "Trouble at Wild Animal Parks? Study Cites Lax US Regulations for Private Exhibitors," *Christian Science Monitor*, August 31, 2006.

55. Ibid.

56. American Society for the Prevention of Cruelty to Animals, the Fund for Animals, and the Animal Welfare Institute, "Government Sanctioned Abuse: How the United States Department of Agriculture Allows Ringling Brothers Circus to Systematically Mistreat Elephants," September 2003, http://www.awionline.org/wildlife/elephants/fullrpt.pdf (accessed June 8, 2007).

57. David Crary, "Greatest Show Elephant Suit Plays On," Associated Press, June 3, 2006.

58. American Society for the Prevention of Cruelty to Animals, the Fund for Animals, and the Animal Welfare Institute, "Government Sanctioned Abuse."

59. Mia McDonald, "All for Show: Ringling Brothers' Circus Claims to Promote Conservation," *E Magazine*, November 15, 2003.

60. USDA, "Inspection Report," http://www.wildlifeadvocacy.org/ programs/ringling/usdadocs.htm (accessed June 7, 2007).

61. The Center for Elephant Conservation Web site notes, "With less than 35,000 Asian elephants left in the wild, and the habitat of those in the wild increasingly threatened, captive breeding programs like the one at the *Ringling Bros. Center for Elephant Conservation* are vital to the future survival of this amazing species." See "About the Center for Elephant Conservation," http://www.elephantcenter.com/about.aspx (accessed June 8, 2007). See also McDonald, "All for Show."

62. See Outdoor Amusement Business Association, "Frequently Asked Questions" http://www.circusnews.com/pdf/oaba-animal-faq.pdf (accessed June 8, 2007). See also the legislation section of Circusnews.com for press releases about the circus industry's efforts regarding circus legislation at http://www.circusnews.com/modules.php?name=News&new_topic=75 (accessed June 8, 2007), and Ken Dixon, "Bullhook Ban Fails in Legisla-

ture," *Connecticut Post*, June 5, 2007, http://www.connpost.com/ci_6069796
?source=most_emailed (accessed June 8, 2007).

63. Assembly Committee on Public Safety Hearing, "AB 3027 Bill Analysis," April 25, 2006, http://info.sen.ca.gov/pub/05-06/bill/asm/ab_30013050/ab
_3027_cfa_20060424_114038_asm_comm.html (accessed June 8, 2007).

64. McDonald, "All for Show."

65. Center for Public Integrity, "Feld Entertainment D/B/A Ringling
Bros and Barnum & Bailey," http://www.publicintegrity.org/lobby/profile
.aspx?act=clients&year=2003&cl=L010120 (accessed June 3, 2007).

66. Testimony of David Rawls, president of Kelly Miller Circus,
before the Subcommittee on Crime of the Committee of the Judiciary, *The
Captive Elephant Act of 1999*, 106th Cong., 2nd sess., June 13, 2000. Transcript available at http://commdocs.house.gov/committees/judiciary/
hju65825.000/hju65825_0f.htm (accessed May 29, 2007).

67. Elizabeth Lawrence, "Rodeo Horses: The Wild and the Tame" in
Signifying Animals: Human Meaning in the Natural World, ed. Roy Willis
(New York: Routledge, 1994).

68. Professional Rodeo Cowboys Association, http://www.prorodeo
.org (accessed September 26, 2006).

69. Lawrence, "Rodeo Horses."

70. Ibid.

71. Some rodeo associations go further with their humane requirements, such as the International Gay Rodeo Association.

72. PRCA, "Animal Welfare: The Care and Treatment of Professional
Rodeo Livestock," ftp://ftp.prorodeo.com/Animal%20Welfare%20Booklet/
ANIMAL%20WELFARE%20B&W.pdf (accessed September 2006).

73. Ibid, p. 17.

74. Alabama Agricultural Experiment Station, "Loss of Horse Racing
May Cost Alabama Millions," press release, February 1, 1991; Robyn Lamb,
"Studs Producing Stakes Winners Command High Fees," *Daily Record* (Baltimore), August 17, 2006.

75. Indeed, the National Horseshow Commission spent $300,000 from
1998 to 2004 lobbying Congress on issues favorable to the horse industry.

76. Takahashi Toshiyuki et al., "Frequency of and Risk Factors for
Epistaxis Associated with Exercise-Induced Pulmonary Hemorrhage in
Horses: 251,609 Race Starts (1992–1997)," *Journal of the American Veterinary Medical Association* 218, no. 9 (May 1, 2001): 1462–64.

77. Bryan Joyner, "Horse Sense: Barbaro and the Sad State of Horse Racing," *New York Inquirer*, July 19, 2006.

78. Ray Paulick, "Death of a Derby Winner: Slaughterhouse Likely Fate for Ferdinand," *Blood Horse Magazine*, July 25, 2003, http://news.bloodhorse.com/viewstory.asp?id=17051 (accessed June 3, 2007).

79. Joseph Sjostrom and Patrick Yeagle, "Illinois Bans Horse Slaughter," *Chicago Tribune*, May 25, 2007.

80. Greyhound Association of America Web site: http://www.gra-america.org/media_kit/press/mediakit.html (accessed June 3, 2007).

81. Mary Jo Pitzl, "Dog Breeder Gets Sixty-Day Suspension," *Arizona Republic*, November 15, 2002.

82. Greyhound Racing Association of America, "The Most Exciting Dogs in the World," http://www.gra-america.org/the_sport/history.html (accessed June 12, 2007).

83. Misty Dean, "Raced-Out Greyhounds Await New Life in N. Texas," *Dallas Morning News*, April 22, 2007.

84. Gary Karasik, "You Can Bet Their Life on It," *Miami Herald Tropic Magazine*, October 21, 1990.

85. "Two Charged in Deaths of Former Race Dogs," Associated Press, January 1, 2002.

86. Jack Douglas Jr., "A Business That Breeds Violence," *Fort Worth Star-Telegram*, August 27, 2006.

87. Diane Jessup, "Dog Fighting: The Truth," http://www.workingpitbull.com/dogfighting2.htm (accessed June 3, 2007).

88. Douglas Jr., "A Business That Breeds Violence."

89. Mike Glenn, "Argument over Illegal Cockfight Leads to Fatal Shooting," *Houston Chronicle*, September 4, 2006.

90. Dan Noyes, "I-Team Uncovers Blood Sport in Bay Area," KGO-TV, February 5, 2006.

91. A bill was introduced in the California Legislature in 2006 that would have banned open coursing after a San Francisco television station filmed a gruesome event in which dogs were awarded points based on how aggressively they pursued rabbits. Unfortunately, the bill was opposed by groups like the National Open-Field Coursing Association and died in committee.

92. John Berger, *About Looking* (New York: Pantheon Books, 1980).

93. Jonathan Burt, *Animals in Film* (London: Reaktion Books, 2002).

94. Jennifer Hile, "Goodall Group Calls for Curtain on Ape 'Actors,'" National Geographic Channel, February 13, 2004.

95. Performing Animal Welfare Society, "Animals in Movies and Television," http://www.pawsweb.org/site/resources/index_fs_movies.htm (accessed June 8, 2007).

96. Have Trunk, Will Travel, "An Endangered Species," http://www.havetrunkwilltravel.com/about2.htm (accessed June 3, 2007).

97. Francis McCabe, "Chips Fall Wrong Way for Chimp's Poker Hopes," *Las Vegas Review-Journal*, July 28, 2006.

NOTES TO CONCLUSION

1. Barbara Ehrenreich, "Will Chimp Life Get Human Rights?" Znet, May 12, 2007, http://www.zmag.org/content/showarticle.cfm?SectionID=80 &ItemID=12805 (accessed June 12, 2007).

2. J. M. Coetzee, "Animals Can't Speak for Themselves—It's Up to Us to Do It," *The Age*, February 22, 2007.

3. James Serpell, *In the Company of Animals: A Study of Human-Animal Relationships* (Cambridge: Cambridge University Press, 1986).

4. Ibid.

5. Jonathan Balcombe, *Pleasurable Kingdom* (New York: Macmillian, 2006), p. 218.

6. Serpell, *In the Company of Animals*.

7. William C. McGrew, "Culture in Nonhuman Primates?" *Annual Review of Anthropology* 27 (1998): 301–328. See also W. C. McGrew, L. F. Marchant, and T. Nishida, eds., *Great Ape Societies* (Cambridge: Cambridge University Press, 1996) and Marc Bekoff, Colin Allen, and Gordon Burghardt, eds., *The Cognitive Animal: Empirical and Theoretical Perspectives on Animal Cognition* (Cambridge, MA: MIT Press, 2002).

8. S. Savage-Rumbah, W. M. Fields, and J. P. Taglialatela, "Ape Consciousness–Human Consciousness: A Perspective Informed by Language and Culture," *American Zoologist* 40, no. 6 (2000): 910–21.

9. John Noble Wilford, "Almost Human, and Sometimes Smarter," *New York Times*, April 17, 2007.

10. Ibid.

11. Alex Kirby, "Parrot's Oratory Stuns Scientists," BBC News, May 1, 2007, http://news.bbc.co.uk/go/pr/fr/-/2/hi/science/nature/3430481.stm (accessed June 12, 2007).

12. Charles Choi, "Hmm . . . Rats Think like Humans," *MSNBC.com*, March 9, 2007, http://www.msnbc.msn.com/id/17537590/?GT1=9145 (accessed June 12, 2007).

13. Amanda Onion, "Studies Show Rats Enjoy Tickling," ABC News, March 31, 2005, http://abcnews.go.com/Technology/story?id=626264 &page=1 (accessed June 12, 2007).

14. Matthew Scully, "A Sunless Hell," *Arizona Republic,* February 19, 2006.

15. Matthew Scully, *Dominion: The Power of Man, the Suffering of Animals, and the Call to Mercy* (New York: St. Martin's, 2002).

16. Ibid.

17. "City Council Approves Foie Gras Ban," *Chicago Sun-Times*, April 26, 2006.

18. Proclamation of Mayor Richard M. Daley, Office of the Mayor, City of Chicago, August 16, 2006. Available at http://www.wlup.com/check_it_out/tom_petty_proclimation.htm (accessed September 30, 2006).

RECOMMENDED READINGS

Alger, Janey, and Steven Alger. *Cat Culture: The Social World of a Cat Shelter*. Philadelphia: Temple University Press, 2003.

Animal Studies Group. *Killing Animals*. Champaign: University of Illinois Press, 2006.

Armstrong, Susan J., and Richard G. Botzler. *The Animal Ethics Reader*. Routledge, 2003.

Balcombe, Jonathan. *Pleasurable Kingdom: Animals and the Nature of Feeling Good*. Macmillan, 2006.

Bekoff, Marc. *The Emotional Lives of Animals: A Leading Scientist Explores Animal Joy, Sorrow, and Empathy—and Why They Matter*. Novato, CA: New World Library, 2007.

Benson, G. John, and Bernard E. Rollin, eds. *The Well-Being of Farm Animals: Challenges and Solutions*. Ames, IA: Blackwell, 2004.

Buckley, Carol. *Just for Elephants*. Gardiner, ME: Tilbury House, 2006.

Burt, Jonathan. *Animals in Film*. London: Reaktion Books, 2002.

Coetzee, J. M. *The Lives of Animals*. Princeton, NJ: Princeton University Press, 1999.

Davis, Susan E., and Margo DeMello. *Stories Rabbits Tell: A Natural and Cultural History of a Misunderstood Creature*. New York: Lantern Books, 2003.

Dolan, Kevin. *Ethics, Animals and Science*. Ames, IA: Iowa State University Press, 1999.

Eisnitz, Gail A. *Slaughterhouse: The Shocking Story of Greed, Neglect, and Inhumane Treatment inside the US Meat Industry.* Amherst, NY: Prometheus Books, 2006.

Greek, Ray. *Sacred Cows and Golden Geese: The Human Cost of Experiments on Animals.* New York: Continuum, 2000.

Green, Alan. *Animal Underworld: Inside America's Black Market for Rare and Exotic Species.* New York: Public Affairs, 1999.

Greger, Michael. *Bird Flu: A Virus of Our Own Hatching.* New York: Lantern Books, 2006.

Grogan, John. *Marley & Me: Life and Love with the World's Worst Dog.* New York: Morrow, 2005.

Grosz, Terry. *No Safe Refuge: Man as Predator in the World of Wildlife.* Boulder, CO: Johnson Books, 2003.

Hancocks, David. *A Different Nature: The Paradoxical World of Zoos and Their Uncertain Future.* Los Angeles: University of California Press, 2002.

Harriman, Marinell. *House Rabbit Handbook.* 4th ed. Alameda, CA: Drollery, 2005.

Herda-Rapp, Ann, and Theresa L. Goedeke. *Mad about Wildlife: Looking at Social Conflict over Wildlife.* Danvers, MA: Brill Academic Publishers, 2005.

Irvine, Leslie, and Marc Bekoff. *If You Tame Me: Understanding Our Connection with Animals.* Philadelphia: Temple University Press, 2004.

Lane, Marion S. *The HSUS Complete Guide to Dog Care: Everything You Need to Know to Keep Your Dog Healthy and Happy.* New York: Little, Brown, 2001.

Leigh, Diane, and Marilee Geyer. *One at a Time: A Week in an American Animal Shelter.* 3rd ed. Santa Cruz, CA: No Voice Unheard, 2005.

Lufkin, Elise. *Tales of Strays Who Landed on Their Feet.* New York: Lyons, 2005.

Lyman, Howard. *No More Bull: The Mad Cowboy Targets America's Worst Enemy—Our Diet.* New York: Scribner, 2005.

Masson, Jeffrey Moussaieff. *Dogs Never Lie about Love: Reflections on the Emotional World of Dogs.* New York: Three Rivers, 1998.

———. *The Pig Who Sang to the Moon.* New York: Ballantine Books, 2003.

Mowat, Farley. *Sea of Slaughter.* Mechanicsburg, PA: Stackpole Books, 2004.

Newkirk, Ingrid. *250 Things You Can Do to Make Your Cat Adore You.* New York: Fireside, 1998.

Noelker, Frank. *Captive Beauty.* Champaign: University of Illinois Press, 2004.

O'Barry, Richard. *To Free a Dolphin.* Los Angeles: Renaissance Books, 2000.

Regan, Tom. *The Case for Animal Rights.* Berkeley: University of California Press, 2004.

Robbins, John. *The Food Revolution: How Your Diet Can Help Save Your Life and Our World.* Newburyport, MA: Conari, 2001.

Rollin, Bernard E. *Animal Rights and Human Morality.* 3rd ed. Amherst, NY: Prometheus Books, 2006.

———. *The Unheeded Cry: Animal Consciousness, Animal Pain and Science.* 2nd ed. Blackwell, 1999.

Rothfels, Nigel. *Savages and Beasts: The Birth of the Modern Zoo.* Baltimore: Johns Hopkins University Press, 2002.

Schlosser, Eric. *Fast Food Nation: The Dark Side of the All-American Meal.* Boston: Houghton Mifflin, 2001.

Scully, Matthew. *Dominion: The Power of Many, the Suffering of Animals, and the Call to Mercy.* New York: St. Martin's, 2002.

Singer, Peter. *Animal Liberation.* Harper Perennial, 2001.

———. *In Defense of Animals: The Second Wave.* 2nd ed. Blackwell, 2005.

Singer, Peter, and Jim Mason. *The Way We Eat: Why Our Food Choices Matter.* New York: Rodale, 2006.

Sunstein, Cass R., and Martha C. Nussbaum, eds. *Animal Rights: Current Debates and New Directions.* Oxford: Oxford University Press, 2005.

Watson, Paul. *Seal Wars: Twenty-five Years on the Front Lines with the Harp Seals.* Toronto: Firefly, 2003.

RESOURCES

American Anti-Vivisection Society
www.aavs.org

American Society for the Prevention of Cruelty to Animals
www.aspca.org

Animallearn
www.animalearn.org

Animal Place
www.animalplace.org

Animal Protection Institute
www.api4animals.org

Animal Welfare Institute
www.awionline.org

Association of Veterinarians for Animal Rights
www.avar.org

Compassion Over Killing
www.cok.net

The Elephant Sanctuary
www.elephants.com

Ethical Science and Education Coalition
www.neavs.org/esec/index.htm

Farm Sanctuary
www.farmsanctuary.org

Grey2KUSA
www.grey2kusa.org

Greyhound Companions of New Mexico
www.gcnm.org

Greyhound Protection League
www.greyhounds.org

House Rabbit Society
www.rabbit.org

The Humane Society of the United States
www.humanesociety.org

In Defense of Animals
www.idausa.org

Johns Hopkins Center for Alternatives to Animal Testing
caat.jhsph.edu

National Anti-Vivisection Society
www.navs.org

New England Anti-Vivisection Society
www.neavs.org

People for the Ethical Treatment of Animals
www.peta.org

Performing Animal Welfare Society
www.pawsweb.org

Petfinder
www.petfinder.org

Pets 911
www.pets911.com

Physicians Committee for Responsible Medicine
www.pcrm.org

Showing Animals Respect and Kindness
www.sharkonline.org

University of California Center for Animal Alternatives
www.vetmed.ucdavis.edu/animal_alternatives/main.htm

Vegan Outreach
www.veganoutreach.org

INDEX